The Bloomsbury Italian Philosophy Reader

ALSO AVAILABLE FROM BLOOMSBURY

Introduction to New Realism, Maurizio Ferraris
The Withholding Power, Massimo Cacciari
Time for Revolution, Antonio Negri
The Sublime Reader, ed. by Robert R. Clewis
Posthuman Glossary, ed. by Rosi Braidotti and Maria Hlavajova
A Philosophy of Struggle: The Leonard Harris Reader, ed. by Lee A. McBride III

The Bloomsbury Italian Philosophy Reader

EDITED BY
MICHAEL LEWIS AND
DAVID EDWARD ROSE

BLOOMSBURY ACADEMIC
LONDON • NEW YORK • OXFORD • NEW DELHI • SYDNEY

BLOOMSBURY ACADEMIC
Bloomsbury Publishing Plc
50 Bedford Square, London, WC1B 3DP, UK
1385 Broadway, New York, NY 10018, USA

BLOOMSBURY, BLOOMSBURY ACADEMIC and the Diana logo are trademarks of
Bloomsbury Publishing Plc

First published in Great Britain 2022

Cover design by Ben Anslow
Cover image: Abstract geometric shapes. (© _Aine_ / Getty Images)

A catalogue record for this book is available from the British Library.

A catalog record for this book is available from the Library of Congress.

ISBN: HB: 978-1-3501-1283-4
PB: 978-1-3501-1284-1
ePDF: 978-1-3501-1282-7
eBook: 978-1-3501-1285-8

Typeset by Deanta Global Publishing Services, Chennai, India

To find out more about our authors and books visit www.bloomsbury.com and
sign up for our newsletters.

CONTENTS

CONTRIBUTORS

Onur Acaroglu is Doctoral Researcher in the Department of Political Science and International Politics at the University of Birmingham. His current research concerns the theme of transition and its temporal complexity in historical materialism. He has written on the Gramscian theory of hegemony as a conceptual tool with which to address the question of state power and Left political strategy.

Andrea Bellocci (Rome, 1980–) graduated with a degree in philosophy and the history of philosophy in 2005 at the University of Rome 'La Sapienza', with a dissertation entitled *Towards a Dialectic of the Tragic. An Essay on Luigi Pareyson*, under the supervision of Professors Paolo Vinci and Marco M. Olivetti. In 2006 he began a PhD in philosophy at the University of Siena (Arezzo) which he completed in 2010. The thesis was entitled *Luigi Pareyson and the Question of the Barthian Dialectic*.

His first monograph, *Implication of Opposites, Aporia of the Identical*, on Luigi Pareyson, appeared in 2012.

After teaching Philosophy at the Istituto Filosofico-Teologico, Viterbo, he took up his current position as professor of theoretical philosophy at the Pontificio Ateneo S. Anselmo, Rome. He is currently working on the philosophical thought of Gennaro Sasso. He has composed numerous essays involving the works of Pareyson, Sasso, Barth and Marco Vannini, among others.

E-mail: andreabellocci@yahoo.it

Lorenzo Bernini is Associate Professor of Political Philosophy at the University of Verona, where he founded the Research Centre PoliTeSse (Politics and Theories of Sexuality, www.politesse.it) which he now directs. His interests range from classical political philosophy (especially Thomas Hobbes) and French thought of the twentieth century (especially Michel Foucault) to contemporary theories of radical democracy, critical race theories and queer theories. Among his books are *Queer Apocalypses: Elements of Antisocial Theory* (2017), previously published in Italian (2013) and Spanish (2015); and *Le teorie queer: Un'introduzione* (2017), translated into Spanish (2018).

Arianna Bove is a political theorist and translator of political and philosophical texts from Italian and French into English, including works by Elettra Stimilli, Manfredo Tafuri, Maurizio Lazzarato, Antonio Negri, Luca Basso and Franco Berardi. She taught Politics and Ethics at Queen Mary, University of London.

Federica Castelli received her PhD from the University of Modena and Reggio Emilia and has been a post-doctoral researcher in Political Philosophy at the University of Roma Tre. She is the editor of the feminist journal DWF and governing council member of Iaph Italia, Italian section for the International Association of Women Philosophers. She is supervisor and scientific coordinator for the master's degree in Studi e Politiche di Genere at Roma Tre. She is the author of *Corpi in Rivolta. Spazi urbani, conflitti e nuove forme della politica* (2015) and co-editor of *Città. Politiche dello spazio urbano* (2016).

Anna Cicogna is a Lacanian psychologist who lives and works in Trieste. She attended Irpa and became a member of Jonas and Telemaco, Trieste, a clinical psychoanalytic centre for childhood and adolescence. Outside of clinical practice, she researches art and literature from a psychoanalytical perspective.

Joseph Farrell is Professor Emeritus in Italian at the University of Strathclyde. He studied philosophy in Rome and has authored, edited and translated several books on Italian society and literature, including *Leonardo Sciascia*, *Sicily: A Cultural History* and *History of Italian Theatre*, co-edited with Paolo Puppa. His most recent book is *Dario Fo and Franca Rame: Theatre, Politics and Life* (2019).

Leone Gazziero (1971–) is a CNRS research fellow at the University of Lille. He has published a book on Plato and Aristotle (2008) and a score of papers (in French and English) on Ancient metaphysics and mediaeval logic.

Jeremy Gilbert is Professor of Cultural and Political Theory at the University of East London. His most recent publications include the translation of Maurizio Lazzarato's *Experimental Politics* and the book *Common Ground: Democracy and Collectivity in an Age of Individualism*. He is currently working on three books: *Twenty-First Century Socialism* (2019), *Hegemony Now: Power in the Twenty-First Century* (2020, co-authored with Alex Williams) and *The Last Days of Neoliberalism: Politics, Culture and Society Since 2008* (2020).

In the spring of 2020 he will be Visiting Professor in the Humanities at the Cogut Center for the Humanities, Brown University, Rhode Island.

Jeremy is the current editor of the journal *New Formations* and has written and spoken widely on politics, music and cultural theory, having given keynotes at numerous international conferences on these topics and on the politics and practice of cultural studies.

Iain Hamilton Grant is Senior Lecturer in Philosophy at the University of the West of England and works in the areas of ontology, post-Kantian philosophy and German idealism, especially Schelling, as well as on the philosophy of nature both historically and in a contemporary context. He has published widely in these areas and is currently writing a monograph on the problem of nature in later Idealism to follow his earlier book, *Philosophies of Nature after Schelling* (2006).

Olivia Guaraldo is Associate Professor in Political Philosophy at the University of Verona. Her field of research comprises modern and contemporary political thought. She has worked extensively on the thought of Hannah Arendt and feminist political theory.

She has edited and introduced the Italian translations of Judith Butler's works, *Precarious Life* (Rome 2004, Milan 2013) and *Undoing Gender* (Rome 2006, Milan 2014). She has also edited and introduced the Italian translation of Hannah Arendt's essay, *Lying in Politics* (Milan 2006).

Among her most recent publications are 'Public Happiness: Revisiting an Arendtian Hypothesis', *Philosophy Today* 62:2 (2018) and the *Gender and Education* special issue, 'If Not Now When: Feminism in contemporary activist, social and educational contexts' (2016) which she co-edited with Angie Voela.

E-mail: olivia.guaraldo@univr.it

Katherine Langley is a freelance translator and postgraduate of the University of Newcastle upon Tyne.

Michael Lewis is Senior Lecturer in Philosophy at the University of Newcastle upon Tyne and General Editor of the *Journal of Italian Philosophy*. He is the author of *Heidegger and the Place of Ethics*, *Heidegger beyond Deconstruction: On Nature*, *Derrida and Lacan: Another Writing*, *The Beautiful Animal: Sincerity, Charm, and the Fossilised Dialectic* and, with Tanja Staehler, *Phenomenology: An Introduction*. He is completing a book on Giorgio Agamben, as well as an account of the history and contemporary forms of Philosophical Anthropology. Educated in philosophy at the University of Warwick and the University of Essex, he has taught philosophy at the University of Sussex, the University of Warwick and the University of the West of England.

Marco Piasentier is currently a postdoctoral researcher in the Department of Social Sciences and Philosophy at the University of Jyväskylä. He obtained his cotutelle PhD at the Scuola Normale di Pisa and the University of Kent. He held research positions at the University of Helsinki and the Centre for Critical Thought, University of Kent. Piasentier is the author of a forthcoming monograph on the question of the human (2019) and the editor of two volumes on philosophy and biopolitics. He is a member of the editorial board of *Il Rasoio di Occam* (*MicroMega*) and the *Journal of Italian Philosophy*.

German Primera is Senior Lecturer in Philosophy and Critical Theory at the University of Brighton. He is an editor of the *Journal of Italian Philosophy* and the author of *The Political Ontology of Giorgio Agamben: Signatures of Life and Power* (2019).

David Rose is Professor of Social Ethics at the University of Newcastle upon Tyne. He has published widely in the area of social and political thought, with a particular stress on Hegelian and Marxist theories, cosmopolitanism, posthumanism, applied ethics, hermeneutics and Italian thought from the Renaissance to the present day, particularly the work of Vico and Vattimo. He has translated the latter into English and is the author of *The Ethics and Politics of Pornography*, *Free Will and Continental Philosophy: The Death without Meaning* and *Hegel's Philosophy of Right: A Reader's Guide*.

Andrea Soardo studied philosophy at the Università Vita-Salute San Raffaele of Milan and lived in Canterbury as a PhD candidate at the University of Kent. His main philosophical interests concern metaphysics, and in particular, he has attempted to define what can be true.

Will Stronge is an ESRC Research Fellow at the University of Brighton. His current research focuses on Gramsci's legacy and the notion of hegemony. He is the editor of *Georges Bataille and Contemporary Thought* (2017) and co-author of *Post-Work: What It Is, Why It Matters and How We Get There*, with Helen Hester (2019).

Francesco Tava is Senior Lecturer in Philosophy at the University of the West of England, specializing in moral and political philosophy, phenomenology and the history of philosophy. Since the completion of his doctorate in 2012, he has held several research fellowships, at the University of Milan, the Czech Academy of Sciences and the University of the West of England. From 2015 to 2017 he was a postdoctoral scholar at the Husserl Archives at KU Leuven. He has written one monograph, *The Risk of Freedom*, on the political phenomenology of the Czech philosopher, Jan Patočka, and has published a series of articles and book chapters on related themes. He is currently working on a research project concerning the idea of political solidarity within the European frame.

Nicholas Thoburn is Senior Lecturer in Sociology at the University of Manchester. He is the author of two books, *Anti-Book: On the Art and Politics of Radical Publishing* and *Deleuze, Marx, and Politics*, and co-editor of *Deleuze and Politics* and *Objects and Materials*. He has published on political theory, media aesthetics, social movements and architecture and is on the editorial board of the journal *New Formations*.

Zoe Waters is a PhD student in Philosophy at the University of Newcastle upon Tyne.

ACKNOWLEDGEMENTS

Many thanks to Liza Thompson, Frankie Mace and Lucy Russell at Bloomsbury for proposing this project in the first place and for seeing it through its protracted gestation.

To Zoe Waters, whose unflagging assistance was offered with an unfailing patience and energy.

Thanks to Katherine Langley for her translation work, to Laura Leonardo for introducing us and to the University of Newcastle upon Tyne for funding this labour.

To Marco Piasentier, for his endless advice and tireless positivity: a generosity of character, time and knowledge shockingly rare in academia. Also thanks to my other fellow editors at the *Journal of Italian Philosophy*, German Primera and Will Stronge.

Thanks to Lorenzo Bernini for putting us in contact with Olivia Guaraldo, along with Adriana Cavarero and Simona Forti, who kindly advised us as to the extracts from their work which they would like to be included in this volume.

To Francesco Tava for advice with respect to translation, help in relation to the Milan School, which went far beyond the text that appears here, and for putting us in touch with Carlo Sini, who composed a new text especially for the Reader.

To Lorenzo Chiesa for opening up huge swathes of Italian philosophy, directly and indirectly, and for advice on certain points of translation and doctrine.

To Alberto Toscano for directing us towards Ariana Bove and Jeremy Gilbert and for his suggestions. Relatedly, by way of Ariana Bove, we must thank Christian Marazzi for his advice on which of his works might be best to include.

To David Webb, Niall Keane, Matteo Mandarini and Alice Gibson for advice on a number of elements in the text.

To Tim Christiaens for the advice and a gracious offer of assistance.

To Silvia Benso and Antonio Calcagno, for the advice, which in some cases stems from a very different approach to the topic, but which was enlightening precisely for that reason, at an early stage in this project's development.

To everyone who has written introductions, giving time that has little chance of being compensated: with thanks for their patience in light of the fact that this project has taken an inordinate length of time to bring to completion. This includes my co-editor, David Rose, whose remarkably uncomplaining, calm and pragmatic solution of problems with a minimum of fuss and without any trace of rancour demonstrated him to be the perfect partner in such an endeavour.

Many apologies to anyone who has helped us and whom we have neglected to mention through forgetfulness or carelessness. Please let us know and we shall rectify it next time.

Michael Lewis

Finally, a massive amount of gratitude to Michael Lewis, who conceived of and energized this project from the very beginning, reaching out to everyone and carrying out a large part of the work himself while I was researching away from the office and only able to drop in virtually every so often. It really wouldn't have happened without him.

David Rose

PERMISSIONS

The editors and publisher gratefully acknowledge the permission granted to reproduce the copyright material in this book:

Cambridge University Press for *Pico della Mirandola. Oration on the Dignity of Man.* Trans. F. Borghesi, M. Papio and M. Riva. Cambridge, Cambridge University Press, 2012.

Oxford University Press for Machiavelli, N., *Niccolò Machiavelli. The Prince.* Trans. P. Bondanella, Oxford, Oxford University Press, 2005. XV, XVII, XVIII, XIX.

The University of Chicago Press *for* Machiavelli, N., *Discourses on Livy,* Trans. H.C Mansfield and N. Tarcov, London, The University of Chicago Press, 1996. I, 41.

Cambridge University Press for Vico, G., *The First New Science.* Trans. L. Pompa. Cambridge: Cambridge University Press. Pp. 9–12.

International Publishers for Gramsci, A. *Selections from the Prison Notebooks,* ed. Q. Hoare and G.N. Smith, International Publishers, New York. PP. 125–7, 169, 238, 323.

Lawrence and Wishart for Gramsci, A. 1987, "Revolution Against 'Capital'" in *Selections from Political Writings: 1910–1920,* ed. Q. Hoare, Lawrence & Wishart, London. pp. 34–7.

Cambridge University Press for Croce, B. *The Aesthetic as the Science of Expression and the Linguistic in General.* Trans. C. Lyas. Cambridge: Cambridge University Press, 1992 [1941], pp. 33–5.

The extract from Agamben was originally published in *The Use of Bodies* by Giorgio Agamben, trans. Adam Kotsko, Copyright © 2015 by the Board of Trustees of the Leland Stanford Jr. University. All rights reserved. Used by permission of the publisher, Stanford University Press, sup.org.

Fordham University Press for Massimo Cacciari, 'Nietzsche and the Unpolitical', pp.92–103, in *The Unpolitical: On the Radical Critique of Political Reason.* Ed. Alessandro Carrera. Trans. Massimo Verdicchio. New York: Fordham University Press, 2009.

Routledge for A. Cavarero, *Relating Narratives. Storytelling and Selfhood*, trans. by Paul Kottman, Routledge 2000, pp. 55–62.

Routledge for Roberto Esposito (2013), 'Community, Immunity, Biopolitics', in *Community, Immunity and the Proper*, Trans. Z. Hanafi, Routledge, 2017, pp. 81–88.

The extract from Maurizio Ferraris, 'Transcendental Realism' in *The Monist* 98(2) 2015, pp. 215–32 by permission of Oxford University Press.

The extract from Forti was originally the introduction to *New Demons: Rethinking Power and Evil Today* by Simona Forti, trans. Zakiya Hanafi. Copyright © 2012 by the Board of Trustees of the Leland Stanford Jr. University. All rights reserved. Used by permission of the publisher, Stanford University Press, sup.org.

The extract from Lazzarato was originally published in Lazzarato, Maurizio. *Experimental Politics*. Translated by Arianna Bove, Jeremy Gilbert, Andrew Goffey, Mark Hayward, Jason Read, and Alberto Toscano. Edited by Jeremy Gilbert. pp. 83–102, © 2017 Massachusetts Institute of Technology, by permission of The MIT Press

Semiotext(e) for Christian Marazzi, *The Linguistic Nature of Money and Finance*. Trans. Isabella Bertoletti, James Cascaito, & Andrea Casson. Los Angeles: Semiotext(e), 2014, pp. 5–47.

SUNY Press for Luisa Muraro reprinted by permission from *The Symbolic Order of the Mother* by Luisa Muraro, the State University of New York Press © 2018 State University of New York. All rights reserved.

SUNY Press for Antonio Negri reprinted by permission from *Flower of the Desert: Giacomo Leopardi's Poetic Ontology* by Antonio Negril, the State University of New York Press © 2018 State University of New York. All rights reserved.

Mimesis for Emanuele Severino. Originally published as *Nihilism and Destiny*. Trans. Kevin William Molin. Ed. Nicoletta Cusano. N.: Mimesis, 2016, Chapter 1. 'Nihilism and Destiny', pp.13–23. © Mimesis International, an imprint of Mim Edizioni srl, Milano-Udine http://mimesisinternational.com/

And we should also like to thank those authors and translators who gave us permission to reproduce their work:

The extract from Giordano Bruno was translated by Scott Gosnell and the full version has been published as Giordano Bruno, *On the Infinite, the Universe and the Worlds*, Trans. Scott Gosnell, USA: Huginn, Munnin & Co, 2014.

Extracts from Luigi Pareyson, *Existence, Interpretation, Freedom: Selected Writings*. Trans. Anna Mattei. Ed. P.D. Bubbio, Aurora: Davies, 2009, pp. 217–29.

Raffaello Cortina for Massimo Recalcati, *The Man Without Unconscious: Figures of the New Psychoanalytic Clinic*. Milan: Raffaello Cortina, 2010, a translation of *L'uomo senza inconscio: figure della nuova clinica psicoanalitica*. Milano: Raffaello Cortina, 2010, pp.3–14.

The extract from Carlo Sini, 'Enzo Paci: From Existentialism to the Things Themselves' Trans, K. Langley with M. Lewis, 'Enzo Paci: dall'esistenzialismo alle cose stesse', *Journal of Italian Philosophy* 2 (2019).

Bollati Boringhieri and Davide Tarizzo, for Tarizzo 'Applauso. L'impero dell'assenso', in Massimo Recalcati (ed.), Forme contemporanee del totalitarismo. Torino, 2007. Trans. Bollati Boringhieri, pp. 83-94.

*We also acknowledge the publishers and translators of the shorter extracts and quotations and those where copyright has expired or is not present which have been republished come under the creative commons licence (*http://creativecommons.org/licenses/by-nc-sa/3.0/).

Extracts from Dante are reproduced from the open access texts available on www.gutenberg.org. Dante Alighieri, *Divina commedia. The Divine Comedy of Dante*. Trans. H. F. Carey. August, 2005 [Etext #1008] Urbana, Illinois: Project Gutenberg. 2005. Retrieved July 3, 2020, from www.gutenberg .org/ebooks/ "Monarchia" Translator: F.J. Church In R.W. Church Dante: An essay. Urbana, Illinois: Project Gutenberg. Release Date: October 30, 2010 Retrieved 3 July, 2020, [EBook #33896].

Dante Alighieri, *Dante Alighieri: Four Political Letters*. Trans. C. E. Honess. London: Modern Humanities Research Association, 2007.

Extracts from Pico della Mirandola: « Giovanni Pico Della Mirandola on the Conflict of Philosophy and Rhetoric », Trans.Q. Breen, *Journal of the History of Ideas*, 13, 1952, p. 395–396 and 398, 40; *Proemium*, P.E. Fornaciari (éd.) Firenze, Edizioni del Galluzzo, 2010, p. 4, 8–10, 32; *Syncretism in the West. Pico's 900 Theses (1486)*, Trans. S.A. Farmer, Tempe, Medieval and Renaissance Texts and Studies, p. 211; and *On Being and the One*, Trans. P.J.W. Miller, Indianapolis, Hackett, 1965, p. 37–38.

The extracts from Silvia Federici, 'Feminism and the politics of the common in an era of primitive accumulation'. In Federici, Revolution at Point Zero, Brooklyn, NY: Autonomedia, 2012, pp. 138–48 and 'The Great Caliban: The Struggle Against the Rebel Body' from *Caliban and the Witch. Women, The Body, and Primitive Accumulation,* Autonomedia, forthcoming, pp. 133–161.

CHAPTER 1

Introduction

Michael Lewis with David Rose

The very idea of Italian philosophy

The question of Italian philosophy seems at first to be bound up with that of a *national* philosophy. Contemporary Italian philosopher Roberto Esposito asks: 'Does such a thing as "Italian philosophy" exist? Even before answering that, is it legitimate to think of philosophy as belonging to a nation or, at least, to a territory?' (2012 [2010], 12). Is philosophy, necessarily or contingently, a discourse which may be divided up into national traditions – French philosophy, German philosophy, English philosophy etc.? And even if this is the case, how important is such a division *philosophically*? Or, in other words, to what extent does such a putative nationality have an impact upon the *content* of the work in question, as opposed to the form in which it is conveyed? It seems likely that there are indeed significant 'traditions' in philosophy, but might the more significant of these not be organized around something quite distinct from nationality?

Italian philosophy gives us a privileged insight into the way in which an identifiable tradition within philosophy may or may not be aligned with a nationality, for it is *both* a philosophy that has its roots in a certain 'country' or geographical territory and yet it cannot simply amount to a *'national* philosophy' – a philosophy that belongs to a nation and constitutes (part of) a national tradition. This is so for the simple reason that Italy was not, for the greatest part of its history, a unified 'nation'. And indeed, for Esposito, it is this delay in the emergence of such a thing as a single Italian nation, the extraordinarily protracted period prior to unification, that best explains the *exceptional* character of the philosophy which grew out of this culture – the so-called Italian Difference (cf. Negri 2009, Chiesa & Toscano 2009).

The unique *political* and *geographic* status of Italy in the sense of its remarkably belated constitution as a nation (which occurred with the so-called *Risorgimento*, the 'resurgence' or 'revival' of the mid-1800s) may be shown to play a significant role in many if not all of the most distinctive features of Italian philosophy, a set of identifying traits which indeed *constitute* that very lineage. To present a vision of Italian philosophy in which its principal defining characteristics derive from its *history* with respect to its *nationality* (or nationhood) is the task to which this chapter will confine itself.

Italian thought has spent centuries dwelling on the question of how to bind a collective together without the help of an encompassing state and a single sovereign ruler. It is therefore uniquely well placed to think not just negatively about the decline of nationhood and statehood, or even more broadly about the deconstruction of the metaphysical–philosophical categories through which politics and indeed the world more generally have been understood; Italian soil will already have given rise to positive, affirmative categories with which we might conceive a real *alternative* to the nation state and sovereign power.

At the end of the history of metaphysics, the closure of which was progressively delineated from at least the end of the eighteenth century (with Immanuel Kant) to the twentieth century (with Martin Heidegger, Ludwig Wittgenstein, Jacques Derrida and many others on the European continent), almost all of continental philosophy has come to realize the limitations of those traits which Italian philosophy had already problematized – or never seriously believed in. The distinction of Italian thought is already to have proposed an alternative, and this partly explains why it has proved such a rich resource for contemporary thinking. Indeed, we might even go so far as to add to Alain Badiou's suggestion that there have been but three great epochs within philosophy – ancient Greece, nineteenth-century Germany and post-war France – by claiming that the twenty-first century may well turn out to be Italian (Badiou 2012, lii).

Having arrived at the rudiments of this prophetic alternative long before or simply in bypassing a certain philosophy, whether it be modern, statist, humanistic or transcendental, Italian thought holds in reserve the potential for an affirmative response to the situation in which we are left abandoned once the various 'machines' that generate the Western way of speaking and thinking have exhausted themselves or 'run out of fuel' (to borrow Giorgio Agamben's phrase). In this regard, and speaking of Giordano Bruno's anti-humanism, Esposito says the following:

> the very lineaments of the human are dissolved [. . .]. The fact that a view of this sort was created within – and at the same time against – a movement of ideas called 'humanism' is further testament to the antinomic force that characterises Italian thought: a force that situates it outside the most recognised confines of modern thought, but also, and for the same reason, close to our contemporary world. (2012 [2010], 70)

In other words, Italian thought has produced a parallel historical tradition, running alongside the mainstream European, another potential that has found today – or will find tomorrow – the impetus for its actualization.

Italy's alternative philosophy will always have lent its weight to a discourse that promotes affirmation and positivity, an affirmation of immanence rather than an expectant reaching for transcendence. It is a thinking which refuses simply to believe that philosophy's only place is within its own margins and its sole remaining task their embroidery, a negative theological delineation of philosophy's 'other', of which it is denied the right to speak.

If Hegelian dialectic attempts to turn everything concrete, material and living into a moment of the concept and to subordinate real life and labour to the ideal life of the mind and its merely conceptual labour, real movement thus being consumed in the immanent unfolding of concepts, Italian thought attempts to remain true to what it perceives as a radical *difference* between life and thought, or at least to do justice in thought to that life which stands beyond knowledge and thinking: 'it provided a radical answer to the question [. . .] regarding the unbridgeable gap between "science and life" – the excess manifested by life in the face of all attempts to understand it conceptually' (Esposito 2012 [2010], 158).

But we do not simply leave this life to itself, as if to protect it from the predations of our thinking; rather, we actively *modify* thought so as to render it compatible with the life that is initially incommensurate with it; in other words, we produce a *non*-dialectical thought, a thought that is *itself* living, or which understands itself as being a part of life. To do justice to that life which is at least at first recalcitrant to conceptualization, without betraying it through idealization – as dialectic is supposed to do – Esposito suggests that the best of Italian thought 'give[s] philosophy the concrete characteristics of life' and thus becomes a 'living thought', endowed with real life, participating in the very process of living, in the flesh rather than the mere tracery of the conceptual skeleton which Hegel depicted so vividly as to mislead us into thinking that we were looking at a real animal.[1]

Thus Italian thought endeavours not to choke life of its vitality with a mesh of concepts that would lacerate it and arrest its movement, instead allowing it to be and indeed actively wading into its many currents in order both to follow them and to re-channel their flow. In so resisting the dialectic, philosophy seeks the assistance of other disciplines which are less prone to murdering that which they love by embracing it too tightly and imposing themselves upon it.

Philosophy would be encouraged by these other disciplines, which also concern themselves with life in its historicity, to resist the philosophical tendency towards self-reflection to the point of self-absorption. Philosophy thereby refuses to confine itself to a meditation on – or deconstruction of – its own nature, by reinforcing another of its tendencies: towards that which lies beyond the concept: 'The material of philosophy is not another philosophy, in a self-referential attitude that closes in on itself, but rather, precisely what is not philosophy because it coincides with life itself in its continuous and unpredictable development' (Esposito 2012 [2010], 160). Lorenzo Chiesa also stresses this point, according to which Italian philosophy seems to distinguish itself from so many other European philosophies, which seem to desire at all costs to retain their sovereign independence and even a certain legislative power with respect to other disciplines, in that it achieves its very identity precisely by opening itself to these other discourses, as if they were its very lifeblood (Chiesa 2011, 2–3).[2]

The coming to life of thought then compels *theory* to understand itself as a kind of *practice*: for thought, in coming alive, has become inherently active, transformative of that which it touches. Thought must admit that to think is inherently political: 'only in this way, through practical action in the world, can philosophy truly revitalise itself, identifying itself in a historicity that is one with the inexhaustible movement of life' (Esposito 2012 [2010], 158/151). Giovanni Gentile, Antonio Gramsci and, in another more paradoxical way, Benedetto Croce are exemplary figures in this regard for Esposito, the first two at the very least sharing in 'the project of making philosophical practice a potent historical force intended to change the world' (Esposito 2012 [2010], 158).

Italian philosophy is, for the most part, a philosophy which dwells on the living core of its historical moment and proceeds to unfold the potentials contained within it. Thus it actively transforms its own time (even to the point of supplying a unity to 'Italy' itself, in the absence of a nation-state). It is a philosophy which deals with its outside, with those other subjects and their objects from which philosophy was for the greater part of its history kept apart. Among other things, it is this openness to a mobile real and its ever-changing conceptualization by non-philosophical disciplines that allows Italian philosophy to forge so many new pathways for philosophy to explore, while at the same time rendering it ambiguous as to whether certain figures may straightforwardly be described as 'philosophers' at all, or indeed whether a reading of the Italian philosophical scene would be possible if it confined itself to 'pure philosophy' alone.

Philosophy in Italy concerns life, its potential, and the political and cultural transformations made possible by this perspective upon life and philosophy's transformative role within it. It seeks not merely to *interpret* life but also to *change* it, and in order to do so, it embraces its own participation in life, and in particular the bustle of civic life.

Who counts as an Italian philosopher? The history and geography of Italian philosophy

Italy, as we know it today, did not always exist. Nor did Italian philosophy.

Before Italy, philosophy did indeed take place on the peninsula which today constitutes the Italian nation, but it was not always something that we would comfortably deem 'Italian': after all, the history of the territory that stretches from the Alps southwards into the Mediterranean between the Iberian peninsula and the Greek, towards North Africa, is intimately bound up with the history of philosophy, as is this whole ocean, on each of its coasts and even in the passages between cultures that the sea's expanse afforded. What we today, and since the 1870s at least, call 'Italy' had an intimate relation with the beginning of philosophy in antiquity: its Adriatic, Ionian, Tyrrhenian and Mediterranean coasts were, like the coast of modern Turkey, dotted with Greek-speaking colonies, and many of the philosophers we know today as 'pre-Socratics' were born or took up residence there – Empedocles on Sicily, where he famously threw himself into Mount Etna, Parmenides and Zeno in Elea, in the Southern part of modern Italy.

As the dominance of Greek culture waned, it was replaced by an empire which stemmed from Ancient Rome. Latin, the language imposed by the empire, would, together with imperial rule itself, colonize the near entirety of Europe and leave indelible marks on the language of philosophy and indeed on the concepts to which this language gave expression. Even after the empire's irreparable decline over the course of the first millennium of our era, the entire Christian Middle ages would employ Latin as the lingua franca for the overwhelming majority of its philosophical production; and in addition to that, many of the earliest European universities, from Bologna in the twelfth century to Naples and Padua in the thirteenth and Florence in the fourteenth, were founded on Italian soil.

But it would be arbitrary in most respects to consider any of the Ancient Greek or Roman philosophers to be 'Italian'. So, at what point might a certain tradition that could rightly be described as 'Italian' begin? Even if we cannot say that it would be concomitant with the outset of philosophical work on the peninsula, nor would it be wise simply to wait until 'Italy' as a nation had finally formed in the nineteenth century before affirming that something distinctively Italian had begun to happen in philosophy. This is because the traits that define the most powerful Italian thought of the nineteenth and twentieth centuries can be seen to have a much longer prehistory in the 'Italy' of the Modern Age (generally understood to begin around the late sixteenth and early seventeenth centuries), the Renaissance (which is to say, the period immediately preceding the Modern Age, and spanning the fifteenth and sixteenth centuries, most prominently in Florence thanks to the work of Lorenzo de'Medici, who retrieved many of the wonders and much of the knowledge that the ancient world had left to posterity, albeit in a scattered and obscure state) and even the Middle Ages (let us say, although nothing is clear here, from the fourth or fifth century to the fourteenth), long before the *Risorgimento*, by even as much as a whole millennium.

The rediscovery of the culture of the Classical world pitted the sole unquestioned authority of the Christian church against the rediscovered works of the pagan masters (Plato and Aristotle). The disagreement between these respective 'truths' forced Italian thinkers to engage with the problems of pluralism and hermeneutics (interpretation) from very early on, a fact attested to by the works of Giovanni Pico della Mirandola and most of Italian Renaissance humanism in its attempt to synthesize all available knowledge into one coherent whole.

Given that one of the defining traits of Italian philosophy is an intimate relation between contemporary thought and the history of that thought, this *genealogical* account of the nature of Italian philosophy may be legitimized by the very subject under consideration. The most striking features of contemporary Italian thought were raised on the foundations – or built among the ruins – of a much older tradition that may date back as far as the Middle Ages, to the time of Dante Alighieri in the thirteenth and fourteenth centuries, if not earlier.

The *absence* of a single Italian nation from the very beginning had a greater significance for the character of Italian philosophy than the founding of the nation itself, which hardly interrupted the development of that philosophy which had emerged outside of the nation and even the State. This implies that describing the contours of such a thing as Italian philosophy may prove to be a delicate task, since one cannot circumscribe it within the boundaries of a nation from the moment of its foundation onwards, or simply allow that national provenance to define what one will call 'Italian' in the realm of philosophy.

As a consequence, the most obvious possibility to consider is that the vernacular Italian *language* will be at least one of the unifying factors for the entire tradition that we wish to describe, for such a tongue was spoken, in various forms, long before the unification of a nation, and indeed – much more important, philosophically – it was employed in the writing of texts that are more or less recognizable as 'philosophy' (even though, as we have seen, this recognition in itself is rarely if ever absolutely clear, in Italian thought more than anywhere else). Roughly speaking, this first occurred in the works of Dante, who was by no means simply the poet he is generally understood to be in the English-speaking world; and in fact, one of the distinctive features that we have already assigned to Italian philosophy begins to reveal itself here, since it is a philosophical tradition which has long been nourished by and existed in close proximity to disciplines and discourses other than that of philosophy in the strict sense in which the academic and scholastic traditions were developing it elsewhere in Europe.

The choice was between the lingua franca, Latin, with its supposedly universal intelligibility (among the international or, as we might put it today, 'cosmopolitan' population of scholars, the educated classes), and the local vernacular. The decision to write in a natural language rather than a technical one almost always has its reasons, together with its incalculable repercussions. Such is perhaps more readily apparent in the case of the translation of religious texts and may most clearly be seen in the case of the Lutheran translation of the Bible, which, at least in its precedent, would transform Northern Europe in the formation of Protestant Christianity. We see such a moment of decision in Dante, in particular, who, most famously in his extraordinary *Divine Comedy*, chose to write his poetic texts in the 'Italian' of his day – so he himself described it – even though his philosophical and political treatises were still composed in Latin.

And yet not everyone who demonstrates the characteristics that we shall identify as among the most salient of the Italian tradition in philosophy wrote in the Italian language, and thus we can say that while the emergence of a vernacular with Dante is helpful in providing us with a rough location of the historical moment of beginning, composing in Italian is neither a necessary nor – even more so – a sufficient condition for belonging to the class of 'Italian Philosophers'.

We have journeyed as far as we can on the terrains of politics, geography, history and language; to say any more about what might unify a single Italian tradition of philosophical thought we must now turn to philosophy itself and attempt to show how this exceptional geographic and political history of the Italian peninsula affected the philosophical thought which flourished in that historical environment. This will retrospectively illuminate the idea of an Italian philosophy and what might be said to create such a unity in the first place.

The philosophical consequences of history and geography

For Esposito, 'it is undeniable that some connection exists between philosophy and territory' (2012 [2010], 12). Italy was for a long time a territory without a nation, and this connection is operative in the case of Italian philosophy understood as that thought which originates in a certain territory not yet unified into a single nation but which in general spoke a certain dialect of Italian when it was not speaking and writing in Latin.

The belated formation of a political unity, along with that nation's subsequent isolation at the time of Mussolini's fascism, gave birth to a unique culture the origin of which Esposito locates, not without a certain vacillation, in Dante, and which runs through the humanism that flourished in Renaissance Italy (Petrarch, Lorenzo Valla, Giovanni Pico Della Mirandola and Marsilio Ficino, among others), into the twentieth century and the present day.[3] Esposito concludes that 'the lack of a profound national vocation and, until the middle of the nineteenth century, a unitary state, is precisely what has given Italian philosophy something more than (or at least different from) other philosophical traditions which have experienced a more direct identification between territory and nation' (2012 [2010], 21).

Thus Esposito wishes to insist on the difference between the idea of an 'Italian philosophy' and a *national* philosophy. Once this distinction has been made, we may arrive at a more accurate understanding of the relation between philosophy and its *territory*, a connection which Esposito describes under the heading of 'geophilosophy', a philosophy relating to Gaia or Geo, the Earth upon which Reason finds its ground: 'we must keep a firm grasp of the semantic difference between territory and nation. Geophilosophy, the territorializing – and therefore, also always deterritorialized – characterization of thought is in no way identical to philosophical nationalism – or even to a strictly national variety of philosophy' (2012 [2010], 14). Italy is unique in this regard:

> Unlike in other European countries – in France, Spain, England, and, with a delay of two centuries, Germany – rather than accompanying or following the formation of the nation-state, the great Italian philosophy of Machiavelli, [Giordano] Bruno, [Tommaso] Campanella, Galileo, and [Giambattista] Vico preceded it by a long time. Italian philosophy neither influenced nor was influenced by the formation of the national state. [. . .] It formed outside the nation and the state [. . .]. The transition from mediaeval villages to the cities of early Humanism and the high Renaissance did not give rise to anything comparable to a territory united by a single political will. (Esposito 2012 [2010], 19)

And even further, this separation from nationality is precisely the *negative* foundation of the *positive* characteristics of Italian thought: 'not only can Italian philosophy not be reduced to its national role, but its most authentic reason for being lies precisely in the distance it takes from that role' (Esposito 2012 [2010], 18).

Speaking of the great cross-border exchanges of culture and thought that took place with an especial intensity during the Renaissance, Esposito suggests that the very lack of a unified Italian state *facilitated* such exchanges and lent Italian thought a certain internationalism and indeed a *European* character which will always have been unmatched:

> For all of them – Italians and foreigners alike – Italy was anything but a nation like Spain, France, or England, which by that time had been consolidated into the forms of their respective state bodies. Without political boundaries and without a centre, Italy remained a formidable land of development, dissemination, and cross-pollination of the great, single European culture whose scope and importance was not national, because it went beyond the nation. (2012 [2010], 20)

This is why Esposito considers Italian thought to be crucial to a contemporary understanding of what Europe itself and as a whole can and should be (cf. 2018 [2016]). But in any case, this orientation to a transnational Europe, which originated in a non-national territory, went for the Renaissance humanists in a way that it apparently did not for the Scholastics who were at least born on Italian soil: in the case of the latter, for Esposito, they eventually escaped the tug of Italy's gravity (were 'deterritorialized') before being recaptured by whatever national or more likely international situation was unfolding at the universities and seminaries of Paris and elsewhere: 'If the highly developed thought of scholasticism already moved entirely outside the confines of the national culture with Thomas Aquinas, gravitating more toward Paris, Humanism as a whole had an external projection that made it an international movement in the strongest sense of the term' (2012 [2010], 19). It was somehow possible for Italian philosophy to remain both internationalist in its outlook and yet quintessentially Italian at the same time.

Stateless philosophy

Not only is Italian thought habituated to thinking outside the confines of a national border but it is also accustomed to thinking political collectives in such a way that their unity does not depend upon the *state* or upon the existence of a single transcendent *sovereign power*: 'Italian thought on politics is pre-statal in its conception and, at times, is even framed in terms of resistance to the state' (Esposito 2012 [2010], 21). This fact finds a very clear expression in some of the most philosophically powerful forms of contemporary Italian thought, since it is among the greatest merits of Antonio Negri, Giorgio Agamben and Paolo Virno, to speak merely of our contemporaries, that they have attempted to think politics beyond the State. In their work this takes place from the standpoint of the Left, despite the latter's traditional tendency to advocate collectivist and communitarian forms of state intervention, regulation and centralized power. This heritage would explain a certain recurrent tendency towards both individualistic liberalism and anarchism (a political organization or absence of the same which rejects any single instance of governing power, any *archē*). Apart from the Leftists we have just invoked, one might also think of Machiavelli in the context of political science and its relation to the question of human nature, Antonio Gramsci from the left, and Benedetto Croce from the right, or even Gianni Vattimo's pluralist liberal-communism.

But even apart from a certain anarchistic suspicion of state- and sovereign power, this political and geographical rooting of Italian thought (as a 'geophilosophy') is precisely what allows it to respond better than other national philosophies to contemporary concerns, given what has happened to the nation-state over the course of the last century or more, which is to say broadly the decline of its power in the face of transnational bodies, institutions and even corporations. A philosophy, the basic traits of which were formed *prior* to the state, is innately better suited to thinking what comes *after* the state's termination or at least in its increasing irrelevance: 'now that the time of the nation is running out – or at the very least, when its assumptions and ends are being called into question – Italian thought can face the future with greater innovative energy' (Esposito 2012 [2010], 21).

Three paradigms

What are the features of the affirmative alternative to the exhausted categories of political and philosophical thinking that Italy is able to offer as a result of its exceptional history and geography? What are the rudiments of this other thinking, which speaks from the distant past while echoing ahead into a future that is still to come?

To organize his account of Italian thought, Esposito identifies three paradigms, which are not described in immediately accessible terms but with some explication reveal themselves to provide a remarkably powerful, philosophically productive, and coherent way of characterizing Italian thought, throughout its history and right up to the present day – a history which the traits themselves may ultimately be responsible for delimiting.

The three paradigms are:

(1) the *immanentization of antagonism* (associated with the name Machiavelli)

(2) the *historicization of the non-historical* (associated with Giambattista Vico)

(3) the *mundanization* – or becoming-worldly – *of the subject* (associated first of all with Giordano Bruno).

Immanentization of antagonism

'Philosophy is its own time grasped in thought' – this much, at least, Italian philosophy took from Hegel. But perhaps in the end, it took little else. And, as Esposito makes clear, Italian philosophy was not altogether content even with that, for the Hegelian conception remains too theoretical; in Italian thought of the twentieth century at least, we have 'something that thrusts the philosophical work into the very heart of the real, [. . .] the rejection of all dualism in favour of an immanence viewed as more and more absolute [. . . which] implies a profound discontinuity with [philosophy's] traditionally speculative form [in, for instance, Hegel]' (2012 [2010], 157). Once again, the owl of Minerva, one of Hegel's favourite animals, arrives too late to really change anything.

The dualism spoken of here is that which separates theory and practice, thinking and acting, but it corresponds, on a Platonic scheme, to the difference between the intelligible and the sensible: indeed, the very first feature of Italian thought identified by Esposito is one in which the Platonic and Hegelian dialectic, that reconciles the intelligible with the sensible, transcendence with immanence (in favour of the former, naturally), is said to be inoperative.

That from which one seeks to differentiate one's self in order for one's identity to be constituted is never entirely overcome, as a certain reading of the dialectic would have it, but rather persists as an indigestible core, a permanent enemy against whom we define ourselves ever anew without ever reconciling ourselves with them, a bone stuck in the throat that precisely calibrates whatever voice we call our own.[4]

Philosophy, then, remains stubbornly lodged at the very heart of the sensuous real, resisting any dialectical idealization that would raise the real to the level of the ideal concept. The difference between real and ideal, practice and theory, is said to elude dialectical reconciliation altogether – it is not simply taken up in a third instance that would encapsulate the essence and truth of the opposition itself, a gesture which Hegel named 'sublation' (*Aufhebung*) (cf. Negri 2009). Esposito calls the non-dialectical relationship between irreconcilable opposites an 'antagonism'.

In politics, antagonism finds its principal place. If the political is a place of order, then this order must distinguish itself from the chaos and disorder of natural animal life outside of the city or the *polis*. Or so it is frequently thought, by figures such as Thomas Hobbes. But it is a distinguishing characteristic of Italian political thought that this distinction remains indistinct and the separation incomplete. The antagonism between order and disorder remains *immanent* to order itself, and there it endures. Esposito suggests that for someone like Machiavelli, this disorder is in a certain way the very *source* of order, just as the political realm is formed by means of a relation to that which stands outside of it – to take one privileged instance, the private life of the reproductive body whose proper place Aristotle had identified in the home (Esposito 2012 [2010], 24).

For Italian philosophy, disorder is immanent *to* political life rather than chronologically prior or simply outside of it, continuously *generating* order rather than being sublated and ultimately cancelled out *in* order.

One important example of this antagonism is the rethinking of the relation between public and private life which goes by the name of 'biopolitics' and originates in the work of Michel Foucault. For a figure like Giorgio Agamben, the exclusion of private life from the public sphere of politics – an exclusion which nevertheless and indeed precisely thereby places that private bodily life in subjection to political power – is the very origin of biopolitics, and the ever more forceful imposition of political power upon these supposedly once separate and private living processes is known as 'biopower'. The assertion of a permanent antagonism in the political order on the part of Italian thought would explain why in recent times Foucault's ideas have so firmly taken root there.

Esposito finds the matrix of this notion in Machiavelli. Power, for Machiavelli, was always twofold in nature: it could issue either in the ruler's expectation of being loved by those who were subjected to his sovereign power, or in the insistence that he be feared by his subjects. And yet, even the rulers, the intended audience of Machiavelli's *Prince* and *Discourses*, were themselves little more than pawns in a temporary stabilization of the infinitely mightier historical forces which were responsible for the recurrent destabilizations and ensuing reaffirmations of all states and kingdoms.

Historicization of the non-historical

One aspect of Hegelianism that *was* to be influential on Italian shores was the supposedly *historicist* character of his thinking. But how are we to reconcile this putative historicism with the resistance to dialectic that we have just outlined? Has Italian thought conceived of a philosophy of history which would *not* be dialectical?

If Italian thought understands *all* identity as dependent upon an enduring and antagonistic otherness at its core, then something analogous is taken to be the case when it focuses more specifically on *history*. The law of antagonism becomes especially apparent in those entities which are historical and hence inherently subject to change, but perhaps *every* identity is ultimately historically constituted.[5]

We should distinguish first of all between history itself and the history of ideas or the history of philosophy. First, let us examine the history of philosophy:

Italian thought enjoys a very peculiar relation with its own history: 'it not only has never severed this tie [with what precedes it], it seeks the form and sense of its own actuality by looking to the origin' (Esposito 2012 [2010], 22). In other words, Esposito suggests that the modern tradition in Europe, and Descartes in particular, began to think precisely by severing all ties with their mediaeval predecessors, as if the modern could define itself only by making an absolutely clean break with the ancient and whatever binds us to it (such as the continuity provided by the Middle Ages).

Italian thought, on the other hand, never treated its origin in such a way: 'all Italian thought, from Bruno to [Giacomo] Leopardi, seeks in the wisdom of the ancients the keys to interpret what is closest at hand' (Esposito 2012 [2010], 23). Esposito speaks of this as Italian thought's 'genealogical vocation' (and obliquely refers to Giorgio Agamben here, as a prime example, without naming him[6]).

Genealogy amounts to the adoption of a certain attitude towards the beginning of that history to which the genealogist belongs: it assumes that such an 'origin' does not exist. There is no one objectively ascertainable chronological moment at which a certain phenomenon may be said to have begun; there are merely retrospective accounts that appropriate certain disparate elements of the phenomenon's prehistory in such a way as to render that phenomenon intelligible. The meaning of the past is not given until it is interpreted in the present and taken as a precursor of that present, as a condition for the very intelligibility of the contemporary moment. Thus, on Esposito's account, genealogy assumes 'that a founding moment [. . .] is structurally absent. Because of this constitutive "inoriginarity" of history, the origin is always latently coeval with each historical moment. This allows it to be reactivated as a source of energy' (2012 [2010], 23).

This is the way in which the *immanence of antagonism* works itself out in the realm of *history*: the split between history itself as the unfolding of events and the (*a*historical) origin *of* that historical unfolding.

The origin of history lies in the non-historical natural order in which the laws and conventions of culture do not yet apply. Thus, the origin is not eliminated with the emergence of what originates; rather it perdures. We shall never altogether escape from nature into history, and indeed this absence of a definitive egress, this conflict within nature, and indeed between nature and history, is the very motor of history's continuing advance into the future.

In history, we thus discover a crucial analogy with the political and its immanent antagonism, 'the intrinsic but equally antinomic relationship with a nonhistorical (or at least not entirely historicizable) element that nevertheless forms a part of it' (Esposito 2012 [2010], 25). This 'historicization of the nonhistorical' was brought to the fore most strikingly by Giambattista Vico: 'Nothing is more deadly, for Vico, than the typically modern idea that we can sever the knot that binds history to its nonhistorical beginning, unravelling it through a process that fully temporalizes life' (Esposito 2012 [2010], 27).

In general, this refusal to cut itself off from the past helps us to explain why the characteristics of historical Italian thought *remain* constitutive for its current form, and hence why Esposito's account of history can so vividly illuminate the present, while also explaining the long and perhaps permanent posterity of some of the earliest established traits of philosophy on the peninsula.

But this relation to a non-historical kernel that endures throughout a historical unfolding also renders intelligible the predominance of another trait that is particularly prominent in some of the most interesting strains of recent Italian thought: *political theology*, the endeavour to trace political concepts such as 'sovereignty' back to certain theological notions (divine transcendence, autonomy, self-causation), as if that heritage could not at all or only barely be eluded. Hence, the very idea of history (common in the rest of modern Europe) as a process of 'secularization' is, if not rejected, then at least problematized in Italian philosophy, since the theological persists at the very core of Western philosophical and political conceptuality.

This remnant of a theological heritage at the heart of concepts which are only apparently secular has allowed Italian thought to entertain a particular relationship with *Christian* ideas. This in part explains the prominence of *nihilism* in Italian thought, for the latter, according to Nietzsche, is the historical outcome of a Christian worldview, understood as a vulgar translation of Platonic metaphysics (cf. Gianni Vattimo and Emanuele Severino, among others).[7]

Becoming-worldly of the subject

We began with a theory of the (antagonistic) identity of all entities and then applied it to history, or, perhaps more precisely, we came to consider this identity as *itself* historical; now we shall apply the same logic to the *agent* of history: the human subject.

The third paradigm (after the *immanentization of antagonism* (Machiavelli and politics) and the *historicization of the non-historical* (Vico and history)) is the *mundanization of the subject*. It concerns a rethinking of the transcendental and reflexive subject that characterized modern thought elsewhere on the continent, as well as a deconstruction of the primacy of the 'person', understood as an individual unit in which one part (the rational, for preference) subordinates another (the animal) – the ideal transcending the real. Both of these notions were put in question by Italian philosophy from the very start and continue to be matters for interrogation.

Outside of Italy, thought was conceived as taking place only in the bracketing of the sensory body, the passions of which were understood to cloud the eye of the mind and distract us from the purely rational activity that would be our eminently human vocation. The first two paradigms involved the coincidence of a historical and political life with the 'living thought' that would attempt to think and intervene within it; but this third paradigm expresses still more directly the intersection of knowledge and life, inasmuch as here the subject is not understood to be founded on a scission between itself and its own biological substance. The soul will no longer be grounded only through its separation from the body; rather, the animal remains growling in the very texture of our most divine words and thoughts.

Italian philosophy, therefore, has a subtly different understanding of the subject in comparison with that of other European philosophies which deploy a model taken preponderantly from Descartes and Kant. This latter subjectivity is described by Esposito as 'transcendental'. Although this term is most frequently associated with Kant, rather than Descartes, Esposito is attempting to capture something which he deems common to both of these quintessentially modern thinkers, and that is the dependence of all representations on a reflexive subject that would in some way stand apart from (and hence 'transcend') the empirical world of nature that it represents (Descartes) or even constitutes (Kant and later transcendental phenomenology).[8]

There is a direct line between casting ourselves adrift from historical presuppositions and the reflexive subject understood as transcendental, which is to say the condition for the possibility of knowledge. In Descartes at least, philosophy begins by cutting itself off from the presuppositions of earlier ancient and mediaeval philosophies, in a certain temporary scepticism, the suspension of presuppositions; it starts afresh, unencumbered by the weight of the past. This is the gesture with which the Cartesian *Meditations* opens: without these historical hindrances, one finds one's self seeking an anchor or a single patch of dry land in the midst of a vast and disorienting ocean: this point of surety is found in one's own consciousness and the certainty that one finds in the reflexive relation that the subject inalienably enjoys with its own existence in thought.

The Cartesian (and later the Kantian) position asserts that the ground of all representations lies within the transcendental subject that could assure itself of its own being independently of the empirical world of nature, and whose being is in this sense prior to and more significant than that of the world in which it only later becomes enmeshed. Such was the beginning of an immensely broad, idealistic and – Esposito will say – 'transcendentalist' turn in philosophy – the subject as severed from the life of the world and confined primarily to a position of disinterested knowledge – to which Italian philosophy provides a positive alternative, from the very beginning.

In Italy, the subject is not understood to be separable from the animal life and natural world in which it partook prior to the moment of reflection, any more than it is to be extracted from the historical world, which Edmund Husserl would later call the 'lifeworld' (*Lebenswelt*).

Thus Italian thought tends to bypass an entire epoch within philosophy in which the subject was taken to be transcendental and primarily epistemological: hence its predilection for a realism which Maurizio Ferraris will have done so much to promote in our day, an attention to the 'actual' that is not subject to the conditions of transcendental subjectivity.[9] In general, it seems to elude the alternative between Kant and Hegel, the two giants around whom philosophy elsewhere on the continent has revolved for over two centuries. Nevertheless, the resistance to a transcendental understanding of the subject has shifted it closer to Hegelianism than Kantianism. And indeed, the type of realism which we find in Ferraris might be said to have certain roots, albeit rather deeply buried, in Gentile's reinterpretation of Hegelianism as 'actualism'.

Esposito associates this envelopment of the subject by its lifeworld with a turn away from the notion of personhood. In his eyes, the notion of a person has historically involved subjection: either a subordination to a power that transcends the subject or a subjugation of one part of the subject to another, as when our reason subdues our animal drives so as to achieve individual autonomy and to leave anonymity and its nameless desires behind. For Italian thought, these latter are in fact considered to be an inherent part of our thought and humanity. This has led Esposito to advocate the notion of the *im*personal, the *non*-individual (cf. 2012 [2010], 30).

A taste for impersonality has characterized Italian thought since at least the Renaissance. It led historically to the surpassing or complexifying of a certain humanism which understood humanity to be the site of a privileged manifestation of life. Giordano Bruno was exemplary in this regard in his attempt to think of an anonymous life that would run through all of creation and sweep up individuated subjects in its wake. Bruno criticized the traditional emphasis on the primacy of human and divine personhood in the name of an infinite and non-individuated life. He rejected the separation of 'body and soul, spirit and nature, subject and object' and introduced, in their stead, 'the idea of a living cosmos without centre or boundaries' (Esposito 2012 [2010], 30). Human subjects were merely part of 'the regenerative process of the world' (an idea we have also encountered in Machiavelli).

This theory of the subject as 'mundane' and impersonal has significant political implications. Italian thought is thus situated on a different plane to that of modern individualism, which still carries such immense weight today. In the tradition of liberalism stemming from John Locke and John Stuart Mill, individuals are understood to be owners of themselves and fundamentally unrelated to one another. 'Person' in this context is a legal notion in the sense that one's individual person is one's own private property (as are all those chattels which it accrues), and we are each free to dispose of it (and them) as we see fit. Such an isolated metaphysical unit is not to be found in the most powerful and original strains of Italian thought, for here the subject is inherently open to others and to an outside more generally, and hence ontologically forms part of a *community* with these others: 'the theme of community, as an opening of subjectivity to its own alterity, is an integral part of nineteenth-century Italian thought [for instance, Gentile, perhaps]' (Esposito 2012 [2010], 30).

This stress on the *common* as opposed to the singular and private explains the prominence of a certain type of communitarian and even communistic thought on the part of a number of the most widely read figures on the Italian Left (and even the Right) in the twentieth and twenty-first centuries in particular. Giorgio Agamben, Antonio Negri, Paolo Virno, Esposito himself and even Gianni Vattimo could be mentioned here in the same breath.

Human nature rethought: Life, language, politics

The 'common' is often understood in naturalistic or quasi-naturalistic terms, as relating to our shared *life* or our *human nature* – a concept reinvented and deployed quite brazenly by Italian philosophy. Our 'commons' are akin to our biological inheritance, which is to say our human nature, even if this humanity is not that of any stereotypical kind of humanism but encompasses the inhuman and the impersonal. In any case, the Aristotelian definitions of man as an animal possessed of language and a political animal are frequently most unashamedly embraced by Italian thinkers, particularly those among the new Left. And yet they are transformed in a way that often involves a rethinking of human nature itself and in particular an especial attention to the 'nature' that is involved in any assertions regarding 'human nature'. Thus, for instance, Paolo Virno will speak of the joint between the biological and the symbolic, with reference to a novel thinking of both language and life which draws upon empirical biology and philosophical anthropology, all the while attempting to avoid conceding everything to a naive naturalism. Virno attempts to trace the symbolic back to the moment at which humanity in its animal form – the 'human animal' – requires symbolic supplementation.

The same goes for the political aspect of this strange animal, as the work of Agamben, for instance, attests. Here, human nature is understood to involve equally life, language and political co-belonging, along with – at least at present, though one works to resist it – the sovereign power which rules over and decides upon the boundaries of the political sphere, incorporating private life into the public realm even when it appears to exclude it, all the better to exercise control over our bodies.

All of this involves a rethinking of the human in regard to both its animality (its natural side) and its linguistic-political character (its cultural and technical aspect).

*   *   *

The present volume

The account we have just given of the history and nature of Italian philosophy, the very idea, stresses above all its most original moments – which is to say its defining and thus individuating traits. We have closely followed the schema provided by Roberto Esposito, which constitutes perhaps the most powerful, comprehensive and genuinely philosophical attempt to define the uniqueness of Italian philosophy: this is why we have chosen to adopt it as our own. It has also been instrumental in our decision as to which writers to include in the present collection.

That said, we have also been influenced by the stricter delineation of what is most fruitful in Italian thought to be found in Lorenzo Chiesa and Alberto Toscano's *Italian Thought Today* and *The Italian Difference*, as well as Michael Hardt and Paolo Virno's *Radical Thought in Italy*, and other related texts. In truth we have focused for the most part on thinkers who are already visible outside of Italy, and indeed, as Esposito and Chiesa both admit, the very notion of an 'Italian thought' is in general one that has been formed *outside* of Italy itself, from the standpoint of an external gaze looking on from afar. This fact inevitably results in a different perspective from those who would centre their understanding of Italian philosophy on the current and predominant state of the Italian academy (the SUNY Series on Contemporary Italian Philosophy might be said to adopt a position somewhat closer to the latter, and we can only refer the interested reader to that series).[10]

Furthermore, we have not hesitated to include thinkers who would be considered by some to be economists, psychoanalytic thinkers, and political theorists, rather than philosophers, not least because one of the most powerful impetuses that Italy has imparted to philosophy is the force of insights gleaned from spheres beyond the philosophical, including politics and economics, theology and law. Only a pre-given definition of what philosophy is would forestall such an admission, and this would be to refuse the inherent plasticity of philosophy's definition, its power continually to redefine itself and its object, an adaptability to the real which Italian philosophy most openly and adeptly exhibits.

With all that said, in the interests of a certain pluralism and the broader audience that we are obliged to provide for in the presentation of a volume such as this, we *began* from that core but have also extended ourselves beyond it in a number of directions, including some thinkers for whom the former would likely have little time and only scant respect.

In general, we have only included those philosophers who are at least minimally known among English-speaking readers or whose works have begun to be or were once translated. As a result, they may feature, if not today then perhaps tomorrow, on curricula adopted within the Anglophone academy. We have incorporated those among contemporary continental thinkers whose work has achieved some prominence in recent times, as well as those among their precursors who would most likely be considered indispensable and 'classic'. In particular, we want to stress again the fact that when it came to the choice between those figures already well known in the English-speaking world and those well known in Italy who have so far enjoyed less exposure in an English-language context, we have erred towards the former.[11] The purpose of the present work is to provide a textbook for those teaching and even more those learning Italian philosophy in an English-speaking context – within or without the walls of the academy – who have to rely on existing translations. The assumption that this book will function largely as an aid to teaching led to the foreclosure of a number of those thinkers who will likely remain obscure – and untaught – for some time to come in our predominantly monoglot culture.

We have nevertheless attempted to allude to as many philosophers as we have space for (and space, however expansive, is always finite in the world of publishing) and have indicated resources for students of the discipline to explore in more depth these and other even more dimly lit passages, at least in the timeline that may be found towards the end of the book.

The choices made as a part of this pluralist gesture were taken partly in response to the many and various views that we solicited and received; and this advice made it all too clear to us that we were, as one adviser put it, 'unlikely to please everyone' (how could it be otherwise in such a politicized – and gigantic – field?). The disparities and conflicts (to the point of straight contradiction) within the suggestions received (to the point of strident demands and absolute strictures) have led us to attempt to make as few decisions as possible in advance, with regard to our selection and the multiple audiences to which the book could potentially speak. This letting-go has brought with it, as is inevitable, a certain measure of contingency and arbitrariness, perhaps larger than we are capable of imagining.

In any case, we assume that in any future editions, the constellation of thinkers which we shall present will change in line with the mobile situation of translations and the conceptual innovations which prove to be most incisive – or influential – at that time.

In summary, we have tried to present what could only ever have been a partial survey of the immense riches available to us, but which draws its selection from the history and prehistory of Italian thought while being focused above all on the twentieth century, with a certain privilege given to the philosophers of the Left – a precedence justified not by their political orientation but by the sheer power and extent of their theoretical inventions. They above all have helped to open a future for philosophy at a time when it continues elsewhere to seem largely moribund or at least stuck in the doldrums. Irremediable contingencies of the time and situation, such as space and expense, as well as the vagaries of one's own contingent education, have also made decisions for us, inevitably.

In short, and in conclusion, we were constrained by every imaginable kind of finitude while constructing the book that you now hold in your hands, but we hope that, at least at times, it will serve some useful purpose, even if it remains unlikely to please everyone.[12]

✳   ✳   ✳

Notes

1 And if this all sounds close to *Lebensphilosophie* or the 'philosophy of life' of Nietzschean heritage, then that is both entirely understandable and inaccurate. For Esposito, there was no philosophy of life in Italy precisely because 'the entirety of Italian thought is traversed and determined by it. And also, because life has always been thought about both in relation to and in confrontation with the categories of history and politics' (2012 [2010], 31). This means that life is constitutive of subjectivity: 'How could politics and, even more, history arise in a world devoid of subjects defined, within the plane of immanence, by their own living singularity?'

2 Esposito speaks of Italian philosophy as inherently 'extraverted' [*sic*] (2012 [2010], 15). This extroversion has at least two distinct but related faces: first of all, it relates philosophy to the non-philosophical in the sense of life, history and politics – 'the unique propensity of Italian philosophy for the non-philosophical' involves 'engagement with the outside world instead of examination of consciousness or the interior dialogue, Italian philosophy has always appeared poised to cross over its own boundaries; but this overstepping is precisely what allows it to achieve a perspective that would otherwise be unattainable' (Esposito 2012 [2010], 11) – but second, it implies an engagement with other disciplines and discourses *on* this 'life' or this 'living present': hence we find Esposito speaking of 'its civil commitment and its being

coloured by other styles of expression' (Esposito 2012 [2010], 11, translation modified).

3　'I do not mean to deny that the idea, aspiration, and prefiguration of unity ran through – and even mobilised – the culture that was created in Italy starting from the inception [*costituzione*] of its language' (Esposito 2012 [2010], 19/20) (cf. Esposito 2012 [2010], 8). Despite its fragmentation at the political level, a certain *idea* of unity, at least, was present in a certain Italian culture thanks (it seems) to the *language* of Italian (Esposito 2012 [2010], 19). The suggestion is perhaps not so much that philosophy has to be written in Italian in order to count as 'Italian Philosophy' but that it develops from a culture which was formed at the time of the emergence of this common language. And yet elsewhere Esposito seems to attribute some importance to the distinction between 'inception' (*esordio*) and 'origin' (*origine*), with the former being located 'between the early sixteenth and the first half of the eighteenth centuries' (cf. ibid., 10/12).

4　The difference between the sensible thing and its intelligible version is to be found within immanence itself. This fact is stressed by Antonio Negri (2009) in a text entitled 'The Italian Difference'. Here Negri opposes this vision of the immanence of antagonism not to Hegel but to those philosophers he describes as 'postmodern', which seems to imply those who still seek a certain transcendence (a messianic future, a utopia, an Other to whom we are obliged, or any form of sovereign power that would govern the present). In this, they remain somewhat idealist and insufficiently materialist, which for him 'shifts any possible critical space towards the outside [of the world]', and away from immanence (Negri 2009, 20).

　　Among the Italian philosophers who resist this gesture, Negri identifies only three: Antonio Gramsci, Mario Tronti and Luisa Muraro. This troika has chosen not to follow 'postmodernism', preferring a position that is 'consistently immanentist and materialist' (Negri 2009, 23).

　　To any concern for a non-material transcendence, Negri opposes 'a longing for reconstruction based on the very affirmation of difference. The fact is that *difference* is *resistance*', an affirmative and internal difference, an immanent power which resists and yet is nonetheless creative: 'Difference has really stopped being separation: it has become creative and is beginning to produce the future' (2009, 21). Immanence itself is a kind of resistance to that which Negri figures as transcendent, and that is perhaps ultimately a single unified sovereign instance, or something which acts like one (2009, 21). This immanence that resists transcendence would be a power belonging to the living body upon the basis of which we can construct a new politics, an 'affirmative biopolitics', as Esposito says of Negri, setting him in opposition to his friend, Giorgio Agamben: 'articulating something like an affirmative biopolitics [. . . is] recognised by Italian philosophy as one of the most urgent tasks of contemporary thought' (2012 [2010], 269).

5　Esposito suggests as much, and indeed links this historicization of identity with *politics*: 'If human life, including the function of language that defines it as such, has become entirely historical, this means it is subject to political practices intended to transform it, and thus, inevitably, it is a matter for conflict' (2012 [2010], 10).

6   Agamben himself – with Esposito, one of the genuine greats of contemporary Italian philosophy – speaks rather little of Italy and the idea of a specifically Italian thought but is clearly not indifferent to the question: the original title of Agamben's *End of the Poem* was *Categorie italiane*, which Agamben's never to materialize Review, conceived with Italo Calvino and Claudio Rugafiori, was to have delineated: 'one section of our review was to be dedicated to the definition of what we called "Italian categories". It was a matter of identifying nothing less than the categorial structures of Italian culture through a series of conjoined polar concepts'. These were to include architecture and vagueness (Rugafiori), speed and lightness (Calvino), and tragedy/comedy, law/creature, biography/fable (Agamben), and later, mother tongue/grammatical language, living language/ dead language, style/manner (Agamben) (Agamben 1999 [1996], xi–xii).

7   'The complex relationship that Italian thought maintains today with Christianity and its corresponding confrontation with nihilism turn out, in the final analysis, to be part of the philosophically irreducible problem of the historicization of the non-historical. A continued engagement, in other words, with the inevitable and insoluble relation between origin and history' (Esposito 2012 [2010], 28).

8   '[L]ife, politics, and history have been the axes of flow for a reflection that has largely remained extrinsic to the transcendental fold [. . .]. Unlike the tradition between Descartes and Kant, which was founded in the constitution of subjectivity or theory of knowledge, Italian thought came into the world turned upside down and inside out, as it were, into the world of historical and political life' (Esposito 2012 [2010], 10).

9   Today in particular, following Nietzsche and Wittgenstein, if its origins are not even earlier, the transcendental takes the form of *language*, or more broadly, symbolic structure, and, as Esposito points out, if Italian thought is not entirely indifferent to language, it still attributes a much less significant role to it than is the case for much of twentieth-century philosophy elsewhere. When language *is* engaged with, it is not so much taken as a transcendental structure but, rather, as something that will have emerged from another, broader realm, often understood to be that of life, or perhaps history: 'rather than being examined in its autonomous structure, language is situated within a broader horizon, described in terms of biology [Paolo Virno], or of ontological realism [Maurizio Ferraris]' (Esposito 2012 [2010], 8). Thus even language is somehow considered to be inextricable from life, as the symbolic is seen to be intertwined with the biological which it supplements: 'It is as if at some point it began to occur to people [. . .] that there was a new "turn" coming after the linguistic one – in some ways encompassing it – that as a whole belonged to the paradigm of life' (Esposito 2012 [2010], 8).

    The great hero of contemporary Italian thought, Michel Foucault, had already 'set out to problematise the transcendental primacy of language' and turned instead to labour and life as two other aprioris, outside of transcendental subjectivity and somehow within the 'world of history' (Esposito 2012 [2010], 9).

10 In making this decision, we are at least provisionally endorsing the following
    passage from Chiesa, which deserves to be quoted at length: 'we must stress
    that discussions of biopolitics are far from being hegemonic in contemporary
    Italian academia; with specific regard to philosophy, in the last fifteen years
    [1996–2011] we have rather increasingly witnessed the strengthening of a
    watered-down adaptation of Anglo-American analytic speculation and the
    more than dubious transformation of vast sectors of "weak thought" (in
    short, the local version of postmodernism that prospered throughout the
    1980s and 1990s) into *consulenza filosofica* (that is, the bleak idea that the
    contemporary task of the philosopher is to act as a consultant to businessmen
    and corporations). The decision to call a patent minority by the name "Italian
    thought" can nevertheless be motivated by the fact that it is precisely the
    investigation into biopolitics that has established the names of a number
    of Italian thinkers worldwide, especially in the last decade [2001–11], and
    that, paradoxically, what remains at an international level a predominantly
    academic, and hence restricted, phenomenon has started being broadly covered
    in Italy by journalists and cultural analysts from major national newspapers
    which are usually indifferent to theoretical debates and innovations'.
        He goes on to suggest that it is in fact quite easy to argue that this
    'minority' are the rightful heirs to the historical tradition of Italian thought,
    as Esposito has insisted. Hence they may indeed have more of a right to be
    described as 'Italian thinkers' than their more institutionally successful peers.
        Chiesa continues: 'Without necessarily going as far as arguing that the
    link between life and politics has always been the privileged target of Italian
    philosophy – from Machiavelli to Croce, Bruno to Gentile, Vico to Pasolini
    – we can cautiously suggest that, perhaps more than any other speculative
    European tradition, Italian thought has time and again been able to connect
    theory with praxis, as well as to be truly open to other disciplines, in ways that
    have given rise to unforeseeable short-circuits' (2011, 2).

11 We were somewhat chided with ignoring those figures, for instance, who
    appear in a recent book of interviews with Italian philosophers (*Viva Voce:
    Conversations with Italian Philosophers*, SUNY Press), and we are happy to
    accept that and simply refer the reader to this text and the series of which it
    forms a part, for more information on this territory, which occasionally strays,
    let us say, somewhat farther from the radical Left than we have often chosen to.

12 For the omitted rest, we refer the reader to the SUNY Press and Bloomsbury
    series devoted to Italian thought, and for more of the same as well as some
    very surprising new thinkers, we can only advert to the new series from MIT
    Press, together with the already established series published by Seagull Books,
    and the series on continental philosophy (frequently Italian) published by
    Stanford University Press and the University of Minnesota Press. SUNY Press
    ('Series in Contemporary Italian Philosophy'), MIT Press ('Insubordinations'),
    Bloomsbury, Seagull Books ('The Italian List'), Stanford University Press
    ('Meridian: Crossing Aesthetics' & 'Cultural Memory in the Present') and the
    University of Minnesota Press ('Commonalities'). A new journal on the subject,
    The Journal of Italian Philosophy, has recently been ventured, and there is
    also, originating in North America, a *Society for Italian Philosophy*.

Further reading

This chapter was inspired unashamedly by the work of Roberto Esposito, and by his *Living Thought*, in particular. He further discusses the nature of Italian philosophy in *Third Person: Politics of Life and Philosophy of the Impersonal* (2007), *Two: The Machine of Political Theology and the Place of Thought* (2013) and *A Philosophy for Europe: From the Outside* (2016). Beyond this, and as Esposito himself notes, there are at least three anthologies in English relating to Italian philosophy, each with its own striking sociological significance. The language in which they are written is not insignificant since it is not unknown to postulate that 'Italian thought' (in a manner analogous to such entities as 'continental philosophy' or 'French thought') could only form a unified entity when seen from outside, from a perspective that is precisely *not* Italian, as we have seen, and perhaps there is something essential to Italian thought *in* this movement towards the outside (which rebounds back and subsequently affects Italian philosophy's own *self*-perception).

Esposito takes up each edition in turn in order to ask about 'the perception of Italian philosophy [from] outside Italy's borders' (Esposito 2012 [2010], 2).

(1) Giovanna Borradori (ed.), *Recoding Metaphysics* stresses the linguistic and historical deficiency of Italian philosophy; its language and the closure of Italian culture during fascism, which according to Esposito's reading result in a conservative historicism; and a translation of other traditions of philosophy and other philosophical figures into a historicist and nihilist schema: 'Italian philosophy is judged to merely translate into its historicist vocabulary hermeneutic or metaphysical questions inherited from European thought' (Esposito 2012 [2010], 2).

(2) Michael Hardt and Paolo Virno (eds.), *Radical Thought in Italy* presents a different picture of Italian thought as an original source of concepts. This shift in perception is allowed in part by its focusing on the *political* thought that has erupted in twentieth-century Italy. From the perspective of the Left and radical thought, the closure of Italy under fascism takes on an entirely different complexion to that presented by Borradori. Fascism's hindering of modernization in fact allowed Italian thought to be 'better equipped than others to deal with the dynamics of the globalized world and of the immaterial production that characterizes the postmodern era'. The contemporary power of 'Italian theory' is thus due to its having been 'influenced by the political and social struggles of the 1960s and 1970s' (Esposito 2012 [2010], 3).

(3) Lorenzo Chiesa and Alberto Toscano (eds.), *The Italian Difference* identifies nihilism and biopolitics as 'the two axes along which Italian philosophy tends to enter into [a] critical confrontation with its time and, at least in some ways, to guide international debate' (Esposito 2012 [2010], 3). Italian thought is here characterized by the ability to span the immense gulf which separates apparently ahistorical, abstract, philosophical concepts (such as nihilism and biopolitics) from concrete historical events: Esposito

speaks of 'the particular capacity of Italian thought to situate itself at the point of tension between highly determined historical-political events and philosophical categories of great conceptual depth' (2012 [2010], 4). Italian thought itself would *be* this 'difference' and 'tension' between two disparate terrains and would thus encompass them in a single glance, 'a split gaze focused on the most pressing current events [*attualità*] and at the same time on the dispositifs ['apparatuses' which guide thought and speech, as well as behaviour] that come with a long or even ancient history' (Esposito 2012 [2010], 4). Thus Italian thought would effect a revealing connection between any number of apparently opposed concepts, which it would refuse dialectically to sublate: 'By projecting the archaic onto the heart of the present [. . .] these categories diagonally connect knowledge and power, nature and history, technology and life' (Esposito 2012 [2010], 4).

In an introductory essay to an issue of the journal *Angelaki* entitled 'Italian Thought Today', Chiesa draws our attention to another important strand of Italian Philosophy: 'Esposito's courageous return to the much broader theoretical question concerning human nature and the human animal. Despite post-structuralism's and deconstruction's extensive critique of the notion of "man" and its humanist biases, early twenty-first-century Italian thought is experiencing a resurgence of interest in this classical philosophical issue' (2011, 1). Chiesa adduces Esposito, Virno and Agamben as exemplary among those who have reopened investigations into 'the relation of dependence between different figures of the subject and their material substratum, or into the ways in which subjectivity opens up an unsurpassable gap in nature, but also and especially an identification of the subject as irreducible to nature [in] its own animality' (2011, 1) – in other words, a kind of philosophical anthropology which introduces at one and the same time a continuity and a discontinuity between the animal and the human, nature and culture. As we have seen throughout this chapter, they remain locked in an antagonistic embrace, as man struggles to forget his past, and yet fails to do so – but something new is created in that very failure.

Works cited

Agamben, Giorgio. *The End of the Poem: Studies in Poetics*, trans. Daniel Heller-Roazen. Stanford: Stanford University Press, 1999. *Categorie italiane: Studi di poetica*. Venice: Marsilio, 1996 (Second edition, Rome: Laterza, 2010, subtitled *Studi di poetica e di letteratura*).

Badiou, Alain. *The Adventure of French Philosophy*. Edited by and trans. Bruno Bosteels. London: Verso, 2012.

Benso, Silvia. *Viva Voce: Conversations with Italian Philosophers*. Albany, NY: SUNY Press, 2017.

Borradori, Giovanna. ed., *Recoding Metaphysics: The New Italian Philosophy*. Evanston, IL: Northwestern University Press, 1988.

Chiesa, Lorenzo, and Alberto Toscano (eds.). *The Italian Difference: Between Nihilism and Biopolitics*. Melbourne: re.press, 2009.

Chiesa, Lorenzo. 'Editorial Introduction: Biopolitics in Early Twenty-First-Century Italian Theory'. *Angelaki* 16, no. 3 (September 2011): *Italian Thought Today*.

Esposito, Roberto. *Third Person: Politics of Life and Philosophy of the Impersonal*, trans. Zakiya Hanafi. Cambridge: Polity, 2012. *Terza Persona: Politica della vita e filosofia dell'impersonale*. Turin: Einaudi, 2007.

Esposito, Roberto. *Living Thought: The Origins and Actuality of Italian Philosophy*, trans. Zakiya Hanafi. Stanford: Stanford University Press, 2012. *Pensiero vivente: Origine e attualità della filosofia italiana*. Turin: Einaudi, 2010.

Esposito, Roberto. *Two: The Machine of Political Theology and the Place of Thought*, trans. Zakiya Hanafi. New York: Fordham University Press, 2015. *Due: La macchina della telogia politica e il posto del pensiero*. Turin: Einaudi, 2013.

Esposito, Roberto. *A Philosophy for Europe: From the Outside*, trans. Zakiya Hanafi. Cambridge: Polity, 2018. *Fuori: Una filosofia per l'Europa*. Turin: Einaudi 2016.

Hardt, Michael and Paolo Virno (eds.). *Radical Thought in Italy: A Potential Politics*. Minneapolis: University of Minnesota Press, 1996.

Negri, Antonio. 'The Italian Difference'. In *The Italian Difference: Between Nihilism and Biopolitics*, edited by Lorenzo Chiesa and Alberto Toscano. Melbourne: re.press, 2009.

Negri, Antonio. 'Giorgio Agamben: The Discreet Taste of the Dialectic'. In *Giorgio Agamben: Sovereignty and Life*, edited by Matthew Calarco and Steven DeCaroli. Stanford: Stanford University Press, 2007.

The historical context

CHAPTER 2

Dante (1256–1321)

Even if Dante's work involves a fair amount of autobiographical material and occasionally fashions itself as a record of personal experiences, his writings reveal surprisingly few facts about his life. With one exception though: Dante's banishment from Florence, which first occurred in January 1302 and soon escalated into permanent exile. As the first excerpt from *Paradiso* shows, it is a testament to the callous expediency with which Dante's enemies took him out of the Florentine political equation that the whole proceeding (criminal conviction and first proscription) was carried out while Dante was on a diplomatic mission to Rome, precisely where his fate – and the fate of other prominent White Guelfs, his political associates within the local pro-papal faction – had been decided ahead of his embassy.

As the second excerpt from *Convivio* also shows, exile marked something of a turning point in Dante's life, a defining moment which he came to embrace both as a man and as a writer. First and foremost, it meant leaving behind everything he held dear, living thereafter in bitter need: blame, hardship and humiliation being then and always the outcast's lot. More to the point, the death warrant, confiscation of property and loss of citizenship which were repeatedly forced upon him (and, eventually, when they came of age, upon his sons) not only crushed whatever hope he had of setting foot in Florence again, but ultimately shaped his mature views on the civil unrest and periodic bloodshed that had plagued Italy's recent history. How to redeem the country from the evils partisan politics had brought upon the Italian peoples became Dante's first concern and constant preoccupation. While the solution he advocated was by no means original and – politically speaking – as much a thing of the past as the Sicilian vernacular that had risen to prominence with Frederic II and Manfred, his answers to Italy's past and current predicaments were rooted in a line of argument whose philosophical breadth, formal rigour and overall coherence were, if not unparalleled, then at least second to none and – philosophically speaking – more compelling than most.

Excerpts from *Monarchia* present us with Dante's plea for peace, the cornerstone of his philosophy of man. The path that leads to peace and the means to maintain and eventually restore it are the keys to Dante's understanding not only of the purpose of authority throughout history but also – and more fundamentally – of man's true nature and destination as a rational being. According to *Monarchia*, peace is the ultimate goal of human society and – by the same token – the very reason why men associate in the first place. Should they live together as one family instead of seeking after goods that benefit some and harm others, then humanity, free from conflict and oppression, would achieve its full potential, which Dante identified with its intellectual progress, intelligence being what sets man apart from every other worldly creature.

Since the core tenets of Dante's thought revolve around the idea that, in order to reach perfection, humanity must be at peace and, in order to be at peace, humanity must be ruled by a single unified authority, it does not come as a surprise that Dante rejected everything that stood in the way of a universal monarchy, be it the greed of clergymen who turned the Church of Christ into a harlot and let the French kings seize her and hold her captive, the short-sightedness of his fellow citizens eager to fight each other as soon as they ran out of external enemies, the cruelty of the warlords who held sway in the North of the peninsula or the pettiness of the German princelings undeserving of their seat on the imperial throne and unable to fulfil their imperial mission. As a result, one would be hard-pressed to find a more staunch supporter of the separation between secular power and temporal government, on the one side, and pastoral care and religious authority, on the other. It would be equally hard to find a more sturdy advocate of the supremacy of the emperor over and against all kinds of local, regional or national jurisdictions.

On the other hand, it might come as a surprise that of all the worthy men whose example prompted Dante to expose his contemporaries' failures and shortcomings, the one who definitely stands out is Manente degli Uberti (known as Farinata), a damned soul Dante meets on his journey through the Underworld. Though it is no accident that Farinata burns in Hell, his demeanour and everything he says in the *Inferno* speak volumes about Dante's political anthropology. As an Epicurean heretic, Farinata may very well feel nothing but contempt for divine justice and retribution; likewise, as a Ghibelline chieftain, he may very well display an unyielding attachment to his party and lineage. That being said, his character possesses – along with honour, courtesy and valour – one redeeming quality, namely an uncompromising love for his homeland which he refused to identify with himself, his power base or his legacy. Whatever Dante deemed that Farinata's ultimate destiny ought to be, he depicted him as a man who – when it mattered most – raised himself above partisan passions and saved the City being torn apart at the hands of his allies who were more than willing to rip their enemies' cause out, root and stem. Even though – in the aftermath of the victory at Montaperti (1260) – strength and right were on his side, Farinata refused to deal a mortal blow to those who had cast him out and chose to share his homeland with them rather than making certain that it would never be theirs again. As the dialogue between Dante and Farinata unfolds, it becomes clear that there's no love lost between them. It also becomes clear that what drives both – the very thing Dante cherished above all and that Farinata lost but managed, almost single-handedly, to pass on to the next generation – is a dream of peace, the only hope men ever had of making a broken community whole again.

Leone Gazziero

Selected writings

Alighieri, Dante. Divina commedia. Paradiso, trans. J. Hollander and R. Hollander and edited by G. Petrocchi. Florence: Le Lettere, [1994] 2007: Dante Alighieri, Paradiso, New York, Doubleday.

Alighieri, Dante. Divina commedia. Inferno, edited by G. Petrocchi. Firenze: Le Lettere, [1994] 2000, trans. J. Hollander and R. Hollander, Dante Alighieri. Inferno, New York, Doubleday

Alighieri, Dante. Divina commedia. Purgatorio, edited by G. Petrocchi. Firenze: Le Lettere, [1994] 2003; Trans. J. Hollander and R. Hollander.

Alighieri, Dante. Purgatorio, Episolae, edited by E. Pistelli. Firenze: Bemporad, 1960, New York, Doubleday

Alighieri, Dante. *The Banquet*, trans. R. H. Convivio and edited by F. Brambilla Ageno. Florence: Le Lettere, 1995: Trans. R. H. Lansing, Dante's Il Convivio, New York, Garland, 1990

Alighieri, Dante. Monarchia, Ed., edited by P. G. Ricci. Firenze: Società Dantesca Italiana, 1965: Trans. P. Shaw, Dante. Monarchy, Oxford, Oxford University Press, 1996.

EXCERPTS

Dante Alighieri, *Paradiso XVII, 46–49*

(Dante Alighieri, *Divina commedia. The Divine Comedy of Dante. Paradiso.* Trans. H. F. Carey. Urbana, Illinois: Project Gutenberg. 2005. Retrieved July 3, 2020, from www. gutenberg.org/ebooks/ XVII, 46–69)

From Athens, by his cruel stepdame's wiles,
Hippolytus departed, such must thou
Depart from Florence. This they wish, and this
Contrive, and will ere long effectuate, there,
Where gainful merchandize is made of Christ,
Throughout the livelong day. The common cry,
Will, as 't is ever wont, affix the blame
Unto the party injur'd: but the truth
Shall, in the vengeance it dispenseth, find
A faithful witness. Thou shall leave each thing
Belov'd most dearly: this is the first shaft
Shot from the bow of exile. Thou shalt prove
How salt the savour is of other's bread,
How hard the passage to descend and climb
By other's stairs, But that shall gall thee most
Will he the worthless and vile company,
With whom thou must be thrown into these straits.
For all ungrateful, impious all and mad,
Shall turn 'gainst thee: but in a little while
Theirs and not thine shall be the crimson'd brow
Their course shall so evince their brutishness
T' have ta'en thy stand apart shall well become thee.

Dante Alighieri, Convivio

(Dante Alighieri, *Convivio*, F. Brambilla Ageno (ed.), Firenze, *Le Lettere*, 1995, I, III, 3–5: Trans. R. H. Lansing, *Dante's* Il Convivio, New York, Garland, 1990)

Ah, if only it had pleased the Maker of the Universe that the cause of my apology had never existed, for then neither would others have sinned against me, nor would I have suffered punishment unjustly – the punishment, I mean, of exile and poverty. [4] Since it was the pleasure of the citizens of the most beautiful and famous daughter of Rome, Florence, to cast me out of her sweet bosom--where I was born and bred up to the pinnacle of my life, and where, with her good will, I desire with all my heart to rest my weary mind and to complete the span of time that is given to me – I have travelled like a stranger, almost like a beggar, through virtually all the regions to which this tongue of ours extends, displaying against my will the wound of fortune for which the wounded one is often unjustly accustomed to be held accountable. [5] Truly I have been a ship without sail or rudder, brought to different ports, inlets, and shores by the dry wind that painful poverty blows. And I have appeared before the eyes of many who perhaps because of some report had imagined me in another form. In their sight not only was my person held cheap, but each of my works was less valued, those already completed as much as those yet to come].

Dante Alighieri Monarchia, I, I, 5—III, 7

(Dante Alighieri, *Monarchia*, I, i, 5 – iii, 7 : Trans. F. J. Church. In R. W. Church *Dante. An essay*. Urbana, Illinois: Project Gutenberg. Retrieved 3 July, 2020, from www.gutenberg .org/ebooks.)

[i, 5] But seeing that among other truths, ill-understood yet profitable, the knowledge touching temporal monarchy is at once most profitable and most obscure, and that because it has no immediate reference to worldly gain it is left unexplored by all, therefore it is my purpose to draw it forth from its hiding-places, as well that I may spend my toil for the benefit of the world, as that I may be the first to win the prize of so great an achievement to my own glory. [. . .]. [ii, 1] First, therefore, we must see what is it that is called Temporal Monarchy, in its idea, so to speak, and according to its purpose. Temporal Monarchy, then, or, as men call it, the Empire, is the government of one prince above all men in time, or in those things and over those things which are measured by time. Three great questions are asked concerning it. First, there is the doubt and the question, is it necessary for the welfare of the world? [. . .]. [ii, 4] Now, since every truth, which is not itself a first principle, becomes manifest from the truth of some first principle, it is therefore necessary in every inquiry to have a knowledge of the first principle involved, to which by analysis we may go back for the certainty of all the propositions which are afterwards accepted. [ii, 5] It must be understood then that there are certain things which, since they are not subject to our power, are matters of speculation, but not of action: such are Mathematics and Physics, and things divine. But there are some things which, since they are subject to our power, are matters of action as well as of speculation, and in them we do not act for the sake of speculation, but contrariwise: for in such things action is the end. [ii, 6] Now, since the matter which we have in hand has to do with states, nay, with the very origin and principle of good forms of government, and since all that concerns states is subject to our power, it is manifest that our subject is not in the first place speculation, but action. [ii, 7] And again, since in matters of action the end sought is the first principle and cause of all (for that it is which first moves the agent to act), it follows that all our method concerning the means which are set

to gain the end must be taken from the end. [. . .]. [II, 8] That therefore, if it exists, which is the ultimate end for the universal civil order of mankind, will be the first principle from which all the truth of our future deductions will be sufficiently manifest. But it is folly to think that there is an end for this and for that particular civil order, and yet not one end for all. [III, 1] Now, therefore, we must see what is the end of the whole civil order of men; and when we have found this, then, as the Philosopher says in his book to Nicomachus, the half of our labour will have been accomplished. And to render the question clearer, we must observe that as there is a certain end for which nature makes the thumb, and another, different from this, for which she makes the whole hand, and again another for which she makes the arm, and another different from all for which she makes the whole man; so there is one end for which she orders the individual man, and another for which she orders the family, and another end for the city, and another for the kingdom, and finally an ultimate one for which the Everlasting God, by His art which is nature, brings into being the whole human race. And this is what we seek as a first principle to guide our whole inquiry. [III, 3] Let it then be understood that God and nature make nothing to be idle. Whatever comes into being, exists for some operation or working. For no created essence is an ultimate end in the creator's purpose, so far as he is a creator, but rather the proper operation of that essence. Therefore it follows that the operation does not exist for the sake of the essence, but the essence for the sake of the operation. [III, 4] There is therefore a certain proper operation of the whole body of human kind, for which this whole body of men in all its multitudes is ordered and constituted, but to which no one man, nor single family, nor single neighbourhood, nor single city, nor particular kingdom can attain. What this is will be manifest, if we can find what is the final and characteristic capacity of humanity as a whole. [III, 5] I say then that no quality which is shared by different species of things is the distinguishing capacity of any one of them. For were it so, since this capacity is that which makes each species what it is, it would follow that one essence would be specifically distributed to many species, which is impossible. [III, 6] Therefore the ultimate quality of men is not existence, taken simply; for the elements share therein. Nor is it existence under certain conditions; for we find this in minerals too. Nor is it existence with life; for plants too have life. Nor is it percipient existence; for brutes share in this power. It is to be percipient with the possibility of understanding, for this quality falls to the lot of none but man, either above or below him. [III, 7] For though there are other beings which with him have understanding, yet this understanding is not, as man's, capable of development. For such beings are only certain intellectual natures, and not anything besides, and their being is nothing other than to understand; which is without interruption, otherwise they would not be eternal. It is plain, therefore, that the distinguishing quality of humanity is the faculty or the power of understanding.

(Dante Alighieri, *Monarchia*, I, IV, 1–2 and 5)

[IV, 1] It has thus been sufficiently set forth that the proper work of the human race, taken as a whole, is to set in action the whole capacity of that understanding which is capable of development: first in the way of speculation, and then, by its extension, in the way of action. [IV, 2] And seeing that what is true of a part is true also of the whole, and that it is by rest and quiet that the individual man becomes perfect in wisdom and prudence; so the human race, by living in the calm and tranquillity of peace, applies itself most freely and easily to its proper work [. . .] Whence it is manifest that of all things that are ordered to secure blessings to men, peace is the best. [. . .]. [IV, 5] Now that we have declared these matters, it is plain what is the better, nay the best, way in which mankind may attain to do its proper work. And consequently we have seen the readiest means by which to arrive at the point, for which all our works are ordered, as their ultimate end; namely, the universal peace, which is to be assumed as the first principle for our deductions.

(Dante Alighieri, *Monarchia*, I, V, 1–10 ; X, 1 – XI, 2 ; XI, 8–12 and 20)

[V, 1] As therefore we have already said, there are three doubts, and these doubts suggest three questions, concerning Temporal Monarchy, which in more common speech is called the Empire; and our purpose is, as we explained, to inquire concerning these questions in their given order, and starting from the first principle which we have just laid down. The first question, then, is whether Temporal Monarchy is necessary for the welfare of the world; and that it is necessary can, I think, be shown by the strongest and most manifest arguments; for nothing, either of reason or of authority, opposes me. Let us first take the authority of the Philosopher in his Politics. There, on his venerable authority, it is said that where a number of things are arranged to attain an end, it behoves one of them to regulate or govern the others, and the others to submit. And it is not only the authority of his illustrious name which makes this worthy of belief, but also reason, instancing particulars.

If we take the case of a single man, we shall see the same rule manifested in him: all his powers are ordered to gain happiness; but his understanding is what regulates and governs all the others; and otherwise he would never attain to happiness. Again, take a single household: its end is to fit the members thereof to live well; but there must be one to regulate and rule it, who is called the father of the family, or, it may be, one who holds his office. As the Philosopher says: "Every house is ruled by the oldest." And, as Homer says, it is his duty to make rules and laws for the rest. Hence the proverbial curse: "Mayst thou have an equal at home." Take a single village: its end is suitable assistance as regards persons and goods, but one in it must be the ruler of the rest, either set over them by another, or with their consent, the head man amongst them. If it be not so, not only do its inhabitants fail of this mutual assistance, but the whole neighbourhood is sometimes wholly ruined by the ambition of many, who each of them wish to rule. If, again, we take a single city: its end is to secure a good and sufficient life to the citizens; but one man must be ruler in imperfect as well as in good forms of the state. If it is otherwise, not only is the end of civil life lost, but the city too ceases to be what it was. Lastly, if we take any one kingdom, of which the end is the same as that of a city, only with greater security for its tranquillity, there must be one king to rule and govern. For if this is not so, not only do his subjects miss their end, but the kingdom itself falls to destruction, according to that word of the infallible truth: "Every kingdom divided against itself shall be brought to desolation." If then this holds good in these cases, and in each individual thing which is ordered to one certain end, what we have laid down is true.

Now it is plain that the whole human race is ordered to gain some end, as has been before shown. There must, therefore, be one to guide and govern, and the proper title for this office is Monarch or Emperor. And so it is plain that Monarchy or the Empire is necessary for the welfare of the world. [. . .]. [x, 1] Wherever there is controversy, there ought to be judgment, otherwise there would be imperfection without its proper remedy, which is impossible; for God and Nature, in things necessary, do not fail in their provisions. But it is manifest that there may be controversy between any two princes, where the one is not subject to the other, either from the fault of themselves, or even of their subjects. Therefore between them there should be means of judgment. And since, when one is not subject to the other, he cannot be judged by the other (for there is no rule of equals over equals), there must be a third prince of wider jurisdiction, within the circle of whose laws both may come. Either he will or he will not be a Monarch. If he is, we have what we sought; if not, then this one again will have an equal, who is not subject to his jurisdiction, and then again we have need of a third. And so we must either go on to infinity, which is impossible, or we must come to that judge who is first and highest; by whose judgment all controversies shall be either directly or indirectly decided; and he will be Monarch or Emperor. Monarchy is therefore necessary to the world, and this the Philosopher saw when he said: "The world is not intended to be disposed in evil order; 'in a multitude of rulers there is evil, therefore let there be one prince.'" [xi, 1] Further, the world is ordered best when justice is most paramount therein [. . .]. [xi, 2] But Justice is paramount only in a Monarchy, and therefore a Monarchy, that is, the Empire, is needed if the world is to be ordered for the best. [. . .]. [xi, 8] Justice is strongest in the world when it is in one who is most willing and most powerful; only the Monarch is this; therefore, only when Justice is in the Monarch is it strongest in the world. This pro-syllogism goes on through the second figure, with an involved negative, and is like this: All B is A; only C is A; therefore only C is B: or all B is A; nothing but C is A; therefore nothing but C is B. [xi, 10] Our previous explanation makes the first proposition apparent: the second is proved thus, first in regard to will, and secondly in regard to power. First it must be observed that the strongest opponent of Justice is Appetite, as Aristotle intimates in the fifth book to Nicomachus. Remove Appetite altogether, and there remains nothing adverse to Justice; and therefore it is the opinion of the Philosopher that nothing should be left to the judge, if it can be decided by law; and this ought to be done for fear of Appetite, which easily perverts men's minds. Where, then, there is nothing to be wished for, there can be no Appetite, for the passions cannot exist if their objects are destroyed. But the Monarch has nothing to desire, for his jurisdiction is bounded only by the ocean; and this is not the case with other princes, whose kingdoms are bounded by those of their neighbours; as, for instance, the kingdom of Castile is bounded by the kingdom of Aragon. From which it follows that the Monarch is able to be the purest embodiment of Justice among men. [. . .]. [XI, 20] The principle assumed being therefore sufficiently explained, the conclusion is certain, to wit, that a Monarch is necessary that the world may be ordered for the best.

Dante Alighieri, *Inferno* XIX 1–6, 112–17.

(Dante Alighieri, *Divina commedia. The Divine Comedy of Dante. Inferno*. Trans. H. F. Carey. Urbana, Illinois: Project Gutenberg. 2005. Retrieved 3 July 2020, from www .gutenberg.org/ebooks/, XIX 1–6, 112–17.)

WOE to thee, Simon Magus! woe to you,
His wretched followers! who the things of God,
Which should be wedded unto goodness, them,
Rapacious as ye are, do prostitute
For gold and silver in adultery!
Now must the trumpet sound for you, since yours
Is the third chasm.

[. . .]

Of gold and silver ye have made your god,
Diff'ring wherein from the idolater,
But he that worships one, a hundred ye?
Ah, Constantine! to how much ill gave birth,
Not thy conversion, but that plenteous dower,
Which the first wealthy Father gain'd from thee!

Dante Alighieri, *Purgatorio* VI, 76–96

(Dante Alighieri, *Divina commedia. The Divine Comedy of Dante. Purgatorio*. Trans. H. F. Carey. Urbana, Illinois: Project Gutenberg. 2005. Retrieved 3 July 2020, from www .gutenberg.org/ebooks/, VI, 76–96)

Ah slavish Italy! thou inn of grief,
Vessel without a pilot in loud storm,
Lady no longer of fair provinces,
But brothel-house impure! this gentle spirit,
Ev'n from the Pleasant sound of his dear land
Was prompt to greet a fellow citizen
With such glad cheer; while now thy living ones
In thee abide not without war; and one
Malicious gnaws another, ay of those
Whom the same wall and the same moat contains,
Seek, wretched one! around thy sea-coasts wide;
Then homeward to thy bosom turn, and mark
If any part of the sweet peace enjoy.
What boots it, that thy reins Justinian's hand
Befitted, if thy saddle be unpress'd?
Nought doth he now but aggravate thy shame.
Ah people! thou obedient still shouldst live,
And in the saddle let thy Caesar sit,
If well thou marked'st that which God commands
　　Look how that beast to felness hath relaps'd
From having lost correction of the spur,
Since to the bridle thou hast set thine hand,
O German Albert! who abandon'st her,
That is grown savage and unmanageable,
When thou should'st clasp her flanks with forked heels.

(Dante Alighieri, *Divina commedia. Purgatorio*, XVI, 106–12 and 127–9)

Rome, that turn'd it unto good,
Was wont to boast two suns, whose several beams
Cast light on either way, the world's and God's.
One since hath quench'd the other; and the sword
Is grafted on the crook; and so conjoin'd
Each must perforce decline to worse, unaw'd
By fear of other.
　　[. . .]
On this at last conclude. The church of Rome,
Mixing two governments that ill assort,
Hath miss'd her footing, fall'n into the mire,
And there herself and burden much defil'd.

Dante Alighieri, *Episolae* V, 1 and 11–14

(Dante Alighieri, *Episolae*, E. Pistelli (ed), Firenze, Bemporad, 1960, V, 1 and 11–14
Trans. C. E. Honess, *Dante Alighieri. Four Political Letters*, London, Modern Humanities
Research Association, 2007)

[1] To each and every one of the Kings of Italy, and to the Senators of the
Holy City, and also to Italy's Dukes, Marquises, and Counts, and to her
people, a humble Italian, Dante Alighieri, a Florentine undeservedly in exile,
prays for peace. [. . .]. [11] Give up the savage ways you have adopted, you
descendants of the Lombards: and if anything should remain of the seed of
the Trojans and the Romans, yield to it, so that, when the heavenly eagle
comes, descending like lightning, he does not see his own chicks cast out and
the rightful place of his offspring occupied by ravens. [12] Come now, you
Scandinavian race, and make yourselves eager to receive, as is your duty, the
one whose arrival you justifiably fear. [13] Do not let yourselves be seduced
by the ploys of cupidity, which, like the Sirens, uses its charm to overcome
the vigilance of reason. [14] Hasten before him and declare your obedience
to him: rejoice in singing a psalm of penitence to him, bearing in mind
that "anyone who resists authority is rebelling against God's decision",
while anyone who rebels against God's decisions is kicking out against an
omnipotent will, and "it is hard to kick against the goad".

(Dante Alighieri, *Divina commedia. Inferno*, VI, 49–87)

> "Thy city heap'd with envy to the brim,
> Ay that the measure overflows its bounds,
> Held me in brighter days. Ye citizens
> Were wont to name me Ciacco. For the sin
> Of glutt'ny, damned vice, beneath this rain,
> E'en as thou see'st, I with fatigue am worn;
> Nor I sole spirit in this woe: all these
> Have by like crime incurr'd like punishment."
>   No more he said, and I my speech resum'd:
> "Ciacco! thy dire affliction grieves me much,
> Even to tears. But tell me, if thou know'st,
> What shall at length befall the citizens
> Of the divided city; whether any just one
> Inhabit there: and tell me of the cause,
> Whence jarring discord hath assail'd it thus?"
>   He then: "After long striving they will come

To blood; and the wild party from the woods
Will chase the other with much injury forth.
Then it behoves, that this must fall, within
Three solar circles; and the other rise
By borrow'd force of one, who under shore
Now rests. It shall a long space hold aloof
Its forehead, keeping under heavy weight
The other oppress'd, indignant at the load,
And grieving sore. The just are two in number,
But they neglected. Av'rice, envy, pride,
Three fatal sparks, have set the hearts of all
On fire." Here ceas'd the lamentable sound;
And I continu'd thus: "Still would I learn
More from thee, farther parley still entreat.
Of Farinata and Tegghiaio say,
They who so well deserv'd, of Giacopo,
Arrigo, Mosca, and the rest, who bent
Their minds on working good. Oh! tell me where
They bide, and to their knowledge let me come.
For I am press'd with keen desire to hear,
If heaven's sweet cup or poisonous drug of hell
Be to their lip assign'd." He answer'd straight:
"These are yet blacker spirits. Various crimes
Have sunk them deeper in the dark abyss.
If thou so far descendest, thou mayst see them.
But to the pleasant world when thou return'st,
Of me make mention, I entreat thee, there.
No more I tell thee, answer thee no more."

(Dante Alighieri, *Divina commedia. Inferno*, X, 1–51 and 73–108)

NOW by a secret pathway we proceed,
Between the walls, that hem the region round,
And the tormented souls: my master first,
I close behind his steps. "Virtue supreme!"
I thus began; "who through these ample orbs
In circuit lead'st me, even as thou will'st,
Speak thou, and satisfy my wish. May those,
Who lie within these sepulchres, be seen?
Already all the lids are rais'd, and none
O'er them keeps watch." He thus in answer spake
"They shall be closed all, what-time they here
From Josaphat return'd shall come, and bring
Their bodies, which above they now have left.

The cemetery on this part obtain
With Epicurus all his followers,
Who with the body make the spirit die.
Here therefore satisfaction shall be soon
Both to the question ask'd, and to the wish,
Which thou conceal'st in silence." I replied:
"I keep not, guide belov'd! from thee my heart
Secreted, but to shun vain length of words,
A lesson erewhile taught me by thyself."

   "O Tuscan! thou who through the city of fire
Alive art passing, so discreet of speech!
Here please thee stay awhile. Thy utterance
Declares the place of thy nativity
To be that noble land, with which perchance
I too severely dealt." Sudden that sound
Forth issu'd from a vault, whereat in fear
I somewhat closer to my leader's side
Approaching, he thus spake: "What dost thou? Turn.
Lo, Farinata, there! who hath himself
Uplifted: from his girdle upwards all
Expos'd behold him." On his face was mine
Already fix'd; his breast and forehead there
Erecting, seem'd as in high scorn he held
E'en hell. Between the sepulchres to him
My guide thrust me with fearless hands and prompt,
This warning added: "See thy words be clear!"

   He, soon as there I stood at the tomb's foot,
Ey'd me a space, then in disdainful mood
Address'd me: "Say, what ancestors were thine?"

   I, willing to obey him, straight reveal'd
The whole, nor kept back aught: whence he, his brow
Somewhat uplifting, cried: "Fiercely were they
Adverse to me, my party, and the blood
From whence I sprang: twice therefore I abroad
Scatter'd them." "Though driv'n out, yet they each time
From all parts," answer'd I, "return'd; an art
Which yours have shown, they are not skill'd to learn."

   [. . .] Meanwhile the other, great of soul, near whom
I yet was station'd, chang'd not count'nance stern,
Nor mov'd the neck, nor bent his ribbed side.
"And if," continuing the first discourse,
"They in this art," he cried, "small skill have shown,
That doth torment me more e'en than this bed.
But not yet fifty times shall be relum'd
Her aspect, who reigns here Queen of this realm,

Ere thou shalt know the full weight of that art.
So to the pleasant world mayst thou return,
As thou shalt tell me, why in all their laws,
Against my kin this people is so fell?"

    "The slaughter and great havoc," I replied,
"That colour'd Arbia's flood with crimson stain—
To these impute, that in our hallow'd dome
Such orisons ascend." Sighing he shook
The head, then thus resum'd: "In that affray
I stood not singly, nor without just cause
Assuredly should with the rest have stirr'd;
But singly there I stood, when by consent
Of all, Florence had to the ground been raz'd,
The one who openly forbad the deed."

    "So may thy lineage find at last repose,"
I thus adjur'd him, "as thou solve this knot,
Which now involves my mind. If right I hear,
Ye seem to view beforehand, that which time
Leads with him, of the present uninform'd."

    "We view, as one who hath an evil sight,"
He answer'd, "plainly, objects far remote:
So much of his large spendour yet imparts
The' Almighty Ruler; but when they approach
Or actually exist, our intellect
Then wholly fails, nor of your human state
Except what others bring us know we aught.
Hence therefore mayst thou understand, that all
Our knowledge in that instant shall expire,
When on futurity the portals close."

CHAPTER 3

Giovanni Pico della Mirandola (1463–94)

Of the Italian Humanists' victims of their own success – and, in Florence alone, there have been more than a few – Giovanni Pico Count of Mirandola (and Concordia) was, already in the eyes of his contemporaries, the most talented one. While he definitely deserved to enter the Renaissance pantheon of thought and learning, Giovanni Pico was just as much, if not more so, the latest in a long line of mediaeval polymaths of genius. Besides being well acquainted with Aristotelian and Averroist philosophy – which was no less true of a number of contemporary despisers of mediaeval lore and technicalities – Pico was conversant with scholastic logic and theology, whose 'Parisian' Latin he spoke without accent, having spent some six years studying the likes of Albert the Great, Thomas Aquinas, Francis of Meyronnes, John Duns Scotus, Henry of Ghent and Giles of Rome, first in Padua and then in Paris. It may well not be the most striking feature of Pico's intellectual personality, but it is nonetheless that which sets him apart from many of his contemporaries and helps to explain the peculiar agenda he relentlessly pursued in his lifetime.

Assuming his whole letter on the appropriate mode of speaking to philosophers–as its occasional reminders in other works are to suggest – is more than an elaborate in-joke Giovanni shared with Ermolao Barbaro, who – presumably – came up with the idea in the first place, and Poliziano, who advertised it soon afterwards (it would be harder to assume that Leonardo Bruni and those who picked it up later were privy to it or, catching on quicker than the average reader, did not give the game away), it makes it pretty clear that – to say the very least – Pico did not care as much as his fellow-humanists did for exquisite writing. As a matter of fact, he had no qualms about using the uncouth, graceless jargon of the

School, which – as it happens – he considered a language unto itself. As he explains, Scholastics spoke their own Latin, which had certainly strayed away from its roots, but deserved – as much as any other dialect, Roman Latin (and its Renaissance revival) included – to be taken on its own terms. Scholastic Latin had been the 'shoptalk' of philosophers for quite some time and, for all his eagerness to bring about great changes, Pico seemed content with it, as his disparaging gibe at his censors plainly implies, for – as Pico claims in *Proemium* – he relinquished the Scholastic style only to indulge the censor's inability to cope with its intricacies familiar to men of philosophical reputation.

Moreover, disputes over eloquence are, in fact, pointless when philosophical matters are at stake: philosophers need neither educated mouths nor educated ears. All they need is an educated mind. Accordingly, they will be better off with a decent tool for discerning things through reason rather than with cosmetic enhancement and ornamentation which will make things look better (or worse) than they actually are. All of which makes excellent sense if we take Pico at his word: even if Philosophy is but one thread in a much larger scheme – which embraced more exotic disciplines (like magic and Qabbalah) as well – its path leads man beyond earth and heaven and ultimately beyond himself. Philosophy will teach man how to check his urges and emotions, it will dispel the confusions of his mind and it will show him the truth of all things, human and divine alike. What it will not do is entertain him. Pico and Pico's man could live with that, and their willingness to forego all spiritual comfort in their philosophical quest for knowledge and wisdom stands as a lasting testament to the greatness of the former and to the dignity of the latter, for – as Pico reminded his friend Ermolao – 'non est humanus qui sit insolens politioris literaturae, non est homo qui sit expers philosophiae'.

Leone Gazziero

Selected writings

Pico della Mirandola, Giovanni. *Syncretism in the West. Pico's 900 Theses (1486)*, trans. S. A. Farmer. Tempe: Medieval and Renaissance Texts and Studies, 1998.

Pico della Mirandola, Giovanni. *Oration on the Dignity of Man*, trans. F. Borghesi, M. Papio and M. Riva. Cambridge: Cambridge University Press, [1486] 2012

Pico della Mirandola, Giovanni. *On Being and the One*, trans. P. J. W. Miller. Indianapolis: Hackett, 1965

EXCERPTS

Giovanni Pico della Mirandola, *900 Theses*

Giovanni Pico della Mirandola, *Syncretism in the West. Pico's 900 Theses (1486)*, Trans. S. A. Farmer, Tempe, Medieval and Renaissance Texts and Studies, 1998, p. 211)

The following nine hundred dialectical, moral, physical, mathematical, metaphysical, theological, magical, and cabalistic opinions, including his own and those of the wise Chaldeans, Arabs, Hebrews, Greeks, Egyptians, and Latins, will be disputed publicly by Giovanni Pico of Mirandola, the Count of Concord. In reciting these opinions, he has not imitated the splendor of the Roman language but the style of speaking of the most celebrated Parisian disputers, since this is used by almost all philosophers of our time. The doctrines to be debated are proposed separately by nations and their sect leaders, but in common in respect to the parts of philosophy – as though in a medley, everything mixed together.

Giovanni Pico della Mirandola, *Oration on the Dignity of Man*

Giovanni Pico della Mirandola. *Oration on the Dignity of Man*, Trans. F. Borghesi, M. Papio and M. Riva, Cambridge, Cambridge University Press, 2012, p. 205)

To begin with our own, to whom philosophy came last, we find in John [Duns] Scotus something lively and meticulous, in Thomas [Aquinas] a balanced solidity, in Giles [of Rome] a neat precision, in Francis [of Meyronnes] a penetrating acuteness, in Albert [the Great] an ancient and grand breadth, in Henry [of Ghent], as it has seemed to me, a constant and venerable solemnity.

Pico della Mirandola. *On Being and the One*

Giovanni Pico della Mirandola. *On Being and the One*, Trans. P. J. W. Miller, Indianapolis, Hackett, 1965, p. 37–8)

Since those who think that Aristotle disagrees with Plato disagree with me, who make a concordant philosophy of both, you asked both how Aristotle might be defended in this matter and also how he might agree with his master, Plato. I said what came to my mind at that time, confirming what you answered to Lorenzo <de' Medici> in the discussion rather than bringing in anything new. But this was not enough for you. Although I am to write at greater length on these topics in the *Concord of Plato and Aristotle* which I am now bringing forth, you entreated me to collect in a brief compendium what I said about this question then in your presence. [. . .] What can I deny you? May I say that you are an almost inseparable companion, particularly in a literary matter? May I also be allowed, through you who vindicate a more elegant language, to use some words which are not yet perhaps legally given to Latin. Still, the newness of the subject makes such expression almost necessary, and therefore you should not look for the allurement of a more elegant style. As Manilius <*Astronomicon*, III, 39> says, "The subject itself refuses to be ornamented; it is content to be taught"

Pico della Mirandola, On the Mode of Speaking Appropriate to Philosophers

Giovanni Pico della Mirandola, "Giovanni Pico Della Mirandola on the Conflict of Philosophy and Rhetoric", Trans. Q. Breen, *Journal of the History of Ideas*, 13, 1952, p. 395–6, 398, 400)

So great is the conflict between the office of the orator and the philosopher that there can be no conflicting greater than theirs. For what else is the task of the rhetor than to lie, to entrap, to circumvent, to practise sleight-of-hand? For, as you say, it is your business to be able at will to turn black into white, white into black; to be able to elevate, degrade, enlarge, and reduce, by speaking whatsoever you will; at length you do this to the things themselves by magical arts as it were, for by the powers of eloquence you build them in such a way that they change to whatever face and costume you please; so that they are not what their own nature but what your will made them. of course they may not actually become what you willed, but if they should not it may nevertheless appear so to your audience. All this is nothing at all but sheer mendacity, sheer imposture, sheer trickery; for its nature is either to enlarge by addition or to reduce by subtraction, and putting forth a false harmony of words like so many masks and likenesses it dupes the listeners' minds by insincerities. Will there be any affinity between this and the philosopher, whose entire endeavour is concerned with knowing the truth and demonstrating it to others? [. . .] It is our business to set in order our minds rather than our delivery; to be careful lest what strays be reason, not speech; that we attain to the word as thought, not to the word as expression. It is praiseworthy to have the Muses in the soul, and not on the lips.

Both of us should know what is that good Latin, which you say is the only debt philosophers owe but fail to pay when it comes to using it in speech. For example, instead of "a sole hominem produci" our colleagues will say "causari hominem". Forthwith you shout: That is not Latin; and so far you are right. More right you are when you say: It is not the Roman way of speaking. But you are wrong when you say: An Arabian and an Egyptian will say the same thing, but not in Latin; but still they will speak correctly. For the names of things are established either by arbitrary convention or by nature. It may happen that a society of men agree on a word's meaning; if so, for each thing that word is among them the right one to use for the meaning agreed on. That being the case, what will prohibit those philosophers you call barbarians from agreeing together on a common norm of speaking? And let it enjoy with them the same respect as does Roman among you. There is no sense in saying that the one standard is wrong and yours right, if this business of name-making is altogether arbitrary. What of it, if you do not wish to dignify our standard by calling it Roman? You may call it French, British, Spanish, or even what the vulgar is accustomed to call Parisian. When they speak to us they will for many things be laughed at and to a great extent will not be understood. The same will happen to you when you speak to them. Remember the saying: "Anacharsis commits a solecism among the Athenians, the Athenians do so among the Scythians". But if the rightness of names depends on the nature of things, is it the rhetorician we ought to consult about this rightness, or is it the philosopher who alone contemplates and explores the nature of everything? And perhaps while the ears reject the names as harsh, reason accepts them as more cognate to the things.

Giovanni Pico della Mirandola, *Proemium*

Apologia Ioannis Pici Mirandulae Concordiae Comitis, P. E. Fornaciari (éd.) Firenze, Edizioni del Galluzzo, 2010, *Proemium*, p. 4, 8–10, 32 Trans. by Leone Gazziero.

Not long ago I came in Rome to kiss, as custom dictates, Innocent VIII's feet, Pope who fully deserves his name through the innocence of his life. True to my habit of always studying literary matters and commenting upon them, with the purpose of doing something for my fellow-men, something both worthy of the city of Rome and agreeable to the Christian leader, something useful to myself and to other scholars, I have expounded nine hundreds theses on divine and natural matters, which I planned to publicly defend in front of an assembly of most learned men. No sooner these theses had been published than a motley mob of detractors started to slander not my discernment or my lore, but my preparedness as far as the good arts are concerned. [. . .] Leaving aside philosophical issues as such, a number of my foes did not approve the very idea of a public debate and blamed it as an occasion for showing off one's talent and lore rather than comparing knowledge with knowledge. [. . .] To the people who hate this kind of debate and the practice of publicly discussing God, nature and morality I haven't much to say: whether this is a crime or not, it is something I have in common with great men of our age – in fact of all ages – distinguished philosophers who shared the conviction that nothing will help us more in our search for truth and knowledge than engaging over and over again in such disputes. [. . .] But why indulge longer in such digressions instead of going straight to the point and make it crystal-clear and utterly uncontroversial that, far from being heretic and impious myself, I have been treated as such by heretic and impious people who did not blush at charging me with such accusations? This I will do not through vociferations and complaints but through the things themselves and the arguments which I have put forward in what I have said, written and thought. [. . .] Let's inquire into the theses those masters condemned as heretical and let's do it by changing the way we discuss them. As a matter of fact, my quarrel is with barbarians and, as the saying rightly goes, stammerers only understand other stammerers.

Pico della Mirandola. *Oration on the Dignity of Man*

Giovanni Pico della Mirandola, *Pico della Mirandola. Oration on the Dignity of Man*, Trans. F. Borghesi, M. Papio and M. Riva, *op-cit.* p. 151–7, 183–9)

If our man would just seek a truce from his enemies, moral philosophy will beat down the unbridled stampede of the manifold beast and the aggression, ire, and arrogance of the lion. Then, if we yearn rightmindedly for the safety of perpetual peace for ourselves, it will come and liberally satisfy our desires; indeed, both beasts having been sacrificed like a stuck sow, it will ratify an everlasting pact of the most holy peace between the flesh and the spirit. Dialectics will calm the tumults of reason agitated and tossed about between the contradictions of speech and the captiousness of syllogisms. Natural philosophy will allay the differences of opinion and disagreements that vex, perplex, and afflict our restless soul from all sides. But it will bring harmony in such a way as to remind us that nature is the off spring of war, as Heraclitus said, and is therefore called "strife" by Homer. Thus, it is said that in philosophy true rest and stable peace cannot reveal themselves to us alone, that this is the duty and privilege of its mistress; that is, of the most holy Theology. She will show us the way to this peace and like a companion will lead us. Seeing us hurrying along from afar, she will call out, "Come to me, you who exert yourselves in vain; come and I will restore you; come to me and I will give you that peace which the world and nature cannot give to you." So gently called, so kindly invited, we will then fly away into the embrace of the most blessed Mother like terrestrial Mercuries with winged feet and will rejoice in the longed-for peace. This is that most holy peace, the indissoluble bond, the harmonious friendship in which all souls, in one mind (a mind that is above all minds) are not only in agreement but, indeed, in a certain ineffable way, inwardly become one. This is the friendship that the Pythagoreans call the end of all philosophy, that peace which God makes in His heavens, which the angels who came down to earth announced to men of good will so that these men would, ascending to heaven, be transformed by it into angels. Let us desire this peace for our friends, for our times; let us desire it for whatever home we enter. Let us desire it for our soul so that in her may be made a house of the Lord, so that, after casting off her impurities through moral philosophy and dialectics, our soul may adorn herself with multifaceted philosophy, as if with royal magnificence, and so that she may crown the heights of her doors with the garlands of theology. And let us desire this peace for our soul so that the King of Glory may descend at last, together with the Father, to make a home in her. If our soul shows herself to be worthy of such a Guest – for His Clemency is immense – she (clad in gold, as in a wedding toga, and surrounded by a diverse variety of sciences) will receive her handsome Guest not merely as a Guest but as a Bridegroom. So as not to be separated from Him, she will wish to be separated from her people. Having forgotten her own father's home – indeed, having forgotten herself – she will wish to die in herself so that she may live in her Spouse, in Whose sight the death of His saints is truly precious. This is the death, I say (if one must call that plenitude of life death), whose contemplation is, according to the sages, the study of philosophy.

· · ·

These are the reasons, most reverend fathers, that have not only encouraged me but even thrust upon me the duty of studying philosophy. And I would certainly not elaborate on them if I were not compelled to respond to those who are accustomed to condemning the study of philosophy, especially in men of high rank or, even more generally, in those of a middling fortune. For philosophizing as a whole (and this is the misfortune of our age!) is now derided and disparaged, instead of being honoured and glorified. Thus, nearly everyone's mind has been invaded by the ruinous and monstrous conviction that either no one or only a very few may study philosophy, as if having before our eyes and at our fingertips the causes of things, the ways of nature, the logic of the universe, the divine plan, and the mysteries of Heaven and Earth were of no value whatsoever unless accompanied by the possibility of garnering some favour or making a profit. Indeed, it has now reached the point (what sorrow!) that only those who reduce the study of wisdom to a business are considered wise. It is like seeing chaste Pallas, who dwells among men out of the generosity of the gods, rejected, hooted off and hissed at, with no one to love or protect her, lest she, like a prostitute who accepts a pittance for her deflowered virginity, deposit the ill-earned profit into her lover's money chest. And I say all these things (not without the deepest grief and indignation) not against the lords of our times but against the philosophers who believe and openly declare that no one should pursue philosophy if only because there is no market for philosophers, no remuneration given to them, as if they did not reveal in this very word that they are not true philosophers. Hence, insofar as their whole life has been dedicated to moneymaking and ambition, they are incapable of embracing the knowledge of truth for its own sake. This much shall I grant myself (and I shall not blush a bit for self-praise in this regard): that I have never pursued philosophy for any other reason than for the sake of being a philosopher, nor have I ever hoped for or sought from my studies, from my queries, any reward or fruit beyond the nourishment of my mind and the knowledge of the truth, something I have always very greatly desired. And I have always been so avid for it and so enamoured of it that, setting aside all private and public concerns, I devoted my whole self to the leisure of contemplation, from which no calumny of the envious, no slander of the enemies of wisdom, has thus far managed to distract me, nor will it in the future. Philosophy herself has taught me to rely upon my own conscience rather than upon the opinions of others, and always to be careful, not so much that people do not speak badly of me as, rather, that I not say or do anything that is in itself bad.

CHAPTER 4

Niccolò Machiavelli (1469–1527)

Confusion verging on chaos aptly describes Italian politics between any two points in time. That being said, the amount of outright violence, political backstabbing and social upheaval Machiavelli had to put up with – as a successful bureaucrat and diplomat first (1498–1512), and later as a disgraced citizen (1512–27) – is, with few if any exceptions, virtually unmatched in the history of Italian philosophy. At any rate, it is conspicuous enough to put him in a league of his own (among political thinkers). All the more so since, in Machiavelli's own words, his claim to originality rested on a return to the things themselves and the 'real truth' they convey through experience, as opposed to the traditional proclivity towards speculation regarding 'imaginary things', most notably by portraying fanciful characters and devising political regimes that can only exist on paper.

Indeed, philosophers had long been lecturing – either in flawless syllogistic fashion or in vivid rhetorical style – both rulers and subjects on how they should behave and interact. However, they had taken little notice of how they actually go about their business. Alternatively, what does unbiased, direct observation of the present and extensive, informed reading of the past teach us about the ways of the world?

Excerpts from *The Prince* provide us with a colourful reminder of Machiavelli's views on what human beings are capable of and how best to deal with them. In a nutshell, when it comes to human relationships, there is no such thing as being too stupid to be wicked. As a matter of fact, ordinary people are guilty as charged on both counts. (One might as well dispense with labels, as Machiavelli does, insofar as non-ordinary people are so extraordinarily few as to make no difference). Men are a sorry lot (they are peevish, greedy, selfish and treacherous) and a credulous bunch to boot (they cannot help rising to the bait when they are told what they want to hear). No wonder Machiavelli offered some peculiar pieces of advice concerning state management and social control.

A couple of straightforward recommendations of his will help us get the gist of (Machiavelli's) Machiavellianism. It should be understood from the start that enjoying an excellent reputation is one thing and being righteous is quite another. It should also be understood that, when they happen to be at odds, Machiavelli urges whoever is running things to surrender moral principles and embrace whatever course of action keeps him ahead of the competition. In other words, for all practical purposes, good politics and bad ethics get on together far better than the other way around. As a matter of fact, to take one's moral notions for political realities is a recipe for failure. So, as far as Machiavelli is concerned, the real issue is not so much whether or not one should get one's hands dirty, since nobody in his right mind would keep them clean when the situation calls for extreme measures. Since it cannot be helped, the only problem one ought to worry about is rather how to get away with questionable practices such as betrayal, assassination and cruelty (three examples Machiavelli treats as a matter of political course).

Even though the vast majority of people do not care much about the way the powers-that-be deliver a reasonable amount of peace and security at home, Machiavelli's golden rule has been met with a certain amount of suspicion. Yet, he definitely had a point and – like every rule of thumb worthy of the name – it makes things a lot easier while reducing the risk of getting hurt in the process. As Machiavelli puts it in devising ways to avoid being hated and despised, rulers should have someone else endorse and especially enforce unpopular policies, whereas they should claim credit for those actions which will increase their popularity. Given the overall purpose of the chapters and their broad moral compass, no stretch of the imagination is required to infer that, in order to succeed, a ruler had better take the merit whenever it is convenient to do the right thing and lay the blame at someone else's door whenever criminal behaviour is in his best interests.

However, what if there is nobody around either to help with the dirty work or, failing that, conveniently to take the fall? Machiavelli spelled out his answer in a number of different ways, but – bottom line – his counsel remains pretty much the same and it emphasizes convenient timing and careful dissimulation. When the time comes to match violence with more violence and subtlety with more subtlety, one should put extra care into keeping up moral appearances, at least until, having no further use for those his previous facade of respectability had deceived, one can afford – on top of dealing with his current foes – to treat old friends as new enemies. In this respect, it is worth noting that it is rather commonplace, albeit inaccurate and somewhat misleading, to saddle Machiavelli with a clear-cut distinction between ethics and politics. True enough, according to Machiavelli, politics has reasons and rules of its own, which morality condemns more than it understands. And true enough again, when push comes to shove, political expediency and moral integrity are mutually exclusive. Still, according to Machiavelli, good faith, mercy and honour, as well as whatever else passes for good manners or helps you win your neighbour's love and respect, are assets as long as they do not become a liability. All these fine qualities have their uses in the political arena, provided we use them: that is, provided we treat ethical concerns as means to an end rather than as ends in themselves.

Granted that the realm of political possibilities is wide enough to include everything short of mindless violence and random destruction and, as a result, it encompasses what is morally acceptable, how do we get to choose whether to stay within the boundaries of either the ethically or the politically correct? Although apparently well formed, questions along these lines rest on a fundamental confusion to the extent that they overlook the basic fact that we do not really carry the burden – or have the luxury, for that matter – of choosing between the two. Of course, there is plenty to be right or wrong about, but one simply does not decide when it is expedient to go rogue and when, on the contrary, it is unwise to push the moral envelope. Eventually, situations sort themselves out and, when the dust settles, the head count provides a reliable indicator of who got his priorities straight and who didn't.

This is, arguably, the most distinctive feature of Machiavelli's talk of skill, fortune, and how statesmen are supposed to prevail through a solid display of the former and a healthy respect for the latter. First of all, it accounts for the remarkable scope of Machiavelli's *virtù*, which is a constant disposition to do whatever circumstances require, be it good, evil or a bit of both. Second, it goes a long way towards explaining why Machiavelli's Prince is so flexible a character that tycoons and gangsters no less than political and military leaders have boasted that they took a leaf out of his book. No surprise there, either: in a world where everything is negotiable and virtue is simply the art of getting the upper hand, it is immaterial whether it takes a good or a bad person to be a successful ruler. As a matter of fact, it is immaterial whether it takes a person at all. While Dante portrayed Farinata as an individual who would have rather died than give up everything he stood for and thus become somebody he could not live with, Machiavelli is the prophet of another kind of humanity altogether. His Prince is less an individual than a calculating force who does not let anything personal – neither his moral scruples nor his nasty habits – interfere with his commitment to success. A model which is as much suited to humans (monarchs, executives, bureaucrats, diplomats etc.) as human institutions (political parties, state cabinets, corporate boards, criminal cartels and any combination thereof). And this alone should be enough to ensure Machiavellianism a place of choice among the archetypes of philosophical wisdom.

Leone Gazziero

Selected writings

Machiavelli, Niccolò. *The Essential Writings of Machiavelli*, trans. Peter Constantine. London: Penguin, 2007.

EXCERPTS

Niccolò Machiavelli, *The Prince*
_____

(Niccolò Machiavelli, *The Prince*, Trans. P. Bondanella, Oxford, Oxford University Press, 2005)

XV:

(Of those things for which men, and particularly princes, are praised or blamed). Now, it remains to be considered what should be the methods and principles of a prince in dealing with his subjects and allies. Because I know that many have written about this, I am afraid that by writing about it again I shall be considered presumptuous, especially since in discussing this material I depart from the procedures of others. But since my intention is to write something useful for anyone who understands it, it seemed more suitable for me to search after the effectual truth of the matter rather than its imagined one. Many writers have imagined republics and principalities that have never been seen nor known to exist in reality. For there is such a distance between how one lives and how one ought to live, that anyone who abandons what is done for what ought to be done achieves his downfall rather than his preservation. A man who wishes to profess goodness at all times will come to ruin among so many who are not good. Therefore, it is necessary for a prince who wishes to maintain himself to learn how not to be good, and to use this knowledge or not to use it according to necessity. Leaving aside, therefore, matters concerning an imaginary prince, and taking into account those that are true, let me say that etc.

XVII:

(Of cruelty and mercy, and whether it is better to be loved than to be feared or the contrary). From this arises an argument: whether it is better to be loved than to be feared, or the contrary. The answer is that one would like to be both one and the other. But since it is difficult to be both together, it is much safer to be feared than to be loved, when one of the two must be lacking. For one can generally say this about men: they are ungrateful, fickle, simulators and deceivers, avoiders of danger, and greedy for gain. While you work for their benefit they are completely yours, offering you their blood, their property, their lives, and their sons, as I said above, when the need to do so is far away. But when it draws nearer to you, they turn away. [. . .] Men are less hesitant about injuring someone who makes himself loved than one who makes himself feared, because love is held together by a chain of obligation that, since men are a wretched lot, is broken on every occasion for their own self-interest; but fear is sustained by a dread of punishment that will never abandon you.

XVIII:

(How a prince should keep his word). How praiseworthy it is for a prince to keep his word and to live with integrity and not by cunning, everyone knows. Nevertheless, one sees from experience in our times that the princes who have accomplished great deeds are those who have thought little about keeping faith and who have known how cunningly to manipulate men's minds; and in the end they have surpassed those who laid their foundations upon sincerity. [. . .] A wise ruler, therefore, cannot and should not keep his word when such an observance would be to his disadvantage, and when the reasons that caused him to make a promise are removed. If men were all good, this precept would not be good. But since men are a wicked lot and will not keep their promises to you, you likewise need not keep yours to them. A prince never lacks legitimate reasons to colour over his failure to keep his word. Of this, one could cite an endless number of modern examples to show how many pacts and how many promises have been made null and void because of the faithlessness of princes; and he who has known best how to use the ways of the fox has come out best. But it is necessary to know how to colour over this nature effectively, and to be a great pretender and dissembler. Men are so simple-minded and so controlled by their immediate needs that he who deceives will always find someone who will let himself be deceived. I do not wish to remain silent about one of these recent examples. Alexander VI never did anything else, nor thought about anything else, than to deceive men, and he always found someone to whom he could do this. There never has been a man who asserted anything with more effectiveness, nor whose affirmations rested upon greater oaths, who observed them less. Nevertheless, his deceptions always succeeded to his heart's desire, since he knew this aspect of the world very well.

XVIII:
Therefore, let a prince conquer and maintain the state, and his methods will always be judged honourable and praised by all. For ordinary people are always taken in by appearances and by the outcome of an event. And in the world there are only ordinary people; and the few have no place, while the many have a spot on which to lean. A certain prince of the present times, whom it is best not to name, preaches nothing but peace and faith, and to both one and the other he is extremely hostile. If he had observed both peace and faith, he would have had either his reputation or his state taken away from him many times over.

XVIII:
Therefore, it is not necessary for a prince to possess all of the above-mentioned qualities, but it is very necessary for him to appear to possess them. Furthermore, I shall dare to assert this: that having them and always observing them is harmful, but appearing to observe them is useful: for instance, to appear merciful, faithful, humane, trustworthy, religious, and to be so; but with his mind disposed in such a way that, should it become necessary not to be so, he will be able and know how to change to the

opposite. One must understand this: a prince, [. . .], cannot observe all those things for which men are considered good, because in order to maintain the state he must often act against his faith, against charity, against humanity, and against religion. And so it is necessary that he should have a mind ready to turn itself according to the way the winds of Fortune and the changing circumstances command him. And, as I said above, he should not depart from the good if it is possible to do so, but he should know how to enter into evil when forced by necessity.

XV: <to be> generous, open-handed, merciful, faithful, fierce, humane, trustworthy, serious, religious.

Niccolò Machiavelli, *The Discourses*

(Niccolò Machiavelli, *Discourses on Livy*, Trans. H. C Mansfield and N. Tarcov, London, The University of Chicago Press, 1996)

To Leap from Humility to Pride, from Mercy to Cruelty, without Due Degrees Is Something Imprudent and Useless. Among the other means badly used by Appius to maintain his tyranny, it was of no little moment to leap too quickly from one quality to another. For his astuteness in deceiving the plebs, pretending to be a man of the people, was well used; also well used were the means he adopted so that the Ten would have to be remade; also well used was the audacity of creating himself against the opinion of the nobility; creating partners to his purposes was well used. But it was not at all well used, when he had done this, as I say above, to change nature of a sudden and from a friend of the plebs show himself an enemy; from humane, proud; from agreeable, difficult; and to do it so quickly that without any excuse every man had to know the falsity of his spirit. For whoever has appeared good for a time and wishes for his purposes to become wicked ought to do it by due degrees and to conduct himself with opportunities, so that before your different nature takes away old favour from you, it has given you so much new that you do not come to diminish your authority; otherwise, finding yourself uncovered and without friends, you are ruined.

(Niccolò Machiavelli, *Il Principe*, XIX)

(Of avoiding being despised and hated). Here, one must note that hatred is acquired just as much through good actions as by sorry ones. And so, [. . .], if a prince wishes to maintain the state, he is often obliged not to be good, because whenever that group you believe you need to support you is corrupted — whether it be the people, the soldiers, or the nobles — it is to your advantage to follow their inclinations in order to satisfy them, and then good deeds are your enemy.

VIII:

(Of those who have become princes through wickedness). One might well wonder how, after so many betrayals and cruelties, Agathocles and others like him could live for such a long time secure in their native cities and defend themselves from foreign enemies without being plotted against by their own citizens. Many others, employing cruel means, were unable to hold on to their state even in peaceful times, not to speak of the uncertain times of war. I believe that this depends on whether cruelty be badly or well used. Those cruelties are well used (if it is permitted to speak well of evil) that are carried out in a single stroke, done out of necessity to protect oneself, and then are not continued, but are instead converted into the greatest possible benefits for the subjects. Those cruelties are badly used that, although few at the outset, increase with the passing of time instead of disappearing. Those who follow the first method can remedy their standing, both with God and with men, as Agathocles did; the others cannot possibly maintain their positions. Hence it should be noted that, in conquering a state, its conqueror should weigh all the injurious things he must do and commit them all at once, so as not to have to repeat them every day. By not repeating them, he will be able to make men feel secure and win them over with the benefits he bestows upon them. Anyone who does otherwise, either out of timidity or because of bad advice, is always obliged to keep his knife in his hand. Nor can he ever count upon his subjects, who, because of their recent and continuous injuries, cannot feel secure with him. Therefore, injuries should be inflicted all at once, for the less they are tasted, the less harm they do. However, benefits should be distributed a little at a time, so that they may be fully savoured.

XVII:

But when the prince is with his armies and has a multitude of soldiers under his command, then it is absolutely necessary that he should not worry about being considered cruel, for without that reputation he will never keep an army united or prepared for any action. Numbered among the remarkable deeds of Hannibal is this: that while he had a very large army made up of all kinds of men that he commanded in foreign lands, there never arose the slightest dissension, either among themselves or against their leader, both during his periods of good and bad luck. This could not have arisen from anything other than his inhuman cruelty, which, along with his many other virtues, made him always venerable and terrifying in the eyes of his soldiers. Without that quality, his other virtues would not have sufficed to attain the same effect. Having considered this matter very superficially, historians on the one hand admire these deeds of his, and on the other condemn the main cause of them. That it is true that his other virtues would not have been sufficient can be seen from the case of Scipio, a most extraordinary man, not only in his time but in all of recorded history, whose armies in Spain rebelled against him. This came about from nothing other than his excessive compassion, which gave his soldiers more licence than is suitable to military discipline. For this he was censured in the Senate by Fabius Maximus, who called him the corruptor of the Roman army.

XV:

Leaving aside, therefore, matters concerning an imaginary prince, and taking into account those that are true, let me say that all men, when they are spoken of — and especially princes, since they are placed on a higher level — are judged by some of those qualities that bring them either blame or praise. And this is why one is considered generous, another miserly [. . .]. One is considered a giver, the other rapacious; one cruel, the other merciful; one a breaker of faith, the other faithful; one effeminate and cowardly, the other fierce and courageous; one humane, the other proud; one lascivious, the other chaste; one trustworthy, the other shrewd; one hard, the other easygoing; one serious, the other frivolous; one religious, the other unbelieving; and the like. And I know that everyone will admit it would be a very praiseworthy thing to find in a prince those qualities mentioned above that are held to be good. But since it is neither possible to have them nor to observe them all completely, because the human condition does not permit it, a prince must be prudent enough to know how to escape the infamy of those vices that would take the state away from him, and be on guard against those vices that will not take it from him, whenever possible. But if he cannot, he need not concern himself unduly if he ignores these less serious vices. Moreover, he need not worry about incurring the infamy of those vices without which it would be difficult to save the state. Because, carefully taking everything into account, he will discover that something which appears to be a virtue, if pursued, will result in his ruin; while some other thing which seems to be a vice, if pursued, will secure his safety and his well-being.

VIII:

Still, it cannot be called virtue to kill one's fellow citizens, to betray allies, to be without faith, without pity, without religion; by these means one can acquire power, but not glory. If one were to consider Agathocles' virtue in getting into and out of dangers, and his greatness of spirit in bearing up under and overcoming adversities, one can see no reason why he should be judged inferior to any most excellent commander. Nevertheless, his vicious cruelty and inhumanity, along with numerous wicked deeds, do not permit us to honour him among the most excellent of men.

CHAPTER 5

Giordano Bruno (1548–1600)

A statue of Giordano Bruno stands in the centre of Rome's *Campo de' Fiori* at the spot where he was burned at the stake by the ecclesiastical authorities. The erection of the statue in 1889 was a deliberate act of anti-clerical defiance by the forces in the newly united Italian state who saw Bruno as a militant heretic and martyr for the independence of science against ecclesiastical dogma. In death as in life, he was a controversial figure.

There is no consensus on the overall interpretation of Bruno's manifold work, nor did his thought develop inside recognizable boundaries or along coherent lines. He belonged to no school and wrote, in an idiosyncratic style replete with extravagant imagery and mythological references, treatises on such varied subjects as theology, philosophy, cosmology and systems of mnemonics, while also touching on Hermeticism and the occult. He lived in an age of great religious, political and social turmoil, as well as intellectual and cultural innovation, was an independent thinker of great originality in many spheres, but his dissident, intellectual energy allied with his abrasive, arrogant character meant that he alienated Catholics, Calvinists and Lutherans and ended up estranged from powers that would have been protective. He inherited the last of Scholasticism and saw the full affirmation of Humanism, came under the influence of Erasmus and Copernicus, was a contemporary of Galileo, participated in the debates over Medieval Aristotelianism and Renaissance neo-Platonism, as well as between Reformers and orthodox Catholic thinkers.

Born in Nola in Campania, he joined the Dominican order and was ordained priest, but the discovery in his cell of an annotated copy of Erasmus, then on the Index of Prohibited Books, meant he had to flee. He turned up in Geneva where according to some authorities he was converted to Calvinism but had problems with them too. In France he enjoyed the patronage of King Henry III, who was intrigued by his work on memory. The year 1528 saw him publish in Latin three treatises on mnemonics, *De umbris idearum (On* the Shadows of Ideas), Ars memoriae (The Art of Memory) and Cantus Circaeus (Circe's Song), whose title is indicative of Bruno's preference for working with allegories and images rather than austere analysis. Reduced to the barest of bones, Bruno advances the idea that there are general categories or mnemonic notes, which he terms 'seals', around which individual objects or ideas can be clustered. The art of memory is one with the very faculty of thought.

The same year he also produced his only play, Il Candelaio (The Candle-bearer), a cynical, irreverent, bawdy comedy in which the candle is, he writes, intended to shed light on 'the shadows of ideas', not least conventional moral ideas held by the mass of human beings, whom he held in contempt. In his introduction, he declares himself 'an Academician of no Academy' and identifies the three themes as 'Bonifacio's love, Bartolomeo's alchemy and Manfurio's pedantry'. The theatrical format, the interest in alchemy and the contempt for pedants, normally adherents of the then dominant Aristotelian philosophy, which Bruno execrated, are features of his Italian dialogues, written in England where he found refuge in the period 1583–5. He associated with such men as the poet Philip Sidney and the alchemist-astrologer John Dee, but a less reputable side of his character was shown by the research of John Bossy who established that he infiltrated Catholic circles to act as a spy for Sir Francis Walsingham, Secretary of State. Bruno settled in Oxford, where he authored the six Italian dialogues which can be viewed as his major works – three largely cosmological in theme and three confronting moral and theological issues.

La Cena de le Ceneri (The Ash Wednesday Supper, 1584) features Bruno's spokesman Teofilo in dialogue with the pedant Prudenzio, the open-minded Smitho and his boisterous servant Frulla. Teofilo scornfully demolishes the credibility of the Aristotelian geocentric system in favour of the Copernican heliocentric universe and advances the belief that the universe is infinite, that the stars are suns, that planets animate beings and that human life was likely to be found elsewhere in the cosmos. These notions were deepened in De la Causa, Principio et Uno (On Cause, Principle and Unity) and De l'Infinito, Universo e Mondi (On the Infinite, the Universe and the Worlds).

Allegory and myth are employed in the extravagantly written, at times impenetrable, De gl' Heroici Furori (On Heroic Frenzies, 1585), the last of his London dialogues. Structured in a poetic-philosophical format which recalls Dante's Vita Nuova, the work is divided into two parts of five dialogues each and features a series of sonnets followed by comments on each one. In its entirety, it constitutes a disquisition on neo-Platonic notions of the final ascent of the soul to attain union with the whole. Christian beliefs of whatever shade are swept aside in favour of an animistic, pantheistic vision of the universe and the human place in it. There is no longer any space for Christian beliefs in the Trinity, the divinity of Christ or the Virgin birth.

It was over these matters, and not his scientific theories, that Bruno found himself arraigned before the Inquisition. He had moved to Venice, where he believed himself safe under the protection of the aristocratic Giovanni Mocenigo, and even applied unsuccessfully for a chair in the University of Padua, which went to Galileo, but was then denounced and later handed over to the Inquisition in Rome. He spent seven years in prison and was tried for holding heretical beliefs, for instance, on the Trinity of God, the divinity of Christ, the transmigration of souls and an anti-biblical belief in the plurality of worlds. He attempted to defend himself by claiming for the philosopher an independence not granted to the theologian, and that his philosophical beliefs did not undermine his religious faith. The defence was rejected and he was committed to the secular arm for execution.

Joseph Farrell

Selected writings

Bruno, Giordano. *Cause, Principle and Unity: and Essays on Magic*, trans. Robert de Lucca, with Essays on Magic, and J. Richard. Cambridge: Cambridge University Press, 1998. (Translations of De la causa, principio et uno, 1584, and of *De magia* and *De vinculis in genere*, 1591)

Bruno, Giordano. *De Umbris Idearum: On the Shadows of Ideas & The Art of Memory*, trans. Scott Gosnell. Columbus, OH, 2013. (Translations of De Umbris Idearum and Arts Memoriae, 1528)

Bruno, Giordano. *On the Heroic Frenzies*, trans. Ingrid D. Rowland. Toronto: University of Toronto Press, 2013. (A Translation of De gl' Heroici Furori, ed. Eugenio Canone, 1585)

Bruno, Giordano. *On the Infinite, the Universe and the Worlds*, trans. Scott Gosnell. Columbus, OH: Huginn, Munnin & Co, 2014. (Translation of *De l'infinito, universo e mondi*, 1584)

Bruno, Giordano. *The Ash Wednesday Supper*, trans. Hilary Gatti. Toronto: University of Toronto Press, 2018. (Translation of La Cena de la Ceneri, 1584)

EXCERPT

Giordano Bruno, *On the Infinite, the Universe and the Worlds*

(Giordano Bruno, *On the Infinite, the Universe and the Worlds*, Trans. Scott Gosnell. (USA: Huginn, Munnin & Co, 2014), *pp. 44--53*).

From the *First Dialogue*:

Elpino: But what's the reason there are many, instead of only one?

Filoteo: Because if it was a bad thing that there should be nothing in our place, and all other places are equal, then that reasoning holds in those places equally.

Elpino: I would say that it's bad, if something similar to what is in our space were in another space, and we couldn't differentiate the two.

Filoteo: This, as I see it, is all one; because the goodness of being of this body, in this particular space, which is equal to what it would be elsewhere, regarded and reasoned as perfect and good in this our space; this is no argument against innumerable other spaces, similar to this one. Moreover, it is made stronger, for if a finite good is a limited perfection, then how much better is an infinite good, because, where a finite good is reasonable and appropriate, an infinite good becomes absolutely necessary.

Elpino: The infinite good certainly is, but is also incorporeal.

Filoteo: In this, we are in accord regarding the incorporeal infinite. But what shall we make less of the good, infinite, corporeal entity? Is it more repugnant to explain that the infinite should be implicated in the most basic of things and the first principles, these faces of the infinite and limitless, these capacious and innumerable worlds; or to explain rather the narrow margins, the infamy of fate that causes this body, which seems to us so great, to appear to the divine presence as a mere point, and in fact as nothing?

Elpino: Since the greatness of God does not rest upon great physical size in any sense (and let us not say that our world adds in any way to it), we should not think that the greatness of His image rests on the greatness or smallness of it.

Filoteo: Precisely well put, but this does not deal with the core of the argument, for I do not insist on infinite space nor does Nature have infinite space for the sake of dignifying scope or corporeal matter, but because the dignity of nature is by species corporeal, there is necessity that this should be presented by incomparably innumerable individuals as a presentation of the excellence of infinity, rather than only by a small and finite number. We must, therefore, see the reflection of the hidden divine countenance in the endless image with countless members, the innumerable worlds, one to the other. But by reason of the innumerable degrees of perfection, which explicate the divine incorporeal excellence through material means, there are innumerable individuals, like enormous animals (one of which is our Earth, divine mother who has given birth to us and nurtured us and will moreover receive us back in time) and to contain these innumerable bodies, an infinite space is needed. Nevertheless, as it is good that we exist and that it is possible that we exist, so too is it good that these others may exist and do exist.

Elpino: We say that this finite world with its finite stars, contains the whole perfection of those many things.

Filoteo: You could say that, but you cannot prove it. For this world, within its finite space, contains the perfection of the finite things within its space, but not of the infinite things, which are able to exist in innumerable other spaces.

Fracastorio: Give thanks and stop there. Let us not become like the sophists, who argue only to win, and by striving for laurels, impede themselves and others from coming to the truth. For I believe that no one else is so great in perfidiousness or pertinaceousness as those who hurl calumny upon the idea of infinite space, and upon the goodness of the individual and numerous worlds that may dwell within it, each of which may, no less than our own world, be well able to contain its own conscious being. For infinite space contains infinite attributes, and in that lies the greatness of its existence, by which the Efficient Cause is not considered deficient, nor its infinite qualities in vain. Therefore, Elpino, let us be content, and hear the further arguments of Filoteo as they occur to him.

Elpino: I can see well enough, to tell the truth, that the world, or as you say, "the universe" is without bounds, that this creates no inconvenience, and that it frees us from many of the constraints that would otherwise envelop us if we were to state the contrary. I am especially clear that what the Peripatetics say has no foundation when they deny the vacuum, whether outside or inside the universe, they try to answer that it is in its parts, for fear of saying that it is not in any location; it is as if one said: Nullibi, Nusquam. But you cannot remove the problem this way, which needs the parts to be in some location, but the whole universe has no location or lies nowhere in space; that is to say, as any can see, this opinion is not founded on any true intention, but signifies rather a pertinacious means of making a quick escape from judging the world and universe infinite, or space infinite; from which position follows a doubled confusion for all who hold them. Say, therefore, that the whole of it is a body, and the body is spherical, and in consequence it has a shape and a boundary, then that boundary borders on infinite space, but if we want to say that nothing exists in that infinite space, we must therefore admit that true vacuum exists, and if this truly exists, we must admit that it is no less reasonable to conceive of the whole of it than of the part that encloses this world; if it does not, then we must admit that it is a fullness, and consequently admit the infinite universe. And it would be no less insipid to say that the world is somewhere, having said that outside the world is nowhere, though the parts are in themselves. It is as if we said that Elpino is somewhere, for his hand is in [or next to] his arm, his eye in his face, his foot in his leg, his head in his torso. To reach a conclusion, I would not be like a sophist who looks at his feet when reaching an apparent difficulty, nor fear to speak what I cannot deny, namely: that space may well be infinite, and contain other worlds similar to our own, or that the universe may have extended its capacity to contain many bodies, if you will, which we call stars, or otherwise that (whether similar or dissimilar to our own world) there it is no less good that either one or many might exist; for there is no less reason that many rather than one should be, and an infinity of them no less than many of them. So, just as the abolition of one of them would be bad, the more so would the nonexistence of multitudinous others.

Fracastorio: You explain this very well, and demonstrate that you well understand the rationale for these things, and are no mere sophist, for you affirm only that which cannot be denied.

Elpino: Also, I would like to hear more about the Principle and Eternal Efficient Cause, what its effects are upon the infinite, and what effects from both should be expected.

Filoteo: This is what I have to add: after saying that the universe is infinite, and has the ability and aptitude of infinite space, and the possibility and convenience for infinite worlds like this, it still must be proved. So both from the circumstances of the Efficient Cause, which have produced the universe as it is, or rather, have always produced it, and from the circumstances of our understanding, we may argue more easily that infinite space is similar to that which we see, rather than like that which we do not see by example, by likeness, by proportion, or by any operation of the imagination which does not destroy itself. To begin: Why should we think the Divine Efficiency to be otiose? What makes us think that despite the fact that the divine goodness can be diffused into all the infinite things, it would nonetheless choose to make itself scarce and reduce itself to nothingness, as all finite things are reduced to nothing when compared to the infinite? Why would you wish for the divine center, which can (it is possible to say) extend infinitely to an infinite sphere, to instead remain sterile, when it can be fecund, fatherly, ornate and beautiful? Why should it be diminished and mute rather than to fulfill its glorious power and plan? Why should the infinite capacity be frustrated, the infinite worlds defrauded, the excellence of the divine imagination be prejudged, when it could be reflected in an unrestricted mirror in all its infinite, immense glory, according to its nature? Why should we affirm this, instead, which presents many inconveniences but does not further laws, religion, faith or morals in any way at all, and distresses the principles of philosophy? How can you tell me that God in His power, act and efficiency (which in Him are the same) be determined and bounded by the convexity of a sphere, moreso than if it were unbounded and limitless? The limit, I say, without limit, to differentiate the two infinites, for He is the comprehensive, whole and complete totality of the infinite (if we may truthfully use the term "totality" where there is neither part nor boundary) while the other infinity [that of the universe] is not total. The one understands boundaries, the second is bounded, but this is not the difference between infinite and finite. The one is infinite totally, the second is infinite but not totally or comprehensively; this would be repugnant to the dimensionally infinite. It is only entirely infinite.

Elpino: I would like to understand this better. I'd like an explanation for that, when you say entirely infinite and totally infinite.

Filoteo: I say the universe is entirely infinite, because it has neither edges, limits or a surface, but it is not totally infinite because each part of it we can comprehend is finite and each of the innumerable worlds within it is finite. I say that God is totally and comprehensively infinite because not only is He without any boundary or limit, but also each of His attributes is one and infinite; I say God is infinite because each part of Him contains and comprehends infinity and totality in contrast to the infinity of the universe, which is only infinite in total, but not in each of its parts (if it is even possible to say "parts" with reference to an infinite whole).

Elpino: I understand. Please continue.

Filoteo: To sum up the argument: just as it is understood that our finite world is fitting, good, necessary, so too must the innumerable others also be fitting, good and necessary; just so, by the same reasoning, the Omnipotence is not envious of existence, and if [one said] the others were not, either because He does not will it or cannot will it, this would be a blasphemy—to permit a vacuum, or if you don't want to say vacuum, then an infinite, empty space— would not only subtract from the perfection of His being, but also from the infinite majesty of His efficiency in the making of things, if they are made, or sustaining things, if they are eternal. What reason are we apt to credit, if the agent who can shape an infinite eternity, were instead to make a finite one? And if He made it finite, how should we believe that He could have made it infinite, since in Him potential and action are one? For He is immutable, and has no contingency in His actions nor in his efficacy, rather, from determined and certain actions invariably flow determined and certain results. Therefore, He cannot be other than He is, nor be other than He can, nor do what He cannot, nor act other than as He wills, nor necessarily make other than what He makes, for power distinct from action befits only mutable things.

Fracastorio: Certainly, there exists no possibility that the power was never, is not, and will never be other than it is, and truly, the Prime Efficiency does not wish to act any way other than as He does. Also, I do not see why some wish to say that the infinite active power does not correspond to some infinite passive power receiving it from beginning to end, which can create the innumerable, infinite and immense essence of action, or necessity—because if this proceeds from His perfectly immutable will, it must be necessary—so will, potential and being are made one.

CHAPTER 6

Giambattista Vico (1668–1744)

Giambattista Vico was born in, and lived his whole life around, Naples working as a professor of rhetoric at the university, but failing in his ambition to be elected to the more prestigious position of professor of law. This failure perhaps led him to keep his eye on his historical reflections rather than his legal ones, and his early works were concerned with the transmission of concepts and ideas from the Etruscan and Ionian languages into Latin, along with the corruptions, distortions and embellishments which such encounters with difference produced in the discourses of reason and the beliefs of culture. The universal tropes, imaginaries and common beliefs he found in these investigations gave birth to his most original ideas and motivated a continuous process of reflection and revision of his new social science, culminating in his magnum opus, *The New Science* (subtitled in the first edition of 1723 as *The Principles of a New Science of the Nature of Nations Leading to the Discovery of the Principles of a New System of the Natural Law of the Gentes*), which was continually revised until his death in 1744, when the much changed third edition was published. The goal of Vico's developing epistemology was to provide a ground for the justification of historical (philological) knowledge as a science.

Vico's philosophical thinking began through a courageous abandonment of the intellectual context of Cartesianism dominant among his contemporaries. Indignantly driven by the perceived affront shown by the French thinker and his followers to history which, for him, had to be raised to the level of a science, his *New Science* was an attempt to delineate those principles of method necessary for the proper and rigorous investigation of historical documents (myth, primitive religions, first-hand accounts) since Vico was aware that different ages and cultures had radically different beliefs and discourses. The fundamental claim made by Vico in the pages of the *New Science* was that history (philology) and the study of societal change (ideal eternal history) constituted a science with its own principles and methods.

However, the Cartesians had adopted one method, and if a discipline could not be rendered intelligible following their deductive rationalism, then it was not to be considered a branch of knowledge. Vico's rejection of Descartes is a development of his own *verum-factum principle* or the theory of maker's knowledge: the identity of knowledge or truth with making. Physics is an imperfect knowledge because the full list of causes, which, for Vico, must include the 'why', is just not available to the mind, since nature was not created by human activity.

Vico clearly distinguishes between what can be known (deductions derived from artificial concepts forming a coherent system of meaning) and what cannot be known (things which are not made by humans: nature, matter etc.). This limitation placed on knowledge severely challenges Descartes's rationalist assumption that human reason is adapted so as to adequately represent reality in epistemological terms, since the very basis of this system – mathematical, geometrical and analytical truths – requires that truths discovered by reason inhere in reality. Vico stated openly that reason does not discover such truths but invents them.

Historical concepts are born from an expressive, non-rational act on the part of primitive human beings. So, for Vico, one can have knowledge about societies because as humans we have created them, just as we can know about the nature of human beings because they emerge from those societies. *Ingenuity*, as a faculty of knowing, is the power to create 'imaginative universals', which is the faculty of the human mind that creates concepts which make experience possible or poetic wisdom (as opposed to more reflective, modern reason). So, the world view of a people is embodied in its myths, metaphysics and ethics, and the historian needs to think their way into that world view rather than merely observing it. A people produces its world view through an expression of mythopoietic creation. The human being as subject of law and morality is created and produced by those institutions, ideas and conceptions of the good.

Consequent to this, purely rational philosophy is corrupted by the 'conceit of scholars' where thinkers judge what is unknown to them in terms of what is familiar and believe it to be an objective description. This leads to inaccurate and approximate knowledge of the beliefs, ideas and desires of historically and culturally different peoples. All the sciences, disciplines of knowledge and arts have arisen from the social existence of the human being, but that does not mean that one cannot understand their causes or explain them. They were made by the human mind, and hence humans can offer a full explanation of why and how our epistemological, metaphysical and ethical doctrines exist, so long as we remember that they do not correspond with reality, but are, in fact, made possible by the social institutions, practices and languages which gave birth to them.

Vico's science is historical, seeking to understand why humans produce social institutions and cultural productions. Vico is convinced that such a science is possible because one can investigate what is contingent in a particular society and what is universal to all men and in all societies. The method Vico proposes is twofold: philological, or historical, and philosophical. The former is the attempt to avoid what Vico saw as the error of his predecessors, the conceit of scholars or the conflation of how we see the world given our historical, social existence and how the world actually is. To explain something, to know it, is to realize that it is a production of men's minds and its ultimate cause is to be located there. In order to make manifest the how, the *why* and the *what* of an event or an idea, one must reveal its origins in those institutions and primitive ideas which make it possible.

The ingenuity of the human mind, the imaginative capacity to make social and cultural truth, forms the concepts which provide the basis for institutions, and since all peoples share common sense or an unreflective disposition for law-governed behaviour, then those institutions which persist and change only in form can reveal ideas which ground the ideas common to all humans. The philological and philosophical investigation of social and civil institutions (the comparison of actual historical structures and forms with the ideal eternal history) will disclose what must be the origins of history and humanity.

Vico's investigations discovered uniform ideas embodied in all civil societies no matter what their geographical or temporal location, and these are manifest through three institutions which are universal to all societies.

First, religion, since civilization and knowledge have to arise from the attempt to explain the cause of reality and cannot originate in any other way. It is with this recognition of divine providence or the essential limitation of humanity that religion arises and with it the first metaphysical descriptions of reality. It becomes possible to offer primitive explanations of the events that occur within everyday life in terms of a coherent system.

Second, marriage sets up a household and the economics of later institutions. It frees the human from the binding desires of hunger and sexual need in a way that is coherent with values derived from the metaphysical and religious structures of the time.

Finally, respect for the dead is universal to every human society and delineates the first instance of value and worth and an explanation as to who matters, again coherent and consistent with the classes, hierarchies and roles distributed by the other two institutions.

These three ideas capture the historical moment at which human beings as opposed to the animal emerge and create a symbolic, meaningful world which is a reflection of their expressive nature. These three institutions are the fundamentals of any historical society but find themselves manifested in different ways, thus giving rise to the general ages of human existence: the age of gods, of heroes and of men. The different epochs structure the systems of power, the relations of class and the patterns of historical change to describe the abstract form of ideal eternal history. Civil institutions and history can be known because they follow the principles of humans and are made by humans, and so the enquirer is potentially capable of listing their causes. The ideal eternal history comprises the universal principles which set out the limits and possible developments of human civilizations and actual historical change; it is the schema of interpretative, historical understanding.

David Rose

Selected writings

Vico, Giambattista. *The Autobiography of Giambattista Vico*, trans. Thomas Goddard Bergin and Max Harold Fisch. Ithaca, NY: Cornell University Press, 1983.

Vico, Giambattista. *The First New Science*, edited by and trans. Leon Pompa. Cambridge: Cambridge University Press, 2002.

Vico, Giambattista. *The New Science of Giambattista Vico* (1744 edition). Including the 'Practice of the New Science', trans. Thomas Goddard Bergin and Max Harold Fisch. Ithaca, NY: Cornell University Press, 1984.

Vico, Giambattista. *On the Most Ancient Wisdom of the Italians, Unearthed from the Origins of the Latin Language*. Including the Disputations with the Giornale de' Letterata d'Italia, trans. L. M. Palmer. Ithaca and London: Cornell University Press, 1988.

Vico, Giambattista. *On the Study Methods of Our Time*, trans. Elio Gianturco. Reissued with a Preface by Donald Phillip Verene, and including 'The Academies and the Relation between Philosophy and Eloquence', trans. Donald Phillip Verene. Ithaca, NY: Cornell University Press, 1990.

EXCERPT

Giambattista Vico, *The First New Science*

_____

(G. Vico, *The First New Science*. Trans. L. Pompa. (Cambridge: Cambridge University Press, 2002), pp. 9–12.)

I Reasons for our meditation on this work

The natural law of the nations was certainly born with the common customs of the nations. Furthermore, there has never been a nation of atheists in the world, because all nations began in some single religion. The roots of these religions all sprang from man's natural desire for eternal life, a desire, common to human nature, which arises from a common sense, concealed in the depths of the human mind, that the human soul is immortal. But however hidden this cause, its effect is equally evident: that, when faced with the final afflictions of death, we wish for a force superior to nature by which to overcome them, a force that is to be found only in a God who is not identical with, but superior to, nature herself, i.e. an infinite and eternal mind. And when men stray from this God, they become curious about the future.

This curiosity, which is forbidden by nature, for [such knowledge of the future] belongs to a God who is an infinite and eternal mind, precipitated the fall of the two great originators of mankind. Accordingly God both founded the true religion of the Hebrews upon worship of His infinite and eternal Providence and punished the first authors of the human race for their desire to know the future, thus condemning the whole race to toil, pain and death. Whence the false religions all rose from idolatry, i.e. from the worship of imaginary deities, falsely believed to be bodies with supernatural force, who give succour to men in their final afflictions. Idolatry shared her birth with that of divination, which was a vain science of the future, through which men believed that the gods sent them certain sensory warnings. Yet this vain science, in which the vulgar wisdom of all the gentile nations must have begun, hides two great principles of truth: first, that there is a divine Providence which governs human affairs; second, that men possess freedom of the "will, through which, if they so choose, they can escape that which, without their foreseeing it, would otherwise befall them. It follows from this second truth that men can choose to live in justice, a common sense that is confirmed by the common desire men naturally have for laws when they are not moved otherwise by the passion of some self-interest.

This, and no other, is certainly the human nature whose practices, always and everywhere, have been governed by these three common senses of mankind: firstly, that Providence exists; secondly, that certain children be bred by certain women with whom they share at least the principles of a common civil religion, in order that they be brought up by their fathers and mothers in a single spirit and in conformity with the laws and religions amidst which they were born; and thirdly, that the dead should be buried. Hence not only has there never been a nation of atheists in the world, but neither has there been a nation in which women did not adopt the public religion of their husbands. And if there has never been a nation that lived in total nakedness, even less has there been one in which people practised canine or shameless venery in the presence of others or indulged it, like beasts, only in stray matings. Nor, finally, has any nation, no matter how barbaric, ever left the corpses of its members to rot unburied on the ground, for this would be a nefarious state, i.e. one that sins against the common nature of men. Hence, to avoid falling into such a state, the nations protect their native religions with inviolable ceremonies, celebrating marriage and burial, above all other human institutions, with elaborate rites and solemnities. This is the vulgar wisdom of mankind, which began in religions and laws and reached its perfection and completion in the sciences, disciplines and arts.

II Meditation on a new science

But though the sciences, disciplines and arts have all been directed towards the perfection and regulation of man's faculties, none of them has yet contained a meditation upon certain origins of the humanity of nations, from which, beyond doubt, they themselves all arose. Nor, starting from such origins, have they established a certain *acme*, or state of perfection, with which to measure the stages through which the humanity of nations must proceed and the limits within which, like all else mortal, it must terminate. Had they done so they would have gained scientific apprehension of the practices through which the humanity of a nation, as it rises, can reach this perfect state, and those through which, when it declines from this state, it can return to it anew. The only possible form that this state could take would be that in which the nations stand fast on certain maxims, both demonstrated by immutable reasons and practised in their common customs, so that the recondite wisdom of the philosophers would aid and support the vulgar wisdom of nations and, in this way, the distinguished members of the academies be in agreement with the sages of the republics. Thus the science of civil things, divine and human, i.e. of religion and law, which constitute a theology and morality of command acquired through habit, would be supported by the science of natural things, divine and human, which constitute a theology and morality of reason, acquired through reasoning. Hence, a life beyond such maxims would be the true (state of) error, i.e. of wandering, of man and beast alike.

[. . .]

The ground of the proofs that establish this Science is the universal language of the universal law of the gentes which has been observed in this great city of mankind. With the language of this Jaw we can explain the mode of the birth of the parts that comprise the entire system of the nature of nations, for science consists solely in cognition of the mode; we can exhibit the times of the birth of the first parts of each kind [of nature], for it is the distinguishing mark of a science that it should reach those origins beyond which it is utterly foolish curiosity to seek others earlier; through these same times and modes of birth we can discover the eternal properties through which alone it is possible to ascertain that their birth or nature was thus and not otherwise; and [we can reveal how], from their first beginnings, they proceeded through an uninterrupted, i.e. continuous, succession of things, in accordance with the natural progress of human ideas. This is the principal reason why, in the 'Idea of the Work', we conceived the present book in accordance with the expression leges aeternas ['the eternal laws'] that the philosophers use to name the parts of law that we have treated here. Moreover, on the basis of the foregoing meditations, this work brings mythologies, which are histories of facts, into agreement with etymologies, which provide a science of the origin of things. Thus it brings to light, recomposes and restores to their proper places, the great fragments of antiquity, hitherto lost from sight, dispersed and displaced, while preserving the reverence owed to the vulgar traditions by discovering the grounds of their truth and the causes whereby they later reached us cloaked in falsehood. Thus the whole of philology is governed with certain and determinate meanings by philosophy and consistency reigns both among the parts and in the totality of the system of these principles.

This Science, conducted in accordance with the foregoing sorts of proof, contains two practices. The first is that of a new critical art, which serves it as a torch with which to distinguish the true within obscure and fabulous history. The second is a diagnostic art, as it were, which, regulated in accordance with the wisdom of mankind, provides the stages of necessity and utility in the order of human affairs, and thus, as its final consequence, provides this Science with its principal end: knowledge of the indubitable signs of the state of the nations.

In exemplification of the above claims we offer the following. The mode [in which the first parts of the system of the nature of nations were born] consisted in the reduction of a few men from bestial venery to human venery.

The first time [in which these parts were born] was when, among the Egyptians, Greeks and Latins, the sky first thundered after the Flood.

The [first parts of its] nature consisted in those properties of the fathers through which they became sages, priests and kings in the state of the families.

The continuity of the succession [of things begins with] the first kings, and they were certainly monarchical kings, who were the fathers in the state of nature. Thus, with the full weight of the word, Homer gives the name 'king' to the family father who, with his sceptre, orders the roast ox to be divided among the harvesters, an event placed in front of the cities on Achilles' shield, on which the whole history of the previous world was described. Next the kings everywhere were aristocratic. Finally monarchical kings were established, and everywhere, both in extent and duration, monarchies were, and are, the most celebrated [kingdoms] in the world.

The eternal properties [of things] are: [first], that the natural law of the nations should be dealt with solely by the civil powers, which should either consist in a ruling order of sages, such as in the aristocratic republics, or be regulated by a senate of sages, as in the free republics, or be assisted by a council of sages, as with the monarchs; [second], that the civil powers should be revered as sacred persons who recognise no superior other than God, like the first fathers in the state of the families, and that they should finally govern their peoples in the manner of the fathers of large families; and [third], that the civil powers should have the right of life and death over their subjects, just as the first fathers exercised it over their children, and that their subjects should, like children, inherit through the fathers of the republics, in order that the fathers preserve the liberty of their great families for their nations and for their children. And even Tacitus; in his history of the Caducarian law, referred to the Roman prince as omnium parentem ['the father of all']. This is the genesis of that eminent ownership of the civil powers, to which, in respect of public needs, the sovereign or despotic ownership of the family fathers over their patrimony must give way. Hence, we can see with how much truth Bodin spoke when he said that sovereign ownership under the sovereign ownership of others was a discovery of the last barbarians, whereas it was from the sovereign ownership of the first fathers that the first republics arose and, with them, civilisation itself!

The stages of utility are: first, the need of states to worship a provident divinity; next, the need for the certainty of family relationships through solemn marriage; lastly, the need to distinguish ownership of the lands by burying the dead in them, from which human custom came the practices whereby citizens erected magnificent palaces and embellished their cities with public buildings for the lustre and splendour of their descendants: thus did the public desire for immortality flower among the nations. Hence, the nations guard the following three human practices above all others with the highest of ceremonies and most elaborate solemnities: their native religions, marriage within their own people and funerals within their own lands. For this is the common sense of the whole of mankind: that the nations should stand firm on these three customs above all others in order not to fall back into the state of bestial liberty, for all three arose from a certain blush of shame, experienced by the living and the dead, in face of the sky.

In the same way, the stages of the utility of recondite wisdom are revealed. For recondite wisdom must serve the vulgar wisdom from which it is born and for which it itself lives, with the end of correcting and supporting that wisdom when it is weakened, and guiding and leading it when it wanders astray. Thus the rule for judging the state of the nations is whether they embrace or reject, and whether their philosophers support or abandon, these three maxims.

CHAPTER 7

Benedetto Croce (1866–1952)

Benedetto Croce is perhaps the best-known Italian philosopher of the twentieth century. Although his influence today is most strongly felt in the fields of aesthetics, philosophy of history and literary criticism, his theory of art was merely one part of an integrated philosophical system, which incorporated aesthetics, logic (conceptual knowledge), economics and ethics.

As the son of wealthy landowners in the Abruzzi of Italy, Croce was born into the enviable position of never having to earn money in order to support his scholarly pursuits. For this reason, he never held an academic teaching post although he did twice serve as Minister for Education in the Italian government, once in 1920–1 and again after the Second World War. After being injured in the earthquake which killed his parents, Croce spent three years in Rome before moving in 1886 to Naples, where he lived until his death. He had a long friendship with Giovanni Gentile, and they collaborated together on the journal *La Critica*, but their relationship finally dissolved when Croce openly criticized the fascist government for whom Gentile had become the official philosopher. Croce, oddly enough, was tolerated by the fascist authorities, becoming the most well-known critic of the regime and, in the eyes of the Italian people, the champion of liberty.

Croce's entire philosophical system began from the consideration of aesthetics and, in particular, the problems of literature and history. Above all, he was fascinated by the debate as to whether history was an art or a science. The answer he was to offer would radically revise the relationship between art and science by promoting art to the level of knowledge.

Life and reality were, for him, history and nothing but history, and this 'historical idealism' was an attempt on his part to make intelligible the Hegelian aspiration to identify what is rational with what is historically actual or real. In framing and responding to his own question in this way, Croce aligned himself with his major influences, Vico and Hegel, and like them held a position that ran counter to the prevailing ideas of the

Enlightenment: truth is not to be described in abstract terms independent of history, but it is rather historical through and through. His thought was an idealism because reality is constructed by the power of the knowing mind, and it was specifically a form of Hegelian idealism because the historical rationalization of reality is truth. When one is aware of the historical process of truth, one recognizes one's philosophy as part of this development and this, according to Croce, is spirit. Spirit is perhaps best comprehended as a harmony between the knowing mind and reality, when the knowing subject knows what is the case and why historically it is the case.

The system of spirit describes the development and ascent of knowledge and is primarily divided in traditional fashion into theoretical reason (describing what is) and practical reason (describing what should be). Theoretical reason is either aesthetics (the cognitive experience of the particular) or logic (cognitive experience of the universal), whereas practical reason is divided into economics (practical experience concerned with the particular) and ethics (practical experience concerned with the universal).

Art for Croce – as it was for both Vico and Hegel – is a primitive form of knowing, but – unlike them – he did not believe it to be rational. However, philosophy and logic are dependent on and determined by aesthetic expressions of reality since these supply the raw material from which the mind is able to conceptualize objects. Philosophy or logic, in turn, supplies the language for economics or the sphere of knowledge in which man renders his wants, volitions and needs intelligible. The main characteristic of economic practical reason is that it describes objects as useful or not in terms of the purposes of men. Finally, the practical knowledge of ethics, that is the universal nature of volition and knowledge of good and bad independent of utility, is derived from the subject's experience of the more primitive economic volitions. Ethics describes what is universally good independent of particular or group purposes. The Good is not to be understood in terms of some universal and impersonal moral law; because all truth is ultimately historical, the Good is understood in terms of the historical processes of spirit.

In order to complete the circle of spirit, one would assume that our new, sophisticated account of the Good would feed back into our understanding of art and begin the progression at a higher level, and although Croce does sometimes seem to suggest this, at others he rather affirms that knowledge of the Good raises the knowing subject to the level of historical knowledge and truth proper. That said, the full elaboration of the progressive schema would perhaps constitute the best way in which to elucidate Croce's philosophy.

The first moment of universal spirit is artistic; knowing, in short, begins with art. Art is the expression of intuitions, but intuition is to be understood in terms of Kant's *Anschauung*: a manifold of experience, which is to say that, even at this level, the mind is active and not passive. One can understand the artistic moment as an attempt on the part of the subject to fix what is real and separate it from what is mere appearance: thus it is a cognitive expression and not a value judgement; the artist is not aiming at beauty, nor at some moral judgement, but is aiming rather at the truth of the particular (much like the expressivist artist).

Art must be expressed in a particular medium, hence the divisions of poetry (words), plastic arts (colour, matter etc.), music (sounds) and so on, but all are equally ruled by feeling. It is feeling in the sense of mood or emotion that structures the form of the image and the image which allows a feeling to be expressed. The active element of a representation at this non-conceptual level is human spirit expressing itself in the way that it structures the experience it is given. It is an immediate and aesthetic experience of reality.

However, to equate Croce with the Romantic elements in Hegel's early philosophy would be mistaken: the feeling or emotion at stake is a particular manner of knowing reality for the subject; it is not a moment of primitive reason which needs to be overcome and reified, as Hegel held. Artistic expression is the a priori synthesis of feeling and representation, and it is equally an immediate, vital and non-conceptual awareness of knowing what is real.

Croce also departed from Hegel's influence in one other major way: the realms of expression and reason are distinct, and the dialectic of the elements is not one of opposition (as it was for Hegel in which art would be overcome by more reified ways of knowing such as religion). Intuition is distinct from pure concepts, much as Kant distinguished the faculty of intuition from the faculty of understanding, rather than an opposition which can be resolved. The concepts of reason require intuitions as raw material from which to form objects, but aesthetics, when concerned with beauty, requires the pure concepts of logic. The dialectic operates between the borders set by the knowledge of pure intuition (aesthetics) and the knowledge of pure concepts (logic).

From the particular expressions with which the knowing subject represents the world aesthetically, one can abstract general concepts which can then be used in science and other realms of knowledge. Although the human being's faculty of logic is separate from his faculty of intuition or immediate experience, the former is incapable of operation without the material supplied by the latter.

The central and most controversial claim of Croce's philosophy of knowledge was the identification of truth with history, although this thesis was already well known to Hegelians. Logic is defined as the knowledge of the universal which uses the particular knowledge of intuitions to form objective truth. Croce held that since any philosophical assertion is made by a subject and that subject exists concretely and historically and not as some abstract entity, then the assertion itself must be historical: when I say, 'My laptop is on', the truth of this statement can be established because it is a matter of historical fact.

The awareness of the historical nature of concepts, that is, their relation to the development of spirit, brings the subject to a new kind of knowledge

– spirit itself. However, art is not a primitive form of reason but the faculty of intuition, which is to say, the way in which the subject immediately apprehends the world. Logic, then, is the faculty of understanding, and the categories which determine the truth of the subject's conceptual objects are not abstract universals but the categories of historical knowledge which determine the four ways in which one can evaluate statements: intuitively, rationally, economically and morally.

Croce dismissed the idea of abstract universals in knowledge because they were, according to him, always in the service of some deeper practical aim. Error arises due to the confusion of pseudo-concepts with concepts proper. A pseudo-concept such as egoism in economic systems of explanation does not describe some universal aspect of human nature. Egoism is true of men only in so far as they are interested in predicting the effect of market forces and regulations on a country's economy. Croce does not deny the practical applicability of pseudo-concepts, but he maintains that, in the last instance, one is mistaken if one raises them to the level of truth when they are more properly conceived in pragmatic terms. The evaluation of pseudo-concepts in terms of utility is not dissimilar to the Marxist critique of ethics: what is good depends on deeper structures: namely, economics. What is true in science depends on something more profound: our scientific concepts often change in tune with our practical, historical goals. Truth, for Croce, is a predicate of statements made by concrete individuals in particular historical situations.

Economics covers the sphere of the operations of practical reason concerned with the matter of the individual: his needs, desires and volitions. Any concept employed in the satisfaction of these needs would of course be a pseudo-concept which could not be universalized. Economic operations presuppose the immediate knowing of the world present in aesthetic experience and the conceptual knowledge of logic.

Controversially for an idealist, Croce locates politics and law within the realm of economics: what is legally right is what is useful; law is essentially amoral. The state, for Croce, is nothing but a process of purposive actions taken by a group of individuals or within the group of individuals, and laws are adopted in order to bring about these useful ends. He saw politics as the dialectical struggle between the distinct entities of power and consent, as well as authority and liberty – a view which is hardly surprising given the fascist structure of Italy which he experienced. Morality could play no part in politics because the moral life of the individual is not geared towards the useful. Croce here follows Machiavelli rather than Hegel, and his rather odd brand of liberalism can perhaps be understood as descending from his compatriot rather than from the ethico-political holism of the German. In many ways, he was a liberal by default since difference, individuality and tolerance were necessary for his dialectic, and liberalism was the only way to secure these values. As far as the democratic ideals of liberty, equality and fraternity were concerned, he viewed them as pseudo-concepts rather than moral ideals, that is, concepts useful for attaining an end rather than prescribing or describing universal values.

In the sphere of economic practical reason, Croce reduces all goods or concepts to pragmatism: they are useful in so far as they bring about the end aimed at by the agent. However, usefulness as a value only makes sense if there is some good or end aimed at, which the science of economics cannot evaluate or supply. It is for this reason that ethics occupies the highest echelon of Croce's system: it gives us universal knowledge of the Good so that we can aim at it. However, Croce was – once again – more Machiavellian than Hegelian: he did not see that moral life could lead to the ethical whole of the state and that law was ultimately economic and not moral.

The moral point of view takes precedence when the economic interests of the agent are trumped by some supreme value which obliges him to act in accordance with it rather than pragmatism. The only origin of such a value is not the Hegelian ethical state, nor the Kantian moral law, but spirit understood as historical experience. One sees that Good is the progress of spirit towards ever more adequate ways of understanding the world, and the truth of a political state can only be experienced historically by the progress of spirit. Thus, Croce seems to be committed to at least a minimal conservatism: one can only evaluate the actions of men in terms of the progress of history and not from some universal moral standpoint.

Croce's philosophy often suffers by being misunderstood as a simple derivative of Hegelian idealism, an accusation which is unjust given the differences listed above. Croce combined elements from Hegel and Vico, but also Kant, and his own original insights, in order to produce a unique form of historical idealism which is much more than a mere theory of aesthetics.

The complete works of Croce are available in Italian, and many of his works have been translated separately into English. The major philosophical ideas can be found in *Aesthetics* (*Estetica come scienza dell'espressione e linguistica generale*, 1902), *Logic* (*Logica come scienza del concetto puro*, 1902) and *Philosophy of the Practical* (*Filosofia della pratica, economia ed etica*, 1909).

David Rose

Selected writings

Croce, Benedetto. *Historical Materialism and the Economics of Karl Marx*. Whitefish, MT: Kessinger, [1900] 2004.
Croce, Benedetto. *Philosophy of the Practical Economic and Ethic*, trans. Douglas Ainslie. London: Macmillan and Co., Limited, [1908] 1913

Croce, Benedetto. *What Is Living and What Is Dead of the Philosophy of Hegel [Saggio sullo Hegel]*, trans. Douglas Ainslie. St Martin's St, London, England: Macmillan and Co, 1915.

Croce, Benedetto. *Theory and History of Historiography*, trans. Douglas Ainslie and edited by George G. Harrap. London, [1920] 1921

Croce, Benedetto. *History as Thought and as Action*, trans. Sylvia Sprigge. London: George Allen & Unwin, 1941.

Croce, Benedetto. *The Aesthetic as the Science of Expression and the Linguistic in General*, trans. C. Lyas. Cambridge: Cambridge University Press [1941] 1992.

Croce, Benedetto. *The Aesthetic as the Science of Expression and the Linguistic in General*, trans. C. Lyas. Cambridge: Cambridge University Press [1941] 1992.

EXCERPT

Benedetto Croce, *The Aesthetic as the Science of Expression and the Linguistic in General*

(B. Croce, *The Aesthetic as the Science of Expression and the Linguistic in General*. Trans. C. Lyas (Cambridge: Cambridge University Press, 1992 [1941]), pp. 33–5.)

That philosophy is the perfect science. The so-called natural sciences, and their limits

The world of what has actually occurred, of concrete things, of the historical, is called the world of reality and nature, embracing both the reality that is called physical and that which is called spiritual and human. All this world is intuition, historical intuition if it is presented as it actually is, imaginative intuition or artistic intuition in the strict sense, if it is presented as merely possible, that is, as imaginable.

Science, true science, which is not intuitive but conceptual, not concerned with 'the individual but with the universal,' can only be the science of the spirit, that is, the study of that which reality possesses of the universal: Philosophy. If, apart from this, people speak of the natural sciences, it must be pointed out that these are not proper sciences, that is, they are aggregates of knowledge, arbitrarily abstracted and characterised. The so-called natural sciences, in fact, themselves acknowledge that they are always bounded by limits: and these limits are nothing other than historical and intuitive data. They calculate, measure, posit equalities, establish regularities, determine categories and classes, formulate laws, show in their own way how one state of affairs arises from other states of affairs; but all their proceedings always bring them up against facts that are learned intuitively and historically. Even geometry now claims to rest wholly on hypotheses, since three-dimensional or Euclidean space is only one of the many possible spaces, chosen for study because it is more convenient. That which is true in the natural sciences is actually either philosophy or historical fact; that which is properly called natural in them is mere arbitrary abstraction. When the natural sciences wish to make themselves into perfect sciences they have to spring from their own proper realm and move on to philosophy: which they do when they posit concepts quite different from naturalistic ones, such as the unextended atom, ether or waves, vital forces, nonintuitable space and the like: truly and properly attempts to philosophise, when they are not words devoid of sense. Naturalistic concepts are, without doubt, very useful; but one cannot extract from them that system, which belongs only to the spirit.

These historical and intuitive facts, which cannot be eliminated from the natural sciences, explain, in addition, not only how, with the advance of knowledge, what was once considered the truth can, bit by bit, sink to the level of myth or fantastic illusion, but also why there are those among the practitioners of the natural sciences who refer to everything in their disciplines which is the cornerstone of their reasoning, as myths, verbal expedients, and conventions. And improperly prepared mathematicians and naturalists who venture into the study of the powers of the spirit can easily carry over these mental habits and talk of conventions in philosophy, which are such and such "because men have so decreed it": truth and morality are conventions, and the supreme convention is the Spirit itself! However, if there are to be conventions, there must be something which does not exist by convention, but which is itself the agent responsible for+ conventions: the spiritual activity of man. The limitations of natural science imply the boundlessness of philosophy.

These explanations firmly establish that there are two pure and fundamental forms of knowledge: the intuitive and the conceptual; Art, and Science or Philosophy. History can be resolved into these, since it is, as it were, the outcome which occurs when the intuitive is brought into contact with the conceptual, that is to say, it is an art that, although receiving into itself philosophical distinctions, remains nonetheless concrete and individual. All the others (the natural sciences and mathematics) are impure forms: mixtures of extraneous elements and practical in origin. Intuition gives us the world, the phenomenal: conceptual knowledge gives us the noumenal, the Spirit.

CHAPTER 8

Giovanni Gentile (1875–1944)

Giovanni Gentile's academic and public writings were nearly always driven by the energy of a commitment to the idea that philosophy ought to influence and determine the cultural life of individuals and the nation. He grossly misjudged the fascist movement and became its official philosopher, ghost-writing Mussolini's *The Doctrine of Fascism*. Prior to his intervention, fascism had no doctrinal theory and Gentile was guilty of giving a brutal and intolerant nationalism a veneer of not just respectability but rationality and, like Mussolini's architectural follies, sought the rebirth of Italian cultural ascendency through a robust and tightly controlled social existence, grounding the philosophical aspects of fascism in the collectivist, corporatist and conservative elements of Hegel's political philosophy.

Gentile held positions at Palermo, Pisa and Rome and was the Minister of Public Education for two years from 1922 under the fascist government, driving through radical educational reforms against what he saw as cronyism in the Italian state. He was executed in Florence in 1944 by the partisans due to the loyalty he showed to the puppet state of the Republic of Salò after the German occupation of part of Italy. However, concentrating solely on his ideas, there was no more motivating philosophical ground for Gentile's support of fascism than for his contemporary and one-time friend Benedetto Croce's rejection of it. In both cases, the support or rejection makes sense only when welded to personal dispositions, convictions and interests.

Gentile's intellectual odyssey begins with Marx's critique of Hegel, which reveals the error of detaching ideas from reality, yet also with a disagreement as to Marx's own resolution. According to Gentile, both thinkers fail to resolve the dialectic between ideas and reality. Whereas Marx criticizes both positivism and metaphysics and returns to materialism, Hegel criticizes positivism and materialism and returns to metaphysics.

Like Croce, Gentile's thought begins from a perceived defect in Hegel's philosophical system which, according to both of them, took the form of a return to transcendental metaphysics. Gentile and Croce sought to locate idealism as different from and opposed to materialism (the reduction of being to the empirical world), positivism (the reduction of what can be known to the scientifically verifiable) and also traditional metaphysics (the reduction of being and truth to transcendental reality). However, Gentile is to be distinguished from Croce in that, whereas the latter seeks to reform the Hegelian dialectic in terms of the actuality of absolute historicism, Gentile sought its resolution in the actuality of absolute subjectivity.

Gentile remains a critical philosopher in the sense that he excludes traditional, pre-Kantian metaphysics, rejecting the description of the world as it is, independent of a subject. The dialectic can be fulfilled only by the development of thinking, that is the actual subject of thought, and not anything outside the subject, be it a metaphysical history or a historical materialism. Thinking, for Gentile, is aimed at truth and motivated by this conviction and commitment; one is just not thinking if one does not have this conviction.

As a result of this conception, Gentile distinguishes between abstract and concrete thoughts. *Abstract thoughts* are borrowed thoughts, which occur within the subject when it *entertains* the ideas of another as true (is not committed to their truth). Such thoughts can be irresistible, which is to say that, if thought, they are thought true and this reflects the very structure of thought which aims always at truth. However, such thoughts have abstract objectivity but not concrete objectivity; their irresistibility does not entail truth, but it does involve one in the dialectic of negation because it aims at a concrete objectivity where the proposition is not just entertained but affirmed. Concrete thinking is *absolutely actual*. For this reason, error cannot be thought, even if it can be irresistible; it remains a content merely *borrowed* from another or a thought simply entertained. The proposition is absolutely actual when it is both irresistible (which all propositions are at first) and incorrigible in that I can only reject it at the cost of my own rational thought. Truths then are thoughts that I cannot but think, that are true if thought. And such judgement is always the judgment of a subjectivity or a pure act of thinking. The notion of Gentile's 'actualism' or actual idealism is contained in the affirmation that no one can leave his or her sphere of thought.

The *I* makes itself actual by thinking, introducing opposition into content, and Gentile wants to present the possibility of reconciliation through reason. So, the distinction between thinking and nature (or facts) at the base of all materialism and metaphysics is a product of thinking. The pure act of thinking is introduced into thought by thinking itself as an act of individuation and hence a product of the pure act. To think is necessarily to think of something, but the object of thought has no reality outside the act of thinking which constitutes and possesses it.

Whereas Croce sought to reconcile Hegel's dialectic through historicism, Gentile takes it back to the idealism of Fichte, Kant and, *almost*, Berkeley.

The act of thinking is creative and productive, or it is best thought of as the producer itself, and there is nothing outside of it which can contain the spontaneity of thinking, nothing to constrain, condition or limit it. The subject is, therefore, universal or ultimate. The empirical subject is an object of this transcendental subject, a created product, in a way reminiscent of Sartre's distinction between the impersonal, pre-reflective field of consciousness and the empirical ego in *Transcendence of the Ego*, and, for this reason, the *I* is prior to reality, being and knowledge. Gentile identifies the reconciliation of thought in the pure act of thinking which is, in many ways, best understood as Kant's transcendental unity of apperception, the formal and contentless possibility of thought, or pure spontaneity.

David Rose

Selected writings

Gentile, Giovanni. *The Reform of Education*, trans. Dino Bigongiari. New York: Harcourt, 1922a.

Gentile, Giovanni. *The Theory of Mind as Pure Act*, trans. H. Wildon Carr. London: Macmillan, 1922b.

Gentile, Giovanni. *Genesis and Structure of Society*, trans. H. S. Harris. Urbana, IL: University of Illinois Press, 1960.

Gentile, Giovanni. *The Philosophy of Art*, trans. G. Gullace. Ithaca, NY: Cornell University Press, 1972.

Gentile, Giovanni. *Origins and Doctrine of Fascism, with Selections* from *Other Works.* edited by and trans. A. J. Gregor. New Brunswick, NJ: Transaction, 2002.

EXCERPT

Giovanni Gentile, *The theory of mind as pure act*

(Giovanni Gentile (1922). *The Theory of Mind as Pure Act*. Macmillan & Co, Ch 1, pp 1–9).

BERKELEY in the beginning of the eighteenth century expressed very clearly the following concept. Reality is conceivable only in so far as the reality conceived is in relation to the activity which conceives it, and in that relation it is not only a possible object of knowledge, it is a present and actual one. To conceive a reality is to conceive, at the same time and as one with it, the mind in which that reality is represented; and therefore the concept of a material reality is absurd. To Berkeley it was evident that the concept of a corporeal, external, material substance, that is, the concept of bodies existing generally outside the mind, is a self-contradictory concept, since we can only speak of things which are perceived, and in being perceived things are objects of consciousness, ideas.

Berkeley with his clear insight remarked that "there is surely nothing easier than to imagine trees in a park, or books existing in a closet, and nobody being by to perceive them; but in such case all that we do is to frame in our mind certain ideas, which we call *books* and *trees*, and at the same time omit to frame the idea of any one who may perceive them." It is not therefore really the case that no mind perceives them, the perceiver is the mind which imagines them. The object, even when thought of as outside every mind, is always mental. This is the point on which I desire to concentrate attention. The concept of the *ideality of the real* is a very difficult one to define exactly, and it did not in fact prevent Berkeley himself from conceiving a reality effectively independent of mind.

For Berkeley, notwithstanding that happy remark, came himself to deny the ideality of the real. In declaring that reality is not properly an object of the human mind and contained therein, nor, strictly speaking, a thought of that mind, but the totality of the ideas of an objective, absolute Mind, whose existence the human mind presupposes, he contradicted the fundamental principle of his whole thought. Berkeley, indeed, even while saying *esse est percipi*, even while making reality coincide with perception, distinguished between the thought which actually thinks the world, and the absolute, eternal Thought, which transcends single minds, and makes the development of single minds possible. From the empirical point of view, at which, as a pre-Kantian idealist, Berkeley remained, it is obvious, and appears incontrovertible, that our mind does not think all the thinkable, since our mind is a human mind and therefore finite and the minds of finite beings exist only within certain limits of time and space. And then, too, we are able to think there is something which exists, even though actually it may never yet have been thought. It seems undeniable, then, that our mind has not as the present object of its thought everything which can possibly be its object. And since whatever is not an object of human thinking at one definite, historical, empirical, moment, seems as though it may be such an object at another such moment, we come to imagine another thinking outside human thinking, a thinking which is always thinking all the thinkable, a Thought which transcends human thought, and is free from all the limits within which it is or can be circumscribed. This eternal, infinite, thinking is not a thinking like ours which feels its limits at every moment. It is God's thinking. God, therefore, is the condition which makes it possible to think man's thought as itself reality, and reality as itself thought.

Now it is evident that if we conceive human thinking as conditioned by the divine thinking (even though the divine thinking does not present itself to us as an immediate reality), then we reproduce in the case of human thinking the same situation as that in which mind is confronted with matter, that is with nature, regarded as ancient philosophy regarded it, a presupposition of thought, a reality to which nothing is added by the development of thought. If we conceive reality in this way we make it impossible to conceive human thought, because a reality which is already complete and which when presented to thought, does not grow and continue to be realised, is a reality which in its very conception excludes the possibility of conceiving that presumed or apparent new reality which thought would then be.

It was so with Berkeley. He had given expression to a clear, sound, suggestive theory, strikingly analogous to modern idealistic doctrine, declaring that when we believe we are conceiving a reality outside the mind, we are actually ourselves falsifying our belief by our simple presence in the act of perceiving; and when we presume ourselves absent, even then we are intervening and powerless to abstain from intervening, in the very act by which we affirm our absence. When he had given expression to this doctrine he himself returned to the standpoint of the ancient philosophy, with the result that he failed to conceive the thinking which truly creates reality, the thought which is itself reality. This was precisely the defect of the ancient thought. For it, thinking, strictly conceived, was nothing. Modern philosophy, after full consideration, puts forward simply, with all discretion, the very modest requirement that thinking shall be something. No sooner, however, does modern philosophy acknowledge this modest requirement than it feels the necessity of going on to affirm thinking, as not simply something, as not only an element of reality or an appurtenance of reality, but as indeed the whole or the absolute reality.

From Berkeley's standpoint thinking, strictly, is not anything. Because in so far as the thinking thinks, what it thinks is already thought; for human thought is only a ray of the divine thought, and therefore not something itself new, something other than the divine thought. And even in the case of error, which is indeed ours and not God's, our thinking, as thinking, is not anything; not only is it not objective reality, but it is not even subjective reality. Were it something new, divine thought would not be the whole.

The Kantian philosophy places us at a new standpoint, though Kant himself was not fully conscious of its significance. With Kant's concept of the *Transcendental Ego* it is no longer transcendental possible to ask Berkeley's question: How is our finite thinking thinkable? Our thinking and what we think are correlative terms; for when we think and make our own thinking an object of reflexion, determining it as an object by thinking, then what we think, that is, our very thinking itself, is nothing else than our own idea. Such thinking is finite thinking; how is it possible for it to arise? It is our present actual thinking. It is, that is to say, the actualisation of a power. A power which is actual must have been possible. How is it possible? Berkeley, in perceiving that this thinking is actual, feels the need of transcending it: and he is right. It is the question which sprang up in the inmost centre of the Kantian philosophy, and to answer it Kant had recourse to the concept of the noumenon. But this concept has really no ground, once we have mastered the concept of thinking as transcendental thinking, the concept of mind as self-consciousness, as original apperception, as the condition of all experience. Because, if we conceive our whole mind as something finite, by thinking of it as a present reality, a present with a before and an after from which its reality is absent, then what we are thinking of is not the transcendental activity of experience but what Kant called the *empirical ego*, radically different from the transcendental ego. For in every act of our thinking, and in our thinking in general, we ought to distinguish two things: on the one hand what we are thinking; on the other the we who think and who are therefore not the object but the subject in the thinking act. Berkeley indeed drew attention to the subject which always stands over against the object. But then the subject which Berkeley meant was not the subject truly conceived as subject, but rather a subject which itself was objectified and so reduced to one of the many finite objects contained in experience. It was the object which we reach empirically whenever we analyse our mental act and distinguish therein, on the one hand, the content of our consciousness, and on the other the consciousness as the form of that same content. Just as in vision we have two objects of the one experience, the scene or the term which we may call the object and the eye or the term which we may call the subject, so also in our actual living experience not only is the object of that experience an object, but even the subject by the fact that it is made a term of the experience is an object. And yet the eye cannot see itself except as it is reflected in a mirror!

If then we would know the essence of the mind's transcendental activity we must not present it as spectator and spectacle, the mind as an object of experience, the subject an outside onlooker. In so far as consciousness is an object of consciousness, it is no longer consciousness. In so far as the original apperception is an apperceived object, it is no longer apperception. Strictly speaking, it is no longer a subject, but an object; no longer an ego, but a non-ego. It was precisely here that Berkeley went wrong and failed and for this reason he could not solve the problem. His idealism was *empirical.*

The transcendental point of view is that which we attain when in the reality of thinking we see our thought not as act done, but as act in the doing. This act we can never absolutely transcend since it is our very subjectivity, that is, our own self: an act therefore which we can never in any possible manner objectify. The new point of view which we then gain is that of the *actuality* of the I, a point of view from which the I can never be conceived as its own object. Every attempt which we make—we may try it at this moment—to objectify the I, the actual thinking, the inner activity in which our spiritual nature consists, is bound to fail; we shall always find we have left outside the object just what we want to get in it. For in defining our thinking activity as a definite object of our thinking, we have always to remember that the definition is rendered possible by the very fact that our thinking activity remains the subject for which it is defined as an object, in whatsoever manner this concept of our thinking activity is conceived. The true thinking activity is not what is being defined but what is defining.

This concept may appear abstruse. Yet it is the concept of our ordinary life so long as we enjoy a certain feeling of life as spiritual reality. It is common observation that whenever we want to understand something which has a spiritual value, something which we can speak of as a *spiritual fact*, we have to regard it not as an object, a thing which we set before us for investigation, but as something immediately identical with our own spiritual activity. And it makes no difference that such spiritual values may be souls, with whom our own soul may not be in accord. The apprehension of spiritual value may be realised both through agreement and disagreement, for these are not two parallel possibilities either of which may be realised indifferently; they are rather two co-ordinate and successive possibilities, one of which is necessarily a step to the other. It is clear that the first step in spiritual apprehension is the assent, the approbation, for we say that before judging we must understand. When we say that we understand without exercising judgment, it does not mean that we exercise no judgment; we do not indeed judge approval or disapproval, but we do judge provisionally for apprehension. A fundamental condition, therefore, of understanding others is that our mind should penetrate their mind. The beginning of apprehension is confidence. Without it there is no spiritual penetration, no understanding of mental and moral reality.

Without the agreement and unification of our mind with the other mind with which it would enter into relation, it is impossible to have any kind of understanding, impossible even to begin to notice or perceive anything which may come into another mind. And we are driven by our thinking activity itself into this apprehension of others. Every spiritual relation, every communication between our own inner reality and another's, is essentially unity.

This deep unity we feel every time we are able to say that we understand our fellow-being. In those moments we want more than intellectual unity, we feel the need of loving. The abstract activity we call mind no longer contents us, we want the good spiritual disposition, what we call heart, — good will, charity, sympathy, open-mindedness, warmth of affection.

Now what is the meaning of this unity? What is this fellow-feeling which is the essential condition of all spiritual communication, of all knowledge of mind? It is quite different from the kind of unity which we experience when, for example, we touch a stone, altogether different in kind from the knowledge of simple nature, of what we call material nature. We find a need to be unified with the soul we would know, because the reality of that soul consists in being one with our own soul; and that other soul likewise cannot meet in our soul what is not essentially its own subjectivity. Life of our life, it lives within our soul, where distinction is not opposition. For, be it noted, within our own soul we may find ourselves in precisely the same spiritual situation as that in which we are when face to face with another soul which we fain would but do not yet understand. This means that the disproportion and incongruence which we find between our soul and other souls, when they appear to us as mute and impenetrable as the rocks and blind forces of nature, is no other than the disproportion and incongruence within our own soul between its own states, between what it is and what we would have it be, between what we can think but yet fail to realise; between what, as we shall see, is our state and what is our act.

CHAPTER 9

Antonio Gramsci (1891–1937)

For Gramsci, at the most basic level, 'all men are "philosophers"' precisely because of the '"spontaneous philosophy"' which is proper to everybody' (1971, 323). This spontaneous philosophy or 'conception of the world' (*concezione del mondo*) is found most obviously in the ways in which we describe the world, that is, through language. Shared descriptions between individuals constitute a 'common sense' (*senso comune*) that becomes sedimented in the form of the quasi-natural 'facts' and beliefs that guide our daily practices. Common sense helps bind a social formation together and gives individuals a 'natural' disposition with which to encounter the world.

Much of common sense's strength and persistence is due to its seemingly spontaneous or self-evident nature; we *feel* like certain beliefs and facts are either the product of our own intellect or that they are so self-evidently true that they do not require questioning. Despite these deceptive appearances, however, Gramsci stresses that all apparently natural beliefs, or conceptions of the world, that we hold, are nevertheless historically determined; common sense is no exception. The question, therefore, is of uncovering 'of what historical type is the conformism, the mass humanity to which one belongs' (1971, 324–6).

This, for Gramsci, is the role of philosophy in a more advanced sense. Philosophy too is to be understood as a particular 'conception of the world' and, in this respect, exists on the same spectrum as common sense. However, philosophy can be distinguished from spontaneous common sense on two fronts: coherence and critique. Philosophy, unlike common sense, is, on the one hand, the name for coherent and non-contradictory world views. On the other hand, it is the tool by which one can uncover the presuppositions that lie behind one's own common-sense beliefs. In this way, we can read Gramsci as part of the same critical tradition as Kant, insofar as the 'Enlightenment attitude' entails unfettering ourselves from our 'self-incurred immaturity'. Thus, philosophy might take the form of the critique of political economy, or the science of climate change, or the historical analysis of race; each sets out to deploy the most coherent account of its object over and against whatever common beliefs we might 'naturally' hold on the topic.

While it might be easy to perceive an intellectual elitism in this position, for Gramsci the situation is not so simple. He argues that each set of common sense 'facts' contains within it some embryonic 'good sense' – what he calls 'the healthy nucleus that exists in "common sense"' (1971, 328). Good sense, which is more akin to the English 'common sense', signifies a more accurate and penetrating world view hidden amongst the fragments of everyday *senso comune*. The good sense in common sense might, for example, identify an injustice in the world ('one rule for them and another rule for us'), a particular mechanism of politics ('the system is rigged') or class divide ('they are only out for themselves'), albeit couched in incoherent claims or expressed as a partial truth.

Gramsci saw that this has implications for political practice. He argued that if one wants to bring about a new, more coherent, popular world view, one *has to* start with common sense, uncover the truths and discard the contradictions found there. Thus, common sense requires philosophy for its reformation and, in turn, philosophy requires common sense for its starting point and living basis. Far from being disregarded as nonsense or as regrettable stupidity, then, 'common sense is a site of political struggle' (Hall and O'Shea 2013, 10) whereby the good sense enclosed within it needs to be 'made more unitary and coherent' (Gramsci 1971, 328). Only in this way, for Gramsci, can a 'new common sense and with it a new culture' emerge (1971, 424). The relationship between philosophy, common sense and good sense is properly political then: establishing and maintaining a widespread common sense on a range of issues is to dispose whole populations in a particular way, and ultimately this is a key part of what Gramsci calls 'hegemony'.

At the time in which Gramsci was writing, the term 'hegemony' had been used in revolutionary Marxist texts to signify short-term tactical class alliances (Anderson 1976, 15). Deploying the term in a novel way, Gramsci expands the concept to encompass broader processes of the reproduction of consent, both as a field of struggle for power and as the fabric of social reality. In his work, hegemony is conceived as a historically specific mixture of consent and coercion, although these two concepts are separated for analytic purposes and do not map so neatly onto lived practice. Gramsci is mindful not only of the fact that consent on its own is not sufficient unless it is buttressed by a coercive framework, but also that there is no purely coercive or consensual practice in social reality. For instance, education could be conceived in terms of the institutional cultivation of consent, yet it also functions as a coercive frame of discipline. Or, prisons would appear to be primarily coercive instruments of domination, yet processes of carceral punishment also work to instil consent to the existing economic and political structures.

Gramsci enjoys the rare merit of being read by Marxists and non-Marxists alike, and this is in part due to the unique mixture of influences upon his work. As an heir of Machiavelli, Gramsci explores the impact of politics as an autonomous field with its own principles. Unlike Machiavelli, however, Gramsci's political writings are angled towards the revolutionary transformation of society rather than providing an amoral handbook for remaining in power. This differentiates him at once from modes of thought that conflate politics and theology, which prefigured much of fascist discourse, as well as the economic reductionism of Marxist orthodoxy. While 'fundamental classes' have economically discernible interests, proletarian revolution cannot simply be explained in the phraseology of *Capital*. The conquest of political power requires cultural legitimacy, which would include a viable economic programme but also the ability to disarm 'common sense' dispositions and assumptions that maintain the status quo. In this way, arranging apparently disparate common-sense beliefs into a coherent programme is both a philosophical and a political activity, involving the analysis of world views and the concentration of force. Such an endeavour must adapt itself to given situations (as Machiavelli knew), and this has the consequence that homogeneous strategies cannot be applied across heterogeneous societies.

Despite recognizing the relative autonomy of politics and culture from economic mechanisms, Gramsci does not reiterate a liberal faith in the expansion of civil society as a parameter of 'freedom'. Rather, he discusses it as a variation of the practice of bourgeois power and uses an East/West dichotomy to demonstrate certain nuances. In the West, Gramsci explains, the power of the state is more diffuse, as its legitimacy is entrenched in the 'outer ditches' of civil society. This was an underlying reason for the failure of revolutionary assaults on the state in Western Europe. On the other hand, the East is characterized by a heavily centralized state which exercises rule in a more directly vertical fashion. The East/West antinomy is more of a theoretical distinction than a geographic description and implicates different strategic approaches for political success. It is one example of the theoretical creativity, against all the odds, of the practitioner of the 'pessimism of the intellect, optimism of the will'.[1]

Onur Acaroglu and Will Stronge

Note

1   The motto 'pessimism of the intellect, optimism of the will' appears numerous times in Gramsci's writings (e.g. 1971: 175), along with the pages of the journal *L'Ordine Nuovo*. It is usually attributed to Romain Rolland.

Cited texts

Anderson, P. 'The Antinomies of Antonio Gramsci'. *New Left Review* 1, no. 100 (1976): 5–78.

Gramsci, A. *Selections from the Prison Notebooks*, edited by and trans. Quintin Hoare and Geoffrey Nowell Smith. London: Lawrence and Wishart, 1971

Hall, S. and A. O'Shea. 'Common-sense Neoliberalism'. *Soundings* 55 (2013): 8–24.

Selected writings

Gramsci, A. *Selections from the Prison Notebooks*, edited by and trans. Quintin Hoare and Geoffrey Nowell Smith. London: Lawrence and Wishart, 1971

Gramsci, A. *Letters from Prison*, trans. Lynne Lawner. London: Quarter Books, 1979

Gramsci, A. *Selections from Political Writings: 1910–1920*, edited by and trans. Q. Hoare, London: Lawrence & Wishart, 1987

Gramsci, A. *Further Selections from the Prison Notebooks*, edited by and trans. Derek Boothman. London: Lawrence and Wishart, 1995

Gramsci, A. *Prison Notebooks* Volume II, trans. Joseph A. Buttigieg. New York: Columbia University Press, 1996

Gramsci, A. *The Gramsci Reader*, edited by D. Forgacs. London: Lawrence and Wishart, 1999

Gramsci, A. *Prison Notebooks* Volume III, trans. Joseph A. Buttigieg. New York: Columbia University Press, 2007

Gramsci, A. *Prison Notebooks* Volume I, trans. Joseph A. Buttigieg and Antonio Callari. New York: Columbia University Press, 2011

EXCERPTS

Antonio Gramsci, *The Prison Nvotebooks*

(Excerpts 1–4 are from Gramsci, A. *Selections from the Prison Notebooks*, ed. Q. Hoare and G. N. Smith, International Publishers, New York. PP. 125–7, 169, 238, 323.)

The study of philosophy

Some preliminary points of reference

It is essential to destroy the widespread prejudice that philosophy is a strange and difficult thing just because it is the specific intellectual activity of a particular category of specialists or of professional and systematic philosophers. It must first be shown that all men are "philosophers", by defining the limits and characteristics of the "spontaneous philosophy" which is proper to everybody. This philosophy is contained in: 1. language itself, which is a totality of determined notions and concepts and not just of words grammatically devoid of content; 2. "common sense" and "good sense"; 3. popular religion and, therefore, also in the entire system of beliefs, superstitions, opinions, ways of seeing things and of acting, which are collectively bundled together under the name of "folklore".

Having first shown that everyone is a philosopher, though in his own way and unconsciously, since even in the slightest manifestation of any intellectual activity whatever, in "language", there is contained a. specific conception of the world, one then moves on to the second level, which is that of awareness and criticism. That is to say, one proceeds to the question—is it better to "think", without having a critical awareness, in a disjointed and episodic way? In other words, is it better to take part in a conception of the world mechanically imposed by the external environment, i.e. by one of the many social groups in which everyone is automatically involved from the moment of his entry into the conscious world (and this can be one's village or province; it can have its origins in the parish and the "intellectual activity" of the local priest or aging patriarch whose wisdom is law, or in the little old woman who has inherited the lore of the witches or the minor intellectual soured by his own stupidity and inability to act)? Or, on the other hand, is it better to work out consciously and critically one's own conception of the world and thus, in connection with the labours of one's own brain, choose one's sphere of activity, take an active part in the creation of the history of the world, be one's own guide, refusing to accept passively and supinely from outside the moulding of one's personality?

Note I. In acquiring one's conception of the world one always belongs to a particular grouping which is that of all the social elements which share the same mode of thinking and acting. We are all conformists of some conformism or other, always man-in-the-mass or collective man. The question is this: of what historical type is the conformism, the mass humanity to which one belongs? When one's conception of the world is not critical and coherent but disjointed and episodic, one belongs simultaneously to a multiplicity of mass human groups. The personality is strangely composite: it contains Stone Age elements and principles of a more advanced science, prejudices from all past phases of history at the local level and intuitions of a future philosophy which will be that of a human race united the world over. To criticise one's own conception of the world means therefore to make it a coherent unity and to raise it to the level reached by the most advanced thought in the world. It therefore also means criticism of all previous philosophy, in so far as this has left stratified deposits in popular philosophy. The starting-point of critical elaboration is the consciousness of what one really is, and is "knowing thyself" as a product of the historical process to date which has deposited in you an infinity of traces, without leaving an inventory.

Note II. Philosophy cannot be separated from the history of philosophy, nor can culture from the history of culture. In the most immediate and relevant sense, one cannot be a philosopher, by which I mean have a critical and coherent conception of the world, without having a consciousness of its historicity, of the phase of development which it represents and of the fact that it contradicts other conceptions or elements of other conceptions. One's conception of the world is a response to certain specific problems posed by reality, which are quite specific and "original" in their immediate relevance. How is it possible to consider the present, and quite specific present, with a mode of thought elaborated for a past which is often remote and superseded? When someone does this, it means that he is a walking anachronism, a fossil, and not living in the modern world, or at the least that he is strangely composite. And it is in fact the case that social groups which in some ways express the most developed modernity, lag behind in other respects, given their social position, and are therefore incapable of complete historical autonomy.

Note III. If it is true that every language contains the elements of a conception of the world and of a culture, it could also be true that from anyone's language one can assess the greater or lesser complexity of his conception of the world. Someone who only speaks dialect, or understands the standard language incompletely, necessarily has an intuition of the world which is more or less limited and provincial, which is fossilised and anachronistic in relation to the major currents of thought which dominate world history. His interests will be limited, more or less corporate or economistic, not universal. While it is not always possible to learn a number of foreign languages in order to put oneself in contact with other cultural lives, it is at the least necessary to learn the national language properly. A great culture can be translated into the language of another great culture, that is to say a great national language with historic richness and complexity, and it can translate any other great culture and can be a world-wide means of expression. But a dialect cannot do this.

Note IV. Creating a new culture does not only mean one's own individual "original" discoveries. It also, and most particularly, means the diffusion in a critical form of truths already discovered, their "socialisation" as it were, and even making them the basis of vital action, an element of co-ordination and intellectual and moral order. For a mass of people to be led to think coherently and in the same coherent fashion about the real present world, is a "philosophical" event far more important and "original" than the discovery by some philosophical "genius" of a truth which remains the property of small groups of intellectuals.

...

Prediction and perspective

Another point which needs to be defined and developed is the "dual perspective" in political action and in national life. The dual perspective can present itself on various levels, from the most elementary to the most complex; but these can all theoretically be reduced to two fundamental levels, corresponding to the dual nature of Machiavelli's Centaur — half-animal and half-human. They are the levels of force and of consent, authority and hegemony, violence and civilisation, of the individual moment and of the universal moment ("Church" and "State"), of agitation and of propaganda, of tactics and of strategy, etc. Some have reduced the theory of the "dual perspective" to something trivial and banal, to nothing but two forms of "immediacy" which succeed each other mechanically in time, with greater or less "proximity". In actual fact, it often happens that the more the first "perspective" is "immediate" and elementary, the more the second has to be "distant" (not in time, but as a dialectical relation), complex and ambitious. In other words, it may happen as in human life, that the more an individual is compelled to defend his own immediate physical existence, the more will he uphold and identify with the highest values of civilisation and of humanity, in all their complexity. [1933–4: 1st version 1931–2.]

...

The modern prince

Brief notes on Machiavelli's politics

3.1 The basic thing about *The Prince* is that it is not a systematic treatment, but a "live" work, in which political ideology and political science are fused in the dramatic form of a "myth". Before Machiavelli, political science had taken the form either of the Utopia or of the scholarly treatise. Machiavelli, combining the two, gave imaginative and artistic form to his conception by embodying the doctrinal, rational element in the person of a *condottiere*, who represents plastically and "anthropomorphically" the symbol of the "collective will". In order to represent the process whereby a given collective will, directed towards a given political objective, is formed, Machiavelli did not have recourse to long-winded arguments, or pedantic classifications of principles and criteria for a method of action. Instead he represented this process in terms of the qualities, characteristics, duties and requirements of a concrete individual. Such a procedure stimulates the artistic imagination of those who have to be convinced, and gives political passions a more concrete form.

Machiavelli's *Prince* could be studied as an historical exemplification of the Sorelian myth — i.e. of a political ideology expressed neither in the form of a cold utopia nor as learned theorising, but rather by a creation of concrete phantasy which acts on a dispersed and shattered people to arouse and organise its collective will. The utopian character of *The Prince* lies in the fact that the Prince had no real historical existence; he did not present himself immediately and objectively to the Italian people, but was a pure theoretical abstraction — a symbol of the leader and ideal *condottiere*. However, in a dramatic movement of great effect, the elements of passion and of myth which occur throughout the book are drawn together and brought to life in the conclusion, in the invocation of a prince who "really exists". Throughout the book, Machiavelli discusses what the Prince must be like if he is to lead a people to found a new State; the argument is developed with rigorous logic, and with scientific detachment. In the conclusion, Machiavelli merges with the people, becomes the people; not, however, some "generic" people, but the people whom he, Machiavelli, has convinced by the preceding argument—the people whose consciousness and whose expression he becomes and feels himself to be, with whom he feels identified. The entire "logical" argument now appears as nothing other than auto-reflection on the part of the people — an inner reasoning worked out in the popular consciousness, whose conclusion is a cry of passionate urgency. The passion, from discussion of itself, becomes once again "emotion", fever, fanatical desire for action. This is why the epilogue of *The Prince is* not something extrinsic, tacked on, rhetorical, but has to be understood as a necessary element of the work — indeed as the element which gives the entire work its true colour, and makes it a kind of "political manifesto".

3.2 The modern prince, the myth-prince, cannot be a real person, a concrete individual. It can only be an organism, a complex element of society in which a collective will, which has already been recognised and has to some extent asserted itself in action, begins to take concrete form. History has already provided this organism, and it is the political party — the first cell in which there come together germs of a collective will tending to become universal and total. In the modern world, only those historico-political actions which are immediate and imminent, characterised by the necessity for lightning speed, can be incarnated mythically by a concrete individual. Such speed can only be made necessary by a great and imminent danger, a great danger which precisely fans passion and fanaticism suddenly to a white heat, and annihilates the critical sense and the corrosive irony which are able to destroy the "charismatic" character of the *condottiere* [. . .]. But an improvised action of such a kind, by its very nature, cannot have a long-term and organic character. It will in almost all cases be appropriate to restoration and reorganisation, but not to the founding of new States or new national and social structures (as was at issue in Machiavelli's *Prince*, in which the theme of restoration was merely a rhetorical element, linked to the literary concept of an Italy descended from Rome and destined to restore the order and the power of Rome).

3.3 An important part of *The Modern Prince* will have to be devoted to the question of intellectual and moral reform, that is to the question of religion or world-view. In this field too we find in the existing tradition an absence of Jacobinism and fear of Jacobinism (the latest philosophical expression of such fear is B. Croce's Malthusian attitude towards religion). The modern Prince must be and cannot but be the proclaimer and organiser of an intellectual and moral reform, which also means creating the terrain for a subsequent development of the national-popular collective will towards the realisation of a superior, total form of modern civilisation.

These two basic points — the formation of a national-popular collective will, of which the modern Prince is at one and the same time the organiser and the active, operative expression; and intellectual and moral reform — should structure the entire work. The concrete, programmatic points must be incorporated in the first part, that is they should result from the line of discussion *"dramatically"*, and not be a cold and pedantic exposition of arguments.

Can there be cultural reform, and can the position of the depressed strata of society be improved culturally, without a previous economic reform and a change in their position in the social and economic fields? Intellectual and moral reform has to be linked with a programme of economic reform—indeed the programme of economic reform is precisely the concrete form in which every intellectual and moral reform presents itself. The modern Prince, as it develops, revolutionises the whole system of intellectual and moral relation, in that its development means precisely that any given act is seen as useful or harmful, as virtuous or as wicked, only in so far as it has as its point of reference the modern Prince itself, and helps to strengthen or to oppose it. In men's consciences, the Prince takes the place of the divinity or the categorical imperative, and becomes the basis for a modern laicism and for a complete laicisation of all aspects of life and of all customary relationships. [1933–4: 1st version 1931–2.]

EXCERPT 4

Ilitch, however, did not have time to expand his formula — though it should be borne in mind that he could only have expanded it theoretically, whereas the fundamental task was a national one; that is to say it required a reconnaissance of the terrain and identification of the elements of trench and fortress represented by the elements of civil society, etc. In Russia the State was everything, civil society was primordial and gelatinous; in the West, there was a proper relation between State and civil society, and when the State trembled a sturdy structure of civil society was at once revealed. The State was only an outer ditch, behind which there stood a powerful system of fortresses and earthworks: more or less numerous from one State to the next, it goes without saying — but precisely necessitated an accurate reconnaissance of each individual country.

Antonio Gramsci, *Revolution against "Capital"*

(Gramsci, A. 1987, "Revolution against 'Capital'" in *Selections from Political Writings: 1910-1920*, ed. Q. Hoare, Lawrence & Wishart, London, pp. 34–7.)

The Bolshevik Revolution is now definitively part of the general revolution of the Russian people. The maximalists up until two months ago were the active agents needed to ensure that events should not stagnate, that the drive to the future should not come to a halt and allow a final settlement — a bourgeois settlement — to be reached. Now these maximalists have seized power and established their dictatorship, and are creating the socialist framework within which the revolution will have to settle down if it is to continue to develop harmoniously, without head-on confrontations, on the basis of the immense gains which have already been made.

The Bolshevik Revolution consists more of ideologies than of events. (And hence, at bottom, we do not really need to know more than we do.) This is the revolution against Karl Marx's *Capital*. In Russia, Marx's *Capital* was more the book of the bourgeoisie than of the proletariat. It stood as the critical demonstration of how events should follow a predetermined course: how in Russia a bourgeoisie had to develop, and a capitalist era had to open, with the setting-up of a Western-type civilization, before the proletariat could even think in terms of its own revolt, its own class demands, its own revolution. But events have overcome ideologies. Events have exploded the critical schemas determining how the history of Russia would unfold according to the canons of historical materialism. The Bolsheviks reject Karl Marx, and their explicit actions and conquests bear witness that the canons of historical materialism are not so rigid as one might have thought and has been believed.

And yet there is a fatality even in these events, and if the Bolsheviks reject some of the statements in *Capital*, they do not reject its invigorating, immanent thought. These people are not "Marxists", that is all; they have not used the works of the Master to compile a rigid doctrine of dogmatic utterances never to be questioned. They live Marxist thought – that thought which is eternal, which represents the continuation of German and Italian idealism, and which in the case of Marx was contaminated by positivist and naturalist encrustations. This thought sees as the dominant factor in history, not raw economic facts, but man, men in societies, men in relation to one another, reaching agreements with one another, developing through these contacts (civilisation) a collective, social will; men coming to understand economic facts, judging them and adapting them to their will until this becomes the driving force of the economy and moulds objective reality, which lives and moves and comes to resemble a current of volcanic lava that can be channelled wherever and in whatever way men's will determines.

Marx foresaw the foreseeable. But he could not foresee the European war, or rather he could not foresee that the war would last as long as it has or have the effects it has had. He could not foresee that in the space of three years of unspeakable suffering and miseries, this war would have aroused in Russia the collective popular will that it has aroused. *In normal times* a lengthy process of gradual diffusion through society is needed for such a collective will to form; a wide range of class experience is needed. Men are lazy, they need to be organised, first externally into corporations and leagues, then internally, within their thought and their will [. . .] need a ceaseless continuity and multiplicity of external stimuli. This is why, *under normal conditions*, the canons of Marxist historical criticism grasp reality, capture and clarify it. *Under normal conditions* the two classes of the capitalist world create history through an ever more intensified class struggle. The proletariat is sharply aware of its poverty and its ever-present discomfort and puts pressure on the bourgeoisie to improve its living standards. It enters into struggle, and forces the bourgeoisie to improve the techniques of production and make it more adapted to meeting the urgent needs of the proletariat. The result is a headlong drive for improvement, an acceleration of the rhythm of production, and a continually increasing output of goods useful to society. And in this drive many fall by the wayside, so making the needs of those who are left more urgent; the masses are forever in a state of turmoil, and out of this chaos they develop some order in their thoughts, and become ever more conscious of their own potential, of their own capacity to shoulder social responsibility and become the arbiters of their own destiny.

This is what happens under normal conditions. When events are repeated with a certain regularity. When history develops through stages which, though ever more complex and richer in significance and value, are nevertheless similar. But in Russia the war galvanized the People's will. As a result of the sufferings accumulated over three years, their will became as one almost overnight. Famine was imminent, and hunger, death from hunger could claim anyone, could crush tens of millions of men at one stroke. Mechanically at first, then actively and consciously after the first revolution, the people's will became as one.

Socialist propaganda put the Russian people in contact with the experience of other proletariats. Socialist propaganda could bring the history of the proletariat dramatically to life in a moment: its struggles against capitalism, the lengthy series of efforts required to emancipate it completely from the chains of servility that made it so abject and to allow it to forge a new consciousness and become a testimony today to a world yet to come. It was socialist propaganda that forged the will of the Russian people. Why should they wait for the history of England to be repeated in Russia, for the bourgeoisie to arise, for the class struggle to begin, so that class consciousness may be formed and the final catastrophe of the capitalist world eventually hit them? The Russian people — or at least a minority of the Russian people — has already passed through these experiences in thought. It has gone beyond them. It will make use of them now to assert itself just as it will make use of Western capitalist experience to bring itself rapidly to the same level of production as the Western world. In capitalist terms, North America is more advanced than England, because the Anglo-Saxons in North America took off at once from the level England had reached only after long evolution. Now the Russian proletariat, socialistically educated, will begin its history at the highest level England has reached today. Since it has to start from scratch, it will start from what has been perfected elsewhere, and hence will be driven to achieve that level of economic maturity which Marx considered to be a necessary condition for collectivism. The revolutionaries themselves will create the conditions needed for the total achievement of their goal. And they will create them faster than capitalism could have done. The criticisms that socialists have made of the bourgeois system, to emphasize its imperfections and its squandering of wealth, can now be applied by the revolutionaries to do better, to avoid the squandering and not fall prey to the imperfections. It will at first be a collectivism of poverty and suffering. But a bourgeois regime would have inherited the same conditions of poverty and suffering. Capitalism could do no more *immediately* than collectivism in Russia. In fact today it would do a lot less, since it would be faced *immediately* by a discontented and turbulent proletariat, a proletariat no longer able to support on behalf of others the suffering and privation that economic dislocation would bring in its wake. So even in absolute, human terms, socialism *now* can be justified in Russia. The hardships that await them after the peace will be bearable only if the proletarians feel they have things under their own control and know that by their efforts they can reduce these hardships in the shortest possible time.

One has the impression that the maximalists at this moment are the spontaneous expression of a *biological* necessity – that they *had* to take power if the Russian people were not to fall prey to a horrible calamity; if the Russian people, throwing themselves into the colossal labours needed for their own regeneration, were to feel less sharply the fangs of the starving wolf; if Russia were not to become a vast shambles of savage beasts tearing each other to pieces.

CHAPTER 10

Phenomenology and Marxism in Milan

'I do not claim that my "Paci" is truer than that of others. This is not what led me to write. I do not recount *him*, but my encounter with him, and I tell of the experience of the immense strength and energy that, investing me from outside, has made me, in large part, who I am on the inside.' With these words, written in his nuanced and yet always transparent language, so hard not to lose in translation, Carlo Sini began his recent book on the philosophy and life of Enzo Paci.[1] This book, as well as the essay that follows this introduction, might seem a curious blend of personal memories and philosophical annotations of the thought of Sini's master: that Enzo Paci who started to teach in Milan in 1957 and who left a permanent mark on a generation of young philosophers who, thanks to him, became acquainted with Husserlian phenomenology, Marxist humanism, and what Paci called 'relationism' – an original development of existentialism in the direction of phenomenology (Maurice Merleau-Ponty) and process philosophy (Alfred North Whitehead).[2] Sini, however, does much more than just recollect his teacher's intuitions. He gives them a very precise shape and sheds new light on the role that Paci played in the history of theoretical thought in the aftermath of the Second World War. The importance of this role is recalled by another philosopher – the Czechoslovakian phenomenologist and political dissident Jan Patočka – who crossed paths with Paci and his students and accompanied them on their way for quite some time. In an interview he gave in 1967, Patočka spoke of the most promising philosophical trends that, according to him, were emerging in those years. On the one hand, in France, Merleau-Ponty had the merit of developing a thought which rejected any abstract understanding of subjectivity and focused instead on corporeality and the embodied subject. On the other hand, in Italy, Paci was following a similar path by emphasizing above all the historical character of contemporary humanity, that is, the importance of the context in which thoughts and personalities emerge, and the impact that human beings, in their capacity as active protagonists of the historical process, are capable of having.[3] This emphasis on history – on the historical and practical relations between individuals within the frame of their lifeworld – is also present in Sini's interpretation. Paci's attempt to address Marxism critically, in contrast to the rigid orthodoxy of his master Antonio Banfi, can be interpreted as a way to enact this renewed understanding of history:

> As Husserl said in the *Crisis*, a science of facts produces 'merely fact-minded people', blind to the intentionality of truth and to the meaning of life, be it scientific or prescientific. Paci applied the same critical remark to Marxism in its political guise, which inspired a supposed science of history that is reduced to a mechanical 'factual' reduction of the relationship between economic structure and cultural or spiritual superstructure.[4]

There is nothing mechanical about history. In this sense, phenomenology provides us with a number of important tools for research since it allows us to reconnect the ongoing historical process with the way in which human beings, in complete freedom, make experiences from such a process and form stable structures of meaning out of it. Sini, alongside other representatives of the so-called Milan School of phenomenology, contributed to the further development of his master's intuitions, and he did so in a highly original way. Looking at the interplay between Paci and Sini's thoughts, the readers of the following section may glimpse the complexity and the historical relevance of this philosophical endeavour, which is currently almost completely forgotten, in Italy and abroad.

Francesco Tava

Notes

1   Carlo Sini, *Enzo Paci: Il filosofo e la vita* (Milano: Feltrinelli, 2015).

2   See, in particular, Enzo Paci, *Dall'esistenzialismo al relazionismo* (Messina-Firenze: D'Anna, 1957).

3   See Patočka, *Češi* (*The Czech People*), Vol. 1 (Praha: Oikoymenh, 2006), pp. 607–29.

4   See the excerpt that follows this introduction.

Selected writings

Carlo, Sini. *Enzo Paci: Il filosofo e la vita (Enzo Paci: The Philosopher and Life)*. Milan: Feltrinelli, 2015

Paci, Enzo. *Il significato del "parmenide" nella filosofia di Platone (The Significance of Parmenides for Plato's Philosophy)*. Milan: Messina, 1938

Paci, Enzo. *Pensiero, esistenza e valore (Thought, Existence and Value)*. Messina-Milan: Principato, 1940

Paci, Enzo. *L'esistenzialismo (Existentialism)*. Padova: Cedam, 1943

Paci, Enzo. *Il nulla e il problema dell'uomo (The Nothing and the Problem of Man)*. Turin: Taylor, 1950

Paci, Enzo. *Dall'esistenzialismo al relazionismo (From Existentialism to Relationism)*. Florence: Messina, 1957

Paci, Enzo. *The Function of the Sciences and the Meaning of Man*, trans. Paul Piccone and Jeffrey Hanson. Evanston, Ill: Northwestern University Press, 1972. (*Funzione delle scienze e significato dell'uomo*, Milan: Il Saggiatore, 1963)

Paci, Enzo. 'Husserl: From Naturalism to the Phenomenological Encyclopaedia'. In *Phenomenology and Natural Existence*, edited by D. Riepe, 131–141. Albany: SUNY Press, 1973

EXCERPT

(Carlo Sini, Enzo Paci: From Existentialism to the Things Themselves)
_____

(Carlo Sini, 'Enzo Paci: From Existentialism to the Things Themselves' Trans, K. Langley with M. Lewis, 'Enzo Paci: dall'esistenzialismo alle cose stesse', *Journal of Italian Philosophy 2* (2019).)

Paci's philosophical path has, notoriously, been divided into three main stages: existentialism, relationism, and finally, the rebirth of Husserl's phenomenology in the wake of existentialism and the relationship it entered into with Marxism.

From a young age, Paci was one of the protagonists in the dissemination of existentialism in Italy. [. . .] In 1940, with *Thought, Existence, and Value* and in 1943 with *Existentialism*, Paci manned the barricades of the philosophy of existence with Abbagnano and Pareyson. In 1950, his existentialist philosophy culminated in the book, *The Nothing and the Problem of Man*, one of his masterpieces, which found itself widely disseminated with the creation of the journal, *aut aut* [*either. . .or*] [. . .].

The reference to Kierkegaard is the first point that I believe needs to be made clear in order to understand Paci's speculative path in its entirety [. . .]. In fact, Paci made his own the motto of Kierkegaard, to 'accentuate existence', and, in essence, he remained faithful to it to the end. Accentuating existence means keeping existence always in mind, and not blocking it from view or demeaning its importance; but the motto also means not ignoring or leaving unspoken the paradox. Existence names the insurmountable fact according to which each of us exists in the unrepeatable singularity of their material and moral situation, which makes every external view upon the world and upon existence *de facto* impossible: the existentialist philosopher, and every human being along with them, is in this way put in question by the very question that he raises: existence, an irresolvable question.

From this imbroglio, Paci wrought the central theme of the relational [*relazionistico*] development within his thought, which centred on the immense problem of time. The Kantian schematism, the organicist conception of temporal duration in Alfred North Whitehead, but also Proust, Joyce and the Eliot of *The Waste Land* formed the site of an extraordinary reflection whose essential point concerned the relation between time and consumption: existence is inscribed in the structure of temporal irreversibility ('Il significato dell'irreversibile', in *Tempo e relazione*, 1954). [. . .] Paci observed that every reflection on time is itself temporal: but this signifies, as Whitehead had insisted, that time is marked by the experience of rhythm. Rhythm testifies to the fact that in every experience both recognition and memory are at play[. . .], but also an irrecoverable loss, because what returns is at the same time the sign of a forgetting: that which returns does not return, since it signals the fact that it is 'new', hitherto unseen and at the same time insuppressible.

[. . .] [Paci was concerned not with] the truth of life and the truth of the world, expressed in mathematical formulae or logical judgments, but the *life of truth*. In fact, the truth is not a thing or the content of a thought, but the very event of existence, whose character is its irresolubility, understood as an always repeated opening to the possibility of being. Therefore, truth does not resemble a formal fact but is rather akin to the inquiry into the sense of human existence, an inquiry which can never be definitive in its formulation or in its answer, because that would be tantamount to the negation of life and of the inescapable mortal condition.

This set of problems spanned the great project of the recommencement of the Husserlian phenomenology after Heidegger's existentialism. In a note written in August 1958, Paci writes:

> Phenomenology is a vision of truth but the truth is infinite [. . .]. Situated between two infinities, existentialism tends to break the relational synthesis between nature and truth, between existence and idea, between sensibility and essence: relationism recovers the synthesis, reconstructing from the ground up the experience of phenomenology and renewing the Kantian schematism. Born from phenomenology, 'positive' existentialism resumes phenomenology on the basis of rational intentionality. It was necessary for me to rediscover the rational intentionality of the corporeal and historical reality of man. For this reason, as early as the 1950's, I was obliged to say that the transcendental is man (*The Nothing and the Problem of Man*). Phenomenology is also a way of feeling, of living, and of discovering, in life, the truth.

This philosophical project became fully transparent in a note that Paci wrote in September 1958 in his fascinating *Phenomenological Diary* (later published in 1961), one of the best liked and most enchanting of Paci's books:

> My aim is to influence philosophy and Italian culture with phenomenology. Mine is a relationistic phenomenology which attempts to take into account the entire history of phenomenological thought and to overcome existentialism. Its principal elements are *time*, as understood by Husserl since 1904–5, and *relation* as it appears in the *Fifth Meditation* and in the *Crisis*. Some of the unpublished works of Husserl on time are a response to *Being and Time*. At this point, we can no longer do without this response. Positive existentialism is transformed into phenomenology as relationism.

Thus was the struggle for Husserlian phenomenology begun, with the journal *aut aut* as its primary means [...]. The advent of phenomenology announced itself progressively throughout Italy and remained in force for approximately fifteen years: it came to involve not only philosophy but the entire culture, from its literature and aesthetics to architecture, music, and finally the natural and social sciences, cybernetics and economics. During these years of great innovation and audacity, the journal *aut aut* addressed in depth the question of how to make philosophy engage with the entire horizon of knowledge and with the living world of society and politics. Naturally, the journal received a great deal of reaction, positive and negative, stances were taken and polemics waged. The final outcome is still awaiting an adequate and above all complex historiographical investigation [. . .]

The main text in which Paci summarises his interpretation of Husserl and the rebirth of phenomenology is *The Function of the Sciences and the Meaning of Man*, which was published in 1963, two years after Sartre's *Critique of Dialectical Reason*: both works highlight the great cultural change which associated phenomenology with Marxism. Paci's book enjoyed a uniquely wide distribution for a stringent work of philosophy. In this book, Paci recommenced his discourse in confrontation with the sciences, making Husserl's criticism of 'naturalism' his own. [. . .]

The invitation to thematise the lifeworld and the precategorical operations as the 'transcendental' foundation of all scientific and worldly categories is placed in a balanced antithesis with both the Kantian and idealist transcendental subject (a 'mythological' subject, says Husserl) and Heideggerian ontology, which establishes entities, being, and their difference as the result of mere intellectualistic abstractions, ignorant of the operations on the basis of which they were constituted. This critique of superstitious 'objectivity', in particular of the logicist mindset, finds its emblematic expression in the Preface that Paci wrote for the Italian translation of [Husserl's] *Formal and Transcendental Logic* [. . .]:

> the sciences, because they fail to comprehend their own operations, as the result of an operative intentionality remaining unthematised for them, are not capable of clarifying the true sense of being in their field and of the concepts with which it is grasped. Consequently, they are not able clearly to determine the sense of the essence of which they speak or which horizons of sense it presupposes, horizons of which the sciences do not speak; and yet these horizons nonetheless participate in the determination of sense. [. . .]

The question can be traced back to the beginning of the Vienna lecture given by Husserl in May 1935 [. . .]. Paci often recalled in his lessons that exemplary beginning, which in fact threw the 'objectivistic' and 'naturalistic' attitude of the modern sciences into crisis. Husserl started from the perennial question of the dualism between the sciences of nature and the sciences of the spirit: a dualism in reality already burdened with prejudices, because there is not and cannot be a comparison between two spheres of real entities such as those of nature and spirit. Husserl writes: 'only nature can be treated by itself as a closed world; only natural science can abstract with unbroken consistency from everything spiritual and investigate nature purely as nature'. If a body falls from a window, natural science can calculate the speed and so on, [. . .] abstracting from the fact that it is, for example, a 'human' body and that there are motives behind the action which could be investigated at the level of 'social', individual, and 'criminal' responsibility, and suchlike. The human-scientist cannot operate the same 'abstraction' of the natural world thanks to which an autonomous world of the spirit, parallel to the natural one, would unfold before the scientist's eyes. The 'animal' spirituality, the spirituality of 'human and animal souls', says Husserl, is based on pre-categorial and material corporeity. The human-scientist cannot investigate his object otherwise than in a descriptive (and not normative) manner, which is to say, taking into account the physical nature in which the subjects being studied live and have lived. For example, an historian of Greek antiquity cannot fail to take into account Greek geography, architecture, economics, and so on.

However, all of this leads to a paradox on which Paci used to insist. On the one hand, the human scientist, for example the historian of Greek culture, has among the phenomena which they study, physical nature:

but this nature, wrote Husserl, is not nature in the sense of natural science but rather that which counted as nature for the ancient Greeks, that which opened up before their gaze, natural reality in the dimension of the lifeworld. More precisely: the historical surrounding world of the Greeks is not the objective world in our sense but rather their 'world-representation', i.e., their own subjective validity, and, within it, all the actualities which are valid for them, including, for example, gods, demons, etc.

Now it is evident that the notion of 'surrounding world' that is lived in a 'historical' mode (the surrounding world as it was lived in ancient Greece and so on) can only be an object of consideration for the sciences of the spirit.

[...] [T]here is no reason for the one who makes spirit *qua* spirit his subject matter to demand anything other than a purely spiritual explanation for it. And so generally: to look upon the nature of the surrounding world as something alien to the spirit, and consequently to want to bolster humanistic science with natural science, rendering it supposedly exact, is absurd.

But now comes the most delicate and decisive point. All of this distinguishing and arguing over the constitutive difference that separates the sciences of nature and the sciences of spirit, [...]

has completely forgotten that the natural sciences (like all science generally) are constituted from a series of spiritual accomplishments: namely, those of natural scientists working together; as such they belong, after all, like all spiritual occurrences, to the region of what is to be explained by humanistic disciplines. Now is it not absurd and circular to wish to explain the historical event of 'natural science' in a natural-scientific way, to explain it by bringing in natural science and its natural laws, which, as spiritual accomplishments, are themselves part of the problem?

[. . .] Paci repeatedly exonerated Husserlian phenomenology of repeated accusations (also stemming from Heidegger) of limited or even no understanding of the original historicity of the phenomenon which it took as the object of thematic description, no understanding of the historicity of the 'things themselves'. Hence Paci's approach, which fell in between the science of Husserl's lifeworld and the New Science of Vico [. . .]. This 'reborn' phenomenology is, in its own way, for Paci, a 'New Science', conscious of its temporal and historical nature, which is linked to concrete historical operations: otherwise put, material and economic. These are the means by which Paci at a certain point posited the unavoidable necessity for a confrontation between phenomenology and Marxism [. . .].

However, to return to Paci's struggle against the superstitions of scientific objectivism, or rather of 'naturalism' [. . .]. As we have seen, [. . .] Paci speaks of the 'positivity' of the sciences, intending thereby to refer to the dogmatic positivistic reduction of scientific knowledge to a mere statement of 'facts': a 'positive' science is a knowledge which has eyes only for 'facts' and fails to pose the problem of how these facts emerged within the historicity of human experience or the transcendental conditions of the very act of cognition. As Husserl said in the *Crisis*, a science of facts produces 'merely fact-minded people', blind to the intentionality of truth and to the meaning of life, be it scientific or pre-scientific. Paci applied the same critical remark to Marxism in its political guise, which inspired a supposed science of history that is reduced to a mechanical 'factual' reduction of the relationship between economic structure and the cultural or spiritual superstructure. In the struggle against official Marxism, Paci was entirely in agreement with Sartre: [. . .] both [. . .] courageously resisted the positivistic trivialisation of Marxism and its reduction to an instrument of political propaganda.

Paci signalled the culmination of this critical path in 1962 upon the occasion of a lecture he was invited to give by the Philosophical Academy of Prague. [. . .] When Paci arrived in Prague, the climate was one of immense agitation: the principles of the revolution of the so-called Prague Spring and of communism with a human face were in full swing. [. . .] In his exordium, Paci recalls certain themes characteristic of the Marx of the *Economic-Philosophical Manuscripts*: the reduction of labour-power to commodities that are bought and sold on the market; the reduction of the worker to abstract labour in which 'value' is reduced to the 'objective' effects serially produced. These effects, abstracted from the concreteness of working operations, are asserted to be the concrete real: commodities take the place of life, oblivious to the fact that commodities are, as Marx had it, 'crystallisations of human labour, crystallisations of social substance'. Paci observed that,

> these crystallisations ignore concrete individuals, and thus fail to make a concrete society possible. The *abstract categories* of economic science, the misuse of such science, means that the value of labour is concealed within the commodity. For this reason, it is very difficult to analyse the commodity.

At the same time, this exchange, this substitution of the fantasy of the commodity for the concreteness of labouring life, suggests to Paci an audacious yet profound reference to phenomenology: even for Husserl it was a question of 'suspending' the naïve trust in common sense when confronted with the phenomena of everyday experience; it was a question of recognising, behind phenomenal appearances, the true reality of experience, behind abstract scientific categories, the 'things themselves'. The entire project of phenomenology (returning to the things themselves, behind appearances and behind scientific intellectualism which remained ignorant of the true meaning of its own operations despite its undeniable successes) is redirected by Paci so as to accord with Marx's path. The mere relationship between things, that is, the commodity and abstract labour, is not the reality, as economic science thinks; it is rather the ideological concealment of the real relationship between concrete persons, those persons which economic science constantly presupposes, without ever thematising them [. . .]. On the one hand, Paci intends to ward off the danger of 'naturalism' in Marx by referring to Husserl, but at the same time, [. . .] he also intends to reconsider Husserl's path in light of Marx.

> Marx reveals the reality of living labour just as Husserl reveals the reality of the living subject and its operations. The misuse of science fails to grasp that all scientific operations, like the operations of labouring in Marx, are carried out by the concrete subject. [. . .] Husserl's task remained interrupted. On the other hand, he has posed the problem of the sciences as a whole, but not the problem of the economy, which is at the centre of Marx's analysis inasmuch as *Capital* is a critique of the economy. The critique of the economy can lead us to view the task that Husserl had set himself in criticising the sciences and the search for their foundation in a new light. [. . .]

The work of Paci culminates in the proposal of a new encyclopaedia of knowledge, against the historical backdrop of the Enlightenment project and the great Hegelian Encyclopaedia: the critical return to reason in a renewed phenomenological sense. In the *Ideas for a Phenomenological Encyclopaedia* (1973), Paci, in fact, took his mark from Vico and from Hegel in order to address the theme of the foundation of the sciences: in particular, anthropology, psychology, psychoanalysis, political economy, the natural sciences and cybernetics: [. . .]

the tendency towards unification on the part of knowledge has always remained present in the history of culture and human civilisation. However, the problems that it implies acquire a particular relief in the current historical situation, a situation which appears to make the unification of every people on planet Earth inevitable. In each case, both the unification of knowledge and the unification of groups and peoples, involve parts that tend towards an open totalisation, and the unification enters a crisis, both in the case where the parts are absolutised and each wishes to impose itself on the others as a whole, and in the case where the totalisation is conceived as definitive and without articulation, in such a form, that is, as not to include within itself the constituent parts as specific parts. Of course, every part contains a potentiality for development and an implicit totality, just as every man has humanity within himself, but as soon as the part is posited as a totality which has already been realised and concluded, absolutising itself, the movement of unification tends towards self-destruction. The problem of unification is by its very nature a dialectical problem, but it is the dialectic of the current historical situation that enables us to understand, in an absolutely peculiar way, the negative and destructive character of the absolutisation of a partial aspect of knowledge, of a given culture, of a given civilisation. No partial form can alone take on the task of unification while, at the same time, every partial form can contribute to a totalisation of knowledge and of an operation guided by knowledge, inasmuch as in all parts an open totality, indeed an infinite totality, is implicit as a potential. Therefore, every part, according to a paradox which has the same structure wherever it presents itself, has an infinite totality in itself, even though it is part of this infinite totality. [. . .] The theme of unification has a universal character and can easily descend into generality. However, the problem of how one part can contain a totality in itself is a problem which concerns all disciplines. Aphoristically one could say: a part can have in itself the whole of which it is a part, and it can therefore be a set, inasmuch as it is organised according to an 'essence' and according to a 'structure'. On the basis of what we have seen so far, we can recognise the very simple fact that the unification of knowledge is always a work in progress.

These thoughts from the late Paci, which have been around for almost fifty years now, are clearly prophetic, both in regard to the unification of politics and the global economy, and in regard to the increasingly problematic nature of this process, destined to ever new conflicts and oriented not at all towards a dialectically unitary solution. At the end of Paci's life, he learned with great anguish of the revelation of the horrors of Stalinism and the political failure of Marxism in Russia. Consequently, Paci wrote in a personal note that the existence of man seems to be inscribed in an insuppressible evil. This is in addition to Paci's active participation in and support of the student movement, together with the struggles inside and outside the university, which essentially concluded in defeat. In Paci's last days, he was in many respects isolated and a survivor. But his works, both profound and far-sighted, continue to reveal to us the fecundity of their inspiration, and they were vital and indispensable throughout the second half of the twentieth century in Italy and in Europe.

Cited Texts

Enzo Paci, *Pensiero, esistenza e valore* [*Thought, Existence and Value*], Messina-Milan: Principato, 1940.

— *L'esistenzialismo*, Padova: Cedam, 1943.

— *Ingens sylva. Saggio sulla filosofia di G.B. Vico* [*The Great Forest. Essay on the philosophy of Vico*], Milan: Mondadori, 1949

— *Il nulla e il problema dell'uomo* [*The Nothing and the Problem of Man*], Turin: Taylor, 1950.

— *Tempo e relazione* [*Time and Relation*], Turin: Taylor, 1954. Extract translated as 'The Philosophy of the Ego and the Philosophy of Relation', trans. Edward P. Mahoney & Ernesto Caserta in Philosophy Today 16:3 (Autumn 1972).

— *Diario fenomenologico* [*Phenomenological Diary*], Milan: Il Saggiatore, 1961.

— *Funzione delle scienze e significato dell'uomo*, Milan: Il Saggiatore, 1963. *The Function of the Sciences and the Meaning of Man*. Trans. Paul Piccone & James E. Hansen. Evanston, IL: Northwestern UP, 1972

— 'Il significato dell'uomo in Marx e in Husserl' ['The Meaning of Man in Marx and Husserl'], in *aut aut* 73 (1963).

— *Prefazione* a: E. Husserl, *Logica formale e trascendentale*, Bari: Laterza 1966.

— *Idee per una enciclopedia fenomenologica*, Milan, Bompiani, 1973

— *Opere di Enzo Paci*, Milan, Bompiani,
Translated by Katherine Langley with Michael Lewis

CHAPTER 11

Luigi Pareyson (1918–91)

Luigi Pareyson's philosophical journey can be divided into three stages, as he himself indicated in the *Introduction* to the fourth edition of *Esistenza e persona* (*Existence and Person*). First of all, he develops a 'personalistic existentialism' (or 'ontological personalism'). In a climate dominated by a rethinking of Hegelian philosophy on the part of Croce and Gentile's idealism, Pareyson's encounter with dialectical theology and German existentialism led to his becoming one of the latter's first proponents in Italy. His turn towards existentialism, therefore, becomes a quest for an alternative philosophical, religious and historiographic model to Hegel's and seeks the dissolution of that system. In fact, Pareyson interprets contemporary philosophy in terms of 'the dissolution of Hegelianism'.

Pareyson conceives of existence as an 'ontological relation', or the coincidence of self-relation and other-relation: to be in relation with the self means to be in relation with Being, with transcendence, with God. According to Karl Barth, God is the 'irrelative' that forms an impossible and paradoxical relationship with man. In this first phase of his thought, however, Pareyson wants to preserve an ontologically and morally positive concept of God and the person, in opposition to Karl Barth and the German philosophy of existence. German existentialism sees man as negative and sinful (thus positing itself as a secularization of protestant theology); conversely, Pareyson argues that man is deficient, and God is the irrelative that relativizes itself and gives itself to man, not by invalidating him but by securing him, compensating for his deficiency and allowing him to be a 'person'. At this stage of Pareyson's thought, his Christian spiritualism clashes with the strong influence of dialectical and Protestant theology; indeed, he is very careful to 'spare' the person from a conceptualization that he sees as invalidating and undermining.

Second, Pareyson develops a theory of hermeneutics that culminates in an 'ontology of the inexhaustible', developed in critical contact with the philosophy of F. W. J. Schelling and Martin Heidegger: being is conceived as an inexhaustible source, an infinite wellspring of meaning, which (even in its irrelativity and ontological difference) relativizes itself by entrusting itself to the work of art, to the artist or to the interpreter, as infinitely interpretable. The truth is unobjectifiable and irrelative, but it is not ineffable; it can be grasped and it gives itself to the interpreter, who nonetheless cannot possess it like an object. The person can choose to reject being and deny the ontological relationship by expressing and absolutizing the self and its history, or they can choose to interpret being and bear witness to the ontological relationship. The former is 'expressive thought', which according to Pareyson should be stripped of its mythical qualities if one is to discover its true origin and hidden meaning; the latter is 'revealing thought', which reveals the person and the truth simultaneously and thus can only be infinitely interpreted.

In the third and final phase of his thought, again in contact with Barth, Schelling and Heidegger, Pareyson develops an 'ontology of freedom' or a 'tragic thought' which may be understood as a 'philosophical rethinking of Christianity': according to Pareyson, philosophy can and must rethink the problem of freedom and evil only by interpreting the myth. Insofar as it persists in looking inwards, philosophy cannot overcome the problem of the relationship between freedom and necessity; and, if it tackles the problem of evil, it minimizes it as a facade, as unreality, and as dialectically necessary for the success of the good. Evil, however, is a negatively positive reality, a revolt against God and a profanation of being. Only in religious myth do evil and freedom manifest themselves in their reality and inseparability, with no camouflage or conceptual distortion.

Therefore, the inexhaustible being of the second phase gives way to God, understood as dialectically ambiguous, and absolute freedom, as the 'reality of chosen good and the possibility of rejected evil' (hence the famous 'Discorso Temerario' [Bold Discourse] on the 'evil in God'). God, as the eternal and original freedom, is to be conceived as 'beginning and choice': he had an 'atemporal beginning'; that is, He could begin only by choosing His very existence instead of the possibility of nothingness and non-existence, by choosing good instead of evil, which lies within Him as an eternally rejected possibility. The alternative between good and evil does not pre-date nor does it follow God: it coincides with Him, and He is the resolved choice.

It is precisely toward the possibility of evil rejected by God that man turns; therefore, man is not the creator, but the author of evil, as he translates the rejected, never actualized evil into a chosen and actualized reality.

Andrea Bellocci

Selected writings

Pareyson, Luigi. *La filosofia dell'esistenza e Karl Jaspers*. Naples: Loffredo. New edn, 1983. *Karl Jaspers*. Casale Monferrato: Marietti, 1939

Pareyson, Luigi. *Studi sull'esistenzialismo.* Florence: Sansoni, 1943. New edn, 1971

Pareyson, Luigi. *Esistenza e persona,* 4th edn. Turin: Taylor, 1950a. Genoa: Il Melangolo, 1985.

Pareyson, Luigi. *Fichte. Turin: Edizioni di 'Filosofia'.* New edn, 1976. Milan: Mursia, 1950b

Pareyson, Luigi. *L'estetica dell'idealismo tedesco.* Turin: Edizioni di 'Filosofia', 1950c

Pareyson, Luigi. *Estetica. Teoria della formatività.* Turin: Edizioni di 'Filosofia'. New edn, 1988, Milan: Bompiani, 1954

Pareyson, Luigi. *I problemi dell'estetica.* Milan: Marzorati, 1966

Pareyson, Luigi. *Il pensiero etico di Dostoevskij.* Turin: Einaudi, 1967. Reproduced in (1993). *Dostoevskij. Filosofia, romanzo ed esperienza religiosa,* 5–121.

Pareyson, Luigi. *Verità e interpretazione.* Milan: Mursia, 1971a

Pareyson, Luigi. 'Giovanni Amedeo Fichte. Introduzione, bibliografia, antologia'. In *Grande Antologia Filosofica,* edited by M. F. Sciacca, M. Schiavone, M. A. Raschini, and P. P. Ottonello, 847–1113. Milan: Marzorati, 1971b

Pareyson, Luigi. 'Federico Guglielmo Schelling. Introduzione, bibliografia, antologia'. In *Grande Antologia Filosofica,* M. F. Sciacca, M. Schiavone, M. A. Raschini, and P. P. Ottonello, 1–340. Milan: Marzorati, 1971c. Reproduced in (1975). *Schelling. Presentazione e antologia.* Turin: Marietti

Pareyson, Luigi. 'Lo stupore della ragione in Schelling'. In *AA.VV. Romanticismo, esistenzialismo, ontologia della libertà,* 137–80. Milan: Mursia, 1979.

Pareyson, Luigi. 'La filosofia e il problema del male'. *Annuario filosofico* 2 (1986): 7–69.

Pareyson, Luigi. *Dostoevskij. Filosofia, romanzo ed esperienza religiosa,* edited by G. Riconda and G. Vattimo. Turin: Einaudi, 1993

Pareyson, Luigi. *Ontologia della libertà. Il male e la sofferenza,* edited by A. Magris, G. Riconda, and F. Tomatis. Turin: Einaudi, 1995

Pareyson, Luigi. *Essere, libertà, ambiguità,* edited by F. Tomatis. Milan: Mursia, 1998

Pareyson, Luigi. *Kierkegaard e Pascal,* edited by S. Givone. Milan: Mursia, 1999 (Complete Works edited by the *Centro Studi Filosofico-religiosi 'Luigi Pareyson'*)

Pareyson, Luigi. *Existence, Interpretation, Freedom: Selected Writings,* trans. Anna Mattei and edited by P. D. Bubbio. Aurora: Davies, 2009

Pareyson, Luigi. *Truth and Interpretation,* trans. R. T. Valgenti, edited by and revised by S. Benso. Albany: SUNY Press, 2014

Pareyson, Luigi. *Thinking the Inexhaustible: Art, Interpretation, and Freedom in the Philosophy of Luigi Pareyson,* edited by S. Benso and B. Schroeder. Albany: SUNY Press, 2018

EXCERPTS

Luigi Pareyson, *Hermeneutics and Tragic Thought*

(Luigi Pareyson, *Existence, Interpretation, Freedom: Selected Writings*. Trans. Anna Mattei. Ed. P. D. Bubbio, Aurora: Davies, 2009, pp. 217–29.)

It is true that the human sciences, such as sociology, psychology, linguistics, cultural anthropology and so on, have grown enormously, but this does not mean that philosophy should consider itself superseded as some would believe. No human science intends to take the place of philosophy. On the contrary, together they have broadened the sphere of philosophy to an extraordinary degree, offering it extremely rich data for new and more complex questions and even encouraging it to pursue its task more closely. And philosophy has not allowed itself to be troubled by the awareness of its own conditionality, however historical, cultural, ideological, psychological or physiological this may be; rather, philosophy makes this conditionality an internal question, thus emerging more critical and astute. It is possible to philosophize on everything: no sphere of experience can escape philosophical reflection, and it is even better if the field has already been ploughed by one of the human sciences. With the opening of these new fields of experience, a boundless field stretches before philosophical research, suitable for that "superior empiricism" which is hermeneutical thought.

The first feature of hermeneutical thought is that it both envelops and penetrates: problematizing and universalizing at the same time. On the one hand, it subjects its field of investigation to such intense interrogation that it causes increasingly urgent and inescapable questions to emerge from it incessantly. On the other hand, it can grasp its truth and discover its meaning, bringing it to a level of clarification that can interest and involve everyone. The difference between the discourse of the human sciences and that of philosophy consists in the fact that philosophical thought is more originary, because — and this is its most profound characteristic — it presupposes an existential choice, that is, it implies a personal perspective of truth. Philosophical thought is absolutely hermeneutical, because it is simultaneously interpretation of experience and interpretation of truth, and it cannot be one without being the other: it is ontological and revelatory and at the same time historical and personal —indissolubly so.

Hermeneutical thought, then, is simultaneously thought of Being and discourse upon beings, suspended between a deep ontological radication and an endless experiential openness. First of all it is true that it is impossible to speak of Being without speaking of beings, but it is equally true that it is not possible to speak of beings without speaking of Being, and it is in this simultaneously single and double frame of reference that hermeneutical thought resides. Moreover it is certain that truth only offers itself within the personal interpretation and the historical formulation it is given, but it is not reduced to them. Rather, when truth coincides with them from time to time, in that same moment it is beyond them, so that it is not dispersed in the flux of history and experience. Philosophy, then, is always realized in an indefinable multiplicity, and likewise the unity of philosophical knowledge is not realized in an all-embracing and definitive way, but transversally and askew. Every philosophy is both a specific and irradiating perspective, a glimpse of truth that is simultaneously neither exclusive nor total.

In my opinion, the future is promising for hermeneutical thought thus conceived, but does not seem to favor those forms of hermeneutics that intend to get rid of truth. Interpretation, it is said, is not interpretation of something: there are no things or facts or truths to be interpreted, but only interpretations, and interpretations of interpretations. I do not think this corresponds to the concept of interpretation, which is either interpretation of something, or it is not interpretation at all: the interpretation which dissolves within itself what it is to interpret, and in so doing replaces it, ceases to be interpretation. So there is nothing left but the diffusion of experience, which in itself is indifferent and devoid of possible distinctions, with no conflicts and no tragedies, but rather comforting and consoling, far from the tragic thought that lurks in the very heart of hermeneutical thought.

The mood of interpretation, constrained to the difficult task of comprehension and as such to the faithful extraction of meaning, is risk, and therefore anguish and doubt. In fact, if it is considered that the only possible path to truth is freedom, which is exercised in a mood of consent and acceptance, but also of denial and refusal, it will emerge that the field of interpretation is a dramatic environment of conflict and contradiction. Insofar as hermeneutical thought refers to an ontology of freedom it is strictly connected to tragic thought. The nature of freedom is unfathomable and ambiguous: in one way, it supposes nothing but itself, and in another, it is always simultaneously positive and negative. Placing it in the centre of the real means introducing duplicity and contrast into the heart of reality, presuming a basis that always denies itself as a basis and focusing on the inseparability of positivity and negation. This induces a recognition of the unfathomable and deep tragedy which is implied in reality itself.

Today the question of evil and sorrow can be faced to good effect only by a hermeneutics of ancient and modern tragedy and of Christian religious experience. This hermeneutics comes down to two principles, which are fundamental to tragic thought. Firstly, evil is not absence of Being, deprivation of good and lack of reality, but reality, positive in its negativity. It results from a positive act of denial: from a conscious act of transgression and revolt, of refusal and abjuration of a former positivity; from an operating negative force, such as negative freedom, since freedom is also free to decide not to be free, and it is indeed in an act of freedom that it ceases to be freedom, and thus becomes the power of destruction. Secondly, there is an indissoluble link between evil and sorrow, represented by expiation, in the sense that sorrow is simultaneously the punishment of sin and its only possible redemption. Nobody is truly innocent, and upon all human beings, united in sin and sorrow by a fundamental originary solidarity, weighs a destiny of expiation, so that even the "innocents," if there are any, are required to suffer for others in order to cleanse the common sin, and so vast is evil that it sets the greatest suffering upon them, at which point the scandal of evil reaches its climax. Evil and sorrow are at the centre of the universe, and the heart of reality is tragic and painful.

Luigi Payerson, Failure of demythologization: Irrationalism of reason without truth

("Pensiero, espressivo e pensiero rivelativo," Giornale critico della filosofia italiana *(2/1965), 177–90;* Verità e interpretazione *(Milano: Mursia, 2005), 28–9.)*

If one wished to persist in demythologizing revelatory thought, one would face the vain dilemma of choosing between a precarious rationalism and an equivocal irrationalism. In one way, it is possible to believe myth can be eliminated with logos, without thinking that this is the greatest rationalistic prejudice [. . .] In another, it would be absurd to draw from the so-called "mythical" nature of revelatory thought the consequence, which only seems plainer and more critical, of a deliberate and programmatic mythology. This means shifting attention from truth to the various ways of approaching it, and mistaking a mere effect for a specific aim, with the result that the word, which would no longer be revelatory, but instead arbitrary and irrational, is lost in the uncertain allusiveness of the cipher.

   In either case, the originary connection between person and truth would be broken, either because, out of a mistrust of thought, the personal aspect is heightened, enclosing it in the incommunicability of an allegory or an experience, or because, out of a superstition of reason, one wishes to suppress the inexhaustibility of thought, thus reducing it in the name of perfect adjustment and complete clarification. In both cases the result is essentially the same—irrationalism—because it entails the loss of precisely that which preserves thought from an irrational outcome, that is, its ontological nature, its grounding in truth.

Luigi Payerson, *Philosophy and Ideology*

("Filosofia e ideologia," in Ideologia e filosofia *(Brescia: Marcelliana, 1967);* Verità e interpretazione *(Milano: Mursia, 2005), 138.)*

The fruitful presence of both the personal and ontological dimensions is also found in "myth," if this is conceived as not only primitive and primordial, but above all as primogenial and originary, that is, as an initial and fundamental understanding of truth, which is indistinct and confused not so much because it is elementary and inchoate, but because it is fruitful and pregnant, and, as such, a common root for the highest human activities, such as art, philosophy, ethics and religion, which draw inspiration from truth without ever exhausting it, and which develop from it without ever suppressing it, and which, far from meaning to replacing it, in fact invoke its continuous presence, which is their only guarantee of constant sustenance and secure inspiration.

Luigi Payerson, *The ontology of liberty*

―――――――――――

("Dal personalismo esistenziale all'ontologia della libertà," *Giornale di Metafisica* 6 (1984), pp. 299–300 and 310–11.)

The profound and originary discourse concerns Being, and not value. Ontology is primary over axiology. The level of philosophy and the level of religious experience must not be confused, as happens when in philosophy God is mentioned and qualified as Value and Person. To consider God *philosophically* as Value and Person means nothing more than making a mythological representation of his generosity and freedom. And one cannot object to this claim by saying that generosity and freedom, considered as attributes of divinity, are just as mythological, if not more mythological. Mythology is one thing, myth another; philosophy is one thing, religious experience another. When God, who is the object of religious experience and not a philosophical concept, is spoken of, any philosophical notion attached to him is mythological—as mythological as it is rational and conceptual—and among these are the concepts of Value and Person. *In religious experience*, the terms "generosity" and "freedom," in reference to God, are not mythological but mythical.

Firstly, religious experience can only be expressed in myth— in the strict sense of the word, which is not mythology—since a language is needed if transcendence, which is beyond discourse, is to be spoken of. The situation is difficult, even painful, because—as Plotinus says (V, 5, 6, 23–25)—"we speak of the ineffable," and difficulty can only be avoided by "naming, only to indicate for our own use as best we may". As a matter of fact, while there remains a sense of inadequacy in Plotinus, it must be admitted that mythical language is quite adequate, and does not bring discrepancies or regrets. In fact, if mythology is essentially allegorical, that is, based on the distinction between and separation of symbol and meaning (and signification is always endowed with an arbitrary element which leads the way towards mystification), myth is instead tautegoric, in that it supposes that the symbol is the signified reality, and vice versa, in a complete identification, or rather, in a concrete originary identity. [. . .]

In philosophy, when there is mismatch between rational expression and the experience that is meant to be clarified, or a partition between the speculative height that has been reached and the philosophical language which tries in vain to keep pace with it but does not succeed due to the inadequacy of its own means, philosophy can do nothing but rely on myth.

Thus philosophy either forms its own myths, or resorts to religious experience, in which case it must adapt itself in some way to mythical language, respecting the tautegoric nature of symbols and exercising caution with regard to the particular eloquence of coded writing. The exactitude of a cipher is very different from that of a rational discourse, but no less inflexible or strict. As Plotinus says, reflection must therefore in some way relax its philosophical rigor, giving preference to substantial meaning and even to the exigencies of communication, and agree to speak in a rationally imprecise way. In short, it must concede that there is a risk of imprecision that has to be taken into consideration, and it must forgive the (eloquent and meaningful) inexactness of words [. . .].

Naturally, if philosophy intervenes, it does so not to translate mythical discourse into rational discourse, which is impossible by definition [...]; but to illuminate universally human themes in mythical and religious discourse, which are of interest to all human beings, even unbelievers—that is, to include religious discourse, which is so intimately linked to personal experience, in a universal and broadly human interlacement, capable of ensuring the widest communication and to guarantee, or at least promise, the possibility for participation by everybody.

Luigi Payerson, *Philosophical reflection on religious experience*

("Filosofia ed esperienza religiosa," *Annuario Filosofico* 1 (1985), 47–50; in *Ontologia della libertà* (Torino: Einaudi, 1995), 142–6.)

If symbolism is not *only* expressive or inventive, but *also* revelatory, this is because it has its roots in a deep and originary area of thought, or, rather, it is immersed in the heart of existence, conceived as the coincidence of relationship with oneself and relationship with Being. At this level, the relationship between name and thing, between image and reality (whether in signification or reference) must no longer be examined in itself, but should be considered in its indissoluble link to the relationship between human beings and Being, as a relationship, no less revelatory than existential and ontological, between human beings and truth. The process of signification becomes the process of revelation; it is no longer a question of language, but of Being. Just as what is important is not having but being, so an utterance carries no weight without Being.

Therefore the deep level pertains to the ontological relationship that human being is within herself, and to the originary interpretation of truth. It cannot be considered irrational, because thought is present in it, in its primary function of interpretation of truth, even though this interpretation is not expressed in clearly conceptual terms; but neither can it be considered explicitly rational, because, within it, thought is inseparably connected with poetry and religion, which have not yet reached a specification of their own, but which are already present in their genuine nature, poetry as invention and expression, and religion as invocation and listening. It is an originary and profound structure, beyond any antithesis of rational and irrational, in which thought, poetry and religion are indivisibly united and interlocked, no less operational and active even though they await their distinction and specification, brought together by the use of the same symbolic language, by an equally revelatory result and by a primogenial contact with the unobjectifiable; an inextricable, dense and fruitful structure, in which thought has a simultaneously poetical and religious nature and in which poetry and religion simultaneously have the task and the function of thought, and for this reason thought, poetry and religion equally conspire to reach and express the unobjectifiable heart of reality and the meaning of things; an originary structure which could not have a more appropriate name than myth, in the most intense and pregnant meaning of the word.

Here, myth must be understood in its originary meaning, in which it can be opposed neither to reality, nor history, nor truth, nor reason, nor revelation, from all of which it is certainly different, but not in the sense of "opposite," as is usually claimed. It is not opposed to reality, because it is an experience of reality in itself, or rather reality itself, as existentially experienced. It is not opposed to history, because it is re-telling and the narration of facts, whether they be historical events or actions of originary freedom or of eras of eternity. It is not opposed to truth, because it is truth itself, as interpreted, possessed as a sensible figure, existentially formulated and symbolically grasped. It is not opposed to reason, because it contains its thought, although it is neither conceptual, nor rationally explicable, but real and substantial. It is not opposed to revelation, because that which distinguishes it is precisely a nature that is not exclusively creative, inventive and expressive, but also, and especially, revelatory: it is *simultaneously* and indivisibly a fabulating operation and a manifestation of truth, mythopoeisis and interpretation of Being. In short, myth is experience of reality and truth; it is experienced truth and reality, which implies total involvement: humanity and transcendence, human beings and God. Its *sense* is deep, beyond *meanings*. Myth is that primogenial interpretation of truth which every human being is to herself; it is truth in that it primarily speaks to everyone; it is memory of origin and the remembrance of the immemorial; it is attentiveness to unobjectifiable transcendence; it is the very revelation of Being, of truth, and of divinity: it is God *insofar as* he speaks to human beings; it is God who speaks to human beings. This is why religious experience must be grasped at a deep level, where it is inseparable from thought and poetry, poetical in its symbolism and truthful in its revelatory power.

And so it is clear what constitutes that philosophical reflection on religious experience which is the purpose of this study, and which is far from the rather abstract idea of analyzing the relations between philosophy and religion considered in their separation and exteriority and lying outside any existential context. Thought, which in its originarity accompanies poetical inspirations and religious inflexions in the originary and living structure of myth, emerges from it as open and conscious philosophy, though it reserves the possibility of returning to it to cast its reflection upon it. If it is considered that faith is to be seen as a specification of the originary religiosity implied in myth, and that it fully maintains the symbolic nature of myth, it will be understood not only how philosophical reflection on religious experience can concern both myth and faith indifferently, but also that, being mindful of the symbolic force originary thought wields in myth, is not inadequate, but rather particularly disposed to penetrate both the originary and the specified religious experience. *Philosophical reflection on religious experience*, then, is nothing but *interpretation of myth,* which itself is already interpretation of truth. It is therefore important to define under which conditions this hermeneutics can unfold with the express hope of understanding the philosophical meaning of myth and of obtaining results from it that are valid in philosophy.

To begin with, it will not, of course, be a question of demythologization, since what must be demythologized are in fact the simplistic demythologizations, whereas myth itself has no need of demystification, as it is revelatory in itself. Interpreting myth does not mean purging it of symbolic language, which is precisely what makes it eloquent, but analyzing and untangling its infinite signification, which is a hard task and a tireless enterprise. Philosophical reflection must respect myth: allowing myth to say what can only be said with myth, and adding nothing else, since to interpret means to make others speak and to be able to listen, not to hush nor *mitsingen.* Safeguarding myth and the symbol that, with its importance, makes it meaningful is the first task of philosophical reflection; and this task is consonant with the critical nature of philosophy, which must maintain everything in *its own* complexity. It is a victory for philosophy itself if the acknowledgement of the revelatory nature of myth prevents transcendence from isolating itself in (mystic) silence, just as it prevents the (objectifying) word from constraining the transcendent. In this way, philosophical reflection may discover that respecting and safeguarding myth as such is a way to say things to which the rational language of philosophy is unsuited, but which must necessarily be said for the sake of philosophy itself.

Of course, neither will it be a simple transposition of religious experience into philosophical terms, as if it were merely a question of translation, or transcription, of contents ready to change their appearance while remaining unchanged in their nature. In their hypothetical philosophical transposition, religious themes run the risk of changing their meaning so radically that the result can only be a series of deplorable misunderstandings, because of the impossibility of establishing which meaning these themes (which had only one meaning in the religious context from which they were removed) shall acquire. The failure of the numerous modern philosophies, which claim to be a laicization of Christianity, or the rationalization of religious faith, or the panlogistic translation of mystic experience, attests to the meager reliability of this agenda. In reality it must be a far more demanding task, that is, an intense problematization, capable of turning such a powerfully and insatiably investigative glance upon religious experience that it transforms it into a tangle of questions that await and demand a philosophical answer, while at the same time encouraging and hinting at one.

Neither will it be an objective and mirror-like reflection, applied to religious experience by placing it in front of itself and examining it from the outside, but a kind of reflection which places itself entirely within such experience without dissolving in it, and there, within it, subjects it to a demanding interrogation and succeeds in obtaining frank and genuine answers, to which it makes no further additions, and which are still valid in the philosophical and speculative fields. In short, philosophical reflection must occur in terms of a superior "empiricism," capable of giving a philosophical account of reality without distorting, transforming or reforming it, but rather letting it be with respectful discretion while also seizing it with inexorable resoluteness – more than what happens, for example, in the more cunning forms of phenomenology and existential analysis. A sort of evocative obedience and revelatory docility would then come into play in the ductility of philosophical reflection, in which the at once penetrating and enveloping nature of thought—of a decidedly hermeneutical kind— would maintain reality in its irreducible consistency while seizing its rhythm and extracting its secret, so as to be able to grasp its meaning and reveal its structure.

Neither, finally, will it be philosophy of religion or religious philosophy, let alone theology or theosophy or apologetics, but pure and genuine philosophy, which could take the form of a philosophical reflection *on* religious experience, working *within* it and emerging *from* it, in which the fact that such experience is personally borne is not sufficient to quell the truly philosophical nature of reflection. Once again, it will be a question of meaning: it will be a question of grasping the *philosophical* meaning of *religious* themes, without allowing these aspects to be confused or exchanged. The religious theme remains religious, but is not taken as such in philosophy, which, for its own part, grasps its philosophical meaning without perverting its religious consistence. It is not a rough and superficial adoption of the content, but the tension of a dialogue that maintains the (religious) nature of the interlocutor in order to obtain (philosophically) meaningful answers through an imperious and yet benign interrogation, and which is able to grasp its eloquent (philosophical) message while allowing it to speak in its genuine (religious) terms.

Contemporary thinkers (Alphabetical order)

CHAPTER 12

Giorgio Agamben (1942–)

Widely regarded as a pre-eminent thinker of biopolitics, Giorgio Agamben's philosophical interests and interventions extend over a wide range of fields, disciplines and philosophical problems, rendering any attempt at introducing his thought necessarily incomplete. Indeed, Agamben's contributions have shed light on debates ranging from iconography to poetics, from aesthetics to philosophy, from theology to politics. Nevertheless, despite the eclectic appearance of his *oeuvre*, there are not only important continuities and crucial resonances between his works – he frequently states that what remains unsaid and unexplored in his works constitutes the point of departure for what is developed in the others – but also a distinctive philosophical method connecting them.

The common thread that runs through Agamben's early works on language and signification is the critique of Western metaphysics. Although this critique is developed in different registers throughout Agamben's works, they all carry out their excavations in the same direction. For instance, in his *Stanzas*, this critique targets the presupposition of the distinction between the signifier and the signified that marks Western philosophy of language and which is crystallized in the notion of the sign. In *Infancy and History*, Agamben explores another manifestation of this metaphysical differentiation (which distinguishes the sensible from the intelligible, the real from the ideal) by questioning the opposition between language and speech and the opposition between knowledge and experience, which permeate Western philosophy. In *Language and Death*, Agamben develops this critique of the metaphysical tradition on the terrain of ethics, through a close reading of Hegel and Heidegger. Here he demonstrates that logic and ethics are constructed on a negative ground and that the human being cannot simply be defined by language (a speaking being) or by death (as mortal).

What is made clear through this critique is that an attempt to go beyond metaphysics should not only question the privileged status it assigns to the signified, identity, and speech, in comparison with the signifier, difference and writing; it should also, and more importantly, call into question the very structures of differentiation that presuppose these two aspects as distinct from one another. It is with this task in mind that Agamben develops a philosophical archaeology, which he makes explicit in *The Signature of All Things*. Unlike Michel Foucault's version of the same, Agamben's archaeology tries to locate the moments at which the metaphysical structures of differentiation become operative and give birth to discursive formations: and the archaeology does so in order eventually to deactivate these structures, or rather the 'machines' that give rise to them. These moments, which correspond to what Agamben calls the *archē*, are not chronologically situated and fixed but are rather a force that continues to act in the present, determining the way in which we understand the world around us. Agamben's archaeology aims precisely at suspending and rendering inoperative these forces which control the intelligibility of Western culture and politics.

It is in this light that we should read Agamben's *Homo Sacer* project. That is, as an archaeological investigation which aims to make explicit and render inoperative the ways in which we understand political power and its effects. The nine volumes that compose the project demonstrate that power operates as a bipolar machine, which encompasses a transcendent pole of sovereignty and an immanent pole of administration, kingdom and government. This is the structure of what Agamben calls the 'governmental machine'. The first volumes of the project focus on the first pole, namely sovereign power, and on the structure of exceptionality that lies at its core (entities are excepted from, or set in opposition to, a certain group, but only in order to be placed all the more decisively under the control of that group's sovereign: one is excluded only in order to be *in*cluded in a subtly new way). Yet, as Agamben suggests, with few exceptions, modern political theorists have failed to recognize the *bipolar* character of the governmental machine and have as a consequence placed their emphasis either solely on sovereignty or solely on governmentality, each to the exclusion of the other. This is the reason why, in *The Kingdom and the Glory*, Agamben launches an archaeological investigation into government, the second pole of the machine, through an analysis of economic theology (an account of the Christian trinity which, in the very earliest period of the Christian church, understood the relation between the three personae by means of the term '*oikonomia*') in order to reveal the *articulation* between sovereignty and *administration*, law and police, the kingdom and the glory – which is to say between *both* poles of sovereignty and government.

A fundamental aim of the *Homo Sacer* project is to reveal the hidden link between the sovereign exception and the production of 'bare life', this production understood as the original activity of sovereign power. For Agamben, bare life is not a concrete referent that can be empirically pointed out; it is not a sociological category that refers to those excluded from the political realm. Rather, it is an empty and indeterminate element made intelligible by the constant process of inclusive exclusion that characterizes Western politics. Bare life, as opposed to political or qualified life, is a life that has been included in the political realm through an exclusion, and as such it is exposed to sovereign violence.

This leads us to *homo sacer* – the one who, according to ancient Roman law, could be killed, but not sacrificed, and whose killing is not considered a crime – as a figure which helps us to understand the fact that political power founds itself on the separation of a sphere of bare life from a set comprised of those belonging to another type of life, in which each living being has acquired a certain 'form' which is deemed to be political – hence Agamben's description of the latter as 'form of life'.

Homo sacer is a paradigmatic figure which acquires a central place in Agamben's archaeological project, but it is only one paradigm among others, which, by allowing its own singularity to be bracketed, explains how sovereign power and biopolitics coincide within the Western tradition – contrary to Foucault's periodization which understood the one to precede the other in a broadly chronological time.

Indeed, for Agamben, biopolitics refers to this process of the exclusion of life that founds political power, a process which can be traced back to the Greeks. In this sense, biopolitics is a power over life – that is to say, a power which separates and divides life, producing a constant form of violence which blurs the boundaries separating law and its outside.

Therefore, one of the conclusions of the *Homo Sacer* project is that the biopolitical machine cannot be deactivated from the inside, by opposing life – creative, productive, precarious, vulnerable – to the power that divides it, as this will ultimately *reinforce* the differentiating structures through which biopolitics operates, rather than suspending them. It is for this reason that, in *The Use of Bodies*, Agamben offers an account of inoperativity which is based on the notion of form-of-life, which is to say, a life that cannot be divided. Against a politics grounded on traditional ontology, which privileges reason as the defining characteristic of the human being, Agamben points towards a politics of inoperativity, based on modal ontology – that is, an ontology for which relationality is primary and constitutive, rendering the distinction between essence and existence inoperative – and an idea of man as devoid of any particular destiny, task or vocation. What Agamben's works offer contemporary politics is therefore not a normative framework or a blueprint for political action, but rather strategic theoretical resources for thinking politics anew.

German Primera

Selected writings

Agamben, Giorgio. 'The Tree of Language', trans. Connal Parsley. *Journal of Italian Philosophy* 1 ([1968] 2018).

Agamben, Giorgio. *The Man Without Content*, trans. Georgia Albert. Stanford: Stanford University Press, [1970] 1999.

Agamben, Giorgio. *Stanzas: Word and Phantasm in Western Culture*, trans. Ronald L. Martinez. Minneapolis: University of Minnesota Press, [1977] 1993.

Agamben, Giorgio. *Infancy and History: The Destruction of Experience*, trans. Liz Heron. London: Verso, [1978] 2007.

Agamben, Giorgio. *Language and Death: The Place of Negativity*, trans. Karen E. Pinkus with Michael Hardt. Minneapolis: University of Minnesota Press, [1982] 1991.

Agamben, Giorgio. *Idea of Prose*, trans. Michael Sullivan and Sam Whitsitt. Albany: SUNY Press, [1985] 1995.

Agamben, Giorgio. 'The Eternal Return and the Paradox of Passion'. In *Nietzsche in Italy*, edited by Thomas Harrison. Saratoga: Anma Libri, [1986] 1988.

Agamben, Giorgio. *The Coming Community*, trans. Michael Hardt. Minneapolis: University of Minnesota Press, [1990] 1993.

Agamben, Giorgio. *Homo Sacer: Bare Life and Sovereign Power*, trans. Daniel Heller-Roazen. Stanford: Stanford University Press, [1995] 1998.

Agamben, Giorgio. *The End of the Poem: Studies in Poetics*, trans. Daniel Heller-Roazen. Stanford: Stanford University Press, [1996] 1999.

Agamben, Giorgio. *Means Without End: Notes on Politics*, trans. Vincenzo Binetti and Cesare Casarino. Minneapolis: University of Minnesota Press, [1996] 2000.

Agamben, Giorgio. *Remnants of Auschwitz: The Witness and the Archive*. (Homo sacer, III), trans. Daniel Heller-Roazen. New York: Zone, [1998] 1999.

Agamben, Giorgio. *Potentialities: Collected Essays in Philosophy*, edited by and trans. D. Heller-Roazen. Stanford: Stanford University Press, 1999.

Agamben, Giorgio. '"I am sure that you are more pessimistic than I am..." An Interview with Giorgio Agamben' trans. Jason Smith, *Rethinking Marxism: A Journal of Economics, Culture and Society* 16, no. 2 (April [1999] 2004).

Agamben, Giorgio. *The Time that Remains: A Commentary on the Letter to the Romans*, trans. Patricia Dailey. Stanford: Stanford University Press, [2000] 2005. Abbreviation: TR.

Agamben, Giorgio. *The Open: Man and Animal*, trans. Kevin Attell. Stanford, CA: Stanford University Press, [2002] 2004. Abbreviation: O.

Agamben, Giorgio. *State of Exception*. (Homo sacer, II, 1), trans. Kevin Attell. Chicago: University of Chicago Press, Abbreviation: SE.

Agamben, Giorgio. *Profanations*, trans. Jeff Fort. New York: Zone, [2005] 2007. Abbreviation: PR.

Agamben, Giorgio. *What Is an Apparatus? and Other Essays* (includes 'The Friend' and 'What is the Contemporary?'), trans. David Kishik and Stefan Pedatella. Stanford: Stanford University Press, [2006–7] 2009. Abbreviations: WA, F, WC.

Agamben, Giorgio. *Nymphs*, trans. Amanda Minervini. Calcutta: Seagull, [2007] 2013.

Agamben, Giorgio. *The Kingdom and the Glory*. (Homo sacer, II, 4 [originally II, 2]), trans. Lorenzo Chiesa (with Matteo Mandarini). Stanford: Stanford University Press, [2007] 2011. Abbreviation: KG.

Agamben, Giorgio. *The Sacrament of Language: An Archaeology of the Oath* (Homo sacer II, 3), trans. Adam Kotsko. Stanford University Press, [2008] 2011. Abbreviation: SL.

Agamben, Giorgio. *The Signature of All Things: On Method*, trans. Luca D'Isanto with Kevin Attell. New York: Zone, [2008] 2009. Abbreviation SAT:

Agamben, Giorgio. *Nudities*, trans. David Kishik and Stefan Pedatella. Stanford: Stanford University Press, [2009] 2011.

Agamben, Giorgio. 'Introductory Note on the Concept of Democracy'. In *Democracy in What State?*, edited by Giorgio Agamben et al., and trans. William McCuaig. New York: Columbia University Press, [2009] 2011.

Agamben, Giorgio. 'Angels' trans. Lorenzo Chiesa, *Angelaki* 16, no. 3 (September [2009] 2011): 117–23.

Agamben, Giorgio. *The Church and the Kingdom*, trans. Leland de la Durantaye. With Photographs by Alice Attie. Calcutta: Seagull, [2010] 2012.

Agamben, Giorgio. (with Monica Ferrando), *The Unspeakable Girl: The Myth and Mystery of Kore*, trans. Leland de la Durantaye and Annie Julia Wyman. Calcutta: Seagull, [2010] 2014.

Agamben, Giorgio. *The Highest Poverty: Monastic Rules and Form-of-Life* (Homo sacer, IV, 1), trans. Adam Kotsko. Stanford: Stanford University Press, [2011] 2013. Abbreviation: HP.

Agamben, Giorgio. *Opus Dei: An Archaeology of Duty.* (Homo sacer, II, 5), trans. Adam Kotsko. Stanford: Stanford University Press, [2012] 2013. Abbreviation: OD.

Agamben, Giorgio. *Pilate and Jesus*, trans. Adam Kotsko. Stanford: Stanford University Press, [2013] 2015.

Agamben, Giorgio. *The Mystery of Evil: Benedict XVI and the End of Days*, trans. Adam Kotsko. Stanford: Stanford University Press, [2013] 2017.

Agamben, Giorgio. *The Use of Bodies.* (Homo sacer, IV, 2), trans. Adam Kotsko. Stanford: Stanford University Press, [2014] 2016. Abbreviation: UB.

Agamben, Giorgio. *The Fire and the Tale*, trans. Lorenzo Chiesa. Stanford: Stanford University Press, [2014] 2017. Abbreviation: FT.

Agamben, Giorgio. *Stasis: Civil War as a Political Paradigm* (Homo Sacer, II, 2), trans. Nicholas Heron. Edinburgh: Edinburgh University Press, 2015. Turin: Boringhieri, 2015.

Agamben, Giorgio. *Taste*, trans. Cooper Francis. London: Seagull, [2015] 2017.

Agamben, Giorgio. *The Adventure*, trans. Lorenzo Chiesa. Cambridge, MA: MIT Press, [2015] 2018. Abbreviation: A.

Agamben, Giorgio. *Pulcinella or, Entertainment for Kids in Four Scenes*, trans. Kevin Attell. London: Seagull, [2015] 2019.

Agamben, Giorgio. *What Is Real?*, trans. Lorenzo Chiesa. Stanford: Stanford University Press, [2016] 2018.

Agamben, Giorgio. 'Foreword: The Vocabulary and the Voice', trans. Thomas Zummer in Émile Benveniste, In *Dictionary of Indo-European Concepts and Society*, trans. Elizabeth Palmer, ix–xx. Chicago: Hau Books, 2016

Agamben, Giorgio. *What Is Philosophy?*, trans. Lorenzo Chiesa. Stanford: Stanford University Press, [2016] 2018. Abbreviation: WP.

Agamben, Giorgio. *Karman: A Brief Treatise on Action, Guilt, and Gesture*, trans. Adam Kotsko. Stanford: Stanford University Press, [2017] 2018.

Agamben, Giorgio. *Creation and Anarchy: The Work of Art and the Religion of Capitalism*, trans. Adam Kotsko. Stanford: Stanford University Press, [2017] 2019. Abbreviation: CA.

Agamben, Giorgio. *Autoritratto nello studio*. Milan: Nottetempo, 2017

(Useful bibliographies for early and other works, particularly those written in Italian and French, may be found in Calarco & DeCaroli (eds.) (2007), and Durantaye (2009) and in Jacopo D'Alonzo's online bibliography, for works in Italian up to 2013 at least: https://www.academia.edu/6672253/Jacopo_ DAlonzo._Bibliografia_di_Giorgio_Agamben._Filosofia_italiana [accessed 22nd October 2018.)

Calarco, Matthew. and Steven DeCaroli, eds, *Giorgio Agamben: Sovereignty and Life*. Stanford: Stanford University Press, 2007

de la Durantaye, Leland. *Giorgio Agamben: A Critical Introduction*. Stanford: Stanford University Press, 2009

EXCERPT

Giorgio Agamben, **The Work of Man**

('The Work of Man', by Giorgio Agamben, from Matthew Calarco and Steven DeCaroli (eds.), *Giorgio Agamben: Sovereignty and Life*, Stanford: Stanford UP, 2007, pp.1–10.)

In the first book of the *Nicomachean Ethics* (1097b, 22 ff.), Aristotle poses the problem of defining the "work *[opera]* of man" *(to ergon tou anthrōpou)*. The context of this definition is the determination of the highest good as the object of *epistēmē politikē*, political science, to which the treatise on ethics represents a sort of introduction. This highest good is happiness. And it is precisely in order to define happiness that Aristotle begins his inquiry into the work of man.

> Just as for a flute player, a sculptor, or any artisan *(tekhnitē)*, and, in general, for all those who have a certain kind of work *(ergon)* and an activity *(praxis)*, the good *(tagathon)* and the "well" *(to eu)* seem [to consist] in this work, so it should also be for man, if indeed there is for him something like a certain work *(ti ergon)*. Or [must we say] that there is a certain work and an activity for the carpenter and the shoemaker, and for man there is none, that he is born with no work *(argos)*?

Ergon in Greek means "labour," "work." Yet, in the passage in question, the meaning of the term is complicated because of the close relation that links it to one of the fundamental concepts of Aristotle's thought: *en-ergeia* (lit. "being at work"). The term was, in all probability, created by Aristotle, who uses it in functional opposition to *dunamis* ("potentiality"). The adjective *energos* ("working," "active"), from which Aristotle takes it, is already found in Herodotus. The opposite term *argos* (from *aergos*, "not working," "lacking *ergon*"; cf. *argia*, "inactivity") already occurs in Homer. That the work of man, therefore, does not, in this context, simply mean "work," but rather that which defines the *energeia*, the activity, the being-in-act that is proper to man, is proved by the fact that a few lines later Aristotle will define happiness as *psukhēs energeia [. . .] kat' aretēn*, the being-at-work of the soul in accordance with excellence (1098a, 16). The question concerning the work or absence of work of man therefore has a decisive strategic importance, for on it depends the possibility not only of assigning him a proper nature and essence, but also, as we have seen, of defining his happiness and his politics.

The question is not simply a rhetorical one. In opposing four types of artisans—the flute player, the maker of *agalmata,* the carpenter, and the shoemaker—to man in general, Aristotle intentionally employs figures in which the work (and the being-at-work) can be identified without difficulty. But the choice of such, so to speak, "menial" examples does not mean that the list could not be continued upward (a few lines earlier, he had mentioned the doctor, the architect, and the strategist). That is to say, the problem has a broader meaning, and involves the very possibility of identifying the *energeia*, the being-at-work of man as man, independently of and beyond the concrete social figures that he can assume. Even if in the form of a paradoxical question, the idea of an *argia*, of an essential inactivity *[inoperosità]* of man with respect to his concrete occupations and functions *[operazioni]* is unequivocally put forward. The modern (or, rather, postmodern) problem of a fulfilled realisation of human work and thus of a possible *désoeuvrement (désoeuvré* corresponds perfectly to *argos)* of man at the end of history here has its logical-metaphysical foundation. The *voyou désoeuvré* in Queneau, the *shabbat* of man in Kojève, and the "inoperative community" in Nancy would then be the posthistorical figure corresponding to the absence of a truly human work. More generally, however, what is at issue in this question is the very nature of man, who appears as the living being that has no work, that is, the living being that has no specific nature and vocation. If he were to lack an *ergon* of his own, man would not even have an *energeia*, a being in act that could define his essence: he would be, that is, a being of pure potentiality, which no identity and no work could exhaust.

That this hypothesis must not have appeared as out of the question to Aristotle is shown by the fact that, in *De anima*, at the moment when he is defining *nous*, human intellect, he asserts that, "it has no other nature than being in potentiality" (429a, 21). For this reason even when it passes into act, thought "remains in some way still in potentiality . . . and is thus able to think of itself" (429b, 9). Moreover, in Greek the vocabulary of inactivity, to which *argos* as well as *skholē* belong, has no negative connotations at all. From the perspective of Aristotle's Christian commentators, however, the hypothesis of an essential inactivity of man could not have appeared as anything but scandalous. For this reason, in his commentary on the passage in question from the *Nicomachean Ethics*, Thomas is careful to specify that "it is impossible that man be by nature idle, as if he had no proper function *[impossibile est, quod sit naturaliter otiosus, quasi non habens propriam operationem]*" (*Sententia libri ethicorum*, 1.10.4).

Nevertheless, in the subsequent passage, Aristotle seems to back away from the hypothesis that there is no work of man as man, and, with a sudden turn, he seeks man's *ergon* in the sphere of life.

Or as the eye, the hand, the foot, and each of the parts of the body seem to have their work, must we then suppose that alongside *(para)* all of these man similarly has a certain work? And what then might this be? The simple fact of living *(to zēn)* seems to be common even to plants, but we are seeking something that is proper to man. We must therefore set aside *(aphoristeon)* nutritive life and the life of growth *(tēn threptikēn kai auxētikēn zōēn)*. Next would be a form of sensitive life *(aisthētikē tis)*. But even this seems to be common to the horse, the ox, and every living thing. There remains *(leipetai)* the form of practical life *(praktikē tis)* of a being who has *logos*. But since this has two meanings, we must consider life in accordance with being-at-work *(kat' energeian)*, which is the more proper sense of the term.

This analogy between the relation of individual *erga* to the work of man and that of the individual parts of the body to the body in its totality strategically serves to prepare for the passage to the sphere of life. Indeed, this passage is not obvious. If individual human activities (playing the lyre, making shoes, sculpting images) cannot exhaust the work proper to man as such, this does not mean that it must necessarily be sought in the sphere of life. That the work of man (on the individuation of which depends the individuation of the end of "political science") is defined as a certain form of life bears witness to the fact that the nexus between politics and life belongs, from the beginning, to the way the Greeks think of the *polis*.

In a typically Aristotelian gesture, the individuation of the *ergon* of man comes about by working a series of caesurae in the *continuum* of life. This *continuum* is divided into nutritive, sensitive, and practical-rational life. The articulation of the concept of life in a series of functions had already been carried out in *De anima*. Here Aristotle had isolated, from among the various senses of the term "to live," the most general and separable one:

> It is through life that what has soul in it differs from what has not. Now this term "to live" has more than one sense, and provided anyone alone of these is found in a thing, we say that the thing is living — viz, thinking, sensation, local movement and rest, or movement in the sense of nutrition, decay, and growth. Hence we think of all species of plants also as living, for they are observed to possess in themselves a principle and potentiality through which they grow and decay [. . .]. This principle can be separated from the others, but not they from it — in mortal beings at least. The fact is obvious in plants; for it is the only psychic potentiality they possess. Thus, it is through this principle that life belongs to living things. [. . .] By nutritive power we mean that part of the soul which is common also to plants. (413a, 20 ff.)

It is important to observe that Aristotle in no way defines what life is: he limits himself to breaking it down, by isolating the nutritive function, in order then to rearticulate it in a series of distinct and correlated faculties (nutrition, sensation, thought). In *De anima*, as well as in the *Nicomachean Ethics* and the *Politics*, nutritive life (or vegetative life, as it will be called as early as the ancient commentators, on the basis of that peculiar, obscure status as absolutely separated from *logos* that plants constantly have in Aristotle's thought) is that on the exclusion of which the definition of man, that is, of the living being that has *logos*, is founded.

The determination of the work of man is achieved, then, by means of the segregation of vegetative and sensitive life, which leaves life in accordance with *logos* as the only possible "remainder." And, since this life in accordance with *logos* can also be seen as in accordance with its pure potentiality, Aristotle is careful to specify that the work of man cannot be a mere potentiality or faculty, but only the *energeia* and the exercise of this faculty.

> If, therefore, the work of man is the being at work of the soul in accordance with *logos,* or not without *logos,* and if we say that the work of this particular individual and this particular good individual is the same in kind (e.g., a lyre player and a good lyre player, and similarly in all cases), eminence in respect of excellence being added to the work (for the work of a lyre player is to play the lyre, and that of a good lyre player is to do so well); if this is the case, we must suppose that the work of man is a certain kind of life (*zōēn tina*) and that this is the being-at-work of the soul and a praxis in accordance with *logos,* and that the work of the good man is these same things, performed well and in a beautiful way, each act in accordance with its own excellence; if this is the case, human good turns out to be the being- at-work of the soul in accordance with excellence, and if there are more than one excellence, in accordance with the best and most perfect.

At this point, Aristotle can proceed to the definition of the "work of man." As was implicit in the immediately preceding passage, this is a form of living, a "certain kind of life" *(zoē tis),* life that is in act in accordance with *logos.* This means that Aristotle determines the highest good—which the entire treatise was aimed at identifying and which also constitutes the end of politics—through the relation to a certain kind of *ergon,* a certain kind of activity or being-at-work. This activity consists, as we have seen, in the actualisation of the vital rational potentiality (and not, therefore, of the nutritive or sensitive potentiality). Consequently, human ethics and politics will be defined by the participation in this function, in general and in accordance with excellence (playing the lyre and playing it well, living and living well, in accordance with *logos*). We should not be surprised if, consistently with these premises, Aristotle's definition of the *polis,* that is, of the perfect political community, is articulated through the difference between living *(zēn)* and living well *(eu zēn)* "originating for the sake of life, but existing for living well" *(Politics* 1252b, 30).

Aristotle's determination of the work of man entails, therefore, two theses on politics:

1. Insofar as it is defined in relation to an *ergon*, politics is a politics of activity *[operosità]* and not of inactivity *[inoperosità]*, of the act and not of potentiality.

2. This *ergon,* however, is ultimately a "certain kind of life," which is defined above all through the exclusion of the simple fact of living, of bare life.

This is the legacy that Aristotle's thought has left to Western politics, An aporetic legacy, (1) because it binds the destiny of politics to a kind of work, which remains unassignable with respect to individual human activities (playing the lyre, making statues, producing shoes), and (2) because its single determination is ultimately biopolitical, insofar as it rests on a division and articulation of *zoē*. The political, as the work of man as man, is drawn out of the living being through the exclusion—as unpolitical—of a part of its vital activity.

In the modern era, Western politics has consequently been conceived as the collective assumption of a historical task (of a "work") on the part of a people or a nation. "This political task coincided with a metaphysical task, that is, the realisation of man as rational living being. The problematicity inherent in the determination of this "political" task with respect to the concrete figures of labor, action, and, ultimately, human life has gradually grown. From this perspective, the thought of Marx, which seeks the realisation of man as a generic being *(Gattungswesen)*, represents a renewal and a radicalisation of the Aristotelian project. Hence the two aporias implicit in this renewal: (1) the subject of the work of man must necessarily be an unassignable class, which destroys itself insofar as it represents a particular activity (for example, the working class); (2) the activity of man in the classless society is impossible or, in any case, extremely difficult to define (hence the hesitations of Marx concerning the destiny of labor in the classless society and the right to laziness claimed by Lafargue and Malevich).

And when, beginning with the end of World War I, the paradigm of the work enters into crisis and it becomes clear for the nation-states that there no longer are historical tasks that can be assigned, a reformulation of the biopolitical legacy of classical political philosophy becomes the extreme outcome of Western politics. In the impossibility of defining a new "work of man," it is now a question of taking on biological life itself as the last and decisive historical task. The "work" of the living being in accordance with *logos* is the assumption and the care of that nutritive and sensitive life on whose exclusion Aristotelian politics had defined the *ergon tou anthrōpou*.

However, a different reading of this passage from Aristotle is possible. This reading is contained in two heterogeneous, though not unrelated, texts. The first is Averroes' commentary on Plato's *Republic,* which has been preserved for us only in a Hebrew translation. The second is Dante's *Monarchy.* Both begin with the Aristotelian determination of human perfection as the actualisation of the rational potentiality; both take up the Aristotelian opposition between man on the one hand and plants and animals on the other. However, both, as we will see, emphasise the moment of potentiality as the specific characteristic of man. Indeed, for both Averroes and Dante, animals in some way participate in rational activity ("many animals," writes Averroes, "have this part in common with men");

what specifically characterises human *logos*, however, is that it is not always already in act, but exists, first and foremost, only in potentiality ("since the rational part," writes Averroes, "does not exist in us from the beginning in its ultimate perfection and in act, its existence in us is only potential"). But let us read Dante's text (*Monarchy* 1.3), which is articulated as an undeclared commentary on Aristotle's determination of the work of man in the *Nicomachean Ethics*, the lexicon and argumentation of which it takes up:

> We must therefore now see what is the end of human society as a whole. [. . .] And to throw light on the matter we are inquiring into, it should be borne in mind that, just as there is an end for which nature produces the thumb, and a different one for which she produces the whole hand, and again an end different from both of these for which she produces the arm, and an end different from all these for which she produces the whole person; in the same way there is an end for which the individual person is designed, another for the household, another for the village, yet another for the city, and another for the kingdom; and finally the best end of all is the one for which God Everlasting with his art, which is nature, brings into being the whole of humankind (*universaliter genus humanum*).

Here Dante takes up Aristotle's example of the relation between the individual parts of the body and the whole person *(totus homo)*; but the accent is shifted from the plurality of human activities to the multiplicity of the forms of community (added to the family, the village, and the city, which are already in Aristotle's *Politics,* are the kingdom and the end, for the moment unnamed, which corresponds to the universality of humankind). It is at this point that Dante reformulates the Aristotelian question concerning the work of man.

Consequently the first thing to bear in mind is that God and nature make nothing that is idle *(nil otiosum facit)*; on the contrary, all things come into being to perform some function *(ad aliquam operationem)*. For in the intention of its creator *qua* creator no created essence is an ultimate end in itself; the end is rather the function which is proper to that essence; and so it is that the function does not exist for the sake of the essence, but the essence for the sake of the function. There is therefore some function proper to humankind as a whole (*humane universitatis*), for which it is designed in such a great multitude *(in tanta multitudine ordinatur),* and no single man, or individual household, or village, or city, or individual kingdom can fully realise it.

Operatio is the Latin term that corresponds to *ergon* in the Latin translation of the *Ethics* that both Thomas and Dante had before them. Thus in Thomas's commentary we read: "Si igitur hominis est aliqua operatio propria, necesse est quod in eius operatione propria consistat finale bonum ipsius [If then man has some proper function, his final good must consist in this function]" (1.10.2). Like Thomas, Dante takes up (and, as we will see, modifies) the Aristotelian motif of the act's superiority over the essence (or potentiality); but for him the determination of this "work" of humankind as such immediately entails the introduction of the figure of the multitude. And just as in Aristotle no single concrete activity of man could exhaust the *ergon* of man as such, in Dante the actualisation of the *operatio humane universitatis* transcends the limits of individual men and individual communities.

> What this function is will become clear once we clarify what is the highest potentiality of the whole of humanity. [. . .] The highest potentiality in man is not simply to be, because the elements too share in this; nor is it to be in compound form, for that is found in minerals; nor is it to be an animate thing, for plants too share in that; nor is it to be a creature who apprehends, for that is also shared by the animals; but it is to be a creature who apprehends by means of the possible intellect (*esse apprehensivum per intellectum possibilem*), which belongs to no creature (whether higher or lower) other than man. For while there are indeed other essences who are endowed with intellect, nonetheless their intellect is not "possible" in the way that man's is, since such essences exist only as intelligences and nothing else, and their very being is simply the act of understanding that which they are; and this occurs without interruption (*sine interpolatione*), otherwise they would not be eternal. It is thus clear that the highest potentiality of humankind is its intellectual potentiality or faculty. And since that potentiality cannot be fully and all at once reduced in act through any one individual or any one of the particular communities enumerated above, there must needs be a multitude in humankind, through whom the whole of this potentiality can be actualised, just as there must be a multitude of things which can be generated so that the whole potentiality of prime matter lies under the act (*sub actu*); otherwise there would be a separate potentiality, which is impossible.

At this point Dante defines the work proper to humankind as such. And he does it by broadening, with respect to Aristotle, the context of the definition of human specificity: not only plants and animals but also inanimate beings (the elements and minerals) and supernatural creatures (the angels). From this perspective, rational activity is no longer enough to identify the proper characteristic of man, since he shares it with the *bruta* and the angels. In keeping with the fundamental motif of Averroes' interpretation of Aristotle's *De anima*, what defines human rationality is now its potential— that is, its contingent and discontinuous—character. While the intelligence of the angels is perpetually in act without interruption *(sine interpolatione)* and that of the animals is inscribed naturally in each individual, human thought is constitutively exposed to the possibility of its own lack and inactivity: that is to say, it is, in the terms of the Aristotelian tradition, *nous dunatos, intellectus possibilis*. This is why, insofar as it is essentially potentiality and can be in act only beginning from an "interpolation" (which, in the Averroist tradition, coincides with the imagination), the work of man requires a multitude, and indeed makes the multitude (and not a people, a city, or a particular community) the true subject of politics.

The motif of the *multitudo* in Dante takes up Averroes' theory of the eternity of humankind as a correlative to the oneness of the possible intellect. Since, according to Averroes, the perfection of man's potential to think is bound essentially to the species and accidentally to single individuals, there will always be at least one individual — a philosopher — who realises in act the potentiality of thought. According to the formulation in one of the theses condemned by Etienne Tempier in 1277, the numerically singular possible intellect, though separate from this or that individual body, is never separate from any body.

Dante develops and radicalises this theory, making the *multitude* the subject of both thought and political life. The *multitudo* is not simply idle, because it is not, like the individual, essentially separated from the one intellect; on the other hand, it is not solely active *[operosa]*, because the passage to the act always depends contingently on this or that individual. *The multitude, then, is the generic form of existence of potentiality,* which in this way always maintains itself in an essential proximity to the act (*sub actu* not *in actu*). The expression *sub actu* is not an invention of Dante's. We find it used in contemporary texts (for example, in Dietrich of Freiberg, whose treatise *De intellectu et intellegibili* Dante could have read) to express the mode of being of prime matter, which can never be completely separate from some form and therefore stands *sub actu*. But while Dietrich explicitly opposes the possible intellect, which is wholly separate from the act, to prime matter, Dante sets up an analogy between the mode of being of the intellect in potentiality and that of matter. Though it can suffer "interpolations" with respect to thought in act, the potentiality of thought is not entirely separate from it, and the multitude is this existence of potentiality *sub actu,* that is, in proximity to the act.

Dante conceives a politics that corresponds to the inactivity of man, one which is determined, that is, not simply and absolutely beginning from the being-at-work of human rationality, but from a working that exposes and contains in itself the possibility of its own not existing, of its own inactivity. From this inactivity, Dante deduces the necessity of the multitude as the subject of politics that exceeds every particular community, and of the Monarchy or the Empire as the regulating principle corresponding to this excess. What other consequences thought can draw from the awareness of its own essential inactivity, and whether, in general, there is a politics possible today that is equal to the absence of a work of man, and will not simply fall back into the assumption of a biopolitical task— this must for now remain in suspense. What is certain, however, is that it will be necessary to put aside the emphasis on labor and production and to attempt to think of the multitude as a figure, if not of inaction, at least of a working that in every act realises its own *shabbat* and in every work is capable of exposing its own inactivity and its own potentiality.

Translated by Kevin Attell

CHAPTER 13

Massimo Cacciari (1944–)

Massimo Cacciari is a leading figure in contemporary Italian cultural debate, both as a philosopher and as a politician. He graduated in 1967 from the University of Padua with a thesis on Kant's *Critique of Judgement* written under the supervision of Dino Formaggio. Between 1967 and 1969, Cacciari was close to the radical leftist movement *Potere Operaio* (Worker's Power), participated in the occupation of Mestre's railway station with the Montedison workers and collaborated with the journal *Classe operaia* (Working Class). After conflict arose between members of the journal, including Toni Negri, Alberto Asor Rosa and Mario Tronti, Cacciari left *Classe Operaia* and founded *Contropiano: Materiali marxisti* (Counterplan: Marxist Materials) together with Asor Rosa. In 1976, Cacciari joined the Italian Communist Party (PCI), becoming responsible for the Industry Committee of the Veneto Regional section of the PCI. He was elected to the Italian parliament between 1976 and 1983, where he also sat on the Industry Committee of the Chamber of Deputies. In 1983, he abandoned his party activism.

In 1985, Cacciari was appointed a full professor of Aesthetics at the Institute of Architecture of Venice. From 1993 to 2000 he was mayor of Venice, with a centre-left-wing coalition. In 2002 he founded (with Luigi Verzè) the faculty of philosophy at the private University San Raffaele (Cesano Maderno, Milan). Cacciari's political career was marked by another important step in 2005 when he was elected mayor of Venice for a second time. After the end of his mandate in 2010 Cacciari left politics, disappointed by the evolution of the Democratic party. Since 2010 he has been president of the Gianni Pellicani Foundation and has taught philosophy at the University of San Raffaele.

Cacciari's writings address the crisis of German idealism and dialectical systems, developing a reading of Western metaphysics in critical dialogue with Nietzsche and Heidegger, and trace the genealogy of negative thought in the classics of late ancient, mediaeval and modern thought. Such a genealogy has covered a wide range of thinkers and disciplines, leading Cacciari to trace connections between theology, political theory and philosophy. During his early period of political activism he published essays such as *Qualificazione e composizione di classe* (1970), *Pensiero negativo e razionalizzazione. Problemi e funzione della critica del sistema dialettico* (1973) and *Piano economico e composizione di classe* (1975), but his first major philosophical contribution was *Krisis, Saggio sulla crisi del pensiero negativo da Nietzsche a Wittgenstein* (1976). Following this, his main works include *Dallo Steinhof* (1980), *Icone della legge* (1985), *L'angelo necessario* (1986), *Dell'inizio* (1990), *Geo-filosofia dell'Europa* (1994), *L'arcipelago* (1997), *Della cosa ultima* (2004), *Tre icone* (2007), *Hamletica* (2009), *Il potere che frena* (2013), *Labirinto filosofico* (2014), *Occidente senza utopie* (with P. Prodi, 2016), *Icone. Pensare per immagini* (2017), *La mente inquieta. Saggio sull'Umanesimo* (2019), *Il lavoro dello spirito* (2020).

After an initial political and philosophical experience developed in close relation with *Operaismo* (Workerism), Cacciari began to develop a negative and anti-dialectical thought, which has become the main focus of his research and it comprises a significant portion of his more recent works. In the first phase of this inquiry, *Krisis* and *Pensiero negativo e razionalizzazione*, he explored the question of negativity through his inquiry into the works of philosophers such as Schopenhauer, Wittgenstein and Nietzsche, together with an analysis of their connections with Viennese culture during the eighteenth and nineteenth centuries. An analysis outlined in the wake of Heidegger on the crisis of scientific and technological reason led Cacciari to conclude that in the modern epoch only contextual processes of rationalization are possible, which, due to their limited nature, leave unanswered the key philosophical question of the origin of meaning.

In what can be considered a second phase of his speculation on negativity, Cacciari has addressed the question of the origin. In particular, in *Dell'inizio* and in *Della cosa ultima* he has developed an inquiry concerning the philosophical origin of negativity with reference not only to modern philosophical traditions such as German Idealism but also to Platonism and Neo-Platonism. His critique of Western metaphysics has always been carried out hand in hand with an analysis of Christian political theology, proposing original perspectives on ideas of power and sovereignty. Within this research path, Cacciari has articulated a critique of the political from what he has defined as an 'unpolitical' perspective. The latter is a reminder of the essential finitude and absence of foundation that characterizes the political.

Marco Piasentier

Selected writings

Cacciari, Massimo. *Architecture and Nihilism: On the Philosophy of Modern Architecture*. New Haven, CT: Yale University Press, 1993.

Cacciari, Massimo. *The Necessary Angel*. New York: State University of New York Press, 1994.

Cacciari, Massimo. *Posthumous People: Vienna at the Turning Point*, Redwood City, CA: Stanford University Press, 1996.

Cacciari, Massimo. *Unpolitical: On the Radical Critique of Political Reason*, trans. Massimo Verdicchio and edited by Alessandro Carrera. New York: Fordham University Press, 2009.

Cacciari, Massimo. *Europe and Empire: On the Political Forms of Globalization*. New York: Fordham University Press, 2016.

Cacciari, Massimo. *The Withholding Power. An Essay on Political Theology*. London: Bloomsbury Academic, 2018.

EXCERPT

Massimo Cacciari, *Nietzsche and the unpolitical*

(Massimo Cacciari, 'Nietzsche and the Unpolitical', pp.92–103, in *The Unpolitical: On the Radical Critique of Political Reason*. Ed. Alessandro Carrera. Trans. Massimo Verdicchio. New York: Fordham University Press, 2009.)

The most authentic reactionary thinking of the German crisis remarked with sound intuition its own distance from the "political" Nietzsche. [. . .] Between the "spirit of 1914" — in all its academic variations, from Wilamowitz on one hand to Troeltsch or Meinecke on the other — and Nietzsche, the critic of Wilhelmine *Sekurität* (that is, the outcome of that Prussian militarism and nationalism that believed itself to have been called "to lead the history of Humanity"), the clash is head-on. The "great reaction" understands Nietzsche's uselessness within its cultural-political project. Its philology is too good to translate *Will to Power (Wille zur Macht)* into *Waiting for the Leader (Führererwartung)*, and to aestheticise Nietzsche's political as *völkisch*. To this aestheticisation — the virile power of *Deutschtum* opposed to European decadence, to the "decline of the West" the definitive answer came from Thomas Mann in 1918, in his *Reflections of a Nonpolitical Man*.

In Mann, Nietzsche becomes the centre of German *Kultur* precisely because he is unpolitical. "The spiritual conversion of Germany to politics" constitutes the process *against* which Nietzsche testifies to the authentic German destiny. Thomas Mann's hatred for any aestheticisation and politicisation of Nietzsche finds here, therefore, its essential motives: Nietzsche is the unpolitical, but this unpolitical is the spiritual power of Germany itself. Therefore, Nietzsche belongs to the heart of Germany. The whole book is but the development of this one theme: Nietzsche read according to Theodor Storm's "renunciation" *(Entsagung)*, educated to the pessimistic German and *bürgerlich* ethics of Schopenhauer and Wagner, belonging to the *Humanität* of the classical-romantic period, of the German *Bildung*.[. . .] The spirit, insofar as it is *bürgerlich* and German, is essentially *Kultur. Kultur* is *Weltbürgertum*, cosmopolitanism; it is the expression, that is, of the substance of *Bürgertum*, universal substance opposed to the Latin concept of the bourgeoisie. The essential meaning of *Weltbürgertum* rests therefore on the concept of the unpolitical. Mann sees war itself, differently from those other greats of the liberal-conservative tradition, as a clash between the affirmation of this idea of *Weltbürgertum [. . .]* and the affirmation of political civilisation controlled by the bourgeoisie. The German mission consists in affirming the power of the unpolitical, and in this consists its supra-Germanity.

This Mannian interpretation of Nietzsche, however, so contrary to the myths of the "spirit of 1914," to the vision of German *Bildung* typical of the latter, so fiercely opposed to the Nietzschean popularisation of reactionary *Deutschtum,* follows the same historicist method that it questions in many of its individual assertions. A deep, strong continuity sustains German history from its classical era — but even before: from the age of the German cities, of the German Hanseatic League, of a Wagnerian Nuremberg more than merely medieval — until the test of 1914. And Nietzsche is supposedly the symbol of this continuity, which is hatred for the political. However, Nietzsche, instead, is precisely the critic of this symbol and this continuity. As Löwith has masterfully pointed out, the Nietzschean position with respect to the "age of Goethe" is completely different from the interpretation given by Mann. Goethe is for Nietzsche an accident without consequences in German history. Far from perfecting a tradition from which Nietzsche himself could draw, his conservative and conciliatory attitude appears in actuality to be the mask with which he detaches himself from the German *Weltbürgertum.* The latter is Hegelian and dialectical, not Goethean — it is dominated by the philosophy of history and by the idol of success sacralised as rational necessity. Goethe's realism seems to Nietzsche to be, in actual fact, a heroic anti-nihilistic attempt at overcoming nihilism, at Dionysian affirmation, absolutely eccentric with respect to the forces of German *Kultur.* This radical misunderstanding of Nietzsche's Goethe on Thomas Mann's part conceals, obviously, an even more substantial misunderstanding of the antihistoricist direction of Nietzsche's thought, absolutely opposed to any continuist reconstruction of the cultural event, to overcoming it in synthetic forms.

[. . .] The real central question posed by Mann's *Reflections of a Nonpolitical Man* is another: Should the political in Nietzsche be understood as an issue of the unpolitical? Is it a question of a reversal of values? And what should we understand by the unpolitical? What is the "thing in itself" that Nietzsche thinks in the question of the unpolitical? It is very clear that Mann understands it as the refusal of the political dimension, as the idea of the will to power as a heroic process of *askesis,* of renunciation in the Protestant sense. The political is for Mann a nonvalue. Its dimension makes impossible the unfolding of that process which is the affirmation of the values of *Humanität* and *Bildung* of the German cosmopolitanism. The unpolitical, therefore, for Mann is an affirmation of value, not its reversal. The political, rather, is the reversal of values. The politicisation expresses the disruption between *Seele* and *Geist,* Soul and Spirit, whereby the *Vergeistigung* [. . .] (the process of spiritualisation or rationalisation of social relations) appears and dominates as *Entseelung* or despiritualisation (the extirpation of romantic individuality, of the cultural individualism of the classic bourgeoisie).

Is this Nietzsche's unpolitical? To be sure, it is radically different from Weber's vision. Mann can prove the utopian character of the conservative reconciliation between *Kultur* and the Prussian state, between spirit and power politics, but his nostalgia for the Weimar myth is entirely powerless with respect to the Weberian analysis of the process of politicisation as necessary despiritualisation. The unpolitical as affirmation of values preceding the era of politicisation, or struggling with its destiny, constitutes the spiritual attitude that more explicitly is opposed to the Weberian disenchantment. To which horn of the dilemma does Nietzsche belong? And can his position throw new light on this contradiction?

Nietzsche's critique is the opposite of the critique of the political as nonvalue. This critique moves already within Weber's necessity [. . .] of politicisation. But, beyond Weber, it questions the meaning of the political as such. It is not enough to record its success, it is not enough to oppose to the praying devout in the old churches the new fetishism of the fact. Nietzsche's unpolitical is the critique of the political as affirmation of value. The unpolitical is not the nostalgic refusal of the political, but the radical critique of the political. It goes beyond the mask of the political (its disenchantment, its necessity, its being destiny) to discover the foundation of values, the discourse of value that still founds it. Its power analyses, and dissolves, that which even in Weber tends to present itself as the totalising method of Western spiritualisation. The unpolitical does not represent the value that frees itself from the nonvalue of the political, but the radical critique of the political as invested with value. The unpolitical is the reversal of value. And only this reversal can liberate the will to power in the direction of politics on a grand scale. Grand politics is not possible where the critique of the unpolitical is limited to affirming the necessity of politicisation. This affirmation is still historicism, tradition. Grand politics is a critique of the values that still form the basis of this politicisation. The unpolitical, in Mann's sense, is but an expression of these values. And here its dialectics ends. Having left home to fight against politicisation, such dialectics finds that it has to defend the same values that lie at the foundation of the still "enchanted," still uncriticised dimension of the political. Such dialectics finds itself in the dimension of the political, in a nutshell. Nietzsche's unpolitical instead develops separately from this political, and from this polar unpolitical, as an analysis of the authentic genealogy of the process of politicisation and of the premises of grand politics contained within it. The unpolitical in Nietzsche shapes up, we could say, as the critical stage of grand politics.

As we have already mentioned, a first test of this thesis could be easily made by reading Nietzsche's critique of the Wilhelmine era. But this would entail an extreme trivialisation of the meaning of the unpolitical. The general theoretical significance of the unpolitical consists in the assertion of the necessity of politicisation insofar as despiritualisation *(Entseelung)* and devaluation *(Entwertung) take place.* Far from coinciding with Mann's refusal of the political, the unpolitical constitutes its greatest assertion within Western nihilism. The unpolitical brings the political back to the acknowledgment of its intrinsic nihilism. This key direction is opened up, above all, by attacking the concepts, the forms, and the conducts that are the substance of the political as value. But this very same *pars destruens* is already a construction of grand politics insofar as it is a nihilistic devaluation.

In the process of politicisation, the political tends to represent itself as total concept. The forms assumed by the politicisation, even in Weber, appear as an articulation of the political as totality. The political intervenes everywhere — its logic constitutes the method of any social relation. And any form of social organisation tends relentlessly to take on the form of a totality, to lock into and to subsume within itself the totality of social interests. The dialectical state expresses these forces organically; it is indeed its outcome. Far from opposing sectarianisms that are represented as such, the dialectical state comprehends the totalising instance that emerges from the combination of forms of politicisation. As totality, this state tends immediately to conceive its own form as the natural form of political organisation. The dialectical state absolutises the concept of state: the historically determined work, which has led to its configuration within the sphere of Western rationalism (nihilism), appears surpassed — now the state counts as pure norm, law. Norm and law point to the universal method on whose basis every subject becomes a totality.

The unpolitical is the work of the deconstruction of this totality. Not in the superficial sense of the "critique of ideology," whereby this totality is said to be "false" — but in the sense that this totality is historically marked and produces the forces of its own crisis, forces whose possibility may definitely be accounted for. In the absolutisation of its being, its totality, the state — the greatest expression of political organisation, the result of the political — defines itself as value: its functions become values. Naming the multiplicity of forces that make up the crisis of that totality, the unpolitical represents the critique of values on whose bases alone such totality is conceivable. Unpolitical does not mean, therefore, suprapolitical: its concept traverses the entire space of the political. It is, in the political, the critique of its ideology and of its determination.

The emphasis is placed on the second term, not on the first. The first unfolds, substantially, by demonstrating the ethical foundation of the absolutisation of the political proclaimed by the modern state. On this side, the political falls once again under Nietzsche's overall critique of ethics. Democratisation and socialism are rather subsumed under the misery of Christian eschatology. This eschatology presupposes a human nature that is to be liberated from the alienation to which the institutions of civilisation have presumably condemned it. This eschatology, however, is not only at the basis of socialism but also at the basis of the idea of democratisation — and, even more generally, of the modern absolutisation of the political. This absolutisation claims to be the redemption of the totality of man, the overcoming of the empirical, contingent immediacy of his figure. If man could resist as an unpolitical partiality, the political could not conclude dialectically in the total state. And, therefore, the strong eschatological tone of the ideas of democracy and socialism is the legitimate heir of the political — it constitutes its necessary unfolding. For Nietzsche, this nature, whose alienation would be revocable, is superstition — better, it is a theological assumption. The absolutisation of the political belongs to the theological dimension of Western thought. But the analysis of its condition is not sufficient: it too represents a determinate and problematic asset of social organisation. In this sense, the critique of the ideas of democracy and socialism is essential since, according to Nietzsche, they unfold the political to the point at which it reveals its own constitutive determinacy and problematic nature.

Democracy makes explicit the origin presupposed by the discourse on the political (the political gives norms and laws that concern the origin and aim at the end of man as totality), but at the same time it makes it possible for any subject as such to express and organise its own force. Precisely insofar as it wants to make explicit the dignity of the common origin, it multiplies the organising of heterogeneous centres of force. This is the process of politicisation itself. It is the generalisation of the political. Any subject, in the dialectics of democracy, can be organised politically — in fact, this is what it is directly called upon to do. But this very same process that appears as absolutisation of the political, defines it in actuality as a field of heterogeneous forces, of contradictions — as a space where endless differences occur. The absolutisation occurs through a loss of centrality and a constant weakening of the system. Far from leading to unity, to common origins, the total politicisation increases the entropy of the system. It undermines the relations of subordination that regulated the course of the different subjects or selected their information. "[Total politicisation] is destined to disappear, because its foundation disappears, namely, trust in absolute authority and in definitive truth. . . In *freer* conditions, one will become subordinate only on condition, as a result of reciprocal contract, that is, with all the reservations of one's own interest" (*Human, All Too Human,* 1:245). But free subordination is the opposite of subordination, which is based on a true social hierarchy and is justified by an overall vision of philosophy of history. It becomes an interest, revocable at any moment on the basis of a right that derives from the relation of force, of an "arbitrary right". This undermines from the foundations the ancient "relation of reverence and piety toward the state." The idea of the state is transformed into an instrument that allows one to avail one's self of one's own right. No-one will see in the law anything other than the determined political organisation that produced it, the contingent power that issued from it. The mission of the democratic idea consists in the perfecting of this decay of the state, of the political as totality, in the concourse of the different subjects that by now autonomously make it up. But this decay is at the same time the greatest extension of the political, the perfection of the *Politisierung:* everybody makes politics and organises himself politically — but only because the political has lost any aura, because it revealed itself as devaluation and despiritualisation. [. . .] None can revere the state, if it ceases to represent the destiny that brings man back home, to the revocation of his alienation, to the conquest (or reformation) of his true nature. If the state appears ultimately as a sectarian organisation of arbitrary laws [. . .] even the last spell is driven away from the idea of the political. The task of the democratic idea consists in the desacralisation of the political. When it fulfils its task and "when every relapse into the old sickness has been overcome, a new page will be turned in the annals of humanity" [. . .]. It is essential to understand the finiteness of the state [. . .]. The state is one of these powers whose process of absolutisation coincides with that of its devaluation. The unpolitical is the recognition of the effective perfection of the political. [. . .]

In the fever that seizes the concept of work, Nietzsche catches the most evident symptom of this process. [. . .] [T]he power of Nietzsche's critique [. . .] is the attack on the very idea of work as value, an attack led on the basis of the concrete, historically determined dissolution of this idea that constitutes, in fact, the motor of dialectical construction. [. . .]

The value of work is founded on the teleological premise of the reconcilability of different operations — and of the necessity of this harmony for the development of the system. This teleology is the object of Nietzsche's critique, but not just because of its general moral character. Nietzsche stresses rather the impracticability, the current powerlessness of the synthesis that it projects. The unpolitical criticises politically the idea of the value of work as law and end of the multiplicity of subjects, as foundation of the progressive-synthetic idea of development. [. . .] Work, therefore, is a multiplicity of practices — and the character of these operations consists in being alienated from the possibility of dialectical synthesis. The unpolitical denounces in small politics the desperate conservation of the regressive idea of a mutual universal recognition of subjects in work as value. But why is this reduction impracticable? Because it appears by now that it is almost impossible to reduce the practices to their mere technical foundation. The doing (doing of *techne* irrevocably severed from *poiein*) is embodied in subjects that enact their own absence of home as a conflictual relation. This doing is political. The value of work is alienated in subjects politically determined. And they see their own operations as alienation — not in the banal and servile sense that this alienation is simply imposed on them, that they are subject to it in messianic expectation of the dialectical synthesis, but in the sense that, within the irrevocable dimension of alienation, they can build their own political interest, can determine their own separateness and division as grand politics. The doing is embodied in the political power of the different class interests. Their contraposition eliminates the teleology of the value of work, whose form is the dialectical state.

[. . .] The dangerous individual is the worker as impossible class, as a class that is aware of its own condition as impossible. But impossible in two senses: both because the conditions of its exploitation are a disgrace — and because its own individuality makes impossible the dialectical process of reduction and mediation, which is a condition of the power of the state form. This form decays.[. . .] Any political nostalgia for the universal foundation of value and the state form is pre-critical. The very same political operation is the dissolution of this form. It is transformation without foundation, that is, it cannot be inscribed in a teleological framework, in a philosophy of history. [. . .] Grand politics has, as its condition, the unpolitical acknowledgment of the non-totality of the political: a radical critique of the state-worshippers.

[. . .] [T]he only glimmer, the only strait gate left to us in the era of the demythologisation of the political, is to keep one's eyes open and to watch and observe well what is going on in the world, in order to work out that dissolution of values of the state that is the intuition of the "philosophy of the morning."

CHAPTER 14

Adriana Cavarero (1947–)

Political philosopher and representative of the Italian 'thought of sexual difference', Adriana Cavarero is one of the most internationally recognized Italian authors. Born in Bra (Piedmont) in 1947, she attended the *liceo classico* in Turin and majored in philosophy at the University of Padua, where she began her academic career. She later moved to Verona, where she was professor of political philosophy until 2016. From 1992, when her book on the feminist reading of Plato was first translated into English (*In Spite of Plato*), to the present, with the publication in English in 2016 of her latest work, *Inclinations*, her work continues to be widely discussed in contemporary debates on philosophy, political theory, comparative literature, feminism and voice studies.

Cavarero's intellectual endeavour, crucially starting with a critical reading of Plato, became progressively centred on the necessity of theoretically questioning the metaphysical tradition in its way of thinking about the subject and the body. By dismissing both the modern notion of the abstract, gender-neutral individual, disembodied and characterized by autonomy and independence, and the post-modern one, which dilutes the supposed compactness of the individual in a fragmented multiplicity, Cavarero elaborates the notion of 'relational ontology' (*ontologia relazionale*). The term refers to a way of framing the self as constitutively in a relation of interdependence with an other concrete, embodied and therefore sexed (*sessuato*) self.

The notion of sexual difference – as originally developed in the work of Luce Irigaray – is crucial to Cavarero's notion of embodiment: the human is never neutral, but always sexed, and in this perspective, femininity, or women's identity, needs to be rethought outside of its role and position within the patriarchal order. By insisting on the elementary given of *sexuation* – the materiality of the sexed body – in its relationship with thinking, sexual difference feminism aims at producing a different symbolic order that does not erase women or subsume them under the falsely neutral term 'man'. Sexual difference is both a material and symbolic dimension that needs to be named, signified and rendered politically active.

Cavarero's philosophical move is to take the philosophical–political enterprise undertaken by the thought of sexual difference *beyond* the boundaries of feminism itself. To think of subjectivity in terms of embodiment, exposure, relationality, in other words, does not serve the sole aim of deconstructing patriarchy and its corresponding notion of femininity; it serves instead to attempt a different framing, a different imaginary for thinking the human and their ethical and political dimension. At stake is a radical philosophical challenge, that of re-signifying subjectivity as structurally relational, contingent and fragile.

The human condition of dependency, claims Cavarero, is visible from birth, where the newborn is exposed to the caring gaze of the mother but also to the possibility of wounding. To thematize exposure, fragility and vulnerability as starting points of a relational notion of the self means, for Cavarero, to find a significant existential scene in which this human condition of dependency comes prominently to the fore. In order to do so, Cavarero often relies on paradigmatic female figures and female stereotypes, that in her works become dislocated from the patriarchal framework of the tradition and re-signified: mothers, servants, lovers, Madonnas are provocatively interpreted as figures of a different symbolic order, which is neither purely matriarchal nor simply feminist, but which challenges both the individualistic paradigm of self-sufficiency and autonomy, and the binary oppositions that sustain it, suggesting ways of conceptualizing subjectivity that neither erase embodiment nor confine it to a pre-semantic sphere.

Cavarero's philosophical–political project, from her early writings on Plato to the latest work on 'inclination', always takes its bearings from a bodily materiality that cannot be reduced to language or to a mere sociocultural construction. The body is an *elementary given* (*un dato elementare*) that Cavarero considers a decisive *source* of vitality, an undeniable *limit* of the self, the locus of relationality, vulnerability and dependency that as such must be taken into account, signified theoretically, and also affect the way in which we conceive of our ethics and our politics.

The anthropological paradigm of the tradition of political thought, namely the autonomous, sovereign self 'in charge of himself', potentially always in a relation of *hostility* with other autonomous selves, needs to be deconstructed and dismissed. The protagonist of the relational scene that Cavarero instead proposes is a self that is embodied and unique, yet neither independent nor autonomous.

The relational dimension of dependence is the crucial feature of Cavarero's works, declined in different contexts with different accents, yet always determining a radical rethinking of subjectivity, ethics and politics. In *Relating Narratives* (Cavarero 1997/2000), Cavarero individuates in the common habit of telling life stories a preferred scene of relationality and dependence: not to tell somebody my story or to write my autobiography, but to tell somebody *their* story is a meaningful narrative practice that responds to what Cavarero calls a 'desire for unity' that each person perceives as essential to their being. Identity in the form of a story is the outcome of a relational practice – between the 'I' and the 'you' – something given to me from another, in the form of a narrative that individuates in my life story a unity and a uniqueness. I depend on you in order to perceive myself as unique: in this context relational ontology becomes framed in a narrative practice that is at once self-confirming and non-individualistic.

In developing this narrative notion of identity, Cavarero relies on Hannah Arendt's notion of uniqueness and also on her critique of identity as sovereignty over one's own acts and deeds. For Arendt, each human being is unique, not in the sense that each possesses unique qualities, but insofar as she/he can give birth to the unpredictable. Uniqueness, for Arendt, can come to the fore only in action, only in a 'space of appearance' in front of others, and it is strictly dependent upon their testimony in order to be. It remains inert, so to speak, if it cannot expose itself to others who, in turn, can tell the story of this active exposure and allow each uniqueness to become tangible, real. In narrative terms, the self cannot be autobiographical, since it is necessarily related to others, to an 'outside' able to testify to and narrate the scene for the appearance of the 'who', namely the uniqueness of the self.

Arendt in fact distinguishes 'who' someone is from 'what' a person is, namely she separates uniqueness from common and abstract features ('qualities, gifts, talents'). 'Who I am' escapes these common features and can be told only in the form of a narrative recounting of my appearance in the world. Cavarero insists, beyond Arendt, that each human being perceives herself as unique but is not able individually to fulfil this desire and therefore needs others; she depends narratively on them.

Moreover, Cavarero further specifies the Arendtian notion of uniqueness by connecting it explicitly to embodiment and therefore connecting the Arendtian perspective with the feminist one: uniqueness is inescapably tied to sexual difference – the *given* of *sexuation* – and therefore the body does not belong to 'what' someone is and plays instead a crucial role in determining their 'who'.

The following extract, from *Relating Narratives*, while discussing the felicitous encounter between sexual difference and narrative practice in the feminist consciousness-raising groups of Italian feminism from the 1970s, also analyses the complex relationship between embodiment, identity and narrative and elaborates on the notion of embodied uniqueness in its relation to both sexual difference and relational ontology.

Olivia Guaraldo

Selected writings

Cavarero, Adriana. *In Spite of Plato: A Feminist Rewriting of Ancient Philosophy*, trans. Serena Anderlini-D'Onofrio and Aine O'Healy. Foreword by Rosi Braidotti. New York: Routledge Polity Press, 1995

Cavarero, Adriana. *Relating Narratives: Storytelling and Selfhood*, trans. by Paul Kottman, London: Routledge, 2000

Cavarero, Adriana. *Stately Bodies: Literature, Philosophy, and the Question of Gender*, trans. Robert de Lucca and Deanna Shemek. Ann Arbor, MI: University of Michigan Press, 2002

Cavarero, Adriana. *For More Than One Voice: Toward a Philosophy of Vocal Expression*, trans. Paul A. Kottman. California: Stanford University Press, 2005

Cavarero, Adriana. *Horrorism: Naming Contemporary Violence*, trans. William McCuaig. New York: Columbia University Press, 2008

Cavarero, Adriana. *Inclinations: A Critique of Rectitude*, 1st ed. trans. Adam Sitze and Amanda Minervini. California: Stanford University Press, 2016

Cavarero, Adriana. *Surging Democracy: Notes on Hannah Arendt's Political Thought*, trans. Matthew Gervase. Stanford: Stanford University Press, 2021

EXCERPT

Adriana Cavarero, *On the outskirts of Milan*

(A. Cavarero, *Relating Narratives. Storytelling and Selfhood*, trans. by Paul Kottman, Routledge 2000, pp. 55–62)

In one of the most famous books of Italian feminism, *Non credere di avere dei diritti* [*Don't Think You Have Any Rights*], a true story gets reported. We are in the 1970s, and the protagonists are two friends with assonant names: Emilia and Amalia. They attend, in Milan, '*la scuola delle 150 ore*'. The story which concerns them appears in the book as a report of Amalia, after the premature death of her friend, who died at fifty-three years of age.

Emilia, in the early days, 'was pretty boring: she went on telling her story umpteen times a day,' says Amalia. The latter has the gift of being able to express things well, whether out loud or on paper, which the other lacks. In their exchange of writing exercises, the gap became evident. 'When I let her read what I had written,' continues Amalia, 'especially when I was talking about my hometown, about the farmers and particularly about my life, she cried.' She too 'needed to tell about her life,' notes Amalia in order to explain this weeping, 'but she wasn't able to connect any of it up, and so she let herself go.' Amalia then decides to take an interesting initiative: 'once I wrote the story of her life, because by then I knew it by heart, and she always carried it in her handbag and read it again and again, overcome by emotion.'

The episode almost seems like a transposition of the Homeric Ulysses on to the outskirts of contemporary Milan. There is the weeping in the listening/reading of a story, and there is the same emotion in the recognition of one's own life-story narrated by another. There is, however, also, beyond the oral or written form of the story, a substantial difference. In the Homeric scene, the rhapsod and Ulysses are strangers: the first does not know that he is singing the story of the second in his presence, and neither had Ulysses ever told the rhapsod anything about himself. Amalia and Emilia, on the other hand, are two friends. The first writes the story of the second because Emilia had continually recounted her story, in the most disorganized way, showing her friend her stubborn desire for narration. The gift of the written story is precisely Amalia's response to this desire. Now Emilia can carry the text of her story with her and reread it continuously — moved every time by her own identity, made tangible by the tale.

Of course, Emilia could have written an autobiography with her own hand — in fact she tried. Like Arendt, we nonetheless begin to suspect that what prevented her from successfully completing the undertaking was not so much a lack of literary talent, but rather the impossibility of personally objectifying the material of her own desire without falling into the perspectival mistake of memory. In other words, the *who* of Emilia shows itself here with clarity in the perception of a narratable self that desires the tale of her own life-story. However, it is the other – the friend who recognizes the ontological roots of this desire — who is the only one who can realise such a narration. This means that Emilia obstinately manifests the desire that the course of her life trace a stork, that her uniqueness leave behind a story. By writing the story for her (not in her place, but for her), Amalia gives it a tangible form, sketches a figure, suggests a unity. Amalia herself, moreover, finds success in autobiographical narration as well. She even makes her friend weep. Her friend weeps because she recognises in that narration the object of her own desire. Autobiography and biography come thus to confront each other in the thread of this common desire, and the desire itself reveals the relation between the two friends in the act of the gift.

As a young maidservant in contemporary Milan would note at this point, women everywhere, and quite often, set themselves to telling their stories to one another, as though through each story there passed their own existence and personal identity. The fact is that this passage does indeed occur. Not only for the reasons that psychoanalytic theory could ably indicate, but also for those reasons that the political thought of Arendt, reinterpreted in the light of feminist experience, helps us to better understand.

As we read in *Non credere di avere diritti*, the aim of women who have returned to school in order to attend the 150-hour adult classes is indeed to 'think that my "I" exists.' Emilia does not seem to have any doubts about the importance of this ontological affirmation. For her, such existence coincides with the very narratability that desires to make itself materialize in a tale. Emilia knows that a life about which a story cannot be told risks remaining a mere empirical existence, or rather an intolerable sequence of events. What is intolerable, therefore, is not so much a life that 'has always been a "no"' and which seems poor at fifty-three years of age, married and without children; but rather the fact that the life-story that results from it remains without narration. She thus passes, from the failed autobiographical attempts, to the biography that her friend gives to her as a gift. This biography is highly tangible, all the more so in so far as it is written. By always carrying it in her purse and rereading it continuously, Emilia can touch with her hand and devour with her eyes her personal identity in a tangible form. She can, like Ulysses, be moved by it.

The paradox of Ulysses functions therefore also in this case, but the comparison between Ulysses and Emilia works only up to a certain point. Indeed, Ulysses is a hero; that is, he has had the Trojan scene as an interactive space for exhibiting his own uniqueness. To use Arendt's language, Ulysses is the archetypal actor who, performing actions in a shared political space, reveals *who* he is to his peers. The life-story that results from these actions corresponds with a specifically human existence in so far as it is political.

Emilia, however, has had no such public scene of reciprocal and interactive exhibition. Emilia, as happens with many women in Italy (and elsewhere), has probably had the domestic scene as the setting for her existence. If the principle — according to which the unexposable is the non-existent — is valid, then Emilia has lived a life in which her uniqueness has remained partially unexposed due to the lack of a shared scene of co-appearance [comparizione], the lack of a true political space.

It is helpful to recall once more that we are using the term 'political' in Arendt's anomalous sense. We are not pointing out the well-known historical phenomenon of women's exclusion from political institutions; but rather the phenomenon through which many women, like Emilia, have no experience of a plural and interactive space of exhibition that is the only space that deserves the name of politics. Actually, the best comparison here is not a Milanese worker [operaio] — the most likely masculine equivalent of Emilia's condition — but rather it is that ancient hero who, despite his suspect virility, keeps us company here. The fact is, as Arendt herself emphasises, it also happens that men too are excluded from participating in a political space of interaction. As many scholars maintain, but as Arendt more than others is able to argue, Western history is a history of depoliticisation. Replaced by the rule of the few over the many; or rather replaced by various models of domination, throughout this two-thousand year history — the political as a shared space of action disappears, or rather reappears only intermittently in revolutionary experiences.

Nonetheless, the dominant social codes, which ascribe different roles to men and women, make this lack-of-politics [impoliticità] different for each. For women, the absence of an interactive scene, where uniqueness can be exhibited, is historically accompanied by their constitutive estrangement from representations of the subject, which rule in the patriarchal symbolic order. As was noted earlier, the tradition which, by ignoring uniqueness, celebrates the glorious accomplishments of Man, is the same tradition that consents only to human beings of the male sex the ability to recognise themselves in this abstract universal. Whether on the level of expression or on the level of representation, women find themselves trapped between a double powerlessness that concerns both *uniqueness* and *quality*. In other words, for women — in addition to the general absence of political spaces where each human being can show to others *who* she or he is — there is the pervasiveness of a symbolic order where the androgynous subject is what defines *what* they are: mothers, wives, care-givers, bodies to be enjoyed . . . the list goes on.

Again, from our point of view, there nonetheless is an appreciable advantage in all of this. Women have somewhat less of a chance of committing that formidable error that consists in exchanging the 'unrepeatable uniqueness' for the abstract 'Man.' In other words, the exhibitive impulse of uniqueness, in the case of a woman, finds obvious obstacles in being erroneously supplied with the representation of a universal subject that is clearly masculine.

Our friend Emilia can testify to this. Her double powerlessness makes it so that she wisely orients her desire where existence finds its only and genuine expressive outlet; namely, towards the scene where uniqueness constitutes itself 'in relation.' This relation does not yet have the luminous characteristics of the public scene, in so far as it arises from the obscurity of the private sphere; but it is first of all in the private sphere that the relations of the feminine experience become a friendship. Contrary to the widely held opinion that maintains that feminine friendship is founded above all on the solidarity of misery and oppression, we are here offered a friendship that has conspicuous narrative characteristics. What is more, we women know how the habitual side of feminine friendship consists in this reciprocal narrative exchange – continuous though interrupted, intense though diverting [*svagato*] — of our own life-stories. For female friends, the questions 'who are you?' and 'who am I?', in the absence of a plural scene of interaction where the *who* can exhibit itself in broad daylight, *immediately* find their answer in the classic rule of storytelling.

This immediacy has its first cause [*causa prima*] in the symptomatic fear that a life led in the absence of a public space of exhibition leaves behind no life-story. *What* Emilia is we could, in fact, try to define with a good approximation: she is a Milanese housewife; she is poor, married, without children... in short, she is a woman like many others who have a difficult lot in contemporary cities. In this sense, she is the champion of a certain sociological 'type.' *Who* Emilia is, on the other hand, eludes this classification. This *who* is precisely an unrepeatable uniqueness which, in order to appear to others, needs first of all a plural — and therefore political — space of interaction.

With respect to Arendt's theory, Emilia and Amalia — or feminine friendship in general — pull off a curious transgression. Arendt would like the narration of the story to follow the actions of the hero from which the story itself results. In other words, Arendt would like the question 'who are you?' to respond to the revealing action of identity; only *after* and *because of* this action does a life-story result, which then needs a narrator. Emilia and Amalia, however, seem to go *immediately* to narration, as do many women in the course of a narrative friendship. The uniqueness, partially unexpressed due to the absence of political scenes of interaction, therefore gets concretized in a narratable self, who entrusts the inalienable sense of her existence to the narration. Emilia, not having had political spaces of exhibition, fears that she may not leave any story behind which is worthy of narration. She wants this narration in the tangible form of a written tale at any cost. It is as if, contrary to Arendt's theory, the narrated story that produces the reality of the self then regards, first of all, the revealing quality of political action, or regards the process of narrating this life-story as if it were already a political action.

Surprisingly, it is.

The typical feminine impulse to self-narration can indeed be recognized even in the phenomenon of 'consciousness-raising groups,' which characterized Italian feminism in the 1970s. This phenomenon is, at its root, the passage of a rather diffuse habit in the everydayness of female relations to the relatively stable and organized form of the group. The desire is still that of expressing *oneself*, in the double sense of actively expressing one's own self and of finding the words that translate that exposition into narrative form. In the practice of 'consciousness-raising,' the feminine custom of self-narration thus finds a political scene — that is, in the Arendtian sense, a shared and interactive one. The thesis 'of an intrinsic authenticity of the personally lived,' which has always sustained the female friendship-relation, can finally make itself explicit and come to an interactive significance that assumes the exhibitive characteristics of action. Nothing, in fact, is lacking, because this experience can, in Arendt's sense, define itself as political: a shared, contextual, and relational space is created by some women who exhibit *who* they are to one another. There is nonetheless an utterly peculiar aspect with respect to Arendt's criteria: the exhibitive action coincides here with a self-narration. Arendt's criteria are thus transgressed — if not the principle according to which the action can consist in a discourse, at least the principle that declares autobiography to be ineffective.

In the practice of consciousness-raising, the narratable self, pushed by the justifiable fear that the partially unexposed is partially non-existent, comes by herself to satisfy her own desire for a narrated story. The life-story, having come into its own tale, puts into words an identity — at the same time and in the same context in which the women present generate a political space that finally exposes them. Put another way, there is a privileging of the word as the vehicle of a desire for identity that only the narrated form seems able to render tangible. And there is, at the same time, the creation of a relational space of reciprocal exhibition, which is clearly perceived and affirmed as political. The insistence on the *relationship between women, on* the *contextuality of the practice* and on *'starting from oneself [partire da sé]'* — that has characterised the feminist political lexicon in Italy since the 1980s — therefore finds a fundamental source in the consciousness-raising groups. Its uniqueness consists in a horizon that sees politics and narration intersect.

Moreover, the exclusively feminine setting of such a horizon in the consciousness-raising group becomes important. The stories of women, which intertwine on the *separatist* scene, allow them 'to deconstruct a point of view on the world, which claims to be neutral, but in reality conforms largely to masculine desires and needs [...] to learn to narrate themselves as women means in fact to legitimate for themselves a definition which is outside the gaze of the other.' Or rather, outside the standards of the gaze of Man. In other words, the relational context, in which the uniqueness of each one can finally expose itself, renders simultaneously visible not only the concrete sensation that pertains to the uniqueness of each one; but also the sexual difference which is shared, and which shows itself capable of working as a point of view that is independent of the masculine one. Since the expression of personal identity comes also to express a gender identity, the fact that each is a woman and not a man risks therefore betraying itself in the super-personal paradigm of Woman. It risks betraying itself in a *representation* of Woman and being satisfied with that. It risks falling into the trap of the Sphinx which old Oedipus avoided (not because he was smart, but because of a defect of memory).

However, the gender identity cannot avoid producing, in this context, a contradictory effect, in so far as it invites the uniqueness of each woman to identify herself with all other women. In the reflection of the one in the other, the very personal identity that is consigned to the tale of an unrepeatable life-story runs the risk of losing its expressive reality and founding itself in the common 'being women' that is represented here. 'I am you, you are me, the words which one says are women's words, hers and mine.' The empathy risks producing a substance. Put simply, *who* I am and *who* you are seem to surrender to the urgency of the question of *what* Woman is.

Even if universalism of the masculine type is amended, the old error of Oedipus returns all the same. The uniqueness of the self sacrifices itself to the hypostatisation of the female gender and, while it gains a critical perspective on the patriarchal tradition, it nonetheless deviates from its original desire. Yet beyond this assimilating effect (which goes on relatively quickly to close the experience of consciousness-raising groups), the phenomenon is still of extreme interest. As Ida Domanijanni writes, 'Here the original figures of the thought of sexual difference come to light, and here one finds that particular form of interaction of the feminine "I" with the order of discourse and representation which constitutes the nucleus of the debate over politics of the symbolic.' Already at the inaugural point of feminist practices, it becomes evident how the usual feminist impulse to self-narration, at the moment in which it generates a political space, roots itself – implicitly or explicitly, spontaneously or reflexively, genuinely or hypothetically – in a self that is constitutively sexed.

Reread in the light of this phenomenon, the Arendtian category of the *who*, precisely in so far as it is expressive and relational, thus is materialized in the specificity of the feminine sex, showing how the uniqueness of human existence deals constitutively with sexual difference *[la sessuazione]*. Not only because, if it is correct to follow Arendt and say that 'men, and not Man, live on Earth and inhabit the world,' it seems even more fitting to say that not Man, but rather men and women live there and inhabit it; but especially because the phenomena in question stage *[inscenano]* the exhibitive impulse of a *who*, which, by distinguishing itself, exhibits at the same time the distinction of its sex. To use Arendt's terms, it must be decided if the fact that I am a woman and not a man belongs to the order of my qualities (*what* I am), rather than to my uniqueness (*who* I am). At the heart of the first alternative there is a subject, unique and unrepeatable, which nonetheless is born 'neutral' as far as sex goes and thus can make of its feminine *quality* a hypostasis that can be entrusted to the realm of representation. At the heart of the second alternative there is a uniqueness, equally unique and unrepeatable; birth shows who the newborn is — namely, sexed [*sessuata*], and given over to the contextual and relational realm of expression.

The maidservant in Milan could therefore once again suggest for us a rather simple summary. From birth, the uniqueness which appears, and which provokes the fundamental question 'who are you?,' is an embodied uniqueness and therefore sexed. Neither the political scene nor the narrative scene, nor their extraordinary coinciding in the consciousness-raising groups, can ignore this sexedness [*sessuazione*] if, on this scene, it is truly the *who* that shows itself.

Beyond the naïve gaze of the housewife, it is above all the advent of feminism that permits us to twist the Arendtian categories towards the concretion of the self. The self-expression of identity reveals itself here to be rooted in a desire which could call itself ontological, since some of the existence of *who* is revealed 'goes' [*'ne va'*] into this desire. Although women live in the world, this is an existence that the patriarchal tradition tends to synthesize within the catalog of feminine qualities that reduce the *who* to the *what*: a mother, a wife, a nurse. Outside of these qualities, or rather outside of the phallocentric representative order, women would end up existing only in the empirical sense, in such a way that their life would be a *zoe* rather than a *bios*. It does not amaze us, therefore, that the in-born [*innata*] self-exhibitive impulse of uniqueness comes together for many women in the desire of the *bios* as the desire for biography.

CHAPTER 15

Roberto Esposito (1950–)

If Italian philosophy, broadly construed, is a strand of thought concerned with the nature of the relation that ties political power to biological life, together with a deconstruction of political theology that reanimates debates on the very notion of secularization and a commitment to think anew the idea of the common, then the thought of Roberto Esposito constitutes a paradigmatic and fundamental example of it. His *oeuvre* can be read as an attempt to think the political from scratch, from its outer limits. The traditional categories which have guided political thought, from representation to democracy, are all called into question by Esposito's genealogical investigations, in order thereby to recover excluded sediments of thought, obfuscated by the liberal tradition, through a meticulous etymological and archaeological procedure.

Although Esposito's thought can be traced back to his writings on critical figures from the history of Western philosophy (notably on Vico, Spinoza, Descartes, Rousseau and Machiavelli), it is with the publication of *Categorie dell'impolitico* (1988) that his research project develops a life of its own. In this book, translated into English as *Categories of the Impolitical* (2015), Esposito engages with Carl Schmitt, Elias Canetti, Hannah Arendt and Georges Bataille, in order to reconstruct an alternative project of critique in relation to the exhausted categories of modern political thought. Indeed, against the autopoietic legitimizing logic of both political theology and contractual theory, Esposito constructs the category of the impolitical.

In exposing the inner connection between power's claims to authority and processes of depoliticization, the impolitical becomes the shadow and the limit of the political in and of itself. The impolitical, in this sense, is a way of thinking politics from its constitutive borders; it is an immanent critique of the political that undermines without negating – and hence its difference from the 'apolitical' – the foundations of modern political thought.

It is in light of this critique that Esposito undertakes the genealogical task of rethinking the notion of the common from a biopolitical perspective. He does so in his trilogy, *Communitas: The Origin and Destiny of Community* (1998), *Immunitas: The Protection and Negation of Life* (2002) and *Bios: Biopolitics and Philosophy* (2008). Contrary to a metaphysical tendency to conceive community as a substance and therefore as theoretically linked to the category of the 'proper', Esposito's starting point is to free the notion of community from any identitarian constitutive bonds and ideas of belonging. Locating himself in a broader tradition that includes Jean-Luc Nancy, Maurice Blanchot and Giorgio Agamben, Esposito develops a notion of community as a radical and irresolvable alterity, giving voice to a critical approach to politics.

The specificity of Esposito's approach to community lies in his focus upon its etymological substratum. By shifting the emphasis from the Latin *cum* – central to Nancy's approach – to the term *munus*, whose ambivalent meaning oscillates between law and gift, Esposito brings to the fore the complex relation of exposing oneself to the other that underpins the notion of community. Indeed, for Esposito, 'to belong entirely to the originary *communitas* means to give up one's most precious substance, namely, one's individual identity, in a process of gradual opening from self to the other' (2013:84). Therefore, the condition for the possibility of community, as indicated by the term *munus*, is a debt, an obligation to the other. It is precisely this focus on *munus* and on its negative etymological derivation (*immunitas*) that allows Esposito to depict the paradigm of immunity: if *communitas* is a collective debt that dismantles the illusions of personal identity, binding its members through a commitment of giving, then immunity is what exonerates us from this debt. In this sense, immunity reconstructs the individual barriers that threaten the constitutive foundation of the common by excluding some from the responsibility of gift sharing.

The reconstruction of community and its paradoxical relation to immunity carried out in Esposito's trilogy lays the groundwork for a crucial contribution to biopolitical theory. Here it is necessary to recall that a theoretical tension marks the limit of Foucault's account of biopolitics: the relation between life and politics in Foucault allows simultaneously for two opposing accounts of biopolitics to emerge – a positive account of biopolitics, that is to say, biopolitics as a power *of* life, which is broadly speaking the path followed by Antonio Negri; and an account of biopolitics as a power *over* life, which is the path followed by Giorgio Agamben. Roberto Esposito's biopolitical theory aims at mediating between these two contrasting possibilities.

The paradigm of immunization makes intelligible the ways in which the body politic, like the individual body, can be immunized against and protected from external threats, by allowing a part of that perceived danger to penetrate some of its boundaries. If modern democratic states are founded on their responsibility for the security, life and health of their subjects, the measures designed to preserve life all too readily serve to redefine boundaries through various mechanisms of exclusion from 'bodies politic', thereby sanctioning the death of some so as to 'immunize' others.

This is why, for Esposito, although immunity attempts to protect life, when pushed beyond a certain threshold, it turns against life and negates it.

However, immunity also carries within itself and requires a different modality. As it is predicated on an opening to an outside, it could also signal a positive dimension that protects life. *Affirmative* biopolitics refers to the intersection between these two processes of the negation and protection of life, implying that political power can never fully capture life and foreclose the possibility of *communitas*.

Esposito's biopolitical theory opens up a line of inquiry into the mechanisms of differentiation and exclusion that are constitutive of Western civilization. One of the pivotal paradigms that emerges from this genealogy is the mechanism of the *person*, a common thread in many of Esposito's latest works: *Third Person: Politics of Life and Philosophy of the Impersonal* (2012), *Two: The Machine of Political Theology and the Place of Thought* (2015) and *Persons and Things* (2015). The aim of these works is to provide a biopolitical critique of the logics of exclusion that underpin the notion of the person within the Roman and Christian traditions and to highlight the urgency of the need to depart from the lexicon of political theology. The purpose of his latest book, *A Philosophy for Europe* (2018), is precisely to offer strategic resources that might make such a departure possible.

German Primera

Selected writings

Esposito, Roberto. *Categories of the Impolitical*, trans. Connal Parsley. New York: Fordham University Press, [1988/1999] 2015. Categorie dell'impolitico. Bologna: Mulino, 1999. First edn 1988.

Esposito, Roberto. *The Origin of the Political: Hannah Arendt or Simone Weil?*, trans. Vincenzo Binetti and Gareth Williams. New York: Fordham University Press, [1996] 2017. L'Origine della politica: Hannah Arendt o Simone Weil? Rome: Donzelli.

Esposito, Roberto. *Communitas: The Origin and Destiny of Community*, trans. Timothy Campbell. Stanford: Stanford University Press, [1998] 2009. *Communitas*. Origine e destino della comunità. Turin: Einaudi, 1998.

Esposito, Roberto. *Immunitas: The Protection and Negation of Life*, trans. Zakiya Hanafi. Cambridge: Polity, [2002] 2011. Immunitas: Protezione e negazione della vita. Turin: Einaudi, 2002.

Esposito, Roberto. *Bios: Biopolitics and Philosophy*, trans. Timothy Campbell. Minneapolis: University of Minnesota Press, [2004] 2008. Bíos: Biopolitica e filosofia. Turin: Einaudi, 2004.

Esposito, Roberto. 'Interview with Timothy Campbell' trans. Anna Paparcone, *Diacritics* 36, no. 2 (Summer 2006): 49–56.

Esposito, Roberto. *Third Person: Politics of Life and Philosophy of the Impersonal*, trans. Zakiya Hanafi. Cambridge: Polity, [2007] 2012. Terza Persona: Politica della vita e filosofia dell'impersonale. Turin: Einaudi, 2007.

Esposito, Roberto. 'Community, Immunity, Biopolitics' trans. Zakiya Hanafi, *Angelaki*, 18 (2013): 3.

Esposito, Roberto. *Terms of the Political: Community, Immunity, Biopolitics*, trans. Rhiannon Noel Welch. New York: Fordham University Press, [2008] 2013. Termini della politica: Comunità, immunità, biopolitica. Milan: Mimesis, 2008.

Esposito, Roberto. *Living Thought: The Origins and Actuality of Italian Philosophy*, trans. Zakiya Hanafi. Stanford: Stanford University Press, [2010] 2012. *Pensiero vivente: Origine e attualità della filosofia italiana*. Turin: Einaudi, 2010.

Esposito, Roberto. *Two: The Machine of Political Theology and the Place of Thought*, trans. Zakiya Hanafi. New York: Fordham University Press, [2013] 2015. Due: La macchina della telogia politica e il posto del pensiero. Turin: Einaudi, 2013.

Esposito, Roberto. *Persons and Things: From the Body's Point of View*, trans. Zakiya Hanafi. Cambridge: Polity, [2014] 2015. *Le persone e le cose*. Turin: Einaudi, 2014.

Esposito, Roberto. *A Philosophy for Europe: From the Outside*, trans. Zakiya Hanafi. Cambridge: Polity, [2016] 2018. Da fuori. Una filosofia per L'Europa. Turin: Einaudi, 2016.

EXCERPT

Roberto Esposito, *Community, Immunity, Biopolitics*

(Roberto Esposito, 'Community, Immunity, Biopolitics', in *Community, Immunity and the Proper*, Trans. Z. Hanafi, Routledge, 2013, pp 83–90.)

Community, immunity, and biopolitics: what is the relation between these three terms through which my recent work has wound its way? Can they be connected together in a relationship that is more than just a simple series of concepts or lexicons? Not only is this possible, in my view, it is also necessary. Indeed, each of these terms takes on its fullest sense only in relation to the other two. But let us start from a historical given, by briefly recalling the transition that the two semantic categories — first community and then biopolitics — went through in contemporary philosophical debate. In the late 1980s in France and Italy, a discourse on the concept of community took form that was radically deconstructive toward the way the concept-term had been used in twentieth-century philosophy as a whole – first by the German organicist sociology on *Gemeinschaft* (community), then by the various ethics of communication, and finally, by American neocommunitarianism. Despite significant differences, what linked these three conceptions was a tendency — which could be defined as metaphysical — to conceive of community in a substantialist, subjective sense. Community was understood as a substance that connected certain individuals to each other through the sharing of a common identity. Based on this understanding, community seemed to be conceptually linked to the figure of the "proper": whether it was a matter of appropriating what is in common or communicating what is proper, the community was still defined by a mutual belonging. What its members had in common was what was proper to them – that of being proprietors of their commonality.

It was in opposition to this conceptual short-circuit — on the basis of which the common was reversed into its logical opposite, namely, the proper — that a number of books appeared in rapid succession, including Jean-Luc Nancy's *The Inoperative Community*, Maurice Blanchot's *The Unavowable Community*, Giorgio Agamben's *The Coming Community*, and my own *Communitas: The Origin and Destiny of Community*. What brought these works into the same arena was a sort of modification of the previous semantic category; in the sense that, quite literally, instead of community referring to a property or a belonging of its members, it alluded rather to a constitutive alterity that also differentiated community from itself, evacuating it of any identity-making connotations. Instead of being united by a substance or *res* (thing), the individuals of a community as it was defined in these works were connected by a fault line that ran through the individuals and reciprocally contaminated them. Especially in the book by Nancy, who had opened up this perspective along a trajectory strongly marked by

Heidegger's *Mitsein* and Bataille's *être avec*, community was not conceived of as that which puts certain individuals into relationship, but rather as the very being of the relationship. To say, as Nancy claimed, that community is not a common "being," but, rather, the being "in common" of an existence that coincides with exposure to otherness, means to do away with all substantialist interpretations, whether particular and universal or subjective and objective in character. However, despite the theoretical fruitfulness of this step, a problem still remained to be solved. By removing community from the horizon of subjectivity, Nancy made its political ramifications extremely difficult to articulate — starting from the obvious difficulty of imagining a politics that stands entirely outside subjectivity — thus retaining it in a necessarily impolitical dimension. For this reason the discourse on community continued to fluctuate between a political approach that ended up being regressive — the one on small homelands of soil and blood — and a theoretically fruitful approach that was inexpressible in political terms. My impression is that at the bottom of this difficulty in expressing the new concept of community in political terms there lay a tendency on the part of its theoreticians, and of Nancy in particular, to look at it from the point of view of the *cum* rather than from that of the *munus*. It was as if the absolute privilege given to the figure of relation, of relationship, ended up eliminating its most important content — the very object of mutual exchange — and then, along with it, its potentially political significance as well.

The personal contribution that I tried to make to the discussion was a genealogical shift toward the origin of the concept. I mean that the idea of community bears within itself the key for escaping its impolitical turn and for regaining a political significance; but only by traveling back through history all the way to its Latin root of *communitas*, and even before that to the term from which this derives, namely, that of *munus*. Starting from this assumption, I set out on an interpretative path that, while motivated by the same need as the French deconstructionists, departed significantly from theirs at least with regard to one point in particular. While assuming the *pars destruens* of their discourse against identity-making communautarisms, and staying within the concept of community, I shifted attention from the sphere of the *cum*, which was the focus of Nancy's analysis, to that of the *munus*, which he had somehow left in the shadows. Its complex, bivalent meaning of "law" and "gift" — and, more specifically, of the law of a unilateral gift to others — allowed me to maintain and even emphasise the expropriative semantic category that had been developed by the deconstructionists: to belong entirely to the originary *communitas* means to give up one's most precious substance, namely, one's individual identity, in a process of gradual opening from self to the other. But at the same time, I allowed myself to take a step forward, or rather sideways, which opened up a possible avenue toward the political sphere.

Central to this passage is the paradigm of immunity, which is difficult to access from the side of the *cum* because it derives its negative or privative meaning specifically from the term *munus*. If *communitas* is what binds its members in a commitment of giving from one to the other, *immunitas*, by contrast, is what unburdens from this burden, what exonerates from this responsibility. In the same way that community refers to something general and open, immunity — or immunisation — refers to the privileged particularity of a situation that is defined by being an exception to a common condition. This is evident in legal terms, according to which someone who has immunity — whether parliamentary or diplomatic — is not subject to a jurisdiction that applies to all other citizens in derogation of the common law. But it is equally recognizable in the medical and biological meanings of the term, according to which natural or induced immunisation implies the ability of the body, by means of its own antibodies, to resist an infection caused by an external virus. By overlaying the legal and medical semantic fields, one may well conclude that if community breaks down the barriers of individual identity, immunity is the way to rebuild them, in defensive and offensive forms, against any external element that threatens it. This applies to individuals, but also to particular communities, which also tend to be immunized against any foreign element that appears to threaten them from outside. Hence the double bind implicit in immunitary dynamics — typical of modernity and increasingly widespread today in all spheres of individual and collective experience, both real and imaginary. Although immunity is necessary to the preservation of our life, when driven beyond a certain threshold it forces life into a sort of cage where not only our freedom gets lost but also the very meaning of our existence — that opening of existence outside itself that takes the name of *communitas*. This is the contradiction that I have sought to bring to attention in my work: that which protects the body (the individual body, the social body, and the body politic) is at the same time that which impedes its development. It is also that which, beyond a certain threshold, is likely to destroy it. To use the words of Walter Benjamin, one could say that immunization at high doses is the sacrifice of the living — of every qualified life, that is — for the sake of mere survival. It is the reduction of life to its bare biological matter. How the category of community can regain a new political significance, without ending up in a substantialist metaphysics, becomes clear thanks to this hermeneutic key. The moment the immunitary dispositif becomes the syndrome of our time, one that is both defensive and offensive, community presents itself as the chosen locus – the real and symbolic form – of resistance to the excess of immunization that relentlessly entraps us. If immunity tends to shut our existence up into non-communicating circles or enclosures, community is not so much a larger circle that contains them as it is a passage that cuts through their boundary lines and mixes up the human experience, freeing it from its obsession with security.

But here is where the second question that we began with gets grafted onto the first: the type of politics that we are speaking about in this case can only be a form of biopolitics. Since the phenomenon of immunity is inscribed precisely at the point of intersection between law and biology, between medical procedure and legal protection, it is clear that the politics that it gives rise to, in the form of action or reaction, must be in direct relationship with biological life. But the relationship between biopolitics on the one hand and the oppositional dialectic between community and immunity on the other is even more intrinsic – because it touches on the otherwise elusive meaning of the various kinds of dynamics bundled together that can all be traced to the biopolitical paradigm. It would be pointless to reconstruct the recent history of this paradigm here, one that originated from courses that Michel Foucault gave in the 1970s and that was pursued mainly by Italian interpreters — initially by Giorgio Agamben and Antonio Negri — who developed the extraordinary insights of the French thinker along original lines.

These authors' different approaches to the category of biopolitics, however, are precisely what point to a difficulty, or better yet, to a fundamental antinomy – one that is somehow recognizable in a latent form in Foucault's works – that consists essentially in a missing, or inadequate, joint between the two poles of *bios* and politics out of which the term "biopolitics" is composed. Rather than being joined into a single semantic block, it's as if they were designed separately and then only later related to each other. What I mean is that the radical difference between a negative, if not apocalyptic, type of interpretation and an opposite, markedly optimistic and even euphoric interpretation of biopolitics is embedded in a semantic breach, already to be found in the writings of Foucault, between two layers of meaning in the concept that were never perfectly integrated and, indeed, that were destined to break it into two parts that are mutually incompatible or only compatible through the violent subjugation of one to the dominion of the other. Thus, either life appears to be seized and seemingly imprisoned, by a power destined to reduce it to mere organic matter, or politics risks remaining dissolved in the rhythm of a life that is able to reproduce itself without interruption beyond the historical contradictions that assail it. In the first case, the tendency of the biopolitical regime is to not deviate from the sovereign regime, of which it appears to be an internal fold; in the second case, it emancipates itself from the sovereign regime almost to the point of losing all contact with its deep genealogy. As we noted earlier, Foucault himself never came to a decisive choice between these two extreme possibilities, and he continued to vacillate from one to the other without ever arriving at a definitive solution. In his categorial apparatus, the relationship between the sovereign and biopolitical regimes as well as that between modernity and totalitarianism remained clouded by this fundamental indecisiveness regarding the meaning of what he himself called "biopolitics" or "biopower" – without attributing any particular significance to this lexical difference — and even more regarding its outcomes. As I have already observed, my impression is that there is something missing from his formidable conceptual dispositif — a link or a joining segment between the two – that is able to connect these different configurations of the concept and, even prior to that, to connect the two polarities of life and politics into a more organic, complex form than the one he created, still hesitantly, in his pioneering work.

This constitutive nexus is what I have sought to identify in the paradigm of immunisation. In its dual appearance in the legal and biological realms, this paradigm is the exact point of tangency between the spheres of life and politics. This is where the possibility arises of filling the gap in principle between the two extreme interpretations of biopolitics — between its deadly version and its euphoric version. Instead of two opposing, irreconcilable ways of understanding the category, they constitute two internal possibilities, in a horizon that is unified precisely by the bivalent character of the immune dispositif, which is both positive and negative, protective and destructive. Once the dual character of the immunisation process has been established – as both the protection and negation of life — the paradigm of biopolitics or biopower can also be defined more congruously by taking immunisation as a starting point. The negative mode that has characterised the biopolitical paradigm is not a result of the violent subjugation that power exerts on life from the outside, but rather the contradictory way that life itself tries to defend itself from the dangers that threaten it, contradicting its other equally prominent needs. Immunity, necessary to the preservation of individual and collective life — none of us would stay alive without the immune system in our bodies — if assumed in a form that is exclusive and exclusionary toward all other human and environmental alterities, ends up counteracting its own development.

At stake, if you like, is the difference — which Derrida brought to the fore in another fashion — between immunisation and self-immunisation. We all know what autoimmune diseases are. They are pathological conditions that occur when our body's immune system becomes so strong that it turns against itself, causing the death of the body. This does not happen all the time, of course. Normally the immune system is limited to a role of preservation, without turning against the body that houses it. But when this does happen, it is not provoked by an external cause but rather by the immune mechanism itself, which is intensified to an intolerable degree. A similar dynamic is also recognisable in the body politic, when the protective barriers against the outside begin to represent a greater risk than what they are intended to prevent. As we know, one of our society's greatest risks today lies in an excessive demand for protection, which in some cases tends to produce an impression of danger, whether real or imagined, for the sole purpose of setting up increasingly powerful preventive defense weapons against it. This logical and historical articulation between the paradigms of biopower and immunization allows us, on the one hand, to clarify the meaning of the concept of biopolitics and, on the other, to establish an internal distinction between its negative mode and another potentially affirmative mode. The fact that the first mode was far more prevalent throughout the course of the last century than the second does not mean that the affirmative mode cannot make a reappearance.

But first things first. It has often been questioned whether the category of biopolitics has any true specificity, since politics has always, in one way or another, been involved with life, even in its strictly biological sense. Weren't agrarian policy in ancient Rome and the use of slave bodies in ancient empires forms of biopolitics? So what distinguishes them, in essence, from what has been called biopolitics? Furthermore, did biopolitics come into being with modernity, as Foucault was inclined to believe, or does it have a longer, deeper genealogy? It could be said in answer to these questions that, looked at from the point of view of its living matter, all politics has taken and will take a biopolitical form. But what caused the first modem intensification and, later on, during the totalitarian phase, its thanatopolitical development, was its immunitary character. As Nietzsche saw clearly, what we call "modernity" is nothing but a metalanguage that has allowed us to respond in immunitary terms to a series of preventive security demands that arose from the very depths of life at a time when the promises of transcendental salvation had vanished. If the paradigm of immunisation helps us to understand the structural link between modernity and biopolitics, that of autoimmunization allows us to establish the relationship as well as the element of discontinuity between modern biopolitics and the thanatopolitics of the Nazi regime. In the latter instance, not only had the racial defense of the Germanic people become the main focus of German politics – in a form that made their survival conditional on the death of their external and internal enemies – but, at a certain point, when defeat seemed inevitable, the order was even given for self-destruction. In this case, the immune syndrome took on all the lineaments of an autoimmune disorder, and biopolitics came to coincide perfectly with thanatopolitics.

As has now become clear, the end of Nazism — and then, nearly half a century later, of Soviet communism — did not mark the end of biopolitics, which has settled permanently in contemporary society in a form that may appear to have replaced the old ideologies. It is not difficult to recognize its growing presence in all areas of domestic and international politics, along a line of growing indistinction between public and private. From the health sector to that of biotechnology, from ethnic issues to the environment, the only source of political legitimacy today seems to be the preservation and implementation of life. It is precisely in this context that the need for an affirmative biopolitics returns with new urgency. This would be something — a horizon of meaning — in which life would no longer be the object but somehow the subject of politics. So what sort of shape would it take? Where would we trace its symptoms? With what objectives? This question, or set of questions, is far from easy to answer. Having experienced negative biopolitics, or even overt thanatopolitics, is not enough in itself to identify its opposite by contrast. You cannot just reverse certain practices with deadly aims into positive ones. What is required is a leap in quality in order to set up the connection between constraints and needs in a totally different way, including the expansion of financial markets and the protection of those who are weakest in social, cultural, and generational terms. In this across-the-board effort, only made possible by a new alliance between national and international politics, between individuals and collectives — including parties and movements — a first point of orientation, one that is not solely theoretical, can be found specifically in the dialectic between community and immunity that we referred to earlier. The task at hand is to overturn in some way — indeed in every way —the balance of power between "common" and "immune"; to separate the immunitary protection of life from its destruction by means of the common; to conceptualize the function of immune systems in a different way, making them into relational filters between inside and outside instead of exclusionary barriers. How? Starting from what assumptions? Using what tools? The problem has to be tackled on two levels: by disabling the apparatuses of negative immunization, and by enabling new spaces of the common.

Let's start from the first point. We have already seen how the abnormal growth in devices of control and subjugation leads to a corresponding decrease in individual and collective freedoms. Dividing barriers, blocks to the circulation of ideas, languages, and information, surveillance mechanisms set up in all the sensitive places: these are increasingly extensive forms of devitalization that, on the one hand, we must remove ourselves from, and, on the other, that we must resist by all legitimate means. This is particularly difficult to do. First, because the contemporary dispositifs — from biometrics taken at border crossings to photoelectric cells that capture us in our every move, to wiretapping that records our words or messages — are also ordered to protect society and ourselves. But there's another, more fundamental reason for the difficulty; namely, because as Foucault has made perfectly clear, the subjectification that gives meaning to our practices always takes place through some form of subjugation – so to escape subjugation always involves a desubjectivizing effect. This is why fleeing the dispositifs, or disabling them, always involves a double outcome – of liberation and isolation, of emancipation and impoverishment. Of course, to live outside the network of the Internet is possible – but at no small cost of alienation and disorientation with respect to the globalised world. What one needs to do, before causing them to shut down, or simply not allowing oneself to be captured by them, is to preventively distinguish between dispositifs of prohibition, dispositifs of control, and dispositifs of subjugation; between systems that facilitate our individual and collective experience, and apparatuses that diminish its vital power. Or even to preserve areas of silence in the midst of communications that are now extended to every moment of our lives.

But this is not enough. This is only the negative aspect — that of individual withdrawal — of a strategy that also has to be played out through positive moves. The untying of the immune bonds must be accompanied by the production of common spaces, spheres, and dimensions, which are increasingly threatened by the interference of their opposite. If you think about the term and the concept of "common," it has three opposites — the concepts of "proper," "private," and "immune" — which differ but converge in their contrastive effect. All three, in different ways, are opposed to the semantics of the common in the differing but converging forms of appropriation, privatisation, and immunisation. These are the three modes by which social ties are dissolved, but even before them, by which the idea of the "common good" is dissolved as well, continually decreasing in intensity and expanse in a world that nevertheless likes to think of itself as global. For some time now, not only philosophers but also legal theorists have started on the task of reconstituting the semantics of the concept of the common good, which is squeezed between the opposing, specular concepts of the private good and the public good. The legal system that arose in ancient Rome as private law was intended to sanction in a legally codified form the originary appropriation of things; but also the appropriation of certain human beings who were reduced to the status of thing by those who proclaimed themselves to be their owners by force. In the modern world, this dynamic of appropriation has been joined by the making public of goods assigned to the control and enjoyment of state bodies. In this way, the space of the common, which cannot be appropriated by individuals or by the state, has become increasingly thinner until it coincides with the legally undecidable area of the *res nullius*, or "nobody's property." When the general immune mechanism was set in motion, this withdrawal of the common — under the converging pressure of the proper, the private and the public — became even more sweeping. Immunity has not merely reinforced the boundaries of the proper, it has gradually assailed the sphere of the public as well. It is no coincidence that sovereignty has revealed itself to be the first, fundamental immunitary dispositif, along with the categories of property and freedom, which were also preventively immunised.

In the twilight of early modernity, when these categories came into direct contact with the horizon of biological life, the erosion of the common good — which was everybody's and nobody's, nobody's because it was everybody's — it became even more intense. Environmental resources were the first to be privatised — water, earth, air, mountains, rivers; then the city spaces, public buildings, roads, and cultural assets; and finally intellectual resources, the communication spaces, and information tools. All of this while waiting for organs of biological life to be legally available for sale and purchased by the highest bidder. Modernity — with the invention of the state, the largest political dispositif — had already intended to exclude the common good, everybody's good; or at least it reduced it more and more in favor of a dialectic between private and public designed to progressively occupy the entire social scene. In reading authors like John Locke, or even Hugo Grotius, one sees how they went about theorising the necessity to break down a world given by God to everybody – in other words, to no one in particular — into what belongs to individual owners and what belongs to the state. For a long period of time, yet to end, the concept of government property, as public property of the state, was not the opposite of private property but a complementary aspect of it. With what we usually define as globalisation, this kind of "making public" [*publicizzazione*] of the private is increasingly intertwined with the inverse phenomenon of the privatization of the public in a manner that seems to exhaust, and even exclude something like a common good from the horizon of possibilities. This becomes even more important when, with the biopolitical turn underway, any property — whether material or intellectual, corporeal or technological — directly or indirectly comes to involve the sphere of biological life, including in the latter all the resources of the intellect and language, the symbolic and the imaginary, needs and desires.

Now it is precisely on this terrain that the battle for an affirmative biopolitics must be braved and possibly won. It must start precisely by breaking the vice-like grip of public and private that threatens to crush the common, by seeking instead to expand the space of the common. The fight that has begun against the planned privatisation of water, the battle over energy sources, or the one seeking to re-examine the patents granted by pharmaceutical companies that prevent the distribution of cheaper medicines in the poorer areas of the planet all go in this direction. This is, of course, a difficult battle — also because we must not make the strategic mistake of abandoning the public space in favour of the common space, and by doing so possibly facilitate the privatization process. But we must not confuse the common good with that pertaining to the sovereignty of the state or government departments and agencies, which are in any case regulated by the prior juridical division between public and private. The problem is that there are currently no legal statutes and codes aimed at protecting the common in relation to the private, the proper, and the immune. In fact, coming prior to adequate legislation, we currently lack even a vocabulary to talk about something — the common that was effectively excluded first from the process of modernisation and then from the process of globalisation. The common is neither the public – which is dialectically opposed to the private — nor the global, to which the local corresponds. It is something largely unknown, and even refractory, to our conceptual categories, which have long been organised by the general immune dispositif. Yet the challenge for an affirmative biopolitics, *of* life and no longer *on* life, is staked precisely on this possibility: on our capacity, even before acting, to think within this horizon, to think around and even from within the common. This is the direction that has been guiding my work over recent years — including through the category of the "impersonal."

Translated by Zakiya Hanafi

CHAPTER 16

Silvia Federici (1942–)

Silvia Federici is a thinker, author and feminist activist. Born in Parma in 1942, she received her PhD in Philosophy from the University of Buffalo in 1967. She then taught at the University de Port Harcourt in Nigeria and the University of Hofstra in New York (where she is Emeritus professor). In 1972 she founded – together with Leopoldina Fortunati, Alisa del Re and Mariarosa Della Costa – the International Feminist Collective and promoted the Wages for Housework campaign. She co-founded the Committee for Academic Freedom in Africa (CAFA) and the Radical Philosophy Association (RPA). She is also a member of the Midnight Notes Collective.

As a Marxist and materialist feminist, she has argued that women's housework is part of the social reproduction of capitalism (1975). Together with the Wages for Housework campaign, Federici not only asked for compensation for unpaid domestic work but also postulated its end. The campaign demanded a wage for the domestic work carried out within one's own household. These activities were at the time unpaid and not considered to be work. In order to attain a social recognition of domestic activities, these feminists started to re-read Marx, who was considered to be both responsible for such disregard and an important source for the analysis: Federici and the campaign frequently adjust and reuse Marxian categories in order to understand these domestic activities. In a society where citizenship is linked to work, the issue of the recognition of activities relating to social reproduction goes beyond the economic dimension: it is, indeed, a political issue. If women's work inside the house is not recognized as work, then women are led to *anomia* and to the impossibility of political identity and representation.

Later on, Federici focused on the transition to capitalism in Europe, pinpointing the emergent capitalist class's urge to control working-class reproduction, namely to eliminate working-class women's control over biological reproduction. Capitalism forced women into unpaid reproductive work in the home by restricting abortions and fuelled the campaign against witches during this period in order to eliminate every form of shared female social knowledge and authority (Federici 2004). In the primitive accumulation process, women and men do not share the same destiny. Women are dispossessed not only of the means of subsistence but also of their practical and social knowledges, their self-determination over their bodies, sociability, relationships, and any form of authority. Gender and race become elements of division and exclusion. Caliban and the Witch become subjects outside of the normal, whose subalternity and subjugation go beyond the exploitation of work and economic dispossession.

Capitalism's *Divide et impera* creates a new dichotomy between productive activities (producing surplus value) and reproductive activities (considered unproductive, even though they make production possible and surplus value all the greater).

Federici highlighted the fundamental role played by feminism and anti-colonialist struggles in their revolutionizing of the traditional categories of the social sciences, whose theories have always tried to provide solutions to existential and social issues. Social sciences can still change societies, as long as they refuse to be immediate instruments of power. For Federici, the link between power and knowledge is inextricable: when power is linked to knowledge, the awareness of those social issues is lost.

Federici has also assessed the world economic development of capitalism as a contradictory force for the liberation of women (2004) and has addressed the restructuring of work and its impact on women and gender culture as an effect of neo-liberal economic adjustments (2008). Precarity and the dangerous shift from welfare to workfare clearly demonstrate the failure of the identification between paid work and citizenship, as well as the idea that women's liberation would arise from the end of the sexual division of labour.

Federici's recent interests revolve around the topic of global capitalism and the link between feminism, reproductive work and the politics of the *commons*. Federici re-reads the issues and the central points of the international debate on commons and identifies commons as a real terrain for a production of new subjectivities, focusing on women's role in the creation, care, resistance and the defence of commons.

Federica Castelli

Selected writings

Federici, Silvia. *Wages Against Housework*. Bristol: Power of Women Collective and the Falling Wall Press, 1975

Federici, Silvia. *Caliban and the Witch: Women, the Body and Primitive Accumulation*. Brooklyn, NY: Autonomedia, 2004

Federici, Silvia. 'The Great Caliban: The Struggle Against the Rebel Body'. *Capitalism Nature Socialism* 15, no. 2. (2004): 7–16.

Federici, Silvia. *Revolution at Point Zero: Housework, Reproduction, and Feminist Struggle*, Brooklyn, NY: Autonomedia, 2012

Federici, Silvia. *Re-enchanting the World: Feminism and the Politics of the Commons*. Oakland, CA: Kairos/PM Press, 2018

Federici, Silvia. *Witches, Witch-Hunting, and Women*, Oakland, CA: PM Press, 2018

EXCERPT

Silvia Federici, Feminism and the Politics of the Common in an Era of Primitive Accumulation

(Silvia Federici, 'Feminism and the Politics of the Commons in an Era of Primitive Accumulation'. In Federici, *Revolution at Point Zero*, Brooklyn, NY: Autonomedia, 2012, pp. 138–48.)

Introduction: Why Commons?

At least since the Zapatistas, on December 31, 1993, took over the zócalo of San Cristóbal to protest legislation dissolving the ejidal lands of Mexico, the concept of the 'commons' has gained popularity among the radical Left, internationally and in the United States, appearing as a ground of convergence among anarchists, Marxists/socialists, ecologists, and eco-feminists.

There are important reasons why this apparently archaic idea has come to the centre of political discussion in contemporary social movements. Two in particular stand out. On the one side, there has been the demise of the statist model of revolution that for decades has sapped the efforts of radical movements to build an alternative to capitalism. On the other, the neoliberal attempt to subordinate every form of life and knowledge to the logic of the market has heightened our awareness of the danger of living in a world in which we no longer have access to seas, trees, animals, and our fellow beings except through the cash-nexus. The 'new enclosures' have also made visible a world of communal properties and relations that many had believed to be extinct or had not valued until threatened with privatization. The new enclosures ironically demonstrated that not only have commons not vanished, but new forms of social cooperation are constantly being produced, also in areas of life where none previously existed, as for example the Internet.

The idea of the common/s, in this context, has offered a logical and historical alternative to both State and Private Property, the State and the Market, enabling us to reject the fiction that they are mutually exclusive and exhaustive of our political possibilities. It has also served an ideological function, as a unifying concept prefiguring the cooperative society that the radical Left is striving to create. Nevertheless, ambiguities as well as significant differences exist in the interpretations of this concept, which we need to clarify, if we want the principle of the commons to translate into a coherent political project.

What, for example, constitutes a common? Examples abound. We have land, water, air commons, digital commons, service commons; our acquired entitlements (e.g. social security pensions) are often described as commons, and so are languages, libraries, and the collective products of past cultures. But are all these 'commons' on the same level from the viewpoint of devising an anticapitalist strategy? Are they all compatible? And how can we ensure that they do not project a unity that remains to be constructed?

With these questions in mind, in this essay, I look at the politics of the commons from a feminist perspective, where feminist refers to a standpoint shaped by the struggle against sexual discrimination and over reproductive work, which (quoting Linebaugh) is the rock upon which society is built, and by which every model of social organisation must be tested. This intervention is necessary, in my view, to better define this politics, expand a debate that so far has remained male-dominated, and clarify under what conditions the principle of the common/s can become the foundation of an anticapitalist program. Two concerns make these tasks especially important.

Global commons, World Bank commons

First, since at least the early 1990s, the language of the commons has been appropriated by the World Bank and the United Nations, and put at the service of privatization. Under the guise of protecting biodiversity and conserving 'global commons,' the Bank has turned rain forests into ecological reserves, has expelled the populations that for centuries had drawn their sustenance from them, while making them available to people who do not need them but can pay for them, for instance, through ecotourism. On its side, the United Nations, in the name again of preserving the common heritage of mankind, has revised the international law governing access to the oceans, in ways enabling governments to consolidate the use of seawaters in fewer hands.

The World Bank and the United Nations are not alone in their adaptation of the idea of the commons to market interests. Responding to different motivations, a revalorisation of the commons has become trendy among mainstream economists and capitalist planners, witness the growing academic literature on the subject and its cognates: 'social capital,' 'gift economies,' 'altruism.' Witness also the official recognition of this trend through the conferral of the Nobel Prize for Economics in 2009 on the leading voice in this field, the political scientist Elinor Ostrom.

Development planners and policy-makers have discovered that, under proper conditions, a collective management of natural resources can be more efficient and less conflictual than privatization, and commons can very well be made to produce for the market. They have also recognized that, carried to the extreme, the commodification of social relations has self-defeating consequences. The extension of the commodity-form to every corner of the social factory, which neoliberalism has promoted, is an ideal limit for capitalist ideologues, but it is a project not only unrealisable but undesirable from the viewpoint of the long-term reproduction of the capitalist system. Capitalist accumulation is structurally dependent on the free appropriation of immense areas of labour and resources that must appear as externalities to the market, like the unpaid domestic work that women have provided, on which employers have relied for the reproduction of the workforce.

Not accidentally, then, long before the Wall Street "meltdown," a variety of economists and social theorists warned that the marketization of all spheres of life is detrimental to the market's well-functioning, for markets too—the argument goes—depend on the existence of nonmonetary relations like confidence, trust, and gift-giving. In brief, capital is learning about the virtues of the 'common good.' In its July 31, 2008 issue, even the London *Economist*, the organ of capitalist free-market economics for more than one hundred and fifty years, cautiously joined the chorus. 'The economics of the new commons', the journal wrote, 'is still in its infancy. It is too soon to be confident about its hypotheses. But it may yet prove a useful way of thinking about problems, such as managing the internet, intellectual property or international pollution, on which policymakers need all the help they can get'. We must be very careful, then, not to craft the discourse on the commons in such a way as to allow a crisis-ridden capitalist class to revive itself, posturing, for instance, as the guardian of the planet.

What commons?

A second concern is that, while international institutions have learned to make commons functional to the market, how commons can become the foundation of a noncapitalist economy is a question still unanswered. From Peter Linebaugh's work, especially *The Magna Carta Manifesto* (2008), we have learned that commons have been the thread that has connected the history of the class struggle into our time, and indeed the fight for the commons is all around us. Mainers are fighting to preserve their fisheries and waters, residents of the Appalachian regions are joining to save their mountains threatened by strip mining, open source, and free software movements are opposing the commodification of knowledge and opening new spaces for communications and cooperation. We also have the many invisible, commoning activities and communities that people are creating in North America, which Chris Carlsson has described in his *Nowtopia*. As Carlsson shows, much creativity is invested in the production of 'virtual commons' and forms of sociality that thrive under the radar of the money/market economy.

Most important has been the creation of urban gardens, which have spread, in the 1980s and 1990s, across the country, thanks mostly to the initiatives of immigrant communities from Africa, the Caribbean or the South of the United States. Their significance cannot be overestimated. Urban gardens have opened the way to a 'rurbanisation' process that is indispensable if we are to regain control over our food production, regenerate our environment and provide for our subsistence. The gardens are far more than a source of food security. They are centres of sociality, knowledge production, cultural and intergenerational exchange. As Margarita Fernandez writes of gardens in New York, urban gardens 'strengthen community cohesion,' as places where people come together not just to work the land, but to play cards, hold weddings, have baby showers or birthday parties. Some have a partnership relation with local schools, whereby they give children after school environmental education. Not last, gardens are 'a medium for the transport and encounter of diverse cultural practices,' so that African vegetables and farming practices (e.g.) mix with those from the Caribbean.

Still, the most significant feature of urban gardens is that they produce for neighbourhood consumption, rather than for commercial purposes. This distinguishes them from other reproductive commons that either produce for the market, like the fisheries of the 'Lobster Coast' of Maine, or are bought on the market, like the land-trusts that preserve the open spaces. The problem, however, is that urban gardens have remained a spontaneous grassroots initiative, and there have been few attempts by movements in the United States to expand their presence, and to make access to land a key terrain of struggle. More generally, how the many proliferating commons, being defended, developed, fought for, can be brought together to form a cohesive whole providing a foundation for a new mode of production is a question the Left has not posed.

An exception is the theory proposed by Negri and Hardt in *Empire* (2000), *Multitude* (2004), and more recently *Commonwealth* (2009), which argues that a society built on the principle of 'the common' is already evolving from the informatization of production. According to this theory, as production becomes predominantly a production of knowledge organized through the Internet, a common space is formed which escapes the problem of defining rules of inclusion or exclusion, because access and use multiply the resources available on the net, rather than subtracting from them, thus signifying the possibility of a society built on abundance — the only remaining hurdle confronting the 'multitude' being presumably how to prevent the capitalist "capture" of the wealth produced.

The appeal of this theory is that it does not separate the formation of 'the common' from the organisation of work and production as already constituted, but sees it immanent in it. Its limit is that it does not question the material basis of the digital technology the Internet relies upon, overlooking the fact that computers depend on economic activities — mining, microchip and rare earth production — that, as currently organized, are extremely destructive, socially and ecologically. Moreover, with its emphasis on science, knowledge production and information, this theory skirts the question of the reproduction of everyday life. This, however, is true of the discourse on the commons as a whole, which has generally focused on the formal preconditions for their existence but much less on the possibilities provided by existing commons, and their potential to create forms of reproduction enabling us to resist dependence on wage labour and subordination to capitalist relations.

Women and the commons

It is in this context that a feminist perspective on the commons is important. It begins with the realisation that, as the primary subjects of reproductive work, historically and in our time, women have depended more than men on access to communal resources, and have been most committed to their defence. As I wrote in *Caliban and the Witch* (2004), in the first phase of capitalist development, women were in the front of the struggle against land enclosures both in England and the 'New World,' and the staunchest defenders of the communal cultures that European colonization attempted to destroy. In Peru, when the Spanish conquistadores took control of their villages, women fled to the high mountains, where they recreated forms of collective life that have survived to this day. Not surprisingly, the sixteenth and seventeenth centuries saw the most violent attack on women in the history of the world: the persecution of women as witches. Today, in the face of a new process of Primitive Accumulation, women are the main social force standing in the way of a complete commercialization of nature. Women are the subsistence farmers of the world. In Africa, they produce 80 percent of the food people consume, despite the attempts made by the World Bank and other agencies to convince them to divert their activities to cash-cropping. Refusal to be without access to land has been so strong that, in the towns, many women have taken over plots in public lands, planted corn and cassava in vacant lots, in this process changing the urban landscape of African cities and breaking down the separation between town and country. In India too, women have restored degraded forests, guarded trees, joined hands to chase away the loggers, and made blockades against mining operations and the construction of dams.

The other side of women's struggle for direct access to means of reproduction has been the formation, across the Third World — from Cambodia to Senegal — of credit associations that function as money commons. Differently named, "tontines" (in parts of Africa) are autonomous, self-managed, women-made banking systems, providing cash to individuals or groups that can have no access to banks, working purely on the basis of trust. In this, they are completely different from the microcredit systems promoted by the World Bank, which functions on the basis of shame, arriving at the extreme (e.g., in Niger) of posting in public places the pictures of the women who fail to repay the loans so that some have been driven to suicide.

Women have also led the effort to collectivize reproductive labour both as a means to economize on the cost of reproduction, and protect each other from poverty, state violence and the violence of individual men. An outstanding example are the ola communes (common kitchens) that women in Chile and in Peru set up in the 1980s, when, due to stiff inflation, they could no longer afford to shop alone. Like collective reforestation and land reclamation, these practices are the expression of a world where communal bonds are still strong. It would be a mistake, however, to consider them as something prepolitical, 'natural,' a product of 'tradition'. In reality, as Leo Podlashuc notes in 'Saving the Women Saving the Commons', these struggles shape a collective identity, constitute a counterpower in the home and the community, and open a process of self-valorization and self-determination from which we have much to learn.

The first lesson to be gained from these struggles is that the "commoning" of the material means of reproduction is the primary mechanism by which a collective interest and mutual bonds are created. It is also the first line of resistance to a life of enslavement, whether in armies, brothels or sweatshops. For us, in North America, an added lesson is that by pooling our resources, by reclaiming land and waters, and turning them into a common, we could begin to de-link our reproduction from the commodity flows that through the world market are responsible for the dispossession of so many people in other parts of the world. We could disentangle our livelihood, not only from the world market but from the war-machine and prison system on which the hegemony of the world market depends. Last, but not least, we could move beyond the abstract solidarity that often characterizes relations in the movement, which limits our commitment and capacity to endure, and the risks we are willing to take.

Undoubtedly, this is a formidable task that can only be accomplished through a long-term process of consciousness raising, cross-cultural exchange, and coalition building, with all the communities throughout the United States who are vitally interested in the reclamation of the land, starting with the First American Nations. Although this task may seem more difficult now than passing through the eye of a needle, it is also the only condition to broaden the space of our autonomy, cease feeding into the process of capital accumulation, and refuse to accept that our reproduction occurs at the expense of the world's other commoners and commons.

Feminist reconstructions

What this task entails is powerfully expressed by Maria Mies when she points out that the production of commons requires first a profound transformation in our everyday life, in order to recombine what the social division of labour in capitalism has separated. For the distancing of production from reproduction and consumption leads us to ignore the conditions under which what we eat or wear, or work with, have been produced, their social and environmental cost, and the fate of the population on whom the waste we produce is unloaded.

In other words, we need to overcome the state of constant denial and irresponsibility, concerning the consequences of our actions, resulting from the destructive ways in which the social division of labour is organized in capitalism; short of that, the production of our life inevitably becomes a production of death for others. As Mies points out, globalization has worsened this crisis, widening the distances between what is produced and what is consumed, thereby intensifying, despite the appearance of an increased global interconnectedness, our blindness to the blood in the food we eat, the petroleum we use, the clothes we wear, the computers with which we communicate.

Overcoming this oblivion is where a feminist perspective teaches us to start in our reconstruction of the commons. No common is possible unless we refuse to base our life, our reproduction on the suffering of others, unless we refuse to see ourselves as separate from them. Indeed if "commoning" has any meaning, it must be the production of ourselves as a common subject. This is how we must understand the slogan 'no commons without community'. But 'community' not intended as a gated reality, a grouping of people joined by exclusive interests separating them from others, as with community formed on the basis of religion or ethnicity. Community as a quality of relations, a principle of cooperation and responsibility: to each other, the earth, the forests, the seas, the animals.

Certainly, the achievement of such community, like the collectivizing of our everyday work of reproduction, can only be a beginning. It is no substitute for broader antiprivatisation campaigns and the reconstitution of our commonwealth. But it is an essential part of the process of our education for collective governance and the recognition of history as a collective project — the main casualty of the neoliberal era of capitalism.

On this account, we must include in our political agenda the communalization/collectivization of housework, reviving that rich feminist tradition that we have in the United States, that stretches from the utopian socialist experiments of the mid-nineteenth century to the attempts that the 'materialist feminists' made, from the late nineteenth century to the early twentieth century, to reorganize and socialize domestic work and thereby the home, and the neighbourhood, through collective housekeeping — efforts that continued until the 1920s, when the 'Red Scare' put an end to them. These practices, and the ability that past feminists have had to look at reproductive labour as an important sphere of human activity, not to be negated but to be revolutionized, must be revisited and revalorized.

One crucial reason for creating collective forms of living is that the reproduction of human beings is the most labour-intensive work on earth, and to a large extent it is work that is irreducible to mechanization. We cannot mechanize childcare or the care of the ill, or the psychological work necessary to reintegrate our physical and emotional balance. Despite the efforts that futuristic industrialists are making, we cannot robotize 'care' except at a terrible cost for the people involved. No one will accept 'nursebots' as care givers, especially for children and the ill. Shared responsibility and cooperative work, not given at the cost of the health of the providers, are the only guarantees of proper care. For centuries the reproduction of human beings has been a collective process. It has been the work of extended families and communities, on which people could rely, especially in proletarian neighbourhoods, even when they lived alone, so that old age was not accompanied by the desolate loneliness and dependence that so many of our elderly experience. It is only with the advent of capitalism that reproduction has been completely privatized, a process that is now carried to a degree that it destroys our lives. This we need to change if we are to put an end to the steady devaluation and fragmentation of our lives.

The times are propitious for such a start. As the capitalist crisis is destroying the basic element of reproduction for millions of people across the world, including the United States, the reconstruction of our everyday life is a possibility and a necessity. Like strikes, social/economic crises break the discipline of wage-work, forcing upon us new forms of sociality. This is what occurred during the Great Depression, which produced a movement of hobo-men who turned the freight trains into their commons, seeking freedom in mobility and nomadism. At the intersections of railroad lines, they organized 'hobo jungles', prefigurations, with their self-governance rules and solidarity, of the communist world in which many of their residents believed. However, but for a few 'box-car Berthas', this was predominantly a masculine world, a fraternity of men, and in the long term it could not be sustained. Once the economic crisis and the war came to an end, the hobo men were domesticated by the two grand engines of labour-power fixation: the family and the house. Mindful of the threat of working class recomposition in the Depression, American capital excelled in its application of the principle that has characterized the organization of economic life: cooperation at the point of production, separation and atomization at the point of reproduction. The atomized, serialized family-house Levittown provided, compounded by its umbilical appendix, the car, not only sedentarized the worker, but put an end to the type of autonomous workers' commons the hobo jungles had represented. Today, as millions of Americans' houses and cars have been repossessed, as foreclosures, evictions, the massive loss of employment are again breaking down the pillars of the capitalist discipline of work, new common grounds are again taking shape, like the tent cities that are sprawling from coast to coast. This time, however, it is women who must build the new commons, so that they do not remain transient spaces or temporary autonomous zones, but become the foundation of new forms of social reproduction.

If the house is the *oikos* on which the economy is built, then it is women, historically the house-workers and house-prisoners, who must take the initiative to reclaim the house as a centre of collective life, one traversed by multiple people and forms of cooperation, providing safety without isolation and fixation, allowing for the sharing and circulation of community possessions, and above all providing the foundation for collective forms of reproduction. As already suggested, we can draw inspiration for this project from the programmes of the nineteenth century 'materialist feminists' who, convinced that the home was an important 'spatial component of the oppression of women' organized communal kitchens, cooperative households, calling for workers' control of reproduction. These objectives are crucial at present: breaking down the isolation of life in a private home is not only a precondition for meeting our most basic needs and increasing our power with regard to employers and the state. As Massimo de Angelis has reminded us, it is also a protection from ecological disaster. For there can be no doubt about the destructive consequences of the 'uneconomic' multiplication of reproductive assets and self-enclosed dwellings, dissipating, in the winter, warmth into the atmosphere, exposing us to unmitigated heat in the summer, which we now call our homes. Most important, we cannot build an alternative society and a strong self-reproducing movement unless we redefine in more cooperative ways our reproduction and put an end to the separation between the personal and the political, political activism and the reproduction of everyday life.

It remains to clarify that assigning women this task of commoning/collectivizing reproduction is not to concede to a naturalistic conception of 'femininity'. Understandably, many feminists would view this possibility as 'a fate worse than death'. It is deeply sculpted in our collective consciousness that women have been designated as men's common, a natural source of wealth and services to be as freely appropriated by them as the capitalists have appropriated the wealth of nature. But, quoting Dolores Hayden, the reorganization of reproductive work, and therefore the reorganisation of the structure of housing and public space is not a question of identity; it is a labour question and, we can add, a power and safety question. I am reminded here of the experience of the women members of the Landless People's Movement of Brazil (MST), who, when their communities won the right to maintain the land which they had occupied, insisted that the new houses should be build to form one compound, so that they could continue to share their housework, wash together, cook together, taking turns with men, as they had done in the course of the struggle, and be ready to run to give each other support if abused by men. Arguing that women should take the lead in the collectivization of reproductive work and housing is not to naturalize housework as a female vocation. It is refusing to obliterate the collective experiences, knowledge, and struggles that women have accumulated concerning reproductive work, whose history has been an essential part of our resistance to capitalism. Reconnecting with this history is today for women and men a crucial step, both for undoing the gendered architecture of our lives and reconstructing our homes and lives as commons.

CHAPTER 17

Maurizio Ferraris (1956–)

It is generally thought that the movement within continental philosophy known as 'Speculative Realism' began in 2006. Maurizio Ferraris, however, had been arguing for what he later deemed a 'New Realism' since at least 1997, in a book entitled *Estetica Razionale* (*Rational Aesthetics*).

Ferraris built his realism on the ruins of three dogmas which characterize the transcendental philosophy he intends to surpass: the first involves a confusion of epistemology and ontology that Ferraris associates with a certain 'postmodern', constructivist combination of Foucault and Kant (nicknamed 'Foukant'), which is understood to issue in an idealism for which only what is thought and spoken about may be said to exist. On this account, any experience of the real is a construction or reconstruction within thought and speech (in *logos*, then) such that the idea of a 'given' prior to its own conceptualization is simply, in Wilfred Sellars's words, a 'myth'.

If in the first dogma of transcendentalism, ontology is subordinated to epistemology, then, in a Kantian vein, most fully developed by J. G. Fichte, transcendental philosophy asserts the primacy of the practical – the priority of practical reason over theoretical reason. This is the second dogma. It entails that epistemology is in turn subordinated to finality or purpose, goals which cannot be met with in experience or 'nature' itself, but which are posited autonomously by reason. This renders the realm of normativity radically distinct from that of nature. That the moral subject is motivated by supernatural 'ideas' ensures that the domain of Reason and indeed the subject itself can operate quite independently of their natural determinations and of the causality to be found in nature.

Just as nature is constructed by reason, so the rational subject is free simply to construct itself, to create and recreate itself.

The third dogma of transcendentalism sublates the first two by affirming that the very entertaining of purposes in the mind can result in the *attainment* of such purposes in reality. In this sense, transcendentalism avers that thinking is ultimately responsible for reality, not just in a theoretical epistemological sense but in a practical sense, such that reason controls, manipulates and even brings about that which it first posited merely as an ideal. Thinking posits being, and what is in being is exhausted by that which can be posited by rational thought.

It is against these three dogmas of an anti-realist type that the realism of Ferraris, along with the other, belated realists in continental philosophy – together with their forebear, F. W. J. Schelling – have directed their efforts.

The realm of rational representation, in which being is correlated with thought, is to be reconceived as merely one *region* among others, in a vaster thoughtless universe. This is to say that rational thought is situated within a broader environment which both conditions thought – together with its correlate (the object of thought) – and transcends it. For Ferraris, in general, 'to exist is to exist in an environment', which amounts to saying that any system will always be encompassed by a greater system.

This environment, to which thought must accommodate itself, and which it is incapable of fully appropriating, is addressed by what Ferraris calls a 'naive physics'. This physics rescues ontology from the clutches of epistemology, for it involves the claim that our perception is not exhausted by those elements within it which may be understood. The non-epistemic element of our perceptual or 'aesthetic' experience reveals itself most vividly when this experience exhibits something new, something which contradicts established knowledge. Nature here demonstrates itself to be unamendable, not amenable to knowledge's strictures, and most certainly not the posit of reason. This is the environment within which the system of thought finds itself engulfed, and at the mercy of which thought stands.

This resistance of the real, of the being which gives thinking, is one aspect of Ferraris's invocation of a certain negativity, which he deploys in opposition to idealism's positivity, the assertion that thinking posits being, and that being is nothing besides that which is posited by thought.

The other aspect of this negativity concerns that which the New Realism is realist *about*: we should not be realist concerning objects or individual things; the fundamental ontological unit is not the thing, but the environment within which such things are said to exist. This environmental real cannot be said to derive from reason and thus remains recalcitrant to its activity. This recalcitrance, this negativity, should be considered as real as the constructed objects which are situated within this broader physical or natural environment that reason could *not* have constructed. Both the real and the ideal, unconstructed nature and (rationally) constructed artifice, are *both* the case – both 'obtain' – in Ferraris's ontology. Such is the extent of its realism, a realism which escapes from the dogmas of both transcendentalism and naturalism.

Iain Hamilton Grant (edited by Michael Lewis)

Selected writings

Ferraris, Maurizio. *Estetica Razionale (Rational Aesthetics)* Milan: Cortina
Raffaello, [1997] 2011

Selected writings in English

Ferraris, Maurizio. *Manifesto of New Realism*. Albany, NY: SUNY Press, [2012]
2014. (Translation of Manifesto del nuovo realismo, 2012)
Ferraris, Maurizio. *Positive Realism*. Winchester: Zero Books, 2015a. (Translation
of Realismo Positivo, 2013)
Ferraris, Maurizio. *Introduction to New Realism*, trans. Sarah De Sanctis. London:
Bloomsbury Academic, 2015b.
Ferraris, Maurizio. 'Transcendental Realism'. *The Monist* 98, no. 2 (2015):
215–32

EXCERPT

Transcendental realism

(Maurizio Ferraris, 'Transcendental Realism' in *The Monist* 98(2) 2015, pp. 215–32.)

First I propose to show that between post-Kantian idealism and postmodern idealism there is only a difference of degree. In fact, both can be traced back to the same root, since both postulate that ontology depends on epistemology. [. . .]

Constructivism is the view according to which we can have certain knowledge about the outside world only if we can generalise the construction processes by means of which geometry derives theorems (i.e., knowledge that is actual and, being deductive, certain) from axioms. Note that on this view both our knowledge of geometry and geometrical objects themselves are constructed through one and the same process. This idea underlies the thesis that prior to any empirical knowledge we have certain *a priori* principles that make possible both our *knowledge* of external reality and the very *existence* of the objects of that knowledge.

Obviously arguments for this thesis can be articulated in many ways, which I will examine in detail. However, all of them are variations of transcendentalism and all follow from the latter's constitutive misunderstanding, otherwise known as the "transcendental fallacy": the confusion between ontology (what there is) and epistemology (what we know, or think we know). [. . .].

The premise of constructivism is what I propose to call the "argument from correlation": objects exist only in correlation with their subjects. This argument, which makes the existence of objects depend on their thinkability or perceptibility by a subject, is the basis of that fundamental character of modern philosophy that has been called "correlationism".

It has been said that correlationism is not capable of accounting for a reality that pre-exists the subject. But a radical correlationist could claim that God created us, with all our memories, just a few seconds ago. In my view, it is more important that correlationism is unable to respond to the objection of solipsism. In fact, if correlationism were true, we would have at least as many mental worlds as there are subjects, and the passage from one mental world to another would be inexplicable. *De facto*, the world of correlationism is made up of just one single monad: a subject representing objects within itself. This, ultimately, is the world represented by Kant in his refutation of idealism [. . .]

Thus, as I will argue below, the fundamental obstacle to correlationism lies not in pre-existence, but rather in interobservation and interrelation — in other words, in the fact that different subjects can observe the same object; different objects, humans and other living things, can interact in the same space. To explain these circumstances by means of correlationism, one would have to invoke some kind of pre-established harmony among all those correlations and this, as we shall see, is a forceful argument in favour of transcendental realism. [. . .] Since a correlationist cannot think that interaction is made possible by properties of both objects and (animal and human) subjects existing independently of this interaction, she has to claim that interaction is made possible by the *subjects*, or rather, by the single *subject*, alone.

In this sense correlationism evolves logically into constructivism. It implies not merely that objects are *known* only in correlation with the subject, but further that objects are somehow *constructed by* the subject. In fact, if correlation does not imply the construction of objects in this way, then the fundamental thesis of correlationism is nothing more than a tautology: when I see the screen of this computer, my knowledge of the screen somehow depends on me (epistemological dependence). If correlationism wants to say something significant, then it has to turn itself into a constructivism of the form: when I see this screen, the existence of the screen somehow depends on me (ontological dependence). [. . .] If correlationism is forced to transform correlation into dependence, then constructivism is forced to clarify what this dependence is and to specify how strong it is, and on this point the three alternatives from which we can choose are, by increasing weakness, causal, conceptual and representational dependence.

Causal dependence is an ontological dependence for which:

if X exists, then X is caused to exist by a subject, that is, this causality is a necessary condition for X to exist.

To my knowledge, the only philosopher who has actually supported this causal dependence thesis is the Italian neo-idealist Giovanni Gentile. Unlike Berkeley's idealism or its contemporary revival, Gentile's philosophy posits that the cause of representations is not God but rather the finite knowing subject [. . .].

Gentile should not be underrated. He says openly what many postmodern philosophers, as we shall see, have said in a more convoluted way. However, if his (and their) theory were true, there would be openly absurd consequences. There would be no difference between introspection and knowledge of the external world. All things past, from dinosaurs to the Sumerians, would be present exactly like the thoughts that think of them. All things future would be no less present than all things past. Everything not present to some subject would be nonexistent; on the other hand, anything he thinks of, including Pegasus, would thereby exist, though only at the exact moment when he thinks of it.

To avoid the problems related to causal dependence, idealists sometimes speak instead of "conceptual dependence."

It is a necessary condition for the existence of X that X is conceptualised by a subject.

This thesis is one of the possible outcomes of Kant's famous statement: "intuitions without concepts are blind." The latter, however, may be interpreted in two ways: (1) The weak form, for which without the concept of 'dinosaur' we would not *recognise* a dinosaur if we saw one. And (2) the strong form, for which without the concept of 'dinosaur' we would not *see* a dinosaur if we saw one. When it comes to defending Kant, it is usually said that he meant only (1): conceptuality is reconstructive of experience in general. But had he meant (1), his philosophy would have been only an epistemology and not an ontology aimed at securing not only the possibility, but also the objective certainty, of knowledge. The only way to counter sceptical objections convincingly is to hold that experience itself is constituted by concepts.

A defender of conceptual dependence thus faces an impasse. In fact, the strong (which is to say, ontological) version of conceptual dependence can be traced back to causal dependence and is subject to the same criticism: by positing that subjects create reality, it has the same absurd consequences as Gentile's theory. On the other hand, the weak (epistemological) version of conceptual dependence is not a real dependence at all, since it is trivially false to state that a Tyrannosaurus rex depends on our conceptual schemes, just as it is trivially true to state that *naming* such a creature "Tyrannosaurus rex" depends on our conceptual schemes. [. . .]

"[R]epresentational dependence" [. . .] posits that:

it is a necessary condition for the existence of X that X is represented by a subject.

Compared to conceptual dependence, representational dependence has the feature of being programmatically vague. While conceptual dependence claims that intuitions depend on concepts, representational dependence suggests that our vocabulary exercises a certain kind of influence over the external world. Notwithstanding this, the problems of conceptual dependence arise here once again. If "representational dependence" means simply that the name "dinosaur" depends on us, then it is a triviality. If it means that a dinosaur's *being* depends on us, then it faces a problem in giving an account of the fact that there were already dinosaurs when we were not yet there. [. . .]

But if, as we have seen, to avoid countersensical outcomes representational dependence has to be related merely to nomenclature, asserting merely that the names of the known objects depend on the knowing subjects, how can representationalists act as if this dependence were something nontrivial (as if it were an authentic kind of dependence)?

For this to happen it is necessary to radically redefine the task of philosophy so that it will be interested not in nature (on which, not by accident, philosophy has had little or nothing to say during the past two centuries) but rather only in culture, regarding it as a "second nature." It is manifest that at this point one can consider representational dependence to be an authentic dependence — indeed some phenomena seem to lead us precisely in this direction in regard to the social world, where changing vocabulary sometimes seems to coincide with changing reality (an idea encapsulated in Orwell's Newspeak).

[T]his attitude is the underlying reason for the popularity of culturalism, whose fundamental assumption is:

> *it is a necessary condition of the existence of X that X is culturally meaningful.*

Philosophical catchphrases widespread in the continental arena such as "language is the house of being" (Heidegger); "being that can be understood is language" (Gadamer); or "there is no outside-text" (Derrida) are nothing more than different formulations of this thesis.

[. . .] In all these cases, one witnesses a form of *esse est concipi*, for which the language used to describe a portion of reality is mistaken for that reality itself. The map is mistaken for the territory. [. . .]

Behind the scenes [. . .] there lurks a very strong implicit ontological commitment, which consists of one or other thesis along the lines of:

> *there is not a subject and an object; there is only the relation between subject and object.*

This, though, raises a crucial problem from the ontological point of view. For the only coherent way to defend (for example) the thesis that *the correlation between knowing and known* is *the only form of existence* (indeed, *esse est concipi)* means embracing an idealism that leaves no room for anything material, since evidently the *relation* takes place only in the mind. The difference between nineteenth and twentieth-century idealism is therefore much smaller than Rorty thought [. . .]. By claiming that the spirit (and its secularised version as "epistemology") is the condition of the possibility of ontology, culturalism turns out to be yet another form of transcendental idealism.

Unlike idealism, the position I call transcendental realism is very sensitive to the difference between observation and introspection. It states that the observer observes in the observed something different and independent of the observer. This thesis is *realist* in so far as it presupposes a reality (above all a material reality) other than knowledge, that is, a reality that does not depend on the subject in any of the ways I have illustrated above. And it is *transcendental* because it regards this reality as the condition of the possibility of knowledge [. . .]. Transcendental realism comprises two components, which I call *negative* and *positive* realism. [. . .] The underlying assumption of negative realism is that ontology is independent from epistemology. [. . .] [T]he fundamental thesis of negative realism is:

> *ontology resists epistemology.*

[I]f external reality (a significant part of ontology) were indeed the result of a constructive activity of the knowing subject (a significant part of epistemology), then there would be no reason to ever encounter resistance in our experience of external reality. If, therefore, we do encounter such resistance, then there are good reasons to think that external reality is not constructed by the knowing subject. [. . .] As we have seen, if transcendental idealism rests on the argument from correlation for which objects exist only in correlation with their subjects, negative realism insists on the resistance of objects. If objects (or at least a good part of them) resist subjects, it means that such correlation as exists between subjects and objects does not entail that the latter causally depend on the former: it is not a case of ontological dependence. Based on this consideration, I propose to criticise the argument from correlation by means of the argument from unamendability [. . .]:

- The argument from correlation states that objects exist only in correlation with their subjects.

- In order for this correlation to entail a real dependence of the object on the subject, it is necessary (as asserted by Gentile) that the subject construct the object by means of thought.

- But we have considerable evidence of the fact that we cannot amend objects by the mere force of thought.

- Therefore it is false that objects causally depend on their subjects.

Given that causal dependence is the only nontrivial type of dependence, and given that representational dependence and cultural dependence are pseudo-dependences, the argument from unamendability demonstrates that the argument from correlation is unsound.

The argument from unamendability plays an essential role in the realist strategy. For otherwise the correlationist, when faced with the thesis that *ontology resists epistemology*, might object that, when *I* experience the resistance of a given object, then *I* am the one who is doing the experiencing, and therefore the argument from correlation is still sound. At this point, however, the realist can ask of the correlationist that he amend the object by means of some act of knowledge. The correlationist will certainly fail in this task [. . .].

So, unlike epistemology, which can always be corrected and improved, ontology is unamendable. From the ontological point of view, resistance thus manifests itself as unamendability: things cannot be corrected or transformed by means of representations. [. . .]

[T]he fundamental thesis of positive realism [affirms] that

epistemology emerges from ontology.

If construction is the cornerstone of transcendental idealism and resistance is the fundamental element of negative realism, then emergence is the basic characteristic of positive realism. Negative realism shows the independence of ontology from epistemology; positive realism shows the dependence of epistemology on ontology.

Positive realism is all about overturning the Copernican Revolution. The answer to the question "How must objects be made in order to be known by us?" is not that knowledge is made possible by a system of conceptual schemes and perceptual apparatuses mediating our relation to the world. Rather, knowledge is made possible by the autonomous features of the objects and agents in the world. This insight yields a form of emergentism that sees ontology as the condition of the possibility of epistemology.

Emergentism as here conceived sees thought as something real that emerges from processes in the organism just as photosynthesis and digestion do. [. . .] Evolution could, certainly, have proceeded differently, and a slight climatic variation might have made the *Critique of Pure Reason* impossible. But it would be very hard to claim that the a priori principles expounded in the *Critique of Pure Reason* are what made possible a world of the type appropriate to allowing its existence.

Now, an obvious objection could be made: How do you prove that the world is organised independently of our representations, given that we know it only through our representations? The answer is simple, and consists of what I propose to call the "argument from interaction." One of our most common experiences is to interact with other beings—cats, dogs, flies, viruses, plants, and inanimate beings — differing more or less radically in the conceptual schemes and perceptual apparatuses with which they are (or in some cases are not) endowed. If such interaction itself *depended on conceptual schemes*, then this simple empirical fact would appear to be miraculous. For interaction between beings with very different conceptual schemes (and perceptual apparatuses, granularities of experience and forms of life) is a very common experience.

[. . .] [I]nteraction is the first step in the process by which epistemology emerges from ontology.

The environment is where interactions between living beings and objects take place—where subjects are but one kind of living being. [. . .]

The environment is not an amorphous platonic *chora*. It is a structured space offering affordances — invitations that belong not to concepts but rather to objects in the world. [. . .]

First of all, the objects in reality are largely autonomous — something that is highly underestimated by constructivism, which takes these objects as (reflections of) a docile colony of conceptual schemes. [. . .]

Secondly, objects manifest a direction of use and offer opportunities for action that are *given*, *directly perceived*, and not merely *thought of*. [. . .] A handle invites one to handle it and this property is not in the subject but in the object.

But now we need to prove the efficaciousness of emergence not only in natural but also in social reality. [. . .]

Positive realism [. . .] differentiates between the socially dependent and the socially constructed. Small portions of social reality are socially constructed: for example, the laws of the United States of America or the price of beer in Parisian bars. [. . .] Laws and prices have to be written down somewhere, and from that moment their existence no longer depends on the intentions of the constructor but on the fact of their being recorded and therefore made permanent, publicly accessible, and textually unchangeable. In other words they become a part of the external world just like tables, chairs, and mountains. Of course they can be amended, but then through other laws and prices that in turn will have to be written down, not by means of mere fantasy or intentionality.

It is also worth noting that the greater part of social reality is not socially constructed but socially dependent: [. . .] there are very important parts (probably the most important parts) of society that are rooted in our animal past and therefore were already phylogenetically formed and ready when our process of hominisation began to be refined.

Also, at the ontogenetic level, our relationship with social reality is not one in which we are constructors but rather passive receptors. In the greater part of our social life we follow the rules blindly without even perceiving them as rules [. . .]

Of course, the transcendental idealist can always ask the transcendental realist what bridges the natural and social worlds and more generally nature and culture, if not collective intentionality. The transcendental realist replies that this function is fulfilled by recording, which exists in nature (think of the genetic code) and underlies culture. Without recording, [. . .] we could not produce science or culture (at least of the sorts with which we are now familiar), since scientific and cultural productions always involve recordings, for example in the form of writing or printing (such as a musical score).

This is why mankind has attached so much importance to the technical prostheses of memory. Aristotle's view that the transition from perception to experience and then science is made possible by memory seems to have had numerous historical confirmations. Some of these were already available in Aristotle's age, including the fundamental role of writing in the transmission and development of knowledge. Subsequently, we had the printing press and, today (in addition to countless recording devices: phonography, photography, cinematography) we have the internet, which has greatly enhanced the possibilities inherent in memory.

[. . .] [T]he reference to recording and to the difference between construction and dependence allows us to exclude transcendental idealism not only from the natural world (from which it was expelled a long time ago) but also from the social world, where it still enjoys surprising popularity.

Although transcendental idealism officially died in or around the year 1830, its effects have been felt up to and including postmodernism. In fact, the philosophical mainstream of the last two centuries has kept alive the fundamental principle of transcendental idealism, namely that reality is constructed by the subject. This statement could appear less radical (and therefore more acceptable) than in its original formulation simply because it has been weakened in a process — culminating in postmodernism — for which an axiological assumption (the world of culture *is important*) is surreptitiously presented as an ontological thesis (the world of culture is constitutive — vaguely and indeterminately — of the world of nature).

[. . .] The positions that I summarised in my presentation of "negative realism" reflect the perspective of many philosophers who, over the last two centuries, have fought against transcendental idealism — such as the realists of the Austro-German school who founded *Gestaltpsychologie*, including Gibson as a late adherent, for whom the outside world has an autonomous organisation independent of the cognitive activity of the subjects who evolve within it. My positions thus have no claim to originality, except perhaps in the form in which they are presented. From my perspective, in fact, negative realism is not limited to rejecting the claims of transcendental idealism; it allows us also to draw essential distinctions between ontology and epistemology, reality and truth, the external and internal world, and between different types of objects.

Positive realism, finally, aims to develop the full potential of ontology as it is revealed by negative realism. At its basis there is nothing but a Darwinian hypothesis: the interaction between different beings has (nonteleologically) caused the emergence of specialised forms of life, social organisation, and knowledge. Here we find the most powerful and definitive answer to transcendental idealism. If the latter regarded epistemology (and its speculative hypostasis: the spirit) as the condition of the possibility of ontology, then transcendental realism does the opposite: it considers ontology to be the condition of the possibility of epistemology. In this sense, the birth date of transcendental realism should be sought in that "strange inversion of reasoning" that Robert Beverley MacKenzie, in 1868, attributed to Darwin:

> In the theory with which we have to deal, Absolute Ignorance is the artificer; so that we may enunciate as the fundamental principle of the whole system, that, in order to make a perfect and beautiful machine, it is not requisite to know how to make it. Mr. Darwin's, by a strange inversion of reasoning, seems to think Absolute Ignorance fully qualified to take the place of Absolute Wisdom in all the achievements of creative skill.

CHAPTER 18

Simona Forti (1958–)

Modern metaphysics has ended: the death of God announced by Nietzsche and the death of Man announced by Foucault have to be mourned. But the invitation to think beyond good and evil can be answered with the stubborn relaunching of the political ethos of philosophy. This is the radical theoretical stance that makes Simona Forti's intellectual production highly original within the Italian and international landscape.

Analytic normative philosophy, even in Italy, obliterates the failure of the project of modernity, by attempting to restore it – rehabilitating its very actor and protagonist, the rational subject. Much of continental philosophy, even in Italy, claims to be Deleuzian, pushing the deconstruction towards an enthusiastic adherence to the vitality of the existent – by promoting the undoing of the subject in the impersonal and irrational flows of becoming-animal, becoming-a-life, becoming-inorganic.

Forti challenges this euphoric optimism, re-engaging seriously with the negative and maintaining that today the more urgent political questions no longer concern the omnipotence of subjectivity, but the attitude towards compliance and indifference. With no nostalgia for normative foundations, she turns the present impossibility of elaborating theories of the good and the moral subject into the effort to think new forms of subjectivation that oppose political evil. For her project, the faculty of political judgment and the courage of freedom are more suitable tools than the formalisms of abstract reason.

Forti's reflections engage with the whole Western canon – philosophical, psychoanalytic and literary. Among her main references, besides Nietzsche and Foucault, we find Primo Levi, Patočka and particularly Arendt. By entering into a dialogue with them, Forti tries to deal with the scandal of a civilization that was promising progress and produced genocides; that used the values of freedom and humanism to justify domination; that, for the sake of life, security and well-being, still produces wretchedness, injustices and death.

Her first book, *Vita della mente e tempo della polis: Hannah Arendt tra filosofia e politica* (1994), immediately became a crucial text on Arendt that underwent numerous new editions. Subsequently, many of her investigations converged in the fundamental volume *Il totalitarismo* (2001), republished many times and incorporated into the volume *El totalitarismo: trayectoria de una idea límite* (2008). Forti's aim is to counter the rhetorical usage of the term 'totalitarianism' as it emerged in the Cold War years, when the Soviet and the National Socialist regimes were equated in order to celebrate Western liberal democracy as the antithesis of both. In her view, totalitarianism as a category becomes all the more valuable when it is understood deconstructively, in order to question liberal democracy – the voluntary servitude which it needs and produces, the securitarian obsessions and paranoid ghosts by which it is haunted. Totalitarianism, for her, is not a menace hovering outside of our political rationality; it is the inner threat which inhabits our political rationality itself.

For instance, in her important 2006 article, 'The Biopolitics of Souls', Forti argues, through a thorough review of sources, that racist theories during Nazism were justified not only on the grounds of positivistic-Darwinian arguments but also through an idealist-inflected anthropology which recovered some traditional philosophical themes dating back to Plato. By no means does this lead her to conclude that Plato is responsible for Nazism, or to formulate a summary condemnation of the philosophical canon. On the contrary, Forti suggests that we both refrain from writing a hagiography of the West and detect the pitfalls of our culture, without giving up on the search – within that very culture – for the resources with which to redirect it onto an ethical path.

The international rise of terrorism, the persistence of war in today's globalized world and the dramatic number of human beings losing their lives in the attempt to reach such alleged bastions of human rights as Europe and the United States are indeed all events that demand an effort of self-reflection. Forti does not falter in the face of such a demand: in her capital, *New Demons: Rethinking Power and Evil Today* (2012, 2015), she reacts to the attempt to dismiss the question of evil in politics as a theological remnant to be overcome.

She masters with virtuosity the history of Western thought in drawing two interpretive paradigms from it. The first, exemplified by Dostoevsky's *Demons*, understands evil as a radical nihilism conceptualized as the death drive, original sin, transgression: as the attempt on the part of the human to replace the creative omnipotence of God with its own finite destructive power. The second paradigm she forges, on the contrary, lingers over the 'grey zone' depicted by Primo Levi in *The Drowned and the Saved*. Here, between the titans of evil and their victims, a large crowd of secondary characters appears: 'mediocre demons' who execute heinous actions not because of an excess in their will but because of their lack of courage, together with their obedience and sense of duty. This is the evil that Arendt deems 'banal' in her

Eichmann in Jerusalem. Forti prefers to call it 'normal' in order to highlight the fact that it does not originate from a flaw in the individual but from the processes through which the individual adjusts to social functionings.

In this regard, Foucault becomes a valuable asset, as he can help us to understand how today's biopolitics, of which totalitarianism is just one of the historical outcomes, produces docile subjects whose sense of responsibility is made dull by promises of safety, health, well-being and hygiene – in the name of life and not death. In addition to this, it is Foucault, together with Arendt and Patočka, who points us towards a way out of the normality of evil, which does not disavow our tradition but passes precisely through it. From different perspectives, these authors find in Socrates' theoretical practices – *parrhesia*, the exercise of the 'two-in-one', the care of the soul – the model for a philosophy which refuses to assume any positive content of truth and appropriates negativity as the condition for freedom: a philosophy that makes itself a critical *ethos*, a dissident way of life. This same *ethos* underlies all of Forti's works and is the main object of her present research.

Lorenzo Bernini

Selected writings

Forti, Simona. *El Totalitarismo: Trayectoria de Una Idea Límite (Totalitarianism: trajectory of a limit idea)* Barcelona: Herder Editorial, 2008

Forti, Simona. *New Demons: Rethinking Power and Evil Today*. Stanford: Stanford University Press, 2015

EXCERPT

Simona Forti, *New Demons*

(Simona Forti, *New Demons: Rethinking Power and Evil Today.* Trans. Zakiya Hanafi. Stanford, CA: Stanford University Press, 2012, Introduction)

What approach can we take to the question of evil as it relates to power today, if the assumptions behind all claims to promoting the good — especially the political good — have been progressively delegitimized? [. . .] Everything depends on whether suffering continues to be a problem for us, and in what way. [. . .] This is not a question of the inescapable reality that inherently accompanies the finitude and vulnerability of our lives but, rather, of what Emmanuel Levinas calls 'useless suffering,' which is produced out of human relations, and which propagates with varying intensity and range on the basis of the social and political context.

Although it is true that evil has been spoken of in many ways, [. . .] there is no doubt that its meaning has swung back and forth between two recurring alternatives that cut across the different historical periods of thought [. . .]. Either, evil is a non-reality, as we would say today, evil is a cultural prejudice, dismantled as soon as it is observed from the perspective of the whole, from the Platonic One to the Deleuzian 'multiple-One'; or it is a reality at war with being, from ancient Gnosticism to the 'theoconservatism' of our day. [. . .]

What direction are we to take, then, if we share the premises of critical and deconstructive thought but also believe that the problem of evil is not only still relevant but also, first and foremost, the a priori in the human animal's search for meaning? What stance can we take if we do not feel aligned or comfortable with the abstractions of a normative political philosophy that believes it can overcome the negative by invoking the 'you must'; and if we feel equally remote from the 'euphoric' currents of an ontological, political immanence for which evil is simply the cumbersome legacy of a theological and metaphysical conception of the world? [. . .]

To redefine the contemporary relevance of the question of political evil, I [. . .] chose to take the byways, so to speak, offered by the genealogical approach. I put it to myself to examine the relationship between evil and power, focusing on the political repercussions of the different philosophical presuppositions. I attempted to recreate the conditions that made it possible to conceive of political evil starting from late modernity, in order to understand how the concepts that have defined it may be kept, reformulated, or discarded.

The point of departure for a journey of this kind can only be Kantian. Immanuel Kant's essay on 'Religion Within the Limits of Reason Alone,' in which he returns to the problem of 'radical evil,' is truly a watershed with respect to the previous philosophical tradition. The definitive distinction that Kant established between physical evil, metaphysical evil, and moral evil allowed the purely theological and metaphysical question of 'Where does evil come from?' to be replaced by the ethical, anthropological, and historical question of 'Why do we commit evil deeds?' Thus, for the German philosopher, moral evil is no longer a substance, but neither is it a nonbeing. It is an act: an act that has to do with freedom. However, although Kant makes it possible to reflect on the complicated interplay between evil and freedom, by his own admission he is pulled up short by the 'inscrutability' of the root of this connection. The possibility of evil actions that intentionally violate the moral law is unthinkable for him; the existence of human beings who pursue evil for the sake of evil is unacceptable.

To push beyond what Kant leaves 'unspoken,' to plumb the 'diabolical abysses' of freedom, was the goal of later philosophical thought, which continued to seek out the 'root' of evil. From Schelling to Heidegger, from Nietzsche to Levinas, from Freud to Lacan — to name only the main figures whose works I will examine — a path can be traced that radicalizes Kant's discovery to the point of overturning it, until transgressing the law, whether divine law or the imperative of reason, became identified as the main objective of evil. In the philosophical thinking of the nineteenth and twentieth centuries, although appearing in radically different versions, the concepts of nihilism, the will to death, and the will to nothingness defined the horizon of understanding of the 'new demons.' Thought of as a disease of the will or as an instinctual drive, as the delirium of reason or as a passion for the absolute, evil in any case always involved the forces of transgression and disorder: in a word, the power of death.

An eloquent, exemplary synthesis of this cluster of concepts appears in what I have decided to call the 'Dostoevsky paradigm.' Not so much because the literary equivalent of a specific post-Kantian idea of evil is to be found in the pages of the great Russian writer — particularly in *Demons* and *The Brothers Karamazov* — but because Dostoevsky's protagonists embody a set of insights, ideas, and concepts whose relationship, although changing, tends toward a clearly identifiable nexus. The schema that takes shape, not always explicitly, [. . .] was for a long time the established condition of conceivability for evil. This paradigm, which I reconstruct, was one that Nietzsche and Freud participated in as well as Heidegger and Levinas [. . .]. The works of these thinkers more than any others were turning points in a possible history of the contemporary idea of evil. However, we should note that this paradigm partly owes its existence to a 'simple' way of reading these authors. I am convinced that another perspective opens up from some of their writings, one that can easily merge into another, alternative genealogy.

There is no doubt in my mind that the expressive power with which the Russian genius gives life to his nihilistic, destructive demons not only definitively names the 'secret' of radical evil that Kant had failed to reveal, but it also clarifies its conditions of possibility, placing evil in relation to the question of power. Maybe what looms up for the first time in *Demons* is the distinction between wickedness and evil, between a subject's way of being and the 'systemic' outcome of the interaction between subjects. [. . .] All the characters misuse their free will in individual ways. But it is certain that for Dostoevsky the various demons, which correspond to the various ways in which evil makes itself visible, share the same absolute desire: to take the place of God and his infinite freedom. However, as finite creatures, since they are incapable of creating, they can only destroy. [. . .]

Will, omnipotence, and nothingness: although no longer framed in Dostoevsky's religious outlook, the correlation between these three terms was taken up and reworked by later philosophers, who continued to think of evil as a result of the perversion of the will in omnipotence, as the result of a sovereign subject — whether collective or individual makes no difference — that by raising itself up to the All creates Nothingness. This is a 'simple,' unidirectional vision of power that remains faithful to the model of sovereign and subjects, whose demonic cypher, also masterfully illustrated by the Russian writer, is depicted most forcefully in the relationship between victim and perpetrator. In other words, on the one hand there stands an omnipotent subject, bearer of death, and on the other, a subject reduced to a mere object, because he or she has been made totally passive by the other's violence.

The same polarized view extends to the collective dimension and allows it to be modeled according to a similar, dualistic structure: on the one hand, a cynical leader who exploits the weaknesses of others, and on the other, the weak masses who are utterly incapable of resistance. The hermeneutic capacity of this schema has been expanded [. . .] to include the key experiences of the twentieth century: total war, planetary, destructive technology, repeated genocides, and above all, Auschwitz. These are the new phenomena by which evil manifests itself in history, and for which there seems to be no better explanation than 'a pure unleashing of the will to death.'

There is no doubt that focusing the gaze on the 'accursed share,' on the abyss of the subject and 'being,' has helped to go beyond the Kantian 'prohibition.' However, this way of thinking about evil and power, as well as about their relationship, is likely to rigidify our understanding of reality into overly schematic, unilateral categories. [. . .]

The time has come, I believe, to let go of the Dostoevsky paradigm. We must leave it behind in order to understand the 'black heart' of the twentieth century, and, even more urgently, to be able to contend with the concerns of today. Our present times no longer allow power to be represented as the simple frontal relation between the state and individual bearers of rights. At the same time, political evil — even the political evil that lurks in our Western democracies — can no longer be purely understood as the result of an unleashing of wickedness. The scene of evil is a complex scene where the will to nothingness and death do not reign supreme. [. . .] We therefore need to dismantle this demonological vision of power and rely instead on an analytical model that no longer attributes evil exclusively to the desire for and will to death. This change of perspective received a significant boost from Hannah Arendt's thought, and above all from that of Michel Foucault, clearing the way to contemporary reflection on biopolitics and biopower. [. . .]

There is no doubt that any attempt to rethink the relationship between evil and power cannot help but return to the historical scene epitomized by Auschwitz, and to how it has been interpreted. Myriad unanswered questions remain, however. What does the status of 'absolute victim' mean in relation to the scientific and ideological obsession for enhancing life? If we start from the premise [. . .] that for a genocide to take place there must first be a process of dehumanization and de-subjectification of the future victim, we must nevertheless look more closely into how this process takes place. Is it really arrived at through the unleashing of a supposedly 'naturalistic' nihilism that goes 'beyond good and evil'? These are the questions I ask myself when revisiting some Nazi texts on racial theory [. . .]. Is it really true, as claimed by many interpreters of biopower [. . .] that in the racist discourse the body of the future victim of extermination is emptied of human and moral meaning? Rather, is it not saturated with a 'hypermoral' meaning that claims to know how to go about separating death from life? I believe that the supposed neutrality of a knowledge that was believed to be scientific, far from foundering in a nihilistic drift, has continued to exert a powerful influence through the traditional dichotomy of good and evil. [. . .]

I certainly do not want to come to the discovery that the perpetrators do not exist, or that they are innocent, and that the victims are guilty. But I think we should break down these logical dichotomies to transform them into a field of forces and tensions, in which the antinomies lose their substantial identity. This is not to oppose the Dostoevsky paradigm to a contrary, specular way of thinking, but to place alongside it another paradigmatic set of concepts that integrates, at the same time as it unblocks, the geometry that is rigidly fixed on the separation between absolute subjects and objects of domination. A different genealogy of the relationship between evil and power can thus be brought to light: a genealogy that finally puts into question the inextricable, recurrent link between transgression, power, and death. This is the approach that was first taken in the third chapter of Genesis, which ever since has continued to conceive of evil as the action of a creature that is essentially rebellious, because deep down it seeks to equal divine omnipotence. I believe that, for a long time now, this anthropological figure is not the one whose dangers we need to guard ourselves from anymore. I think that today, more than ever, what needs to be questioned instead is the desire for rules and conformity that cements our lives in irresponsibility and indifference, a desire that philosophy, apart from a few exceptions, has not wanted or known how to take on.

I thus seek to tie the threads together so as to outline a different way of thinking about the hendiadys of evil and power and to propose a new paradigm: that of 'mediocre demons' or 'the normalcy of evil.' My intellectual debt to Arendt's famous work on Eichmann's trial is evident. [...] However, [...] Arendt did not have time to develop the set of ideas that connect evil to an absence of judgment and to conformity. And rather than provide a reasoned argument on this association, she tied its conception to an expression, [...] — 'the banality of evil' — which has left us with a long list of unanswered questions. [...]

Thinking within the paradigm of mediocre demons means primarily putting into question the exclusive role of the will to and desire for death, and instead viewing the scenes of evil as powerfully inhabited by the will to life, as the result of an attempt to maximize life itself. It also means focusing less on the 'guilt' of the transgression and more on the devious normativity of nonjudgment, endorsed and celebrated by the morality that has so often taught us that judging is a sign of pride, that it is the shadow of that first sin committed by our first parents: the sin of disobedience. Mediocre demons do not replace 'absolute demons,' of course. Absolute demons exist, and still exist today; but if their efforts are successful it is because they seamlessly integrate into the desire of all those who, being too occupied with consolidating their life opportunities, adapt without reacting. For this reason, today, rather than pursuing the impossible goal of saying goodbye to the subject [...], it is important to ask how power and subjectivity constitute each other and are mutually reinforcing; to question not so much why we become wicked subjects but rather, above all, how we become obedient subjects. [...]

A genealogy of mediocre demons [...] must weave together the philosophical contributions of texts that, perhaps not always explicitly, have asked themselves these very questions. Accordingly, I track down the passages in Nietzsche's thought in which the critique of democracy, passivity, and conformism is not 'simple' in the least, and in which the will to life plays an extremely ambivalent role. [...] I then search the work of Foucault, his personal continuation of the Nietzschean genealogy, for the possibility of naming political evil and of locating it at the highest point of subjective dependency, in those 'states of domination' that suppressed the movement between freedom and power. I draw arguments from his writings on governmentality and pastoral power, and even more from the lectures of his later years devoted to the 'care of the self ' and parrhesia, to try to formulate some partial answers to the questions that are key to the paradigm of mediocre demons. First of all: [...] What kind of subjectification was introduced in the Christian West so as to make the relationship of care and protection a perfect mechanism for the production of generalized dependency? And also: How are the conditions of possibility for resistance to political evil to be conceived? Why was an entire field of experience, from the 'care of the self ' to parrhesia, removed from the spectrum of examples on which to model our ethical and political conduct? In a word, does another way of becoming subjects exist? If so, it can only stem from an ethos that changes the perception of life and death and of their relationship; from a 'way of life' that never silences its inner duality and that does not reify it into an internal essence of the good and an external substance of evil. What I seek to demonstrate is that these questions and their possible answers are not only significant for individual ethics; they can also be directly transposed onto the political and collective planes.

This is what I try to show by reconstructing the theoretical ties that Foucauldian thought has forged with what has been called the philosophy of dissent from Central and Eastern Europe, especially with several Prague thinkers — from Patočka to Havel — who were engaged in the Charter 77 experience. My interest lies in finding a 'testing ground,' so to speak, of the revolutionary character of thinking as a way-of-life; of an ethos that always confronts itself anew with the infinite and unsolvable problem of the meaning of a 'life-in-the-truth.' Because in actuality, living in-the-truth—a prerequisite for the practice of parrhesia—is simply the witnessing of a life that ruthlessly questions itself on its own internal conflicts, and for this reason decides to make 'inner anarchy' the terrain on which to cultivate a different political virtue, with the hope that this can be transmitted, by contagion, to the collective dimension. [. . .]

Ultimately, what Primo Levi also courageously examined were the political repercussions of a fatal, dualistic opposition between life and death. [. . .] Everything in Levi's last work, *The Drowned and the Saved*, can be read as a refutation of *Demons* and the legend of the Grand Inquisitor, of that Manichean conception of power that opens up an abysmal distance between the feverish will of the wicked for power and death, and the passive obedience of the masses. Everything in *The Drowned and the Saved* forces us to take note of the normal, and yet at the same time perverse, functioning of the grey zone, which, unfortunately, does not only connect the opposite poles of the fence at Auschwitz. [. . .] Even in far less 'extreme' situations, the gesture that separates life from death, absolutizing them in their opposition, always runs the risk of bringing along with it the conditions of evil. Or at least this is how I think *The Drowned and the Saved* should be read.

CHAPTER 19

Maurizio Lazzarato (1955–)

Maurizio Lazzarato is among the most influential and innovative thinkers to have emerged from the radical activist milieu of 1970s Italy. Active in the *autonomia operaia* movement, he was among the generation to be forced into effective political exile in Paris at the end of that decade, as the Italian government attempted to prosecute leftist intellectuals (including both Lazzarato and Antonio Negri) for the crimes of the *Brigate Rosse* (*Red Brigades*), on entirely trumped-up charges. Since then, his work has evolved in dialogue with key figures of radical French philosophy and with various social movements and political projects.

He is still best known in the English-speaking world for his concept of 'immaterial labour': a concept that he himself claims to have abandoned (and certainly made no further obvious use of) some months after the essay of that title was written, in the mid-1990s. For many years subsequently, however, that essay was the only work of Lazzarato's available in English, and its influence on some of Hardt & Negri's arguments in *Empire* led to its widespread citation. The term generally designates forms of work which do not produce tangible material products, and the tendency of such forms of work to become generalized within post-industrial economies. It was never intended to suggest that all labour had become immaterial or non-physical, or that manufacturing and physical labour do not remain fundamental to the global capitalist economy; although critics have routinely tried to claim that it was.

His work since that time has moved through a number of phases and covered a range of topics, from visual media to political ontology. Among the most important of his untranslated works, *Les Revolutions du Capitalisme* presents a fascinating post-Marxist theory of politics which draws on the ideas of thinkers such as Leibniz and Tarde to set out an understanding of political and aesthetic struggle as the contest over 'possible worlds'.

Lazzarato has been involved with a number of important political projects and interventions in France, including the founding of the theoretical journal,

Multitudes and the organization of the movement of *intermittents* (a special category of worker in the French entertainment industry) to defend their unique, mutually owned unemployment-insurance scheme from neoliberal attack in 2003. The latter is the subject of his 2011 book (published in English in 2017), *Experimental Politics*, which offers one of the most rigorous analyses to date of neoliberalism as a system of contemporary power relations, while also examining the distinctive politics of the *coordinations* (semi-autonomous coordinating groups) of the *intermittents'* movement, and the politics of creativity in the era of the knowledge economy. The extract presented here is from a core section of that work.

Since that time, his work has developed along similar lines while also taking on new dimensions. In *Signs and Machines*, he sets out nothing less than a coherent theory of culture and signification, drawing directly on the work of Deleuze and, above all, his great friend and inspiration, Félix Guattari. In *The Making of Indebted Man*, he offers an astute account of the role played by debt in contemporary capitalist society, and in particular the ways in which debt is used to secure compliance from workers and citizens. In his most recent work, *War and Capital*, written with his friend and collaborator, Éric Alliez (also a member of Guattari's circle in Paris and co-author of several of his works), the authors try to distance themselves from what they see as the failed political and theoretical legacy of 1968. In this volume, they argue for the importance of understanding the centrality of military technology, institutions and goals to the development of the modern state, and for a recovery of the revolutionary ambitions and strategic determination of the early twentieth-century labour movement.

Overall, Lazzarato's *oeuvre* stands as one of the richest and most astute bodies of contemporary political theory and deserves far more attention than it normally receives outside of avant-garde circles.

Jeremy Gilbert

Selected writings

Lazzarato, Maurizio. 'Immaterial Labor'. In *Radical Thought in Italy: A Potential Politics*, edited by Paolo Virno and Michael Hardt, 133–148. Minneapolis, MN: University of Minnesota Press, 2010

Lazzarato, Maurizio. *The Making of the Indebted Man*. Los Angeles, CA: Semiotext(e), 2012

Lazzarato, Maurizio. *Signs and Machines: Capitalism and the Production of Subjectivity*. Los Angeles, CA: Semiotext(e), 2014

Lazzarato, Maurizio. *Governing by Debt*. South Pasadena, CA: Semiotext(e), 2015

Lazzarato, Maurizio. *Experimental Politics: Work, Welfare, and Creativity in the Neoliberal Age*, trans. Arianna Bove, Jeremy Gilbert, Andrew Goffey, Mark Hayward, Jason Read, and Alberto Toscano. and edited by Jeremy Gilbert. Cambridge, MA: MIT Press, 2017

EXCERPT

Maurizio Lazzarato, *The dynamics of the political event: Micropolitics and the process of subjectification*

(Maurizio Lazzarato, *Experimental Politics: Work, Welfare, and Creativity in the Neoliberal Age*. Trans. Arianna Bove et al. Ed. Jeremy Gilbert. Cambridge, MA: MIT Press, 2017, ISBN 9780262034869, Ch. 2, pp. 83–102)

In this chapter we ask what "revolutionary politics" and the "revolutionary subject" have become, in light of the micropolitics of Deleuze and Guattari as well as Foucault's microphysics of power, and draw some lessons from the struggle of the *intermittents,* both very distant from and very close to these theoretical questions.

[. . .] [M]icropolitics and microphysics can be said to be the first great theories that have really problematised the neutralisation of "revolutionary politics" and the "revolutionary subject" that capitalism has been carrying out since the Soviet revolution. According to Foucault, power and politics as they developed in Christian Europe were radically disrupted by the birth of political economy. At the end of the nineteenth century, the workers movement, especially its Marxist wing, and the revolutions that broke out at the end of World War I, managed to exploit the problematic relationship between the economy and the political, and turn it against capitalism. [. . .] By the time Foucault engaged with the liberal theory that emerged after the Soviet revolution, and read its transformation of power and politics, the problem had completely shifted. After the 1970s, the working class that had been previously integrated in industrial society in the interwar US New Deal and the Fordist pact after World War II was defeated and "de-proletarianised" (as the ordoliberals would say), while industrial society was being dismantled as the centre of the world economy. The introduction of a "new domain, a new field," which Foucault calls the "social," now "neutralised" (or depoliticised) the problematic relation between politics and the economy, which the "revolution" had exploited and overturned. [. . .] According to Foucault, by means of overlapping apparatuses of sovereignty, discipline, and biopolitics that simultaneously give rise to and produce large binary divisions (classes, sexes, etc.), and through the "optimisation of systems of difference" — similar to the macro- and microphysics of power that constitute the two inseparable sides of governmentality — power is configured as the government of "subjects of rights" and "living subjects." Similarly, according to Deleuze and Guattari, in contemporary capitalism power is exercised through molar and molecular apparatuses, constituting distinct but inseparable moments. The social subjection that assigns roles, functions, and identities to individuals is coupled with the machinic subjugation that traverses both the pre-individual dimension of affects, perceptions, and desires, and the realm of their transindividuality. The techniques and apparatuses that "neutralised," continuously defused, and newly instituted the dualisms of class that revolutionary politics was able to turn into a "class war" are both macro- and micropolitical, and tie the economic, social, political, cultural, and technological together, displacing the field of struggle and requiring new weapons.

[. . .] How should a "war machine" function when the objective is not war (or the seizure of power in its institutional or armed forms)? When the power it confronts manages dualisms through the optimisation of differentiations and individualisations? How does subjectivity act at the molar and molecular level to subtract itself from the designations of the government of conducts and subjugations? How does it affirm itself both as a political and an existential subject? What is the relationship between ethics (the transformation of the self) and politics given the conditions of contemporary capitalism?

Micropolitics and microphysics have another important function. They substantiate what had been rediscovered in 1968 — that "the revolution in modern Europe was not only a political project but also a form of life" — and what 1968 had affirmed politically — that changes in individual conducts and changes in the configuration of the world go together. In the twentieth century, Communism had dulled the relationship between politics and ethics, politics and "lifestyle," and Stalinism had wiped it out. The "care of the self and others" that Foucault refers to, and the production of the world and subjectivity that Deleuze and Guattari wrote of, activated a "new activism" that is deeply rooted in the history of the West. The movement of the *intermittents* was invested by all these questions, and rooted in a specific situation, its responses were partial but meaningful.

The first great innovation introduced by the micropolitics and microphysics of power is the theory of the event, which questions the relation between time and history in order to distance action from the idealism of the philosophy of history. [. . .] The event is what crops up in history and sinks back into history without being itself history. The event is immanent to economic, social, and political history, but not reducible to it. What is called "history" here must be understood as the product of the multiplicity of discursive and non-discursive devices of subjectification and subjugation that we have already described. As far as the conflict of the *intermittents* is concerned, these are: the condition of their employment, work, and life; the processes of subjectification in which they are caught (waged, entrepreneur, poor, or unemployed); and the public space as it is constituted and codified by the logics of representation and mediation. [. . .]

The movement of the *intermittents* of course has its own historical, social, economic, and political conditions, but in its emergence as an event, it departs from those conditions to create something new: new possibilities of action and new modes of subjectification. There is something in the event that cannot be reduced to the social determinisms of causal series, in the sense that its conditions do not contain all its effects. The *coordination* of *intermittents* and precarious workers, and its practices, its way of doing and speaking, are neither directly deducible from their conditions of work, employment, and unemployment, nor can they be reduced to the codifications of existing social and political spaces, or their devices of subjectification and subjugation. For them, the question is to understand the continuities and discontinuities (of action, problems, and practices) that the socio-economic and political situation entertains with the event. Therefore, the event cannot be *completely* deduced from history, from whence it comes and in which it inscribes itself anew.

[. . .] The event does not affect the state of things it emerges from, without first *affecting the subjectivities* that take part and position themselves in it saying "no." Something changed in life and society that asks of subjectivity, What has just happened, what's happening, and what's going to happen? This instantaneous subjective change is an act of both resistance and creation: resistance to power, and creation of possibilities whose limits are not clearly established. These possibilities are not just possibilities "pure and simple," or in an abstract sense; they are "living possibilities" because they are already engaged in a given situation, in the specific conditions of *intermittence*, the cultural labour market, the refoundation of the social, the treatment of unemployment by the activation of passive spending, etc. For this reason, they are not already there, prior to the event, but are created by the event and emerge with it. [. . .] The event is an opening, a possibility for self-transformation, and consequently, for changing the socio-political situation. A new universe is opened up, and those who cross this threshold can engage in new relations, new modes of thinking and doing, and new knowledge and affects.

These possibilities are first and foremost *felt* rather than *conceived*, because the subjective mutation is primarily non-discursive. [. . .] It comes as an existential rupture that does not merely transform consciousness and discourse. [. . .] The event is a source of desires and unknown beliefs to the extent that adding itself to the world, it must measure itself against what is already there, already instituted. The event and its effects add something to the world, and this can change what is already constituted. *Political action entails building the conditions for a transformation of what is, starting from the new possibilities contained in the event.* These conditions for the realisation of the possible are not identical to the conditions of its emergence, because the two are open to a process of subjectification that reorients action and changes power relations. Among the actual conditions of the world, some create obstacles; others are favourable to the realisation of these possibilities. Among the favorable conditions, some are already there; others must be invented and built; others must be seised in the becoming of the social and political conjuncture. After the first moments of the event (its emergence), a second and problematic moment occurs: the possibilities that have emerged with the event must now actualise themselves in the existing state of things and subjectivity.

The collapse of the event back into history (the counteractualisation of the event) occurs at the crossroads of at least three different processes of singularisation: (1) the political struggle with different apparatuses of power (political, economic, media, welfare state, etc.), which in their turn manage to counteract the event; (2) the political struggle between constituted political forces (unions, Trotskyists, Communists, Maoists, etc.) and the forces that are in the process of being constituted (the *coordination*) inside the movement itself, which are about meeting objectives, modes of organisation and struggle, building alliances, and implementing strategies; and (3) the relation between this level of molar subjectification and the processes of molecular subjectification that emerges from working practices, unemployment, wage labour, and the life of the *intermittents*. [. . .]

The movement of the *intermittents* deploys its political experimentation outside the classical Communist hypothesis because it is forced to conceive of the relation between the molecular action of employment practices, unemployment, work, and life and the molar action in the institutional public realm, as one between two levels of political subjectification that are both distinct and inseparable, heterogeneous and yet communicative, rather than as a relation between the economy and politics.

The second movement of the event (its subsiding back into history) is very important as it opens onto a process other than one of simple verification: political experimentation does not bring about a fidelity to the event but rather something new — a social and political creation. The new nascent subjectivity must, on the one hand, change the conditions of employment, work, unemployment, and the apparatuses of subjugation (to the wage, "profession," or "artist") that it is enveloped in. On the other hand, it must introduce institutional changes (the "rewriting" of unemployment welfare, democracy and its institutions, a new production of knowledge, etc.). This is necessary not only to change its economic and political situation but also, and above all, to open up spaces or build collective agencies capable of operating a "subjective reconversion." In order to measure up to what is already there — for instance, labour rights, social security, the cultural labour market, assigned roles and functions, and the democracy of institutions — it is necessary immediately to invent and build modes of saying and doing, modes of "being together" (the desire to self-govern) and modes of "being against" (the will not to be governed) that are adequate to the discontinuity introduced by the event.

The subsiding of the event into history and its inscription in the existing state of things determines a new political situation: the mode of this subsiding; this inscription in a scene where it barges into social, economic, and political institutions, and subsequently becomes integrated without friction; the mode in which it questions or legitimates the dominant "discourse" on employment, unemployment, and work; or the way in which it eventually defines "these problems" otherwise are all relevant to a "political" struggle. These are questions of political strategy and tactics, of confrontation between heterogeneous points of view.

[. . .] [T]his subsiding occurs in a time span that is normally unfavourable to movements: the long term of unions and political institutions, the term of the "professionals" of politics, the time span of those who have time for politics. Starting from this question of the development of the event and history, where history is no longer configured as a leading idea, a guide to action, it might be possible to understand the deep crisis affecting political action today, in both its "revolutionary" and "democratic" forms.

[. . .] The three moments or temporalities of the event define three heterogeneous political situations that demand different treatments and modes of expression and action. The event is the condition or the occasion for a political "constructivism" that the *coordination* [of the *intermittents*] seems to have adopted.

The political event returns the world and subjectivity to us. It returns the world to its true nature: the world shows those who have been opened and ripped apart by the event that it is not merely *what it is* but something *in the course of making itself* and *something to be made*. The event gives us an open, unfinished, and incomplete world, and in so doing calls on subjectivity, because we can inscribe our actions and exercise our responsibility in this incompleteness [. . .].

The world in the process of making always requires an ethical perfection, is always searching for an existential closure. In this sense, the opening of the event gives us access to the process of production and transformation of subjectivity. Like the world, individual and collective subjectivity are not given; they are in the process of making and are open to being made. The event returns the world to us as a "matter of choice," and subjectivity as a "crossroads of *praxis.*" What is happening to me there? What can or should I do, and how to start from that place there? Am I responsible for what is going on? Am I responsible for what is going to happen? The event brings subjectivity face-to-face with alternatives, decisions, and risks. [. . .]

The world and subjectivity are not already given; everything is far from being decided, contrary to the discourse on "the end of history" that has been repeated to us since the 1990s. The US Department of State decreed that history ended when the Berlin Wall fell, Communism expired, and the "working class" became fragmented in a new sociology of social classes. This talk of an "end of history" proclaims that the possible does not overflow the real but is equal to it; more precisely, the possible amounts to what is on offer on the market. The arrogance of the "victors" expresses that any possible that is not already involved in the market does not exist. Therefore, our time is certainly not the end of history but a time when we should pay attention to the way history acts in relation to what is not historical — the event — in a manner that does not sketch out in advance the future of the world.

In order to determine the relations of continuity and discontinuity between "history" and the "event," we must first return to the description of the socio-economic and subjective conditions of emergence of the event. We have analysed the transformations and mutations of the government of conducts, and the discursive and non-discursive apparatuses through which it is exercised, but so far we have neglected what Foucault calls "counter-conducts"—that is to say, modes of life and behavior animated by the will to not be led by others, not be governed, govern differently, or even self-govern. In this analysis we must carefully distinguish between two types of counter-conduct: the counter-conduct of the *intermittents,* exercised and expressed in their condition of work, employment, unemployment, and life, which we call "molecular"; and the counter-conducts expressed and exercised in the public space of political, union, and social institutions organised and practised by the *coordination,* which we call "molar." Finally, we ought to consider the way these molecular and molar counter-conducts open up to processes of subjectification.

On the one hand, molecular resistances and inventions express themselves as the outsmarting — an escape and a deviation from — the codes and norms that sustain the market for cultural labour. On the other hand, molar counter-conducts, exercised by the *coordination,* try to reverse the situation, and build conditions of open conflict and polemical interlocution with economic, social, political, and media institutions. They demand "new social rights" and work toward the development and institution of a different system of indemnity for unemployment for all precarious workers as well as the "democratic" transformation of the institutions that regulate them. Having said that, molecular counter-conducts cannot be reduced, following the dominant logic of the workers' movement, to simple economic behaviours that require the intervention of a trade union organisation and a party in order to qualify as being political, because they directly undermine the distribution of places, roles, functions, and apparatuses of subjection at work in the market (the injunction to be waged and self-enterprising). By tackling the effects of the power of laws, norms, and rules, they de-structure the functions of command and obedience, the subordination and autonomy of organisation of the labour market. Molecular resistance also manifests itself as a practice of invention and experimentation. Molecular counter-conducts add to the refusal of modes of subjugation and the shifting of codes and rules, the invention of modes of life setting out new temporalities assigned to them (times of work, times of employment, times of unemployment, and times of life). According to Deleuze, under capitalism, all social transformations entail a "reconversion of subjectivity" and the emergence of a "new self" as a pocket of resistance. [. . .]

[M]olecular counter-conducts are not only practices of resistance, but also inventions of new modes of working and living, and a self-transformation that takes place in a space that is only partly institutionalised, somewhere where power relations are in the process of being made and unmade. According to Deleuze, the "movements of subjective reconversion" that occur in the course of all social transformations are "pockets of instability," because they are bearers of "ambiguities" and "potentialities." With Foucault, we can define the nature of this ambiguity, or rather this ambivalence, with much precision: the relations that characterise what he defined as microphysics of power are "unstable, reversible and mobile." They are not completely fixed by norms, laws, and regulations because they partly express "new" relations, and partly elude current modes of subjugation and codifications. These new relations are in the process of being made, and their identity is not fixed; they can still be "here or there." Their reversibility, mobility, and instability give them that character of "ambivalence" that Deleuze speaks of. The nature of social transformation, the "ambivalence" of proliferating counter-conducts, has been perfectly seized on by the *intermittents* that we investigated in our inquiry, insofar as they produce and are subjected to them.

An actor we interviewed during our research sums it up well: "Intermittence presents two faces, one libertarian; the other ultraliberal." The regime of intermittence sweeps across all spaces: "I work when I want, where I want, as I want," and "I work when I can, when they want, as they want." On the same topic, an editor remarks: "The positive aspects should not be forgotten: totally free time, absence of routine, multiple encounters"; and these also have a negative side: "Total irregularity and displacement (therefore, the impossibility of investing oneself in outside activities: sports, music, or social life)," and above all, the constant stress due to precariousness, especially when they realise that they are no longer "assisted by social structures."

The spaces of autonomy and subordination are not fossilised; not everything is immediately fixed by the codes of work or social welfare; they are unstable, mobile, and reversible. New practices of domination and freedom grow, split, superimpose themselves, and produce and reproduce themselves together. These practices of freedom or subordination are dependent on specific, singular relations, and above all, on power relations established between the employer and the employee, and between the latter and the institutions that regulate unemployment benefits. Here more than elsewhere, laws, norms, and regulations are subject to interpretation, uses, and practices that make one or the other side of intermittence more prevalent.

We find the same ambivalence in the question of "time" that, as we have already suggested, and as the interviews show, is the real political issue of the dispute. More often than not, interviewees refused to regard unemployment as a pure absence of employment, as empty time. On the contrary, they conceived it more as a "full" time, but this fullness is very ambiguous because it refers to different things [. . .]. Unemployment is the time emptied of employment that *intermittents* fill with things other than job-seeking. But it is also possible to read a new temporality here that allows one to make the whole lifetime productive and to exploit unpaid time. [. . .] The same "ambiguity," the same reversibility, can equally be said to apply to practices of waged labourers: on the one hand, they express the will to not be governed, to govern themselves, and the desire to escape from subordination to the wage; on the other hand, the model of the self-entrepreneur at work in these practices is the very outcome of capital as a machine of subjugation. From this perspective, the reform seems to be an apparatus destined to substitute the play of antagonistic actions, tricks, escapes, diversions, and reversible power relations, with techniques (norms, laws, and technologies) that fix and guide the conduct of *intermittents* in a constant manner, and with sufficient certainty and security. Seeing the "ambiguities," instability, reversibility, and mobility of these power relations, it is important to point out that counter-conducts have really transformed the attitudes to work, employment, and life, and the subjectivity of those who work. These transformations are under way — "subjective reconversions" that will go much further.

The "subjective reconversion" does not simply take place in the temporality of the political event, as Rancière or Badiou seem to believe. It is produced day by day in the mode of resistance to the law and existing codes that aims to push toward unwritten objectives. Despite their ambivalence, like micro-events, molecular counter-conducts participate in the struggle for a new subjectivity and the constitution of a new self, because they express a resistance to two actual forms of subjugation: one consisting of individuating us according to the needs of power, and "the other of attracting each individual to a known and recognised identity, fixed once and for all." In practice, these counter-conducts experiment with new attitudes, a new *ethos* in relation to work, employment, and unemployment that heralds new modes of existence. Molar counter-conducts in the *coordination* do not function as the "consciousness" or the "politicisation" of these molecular practices that, in any case, can be collective in themselves. It is a question [. . .] of heterogeneous levels of subjectivity, which must be coordinated even while their disparities are preserved.

CHAPTER 20

Christian Marazzi (1951–)

Christian Marazzi was born in Lugano, Switzerland, in 1951. He graduated with a degree in political science from the University of Padua before going on to study for two degrees in economics in London: a master's at the London School of Economics and a PhD at City University. He has held positions at the University of Lausanne, Padua, New York and Geneva and is currently professor and research director in socio-economics at the Scuola Universitaria della Svizzera Italiana.

In the 1970s, in Padua, Marazzi was an active member of a study group on money organized around the magazine *Primo Maggio*, which opened with Sergio Bologna's seminal article on 'Money and Crisis'. The group worked closely on the impact of the declaration of 15 August 1971 on the inconvertibility of the dollar into gold, which sanctioned the end of the Bretton Woods system masterminded in 1944 by John Maynard Keynes, adviser to the British Treasury, and Harry Dexter White, chief international economist at the US Treasury Department.

The monetary turn, the end of the Gold Standard, threw up new questions for Marxian analysis, especially as to the function of money as capital and universal equivalent. The latter function would take a secondary role, giving way to the emergence of money as primarily a fiduciary script or sign of debt, thus magnifying its performative function. Performativity rules govern the manner in which financial markets operate, a manner which has also been analysed, in behavioural finance, as the irrational rationality of traders, a primarily gregarious activity that, much like language, acts through words. Marazzi develops these insights throughout his subsequent work, but unlike most behavioural finance economists, when studying the performative function of money, he insists, with Marx, that money is always also capital that commands labour.

Language and communication are structurally and contemporaneously present throughout both the sphere of the production and distribution of goods and services and the sphere of finance, and [. . .] it is for this very reason that changes in the world of work and modifications in the financial markets must be seen as two sides of the same coin. (Marazzi, *Capital and Language*)

The workers' side of the coin never falls out of sight in his analyses, where much emphasis is placed upon the deeply interconnected nature of the processes of dismantling welfare, privatization of public assets and the financialization of everyday life – all of which sought to mould a more supple labour force.

According to Marazzi's more recent analyses, debt relations have become the primary mode of meeting social needs. Because of this, contemporary financialization exploits 'human raw materials'. The bare life of workers who have nothing but themselves to offer is this raw material, in a turn where poverty and destitution are made profitable and, from a question addressed by welfare provisions, turned back into a resource for surplus extraction, effectively marking the end of the historic compromise of the Fordist era.

In line with other political economists in the tradition of *operaismo*, Marazzi furnishes us with a compelling contemporary translation of the notion of the social factory – an expression that signalled the moment at which society began to produce before it had even entered the factory and outside of it, the breakdown of the borders delineating a privileged place of production, but also a significant externalization of production costs, which in itself initiated a process of profit's becoming-rent. The social factory is now named the production – and therefore the exploitation and surplus value extraction – of the common. The set of resources, skills, human faculties and abilities, information, signs, sociability, affects common to all humans are the substance of the production of value and the extraction of surplus. This means that financial crises, and here crisis is a systemic failure that involves the destruction of capital, also call for the destruction of society, hence the violence.

In Marazzi's view, financial cycles cannot be understood independently of class struggle, whether in terms of capital's response to it or its prevention and pre-emption. His emphasis on the essential role of subjectivity in the system leads Marazzi to oppose the commonplace separation between a 'real' or productive economy and a financial one. Financialization spreads across the entire economic cycle rather than either substituting or usurping the primary role of the so-called real economy. For Marazzi, it is no 'parasitic deviation' but a form of capital accumulation consubstantial with the rest of the economy.

Marazzi is undoubtedly best known and appreciated as an acute observer of and commentator on economic crises, often praised for his powers of anticipation. For social movements, he is the go-to intellectual for intelligible explanations of the latest bust from the standpoint of the people, and the performativity of his own analyses has at times landed him in trouble with the powers that be. Over time, he has greatly contributed to dispelling the obscurantist tendencies of economists' language, and in this he is a militant public intellectual.

In style, he infuses chronicles on economics and finance with philosophical poetry and imbues his dispatches on the global economy with wit. His best moments often furtively lurk between the lines. Perhaps Marazzi is really a philosopher who singularly expresses the world's economy in poetic form, and it is his poetic ability that occasionally makes possible fleeting glimpses of the totality.

Arianna Bove

Selected writings

Marazzi, Christian. *Capital and Affects. The Politics of the Language Economy*, trans. Giuseppina Mecchia. Los Angeles, CA: Semiotext(e), 2011. A translation of *Il posto dei calzini* [*The Place for Socks*], *La svolta linguistica dell'economia e i suoi effetti sulla politica*, Lugano and Milan: Casagrande, 1994.

Marazzi, Christian. *E il denaro va – Esodo e rivoluzione dei mercati finanziari* [*And So the Money Goes: Exodus and Revolution of the Financial Markets*]. Bellinzona: Casagrande, 1998.

Marazzi, Christian. *Capital and Language: From the New Economy to the War Economy*, trans. Gregory Conti. Los Angeles, CA: Semiotext(e), 2008. A collection of lectures on 'Science, Technology and Society' given at the University of Calabria.

Marazzi, Christian. *Il comunismo del capitale: finanziarizzazioni, bio-politiche del lavoro e crisi globale*. Verona: Ombre Corte, 2010. Includes articles published in Multitudes, Posse and Il Manifesto, classic essays such as 'Money and the World Crisis: The New Basis of Capitalist Power' from *Zerowork* 2, 1977, the excellent essay, 'The Manager's Dyslexia' translated into English for Angelaki 16:3 (2011): pp. 19–32 as 'Dyslexia and the Economy', and 'The Violence of Financial Capitalism', published as a standalone book, *The Violence of Financial Capitalism* (2011), trans. Kristina Lebedeva & Jason Francis McGimsey. Los Angeles: Semiotext(e).

Marazzi, Christian. *The Linguistic Nature of Money and Finance*, trans. Isabella Bertoletti, James Cascaito, and Andrea Casson. Los Angeles, CA: Semiotext(e), 2014.

Marazzi, Christian. and Sylvère Lotringer, eds, *Autonomia: Post-Political Politics*. Los Angeles, CA: Semiotext(e), 2007, about the Autonomia movement, a rich anthology of first-hand documents and contemporaneous analysis from Autonomia's most influential theorists and associates.

EXCERPT

Christian Marazzi, *The Linguistic Nature of Money and Finance*

(Christian Marazzi, *The Linguistic Nature of Money and Finance*. Trans. Isabella Bertoletti, James Cascaito, & Andrea Casson. Los Angeles: Semiotext(e), 2014. ISBN: 978-1-58435-142-9, pp. 5–47.)

The "linguistic turn" of the post-Fordist economy and the concurrent process of financialisation, its growing pervasiveness, which have characterised the new capitalism for the last three decades, have radically altered the relationship between money and language. The entrance of language directly into the processes of production, "putting language to work," the transformation of the places of the production of goods and services into "loquacious factories," on the one hand; financialisation as the modality of the production of "collective conventions" for the appropriation of wealth in which the mimetic-communicative function of the multitude of investors is central, on the other — allow us to speak of the *linguistic nature* of money. What we are witnessing here is a real and true overtaking of the classical circular relationship between money and language which, from John Locke to J. M. Keynes, from Saussure to the most recent theories of money, in a game of reciprocal cross-references and searching for isomorphisms, has characterised the theory of money and that of language as distinct spheres of analysis. Today, money and language *overlap* to such a degree that the *moneyness* of money as "absolute convention" is inseparable from praxis and communicative-linguistic strategy. The form of the value of goods is *simultaneously* monetary and linguistic. We have arrived at this historical result by way of the progressive *de-isasubstantialisation* of the value of goods—be it Marxist labour-value or neoclassical utility-value — just as we arrived at the performative becoming of language, at the linguistic capacity for "making things with words." Value lies not in the objects, material or immaterial, but in a collective production, an institution, which more or less permits the organisation of a life in common. The social validation of wealth is actualised in the production of collective beliefs (conventions) such as the rational (and not only "behavioural") modality of the functioning of financial markets. The conventions are, by definition, "cognitive constraints" which act upon the multiplicity of subjects operating upon financial markets by way of a communicative-linguistic function. The *crisis* of contemporary financial capitalism requires that we question the *limits* of the linguistic nature of money, the structural contradictions of an economic-financial system in which the very *performativity* of the monetary-communicative strategy comes into play.

[. . .] In order to begin our discussion on the linguistic nature of money, called "unconventional monetary theory," and financial capital, it will be useful to start with the "regime change" in the monetary policies of the major central banks which has taken shape in 2013. Let it be clear that there is nothing transcendental here; but there is something indicative of the *impasse* at which financial capitalism has found itself since the time of the crisis which, from August of 2007 to the present, seems impermeable to any attempt at creating a solid and enduring economic recovery on the part of the monetary authorities. The new thing, so to speak, is called "*forward guidance*" (long-term guidelines) and it consists of rendering *explicit* the guideline, on the part of the central banks, for how the interest rates will presumably be changed within a rather long time span (in some cases, by 2016, for the moment) in hopes of being able to stimulate the aggregate demand and economic activity in general. [. . .]

[F]orward guidance is a political monetary strategy which seeks to influence the expectations of the multitude of economic subjects. And, above all, it is a *communicative* strategy, if it is true that it is based upon indicators which are not at all clear or consistent. Someone has said that it should be called "forward guessing" rather than "forward guidance." In particular, the goal of keeping interest rates low, with reference to what will happen in the labour market, collides with the more mysterious events of the last five years [from *c.* 2013] (in England, for example) — namely, the reduction in the productivity of labour *in spite of* the increase in unemployment, which means that there are still margins of growth in the utilisation of productive capacities without any need for increasing employment. It is difficult to imagine a reduction in unemployment, in the short to medium-term, based upon what has happened in recent years. Even less clear is what the banks would do if inflation were to give even a hint of taking off, although this is hardly probable (in the United States it is actually diminishing). It is a fact that the institutional mandate of the central banks is to regulate the creation of liquidity, based upon fixed price control. Moreover, it is on the basis of this mandate that the central banks define themselves as "independent institutions." If prices were to rise, for one reason or another (especially in a world flooded by liquidity), it is difficult to imagine that the markets would be able to continue to believe that the central banks will maintain low daily rates by virtue of their proclaimed forward guidance. [. . .]

If we have chosen to begin our discussion with the latest measures assumed by the monetary policy of the central banks, we have not done so with the intention of opening a debate on their greater or lesser effectiveness, or of giving evidence of their particularly innovative qualities. In any event, it is too early to say anything about the effects of these measures, even if some doubt is more than justifiable [. . .]. Instead, it is interesting to highlight the linguistic-communicative dimension of the actions taken by the monetary authorities, the top institutions which regulate the monetary and financial markets. The fact is, of course, that it is the markets, with their demand for liquidity, which ultimately influence the decisions of the central banks; they do so in such a way that the banks, in turn, are forced to support these decisions, monetising the debts generated and accumulated by the markets — also considering that the United States is among the first and largest of indebted subjects. The fact remains that the central banks, with their monetary policies, make it their goal to intervene in the behaviour and choices of the multitude of subjects operating upon the financial markets, attempting, so to speak, to change the historically determined *grammars* at the centre of the financial communities when these communities show themselves to be dysfunctional or destructive to the whole of the economic interests of collectivity. And the grammar in force has a lot to do with the relationship between public debts, the creation of liquidity (*quantitative easing*), the risk of a financial bubble, the rate of unemployment and economic recovery. It is a fact that since the time when the Fed simply *said* that in the near future it could slow the pace of its bond buying stimulus, the yields on government securities have actually increased; *and this has happened without the Fed having to change anything whatsoever in the meantime.* [. . .]

The communicative-linguistic nature of monetary policy actions consists not so much, or solely, in communicating [. . .] the elaborated objectives of economic policy beginning with a series of economic-statistical data [. . .] There is nothing new in this; that's the way it's always been, at least since the inception of the central banks, and even before that. If anything, this has been the case since the time when the financialisation of the economy took the upper hand and imposed itself in terms of overall *governance*; what is verified here is an increase in the opacity, in the entropy (of the complexity) relative to the data upon which the monetary authorities are called upon to intervene. The monetary measures of the central banks, given this profile, are more in the nature of (one hopes) *performative* "speech acts," dialogical interventions for "making things, or having them made with words" — so as to make an impression on the general mood, to induce re-orientations with regard to conforming to the multiple whole of the investors (as in the case of *forward guidance*, where the goal is that of generating trust in the endurance of the daily interest rates). [. . .]

One should note that the communicative function of the monetary authorities was put to a hard test in recent years because of the intrinsic *instability* of the financial markets (there have been more than 160 bank crises since the 1970's, and the financial crises, the bubbles, have become, by now, a constant in the trend of the financial markets), such that the interventions of monetary policy are clearly of an *emergency* nature, moments in which the monetary authorities are forced to make decisions (by means of urgent summit meetings, teleconferences between deeply anxiety ridden, panic stricken leaders of central banks) without being able to base their decisions upon solid statistical bases, without the backup of predictable mathematical models. [. . .]

It is impossible not to see how this real trend of monetary policies is in clear conflict with neoclassical and neoliberal monetary theories which, for the last thirty years, have represented the philosophical framework, so to speak, of governmental policies and the credo of the financial markets. From Léon Walras onward, neoclassical theories have aimed at rendering money *mute*, at "silencing it," in such a way as to *immunise* the so-called real economy, according to the model of perfect concurrence of the contractual kind. For neoclassical economists, money is a disturbing element, an "ideological scandal," an exogenous factor of instability which disturbs the general equilibrium between supply and demand. For neoclassical theoreticians and Milton Friedman-style monetarist economists, the message is this: When money talks, it's no longer the language of the economy that is spoken, but always the language of sovereignty, something quite different. In other words, it's a question of *depoliticising* money, rendering it independent of the arbitrary action of the State, and, with that goal in mind, of transforming money into a pure technical instrument (simply the "veil" of real monetary exchanges), solely at the service of competition. Nevertheless, and this is the most striking paradox, historical evidence shows that policies of neutralisation, of reduction of the rate of monetary sovereignty or governability, fail from time to time, especially in times of crisis.

A recent example of such a "failure," in the neoclassical sense of the term, concerns the ECB which, through a decision made by its president, Mario Draghi, took it upon itself to acquire part of the sovereign debt of the peripheral nations most exposed to the risk of default within the Eurozone, in perfect contradiction to the doctrine [. . .] according to which the emission of money should be radically separated from politics, independent of it, so as to allow the central bank to deal exclusively with the money supply, relative to rates of inflation without the intrusion of political interests. These interventions on the part of central banks are certainly of an emergency nature, intended to save the economic and financial system from collapse. But both the emergency and the rules which one is "forced" to introduce, from time to time, in order to allow the market economy and the banking system itself to function, are *consubstantial* to the functioning of the economic system. Sovereignty, the political dimension of money, is not, in other words, exclusive to moments of disfunctionality, of temporary imbalance in the markets, an exception which would confirm the rule of the economy of the competitive market. Monetary sovereignty emerges, instead, from the very functioning of the market economy; it is, as we shall see, internal and external to it, at one and the same time; it is its direct and inevitable public-collective product. Monetary sovereignty is, above all, of a *dialogical* nature, impregnated by "communicative experiments" intended to forge that intangible "public trust" which is indispensable to the functioning of the entire economic-monetary machine. [. . .]

The thesis we intend to maintain, moreover, is that the linguistic nature of money, if it clearly has to do with the process of financialisation of the capitalist economy, must, however, be seen *also* as the result of a historically determined process of transformation of the modes of the production of goods. The linguistic turn of the economy, in other words, has its beginnings in the factories, in the places where social wealth is produced, and then finds its most potent manifestation in the process of financialisation. [. . .]

The financial markets are able to function thanks to the systematic creation of collective *conventions*, *beliefs* or "cognitive constraints" which, beginning with money as "absolute convention," determine the function of the multitude of economic subjects. The Internet convention, the "emerging nations" convention, the *subprime* convention, the sovereign debt convention, just to name the most recent of these in chronological order, are all conventions created by the "power of the multitude" of the investors in order to determine spheres of fulfillment of monetary profits. [. . .] In this process of financialisation, the money that is created and injected into circulation to monetise the purchase of financial assets becomes entirely *self-referential*, while profit, which prompts investors' decisions, becomes detached from any underlying value. These investment preferences, in turn, are not driven by information related to the fair value of this or that asset (as still advocated by neoclassical theory); they are the result of processes of *imitation*, of *gregarious* processes by means of which an investment strategy is established by looking at what *others* decide to do. [. . .]

Mimetic behaviour, looking at what others are doing, is based on a deficit of information (on an "absence of being") which affects each investor, a structural deficit regarding the nature of wealth as it is *unanimously* recognised. Mimetic behaviour is the *process* of constructing a universal idea of wealth. In other words, on the financial markets, communicative behavior, deferring to others' decisions, and imitation determine conventions or collective opinions (first and foremost, about liquidity as an absolute convention) *regardless* of the fair value underlying the assets in which one invests or upon which one speculates. [. . .] While many would agree completely, at least from the standpoint of the *description* of the "behavioral" operation of the financial markets, with this analysis of the modality of the creation of liquidity and of its "linguisticity," it ignores one important feature: the creation-integration of money into the directly productive cycle of goods. It is likely that this "partiality" in the study of the linguistic evolution of money is due to the power of the processes of financialisation as they have developed in the last thirty years. Financialisation facilitates, so to speak, the "liquidation" of the problem of value-substance by virtue of the self-referentiality of the processes of creation of monetary wealth and, *also*, as a consequence of issues, still unresolved, within a "physiological" (as expenditure of *psychophysical* energy) Marxist substance-essence framework and within *historically determined* and always changing capitalist modes of production.

Without delving into the details of this old debate, for the purpose of this study it suffices to recall that the issue of the relationship between abstract labour as substance and historically determined modes of production is viewed as a *contradiction* between labour-force, that is, the *power-potential* of labour (biological, innate) and *living labour* put to work by the capitalist enterprise, by the historically given and always changing modes of production. The result is that desubstantialisation impacts, first of all, upon the development of productive forces, of technical-scientific knowledge — in other words the *general intellect* crystallised in the machine system which, historically, has turned living labour itself into the "wretched base" of the value of socially produced wealth, as foreseen by Marx in his *Grundrisse* (the famous "Fragment on Machines"). The crisis of Fordism and its evolution into post-Fordism and into financial capitalism can be explained in light of the crisis of labour-as-substance, but *also* as a transition to a new incarnation of capitalism where the most natural and *common* qualities possessed by the linguistic animal (such as linguistic faculty, communicative-relational capacity, capacity to react to unforeseen circumstances, etc.) are *put to work*, controlled by value-mining devices which reach across the spheres of production and the circulation-reproduction of goods.

[. . .] In other words: convention *and* materialism, desubstantialisation of the value *and* materiality of the new processes of valorisation (of value-mining) distributed throughout the entire society are two faces of the same coin, indivisible if one wants to study the linguistic nature of money. On August 15, 1971, the declaration of the inconvertibility to gold of the US dollar sealed the conclusive transition, which had been taking shape during the Sixties, to a fully dematerialised, *desubstantialised* monetary system whose flexibility (in flexible trading, to be precise) had been made necessary by the inflexibility of wage negotiations. The linguistic turn of capitalist modes of production, ushered in later, at the end of the 1970's, as the answer to the crisis of Fordist overproduction and to the decline in profit margins, would further contribute to the desubstantialisation of value, redefining the coordinates of the exploitation of living labour. And it is with this crisis in the Fordist model that a veritable financialisation is rolled out: the creation of additional income by means of wage reductions, by way of increased private debt (both of businesses and of families); the privatisation of Keynesian public *deficit spending* through the proliferation of synthetic financial instruments (the famous derivatives); the deregulation and liberalisation of both labour and capital markets.

Money that is created and integrated into the productive processes of mature capitalism is money created *ex nihilo*, that is, generated on the foundation of a nonexistent amount of pre-existing capital, without any preventive connection to the universe of goods. [. . .]

This money, issued by the banking system as debt-credit and integrated into the economic cycle as an advance on wages and earnings, is the manifestation of a value *yet to come*: it is the aggregate of the devices of capitalist valorisation which transforms money *ex nihilo* into a general equivalent, after having transformed the labour-force into *actualised* living labour. The measure of the value of money (both gold-money and paper-money) is the *capacity to generate work.* "To have worth" means to be effective, and in this sense money and language are totally similar, since both have no effect other than that of generating action. In reality, it is money that *controls* living labour (in the same way as a system of machines does), that validates it socially and that, in doing so, makes it possible to render the value of goods commensurate, *a posteriori.* The monetary measure of value (its "*nominal* measure"), established through the determination of the prices of goods and of wages (the price of the labour-force), is itself, in the era of financial capitalism, a *convention* because it functions as a (capitalist) collective evaluation of the total value of power, of control over the living labour which is necessary to the valorisation of capital. It is in the light of money as control over living labour that we can explain phenomena relative to the increased flexible-temporary nature of work, essentially its *devaluation* in relation to the production and capitalist appropriation of wealth. In this case it is legitimate to speak of a "convention of devaluation" of labour.

This digression on money created-integrated into the cycle of valorisation of capital allows for the inclusion, in the theory of self-referential finance, of the linguistic-communicative functions of *living labour.* The power of the multitude, as Frédéric Lordon has defined it with an explicit reference to Spinoza, does not concern exclusively the multiplicity of investors-financiers searching for a collective convention to ensure the liquidity of their investments in financial profits. The multitude controlled by money is a multitude that *works by way of communication,* that puts to work its linguistic-rational competencies, knowledge crystallised into bodies, bodies which then become machines, fixed capital. Money created *ex nihilo* in order to remunerate the work of the multitude monetises a labour activity in which language, communication, knowledge, and cooperation are productive factors which are strategic for capital, to the point that we have been speaking of "human *capital*" for quite some time now. In this sense we can speak of money as a *form of linguistic value,* that is, a form of the productive function of living labour, of the production of goods by way of language. [. . .]. The *circular* relationship, to put it in Aristotelian terms, between money and language, which over time has been analyzed alternately from the perspective of monetary theories, and at other times from the perspective of the philosophy of language, must be studied with caution. In the continuous references to money and language from both of these perspectives, with references to the disciplinary research of isomorphisms, and of "homologies" between money and language, one can catch a glimpse of the concrete, *material* history of the relationship between money and language.

But what happens when, as is the case today, money and language actually overlap? A first approximation might lead us to say that it is correct to see today's money, as John Searle does, as a demonstration of John Austin's speech acts [. . .]. When, for example, The United States Treasury writes on a 20 dollar bill, "This note is legal tender for all debts, public and private," not only is this de-scribing a fact; in reality it is *creating* one. This is a speech act in which the act of *saying* something makes that something real. Just as is the case in today's monetary policies of forward guidance [. . .].

What is a speech act? To the extent that we use the term X to represent the state/function of Y, we use X symbolically; we use it as a linguistic device. When, however, the term X does not have a physical (substantive) support to which it can refer linguistically, the linguistic act (*saying* X) becomes productive "in and of itself," *constitutive* of the Y function. For the words "chair" and "knife," their functional use is inscribed in the physicality of the chair and of the knife. But there is no physical support, no substance, for "money," or for "I take this woman as my lawful wedded wife," or for stocks, to allow for these states/functions to materialise. The linguistic-communicative act is *constitutive* of money, as it is of marriage and of stocks.

The efficacy of "performative money," as Emile Benveniste says with regard to performative utterances, depends on the *legitimacy* of the speaker; that is, it depends on the *power* and the *legal* designation of whoever "speaks monetarily." In the monetary system there exists, at all times, a "last resort," which could be called an "absolute performative act," one that reveals itself in moments of crisis. Let us bear in mind that roughly 95% of the money in circulation, is in fact, *scriptural* money, while the remaining 5% is *fiduciary* money, that is, money which we keep in our pockets and which represents, as a "last resort," money as a universal equivalent of goods. We can then assert that nearly the entire monetary system is, by nature, a debt system, and as long as the circulation of merchandise (goods and services) assures its commensurability, this will not cause a scandal. When the sequence of exchanges is interrupted for some reason (over borrowing by businesses and individuals, excessive speculation on raw materials, over production in certain sectors such as the automobile industry, the housing sector, the high tech sector, currency crises, etc.), the demand for fiduciary money prevails (this is known as "liquidity preference"). The "run on the banks," the rush to redeem book-entry securities (so to speak) for money that "jingles," reveals the imbalance between the process of socialisation of capital transmitted by the debt leverage and the capacity of the system, as a whole, to satisfy this demand for jingling-fiduciary money. In such situations of crisis, the money created "as a last resort" by the central monetary authorities can truly be called an absolute performative act. [. . .]

The distinction between ordinary performative acts and absolute performative acts within the theory of language is particularly useful for articulating a linguistic theory of money. In the case of ordinary performative acts, such as "I take this woman as my lawful wedded wife," we reference a reality generated *by the* utterance or *in the* utterance. Translated into money, the ordinary performative act is the normal-ordinary creation of money carried out by the banking system. For all intents and purposes, this is scriptural money, certainly created *ex nihilo*, but integrated into the flow of wealth production (material and/or purely financial). In the case of the absolute performative act, on the other hand, the "I speak," the *fact-that-we-speak*, the *fact-that-the-central-bank-speaks*, we are referring to the creation, as a last resort, of *fiduciary* money necessary to avoid catastrophe, whether monetary or financial. Certainly it can be maintained that the creation of fiduciary money on the part of the central banks is also a form of debt, given that this money is injected into the banking circuits through the purchase of Treasury bonds, or of government debt securities (such that the creation of liquidity entails the accumulation of debts in the central bank's balance sheets). But this infinite regression [. . .] calls into being the "*that's enough*" stance of the central monetary authorities. In crisis situations, the monetary "that's enough" stance is, *always*, an attempt to reestablish faith in the collective, in the capitalist system's ability to save itself. [. . .] In recent years we have witnessed the proliferation of "cycles of flight" from official monetary practices contested by those social groups aiming explicitly and actively at creating spaces for a communal economy *without money*. From the "systems of local exchange," to time banking, up to the most recent digital *bitcoins*, the by now innumerable experiments in building parallel horizontal economies have as a common denominator the will to escape from the empire of the monetary system, from the authority of the central banks, and from the right of seigniorage (via interest rates, the manipulation of exchange rates, etc.). As for the quest to establish economies of solidarity *without money*, paradoxically, but not accidentally, the quest nevertheless always entails the establishment and emission of localised and circumscribed money. This money guarantees the "communal affect" and the social cooperation pervasive in these communities. Their distinctive, and to put it in Marxian terms, utopian trait consists of their desire to reform monetary exchange by way of a simple and exclusive modification of the instrument of exchange and of the measurement unit of exchanged goods, thus never interfering in the larger sphere of capitalist production of goods. In these attempts, noble as they might be, one cannot help but catch a glimpse of a certain neoclassical mindset, that is, the will to "silence" money, to make it function as a simple *veil* of exchanges, a mere technical instrument used to bring about a more equitable distribution of wealth, yet failing to chip away at the root those inequalities which originate from within the processes of the *production* of wealth itself.

These ideas of "Communal currency" are clearly reminiscent of Proudhon's proposal to create a labour-money, time chits, time-based money, a currency that can be *immediately* credited to the work produced by individuals in their role as social workers, without needing to first jump through the hoops which come with the exchange of goods produced in the sphere of the monetary circulation-realisation of goods. Marx's criticism of

Proudhon does not refer at all to the *institutional* dimension necessary for guaranteeing the mutualistic structures of social organisation, but rather to the danger of their becoming subaltern to the dominant logic of capital and of the State. In other words, the question of Communal money, first of all, sends us back to the *nature of labour* within the determined modes of the production of wealth: is Communal labour capable of *instituting* its own monetary organisation and of restoring a more equitable distribution of created wealth?

The liquidity of the Communal can only be the result of the power of the multitude which institutes its unit of account (and also the organisation of its emission). If it is true that the linguistic-relational nature of labour brings about its own increasing degree of autonomy from the capitalist organisation of production and the appropriation of social wealth, it is equally true that this autonomy, in order to remain such, needs its own voice, its own words, and the ability to set boundaries. It needs to say: That's enough.

CHAPTER 21

Luisa Muraro (1940–)

Luisa Muraro is an Italian feminist philosopher, founder of the philosophical feminist group *Diotima* in Verona, and one of the most relevant voices of Italian Sexual Difference Theory.

She encountered feminism in the 1960s, after a collaboration with Elvio Fachinelli on a project for an anti-authoritarian school, from which arises the journal *Erba Voglio [The 'I-Want' Plant]*. Across the 1960s and 1970s, she meets the first feminist groups in Milan and becomes part of the *DEMAU (Demistificazione Autoritarismo Patriarcale)* group. Here she meets Lia Cigarini, and together with others, she founds, in 1975, the *Milan Women's Bookstore Collective (Libreria delle Donne di Milano)*, an extremely important feminist cultural and political space, still flourishing, and its journal *Via Dogana*. In 1984, Muraro founds the philosophical community of *Diotima*, together with Chiara Zamboni, Wanda Tommasi and Adriana Cavarero. The group is named after Diotima of Mantinea, Socrates's teacher, as he reveals in Plato's *Symposium*.

Luisa Muraro taught theoretical philosophy at the University of Verona from 1976 to 2006 and collaborated with the Duoda Women's Research Centre at the University of Barcelona. Her works are linked to so-called second wave feminism, born at the end of the 1960s, between the United States and Europe, which has to be distinguished from nineteenth-century feminism which devoted itself largely to the pursuit of equal civil and political rights. Italian second wave feminism has been deeply marked by the political analysis of Carla Lonzi (and her collective, *Rivolta Femminile*) whose influence upon Muraro was considerable and readily apparent. Second wave feminism does not demand inclusion for women in society as it stands or simply provide a radical critique of given societies as patriarchal and sexist, as in the nineteenth century. The irreducible differences between men and women can give rise to a more transformative politics than the struggle for abstract equality. Women and men may be equal before the law, but sexual difference between women and men is a fulcrum for radical change in societies.

This is why Muraro's approach has been recognized as part of Sexual Difference Theory, or Difference Feminism, stemming largely from Luce Irigaray's works (whose most important books were translated into Italian by Muraro). This denomination has often led to confusion and ambiguities, since it seems to suggest that for Muraro there would be some fixed elements common to all women that would distinguish them from men in an essentialist way. In fact, difference between men and women is to be understood as a political operator capable of redefining social categories, hierarchies, dichotomies.

Her approach to both philosophy and politics has been marked by a focus on sexual difference and women's freedom. She has also worked on the topic of Women Mystics in Christianity and their relevance for contemporary philosophy.

In her work, *The Symbolic Order of the Mother*, Muraro identifies the bond between mother and child as a key political moment, ontologically fundamental to the development of culture and politics (since this relationship gives life to both corporeal development and language acquisition, the sources of all thinking, culture and social organization). The mediating power of the mother tongue, which we all learn from our mothers, constitutes a symbolic order that comes before all others, for both women and men. However, in a world whose civilization, culture and societies have been defined by men, a woman can feel admiration, envy and the desire to be included in that cultural landscape, as happened to Muraro herself, who desired to become a philosopher and an independent woman, and this can lead women to set themselves in opposition with their mothers. This conflict between philosophy (and culture) and the mother constitutes a fundamental root of patriarchy's symbolic disorder and undermines the possibility of freedom for both women and men. This leads Muraro to advocate a feminist practice of gratitude to the mother and to appeal for the recognition of the mother's authority as a model of unconditional nurture and support, as well as proposing that the symbolic order of the mother must overcome the disorder of patriarchy.

Federica Castelli

Selected writings

Muraro, Luisa. *La signora del gioco. Episodi della caccia alle streghe (The Lady of the Game. Episodes of the Witch Hunt).* Milan: Feltrinelli, 1976

Muraro, Luisa. *Diotima: Il pensiero della differenza sessuale (Diotima: The Thought of Sexual Difference).* Milan: La Tartaruga, 1987 New edition 2003

Muraro, Luisa. *Il Dio delle donne (The God of Women).* Milan: Mondadori, 2003

Muraro, Luisa. *Tre Lezioni sulla differenza sessuale e altri scritti (Three Lessons on Sexual Difference and Other Writings)*. Naples: Orthotes Editrice, 2011 [1994]

Muraro, Luisa. *Lingua materna, scienza divina. Scritti sulla filosofia mistica di Margherita Porete (Mother Tongue, Divine Science. Writings on the Mystical Philosophy of Margherita Porete)*. Naples: D'Auria, 1995

Muraro, Luisa. *The Symbolic Order of the Mother*, trans. Francesca Novello. Albany, NY: State University of New York Press, 2018 [1991]

EXCERPT

Luisa Muraro, *The abyssal distance*

(Luisa Muraro, *The Symbolic Order of the Mother*, Trans. Francesca Novello. Ed. Timothy S. Murphy. Albany, NY: State University of New York Press, 2018, pp. 85–98.)

For many years, ever since I became an adult, all around me I have heard talk of the contrast between children's need for approval and an adult duty to think independently. [. . .]

[F]rom deep inside of me a new thought arose. I came to think that, in the first place, I do not want an adult independence of thought or of anything else because more than that, I want a correspondence between (my) thinking and (my) being. It is only in this correspondence that I feel good. Only then can I actually say I, me, and mine. Second, I came to think that the correspondence I am looking for begins for me in recognizing the insurmountable feeling of dependence I have inside me, and in accepting it in spite of what is usually taught. So, to conclude, having become capable of an independent thought, I find myself in a new combination of dependence and independence in which the latter grows stronger through acceptance of the former.

[. . .] A child's feeling of dependence is still intact inside me [. . .].

Women before me have carried out careful and balanced feminist investigations that resulted in justifiably refuting the idea of an opposition between dependence and autonomy according to which the one excludes the other. [. . .] What exists reproduces itself not because it is considered good but because a mechanism stronger than our intentions and criticism propels it, no matter how justified those intentions and criticisms are. The problem, then, is to break this mechanism of repetition. As long as this mechanism operates, it uses everything for its own benefit, including our yearning for the good and the true, and including our longing to be free of it.

It is neither a moral nor a psychological problem. It is a problem of symbolic order. If the authority of the mother has no place in the symbolic order we obey, the result is that the behaviour of the mother will regularly be considered intrusive or, vice versa, yielding, or, more often, both intrusive and yielding at the same time. This is because in the absence of a recognized necessity, her authority has no standard for its exercise or its acceptance. Until we break the vicious circles of a certain symbolic order, which for women is rather a symbolic disorder, reality will continue to bet in favour of phallic power and of the rigid opposition between autonomy and dependence [. . .].

The greatest disorder, which casts doubt on the possibility of women's freedom, is ignorance, women's included, of a symbolic order of the mother. Many women imagine their mothers in exactly the same way that Aristotle and Plato depicted her in their cosmologies two thousand years ago. That is, the mother was represented as a formless power and/or an obtuse interpreter of established power.

Time does not have the power to change the symbolic order, though it does change material reality. I have come to the conclusion that time and the symbolic order are equal necessities in that both of them mediate, both of them make the real thinkable. [. . .] It is not easy to understand the symbolic. It is positive because it gives us what is positive of our experience. But it is in this act of giving that the symbolic hides itself. Therefore, we must inevitably explain the symbolic by subtraction. The way I prefer to proceed is to subtract its psychological content. I came up with this idea when I presented to an audience of women the thesis that only gratitude toward the woman who brought us into the world gives a woman an authentic sense of herself. By 'gratitude toward the mother' I do not mean a feeling that may or may not be there, but I mean the pure meaning of those words, which is present in my mind even if I don't recognise her or if I have hostile feelings toward her. So I realized that by subtracting the psychological content from a word that is apparently solely psychological, like *gratitude,* I was not performing a metalinguistic operation that aimed to consider what 'gratitude to the mother' meant in the Italian language. In fact, I discovered that the word also had another reference at the level of symbolic order. [. . .]

Similarly, we can characterize the symbolic order by subtracting all ethicality and logicality from it. This does not mean that the symbolic order is immoral or illogical, as Europeans thought of cultures different from theirs when they came in contact with them, and about which they had no desire to learn. In general, the symbolic order cannot be judged because it precedes and prepares judgement. That is, it is the self-presentation of the real according to an autonomous order of self-presentation itself (and *not* according to an autonomous order of the real).

[. . .] Once again we must face the difficulty of distinguishing act and contents. To understand what a revolution is, we must not consider the symbolic order as limited to codes (such as the economic system, the political system, the law, etc.) which can be reconstructed and from which it is relatively easy, at least for those who do intellectual work, to take their distance and to plan their modification. We need to consider the symbolic order in its actuality, as the system of mediations on which I depend in order to say what I am saying and for what I am not able to say, and in general for all that I can say and wish to say, and so on.

It is at this level of determined/determining mediation, in which I am spoken/speaking, acted-on/acting, and so forth, that the symbolic order reproduces itself and can also change. It is the level of the necessity of mediation at which the absolute intent to say intertwines with the means of saying, the immediate with the mediate. So effects become causes, facts become principles. At this level, experience stops laying itself open to external interpretations, and it produces its own interpretation. The real stops appearing as mere effect and becomes a principle. In plain words, it is at this level that there is freedom, if there is freedom.

The question is: can we plan to change the symbolic order? It is certain that the symbolic order can change, since history shows us it can. But is it sensible to conceive of a politics of modification of the symbolic order based, as I am suggesting, on the politics of women?

I think so. [. . .]

The French historian Fernand Braudel promoted the idea of 'unconscious history.' [. . .] Braudel makes an important observation for the understanding of our time. He observes that today, in fact, people's awareness of a slower and deeper history has grown so acute that we can speak of a revolution, which Braudel calls an intellectual revolution. This revolution consists in openly confronting the semi-obscurity of that deeper and slower history in order to give it an increasingly large place next to and to the detriment of current history. [. . .]

But why should the symbolic revolution be called political? [. . .] Whatever concerns the symbolic order is also part of politics because the social order depends, in part, on it. Without symbolic relevance, a material power, however great it may be, would have little importance. [. . .] There is a contradiction within every regime of mediation that I must now try to formulate. In very general terms, it is the contradiction between presence that speaks for itself and the necessity of mediation. Therefore, the contradiction concerns the originary structure of knowledge with its intertwining of experience and logic. [. . .]

[A] characteristic of perhaps every regime of mediation [. . .] is that its rules fulfill the requirements of communication-signification, and they *also* fulfill other social demands. Consequently, the question of sayability is always and also a question of symbolic order. [. . .] If this is the case, we must think that the pure circularity of experience and logic does not constitute the originary structure of knowledge. Sayability is thus a question of symbolic order that is historically determined. Sayability depends on the set of mediations provided by a given culture. What can be said, therefore, is a historical instance that cannot be distinguished from a logical instance. The language we speak proves that thinking is language and language is historically determined.

I believe that when Saussure spoke of the arbitrary nature of the linguistic sign, he grasped this aspect of mediation. That is, mediation is logically necessary but its forms are not. [. . .]

This leads us to conclude that, first of all, between experience and its signification, no matter how faithful, there is an abyssal distance [. . .]. Second, the imperfect circle of mediation brings up a problem concerning symbolic power, which is a political problem in the most everyday sense of the word.

In fact, who or what decides what is sayable, if experience and logic are not enough? What actually keeps alive or kills the circle of mediation that language in itself guarantees me? How are the historically determined forms of mediation connected to its logical necessity?

Several women thinkers have responded to the systematic isolation of their attempts at autonomous female thinking by trying to adapt as much as possible to the rules of communication-signification in force. [. . .] I came to think that we must take the opposite direction, which does not mean that we should become estranged (with the result of marginalizing ourselves) but, instead, that we should make a new symbolic order necessary. I start from this simple thesis: thought is mediation and the social order is a set of mediations that are more or less coherent, but in any case functioning. If the experience of a woman is not a true point of view, if female grandeur is difficult to sustain, if female freedom is considered a luxury like having a second or a third car, the most effective response will consist in increasing the demands for truth, grandeur, and freedom to make the need for mediation greater and greater. Perhaps it is our self-moderation that makes the issue of women's freedom, and consequently women's autonomous way of thinking, superfluous to the social order. Superfluous, and therefore nil: thought and freedom, in fact, respond to the order of necessity.

[. . .] Based on my personal history and reasoning, I think that women's self-moderation is due to an unresolved conflict with the mother that makes the viewpoint of the originary relationship impracticable. Until I brought to light the aversion I felt for my mother and any other mother figure; until I realised the great love I felt for her together with my need for her approval and my fear of not obtaining it; until I solved this problem of the maternal principle of mediation, the vehemence of my intent to say what I wanted to say fell into a circle with the submission to the established rules, as I have already explained. I ended up saying only what seemed plausible, no matter whether it was true, made up, likely, or sincere, since all circumstances were made irrelevant by the iron constraint of the circle of self-moderation. For me as for others, what was present to me became literally insignificant, although it was still present in the unhappy form of an experience without sense.

The real without the symbolic is less than nothing. [. . .] This situation corresponds to that of the child who is separated from the mother and cannot find the originary common place she or he had with her. That is, the child is not able to speak if we regard speaking as a way of finding again the point of view the child used to share with the mother. Due to the abyssal distance between everything we want to say and the means of sayability, we would never be able to find that point of view again if there were not someone who asked us to speak and assured us that they understand what we wanted to say.

A woman discovers the symbolic need for the mother when self-moderation ends. [. . .]

Earlier I asked myself: who or what decides what can be said if logic and experience are not enough? We must recognize that from the truth-confirming point of view there are no instances equal to logic and experience. It is just that they are not enough. On the one hand, experience in a pure state does not take place, and in any case it requires demonstration and representation. On the other hand, the mode of mediation is historically determined. Languages, scientific societies, churches, radio stations, television, newspapers, and even school principals, editors, and so on, are a series of instances that in many aspects can be considered contingent but that as such are never completely so, because mediation is necessary even between me and myself, and the abyssal distance passes through me, dividing me into two parts. I am not thinking of soul/body, although in the past this duality was a way to smooth over the problem. I am divided in every fibre and cell of my organism by the very regime of mediation: by its necessity and its inadequacy, which are inseparable, like the jaws of pincers we cannot escape. Except for the fact that we know it, and we explain it.

I began this symbolic operation of explaining the regime of mediation by saying that I neither brought myself into the world nor did I teach myself to speak. This led me to find once again the originary relationship with the mother.

Therefore, when I am asked who or what decides what can be said, I answer that in the first place it is the authority of the mother. The mother tongue, first mediator and first code, is proof of this. Scientific communities, parliaments, courts, markets, and other social institutions of the same kind, including my school of philosophy where they taught metaphysics, are valid instances, but they are secondary. They come after the mother.

This takes us back to my 'clause' about the primacy of the mother, which shows us that it is enough to respect her in order to create a symbolic order in a historically given reality, whatever reality one might find oneself in. The maternal principle builds a bridge over the abyssal distance between the logical necessity of mediation and its historical forms, which can always be modified and in an unquantifiable sense are always arbitrary. I do not put the principle of the mother outside history: my history begins with the relationship with my mother. But I place it above authorities and powers whose codes make up both the symbolic and social order, any historical order in which one happens to live, we might say by chance if it were not for the history of our birth.

[...] We must choose whether we want to identify symbolic authority with established power, since it assures (or in the case of the established opposition it promises to assure) some kind of social synthesis, or whether we want to acknowledge the authority of the woman who brought us into the world and taught us to speak. It is because of our relationship with her that the mother is entitled to authority that, instead, established powers usurp from her [...].

In fact, at this level there is a choice and those who choose to grant symbolic authority to established power, which assures a social synthesis (on its own terms, of course), will not speak of usurpation but instead they will talk about substitution, and they will argue that after childhood we must learn to do without the mother. To my way of thinking, we do not have to, but we can do without her. Undeniably there is a symbolic order that is not that of the mother. I have chosen to substitute for childhood attachment to the mother knowing how to love her, and I have chosen to consider the language I learned from her as the first (archetypal) form of that knowing. I know of other women and men who have made this choice. On the other hand, yet other women and men prefer to substitute for the attachment to the mother an obligation within the regime of mediation, devoting themselves completely to their labour, to the state, to their family, to their religion, and so forth. They prefer languages they learned later, or artificial languages, or money, to the language of the mother. This can also be a choice.

At a deeper but very common level, there is no choice. At this level there is a female, and not only female, experience, the signification of which does not find in the given symbolic and also social order either a meaningful, a supportive, or a rejecting interaction, but only fortuitous reactions that can cause chaos or, if you prefer, hell. A frightening example of the lack of meaningful interaction between female experience and codified culture can be found in the history of the persecution of witches, which remains unexplained although extensive historical research has been carried out.

There is the social body, which finds some kind of synthesis, and there is the wild body. I give this name to that part of human experience that goes beyond what a given symbolic-social order can mediate and that, consequently, remains outside of the social synthesis or enters into it as an object of interpretation and of other people's interventions. Before the politics of women, female experience was this wild body.

I believe that for the type of human experience that is outside the social order, or is unhappily within it, there is only one possible symbolic order. This is the symbolic order that can refer experience to the authority of the mother. As a matter of fact, the authority of the mother represents the principle that has in itself the greatest capacity for mediation because it is able to put into the circle of mediation both our being body and our being word. [. . .]

We must fight to prevent the social synthesis of established power from substituting something for the maternal principle. We must give a social translation to maternal power in order to prevent social synthesis from closing up. We must fight to keep social synthesis open to anything we want to say, however distant or abnormal that may be.

For me, keeping the social synthesis open is the condition of freedom.

CHAPTER 22

Antonio Negri (1933–)

Born in Padua in 1933, Antonio Negri studied political science in the Faculty of Jurisprudence at the University of Padua in the 1950s. Then, having been exposed to the critical theory of the Frankfurt School in Germany, he returned to Italy and joined the working-class movement in the North. During the 1960s and 1970s waves of anti-capitalist uprisings against trade unions, the Communist Party and industry were met with violent police repression. An active participant in these struggles, Negri argued for a form of Marxism conceived of as an open materialist theory with a changing real referent and no internal continuity: a philosophy of praxis for a changing subject.

At the University of Padua, in the 1970s he was offered the position of Professor of State Theory and became chair of the Institute of Political Science. There, he animated what became known as the current of *operaismo* or workerism, which used militant sociological inquiry as a device to both research and organize workers. With students, colleagues and fellow militants, Negri investigated class composition: the political, economic and social character of a changing subject and the expressions of its insurgent practices. In this period, he held lectures on Lenin which resulted in *Factory of Strategy*, where he defended a Leninist 'method' and epistemology to radically reinvent communism in the face of new class formations.[1]

For Negri, Marxism is a political epistemology, a form of perspectivism anchored in realities that are all but predestined. 'The concept of asymmetry (of proletarian power versus capitalist development) means that the autonomy of class is not recognizable if one looks for it through the categories of capital.'[2] Against objectivist interpretations of Marx that emphasized continuity and synthesis, Negri speaks of ruptures and metamorphoses.

As unrest spread across society, the Italian government clamped down and arrested over 10,000 militants from the extra-parliamentary left. Negri was one of them. From 1979, he spent four and a half years in various special prisons awaiting trial, before being elected MP and using parliamentary immunity to flee to France in 1983.

During his time in jail, he wrote his most densely philosophical essays and traced the emergence of another modernity, found not in the apologetics of the bourgeoisie, René Descartes, Jean-Jacques Rousseau and Georg Wilhelm Friedrich Hegel, but in immanent materialism, a legacy left by Niccolò Machiavelli, Baruch Spinoza, Giacomo Leopardi and Karl Marx. This opposition between immanent materialism and a transcendental view of sovereignty informs Negri's writings on ontology and epistemology, which often take the form of dense, close, political readings and intellectual histories.

Most importantly, in the face of escalating levels and changing forms of social antagonism, Negri declared the theoretical and political inadequacy of radical humanist interpretations of dialectics. Dialectics sees negation as a moment to be overcome in order to achieve fullness of being, whereas for Negri resistance is immediately productive. Far from negation, antagonism is self-affirmation and valorization; in so far as the relation between capital and labour is asymmetrical and heteronomous, it cannot be resolved or overcome: it can only be replaced by a social revolution. 'Dialectics, in as much as it forms transcendental thinking, denies the decision the power to generate *ex nihilo* (and to produce plenitude, fullness of being in the void, against the void).'[3]

Negri's position on modernity is spelled out in *Political Descartes. Reason, Ideology and the Bourgeois Project*, *The Savage Anomaly: The Power of Spinoza's Metaphysics and Politics* and *Flower of the Desert: Giacomo Leopardi's Poetic Ontology*.

In *Political Descartes*, Negri situates the thought of the father of modern rationalism in the first historical crisis of the bourgeois project. Negri interprets Descartes's rationalism and dualism politically. Philosophies of transcendence emerge as a reactionary response to crisis – in this case, the failure of the humanist project of the Renaissance to free humankind from religious dogma and authority and assert its power to make history and give meaning to its own affairs. In Negri's view, Renaissance utopianism was driven by the dynamics of appropriation of the world of things, nature and history; but the first liberal bourgeois project failed to give itself a political form and resolve these dynamics in a philosophy of praxis. Finding no correspondence to ontological individualism in reality, Descartes fictionalized it in an abstraction. For Negri, the betrayal of the bourgeoisie consists in this politics of mediation, falsification and transcendence, in hiding the violence of mechanisms of appropriation and presenting the realm of circulation and the market as a universal and undivided, second nature.

Negri's discussion of Spinoza as a materialist thinker of immanence in *The Savage Anomaly* carries forward this critique: in Spinoza, the elucidation of connections in logic does not merely serve the purpose of clarity of thought. Spinoza believes that the order and connections of ideas can be treated as the order and connections of things. For a philosophy of immanence, there is no external cause to the world: the world contains its own explanation.

For Negri, the Enlightenment, like the Renaissance, was a social revolution betrayed. The poet Leopardi, discussed in *Flower of the Desert*, was for Negri exemplary of a European Romanticism that embraced a cosmic view of the world instead of retreating into variants of aesthetic individualism in search of the absolute. Here Negri reads Leopardi against Hegel.

One topic that recurs throughout Negri's intellectual histories is the attempt to explain the inability of society to give itself forms of organization that remain true to its political ideals and the spirit in which social revolutionary subjects are formed: in other words, the transitions from constituent to constituted power.[4]

During the 1980s in Paris, Negri held a series of lectures on the *Grundrisse* which resulted in the seminal study, *Marx Beyond Marx*. In 1987 he published *Fabbriche del Soggetto*, an as yet untranslated text, which also aims to dispel the allure of self-abstracting ideologies – this time, contemporaneous ones:

> Optimism of the will becomes a technique for the reduction of social complexity. This operation consists in abstracting antinomies that have an ontological foundation, and relocating them in a project of simulation, requalifying them in a scenario that is substitutive of reality. The process of simulation (in postmodernity) becomes the process of the substitution of the real. (*Fabbriche del Soggetto*, p. 212)

In the late 1990s Negri returned to Italy to serve part of his sentence under house arrest, and in 2000 he published *Empire*, the first of a series co-authored with Michael Hardt that brought a great deal of international attention to his body of work. Previous books began to be translated, and his interventions, past and present, found fertile ground in an intellectual environment that seemed impervious to ongoing struggles and the reality of new political subjectivities. Negri's collaboration with Hardt in *Empire*, followed by *Multitude*, *Commonwealth*, *Declaration* and *Assembly*, contributed enormously to updating the analysis of class composition and political governance in a world that was half-heartedly embarking upon a globalizing journey from which it would never return.

The 'multitude' is the name Hardt and Negri give to a new political subject, and also the protagonist of Negri's recent theatre plays, *A Trilogy of Resistance*, that treats of the relationship between the production of the common and violence.

Negri's affirmative politics has been influenced by and has in turn influenced two if not three generations of militants, from autonomist workers to the anti-capitalist movement and beyond. This symbiotic relationship has contributed to a revival of critical theory as a political task, and, for this, Negri's contribution cannot be underestimated. His writings on ontology, his lineage of revolutionary thinkers otherwise forgotten, the productive encounter of Marxology and post-structuralism, and his intervention in the politics of theories of modernity breathed new life into the otherwise stale and cynical debate on the post-modern. His is a political epistemology that does not formalize the workings of reason to impose them on reality but intervenes critically in the real to identify its potential.

Negri's work ranges from philosophical exegesis, Marxian political economy, political pamphleteering to playwriting, and his writings span a period of sixty years; but if anything binds together this vast and differentiated body of work, it would be the search for the logic of social ontology: a movement that is incommensurable, unstoppable and non-teleological. As he puts it, 'the desire for liberation has an irreducible ontological logic of its own.'

Arianna Bove

Notes

1 Investigating class subjectivity in the hidden spontaneous forms of antagonism in factories, adopting the subjective standpoint of labour, Negri found that, beyond wage demands, struggles took the form of refusal, wild cat strikes, sabotage, absenteeism and moving from one employer to another, all of which occurred autonomously with respect to the political exigencies and programmes of the representative structures of trade unions, the communist party and the state.

2 Negri, '20 Theses on Marx: Interpretation of the Class Situation Today', in S. Makdis, C. Casarino and R. E. Karl (eds.), *Marxism Beyond Marxism*, (New York: Routledge, 1996), pp. 149–80.

3 Negri, *Time for Revolution*, trans. Matteo Mandarini (London: Continuum, 2003 [1982–2000]), p. 251.

4 This dynamic is spelled out in *Insurgencies: Constituent Power and the Modern State,* trans. Maurizia Boscagli (Minneapolis: University of Minnesota Press, 1999 [1992]), and *The Labour of Dionysus: A Critique of the State Form* (co-authored with M. Hardt), (Minneapolis: University of Minnesota Press, 1994).

Selected writings

Hardt, Michael. and Antonio Negri. *Empire*. Cambrdige: Harvard University Press, 2000

Hardt, Michael. and Antonio Negri. *Commonwealth*. Cambrdige: Belknap Press of Harvard University Press, 2009

Negri, Antonio. *The Politics of Subversion: A Manifesto for the Twenty-First Century*. Cambridge: Polity Press, 1989

Negri, Antonio. *The Savage Anomaly: The Power of Spinoza's Metaphysics and Politics*, trans. Michael Hardt. Minneapolis, MN: University of Minnesota Press, 1991

Negri, Antonio. *Time for Revolution*, trans. Matteo Mandarini. New York: Continuum, 2003

Negri, Antonio. *Subversive Spinoza: (Un)Contemporary Variations*, trans. Timothy S. Murphy, Michael Hardt, Ted Stolze, and Charles T. Wolfe, and edited by Timothy S. Murphy. Manchester: Manchester University Press, 2004

Negri, Antonio. *Political Descartes: Reason, Ideology and the Bourgeois Project*, trans. Matteo Mandarini and Alberto Toscano. New York: Verso, 2007

Negri, Antonio. *The Porcelain Workshop: For a New Grammar of Politics*, trans. Noura Wedell. California: Semiotext(e), 2008

Negri, Antonio. *Insurgencies: Constituent Power and the Modern State*, trans. Maurizia Boscagli. Minneapolis, MN: University of Minnesota Press (Reprint Edition), [1999] 2009

Negri, Antonio. *Flower of the Desert: Giacomo Leopardi's Poetic Ontology*, trans. Timothy S. Murphy. New York: SUNY Press, 2015

EXCERPT

Antonio Negri, *Materialism and poetry*

('Materialism and Poetry', 'A Lyric Machiavelli' from *Flower of the Desert: Giacomo Leopardi's Poetic Ontology*. Trans. Timothy S. Murphy. New York: SUNY Press, 2018, pp. 257–71.)

I would like to demonstrate three theses. First, that as a general rule, only a materialist conception of the world allows us to give an adequate account of poetry and its creative force. Second, that from the modern era to the present, immersed in the crisis of Enlightenment and reason and dazzled by postmodern indifference, materialism increasingly becomes the only weapon we have in the attempt to give significance to the world and to transform it — and poetry above all is implicated in this. Third, I would like to characterise Leopardi's path in materialist terms: his poetry precisely accompanies the passage from the modern era to the present, anticipates its outcome, and experiences its entire dynamic, while constructing a beyond and alluding to truth.

Poetry is inseparable from materialism. What does this mean? It means that as production, poetry is conceivable only outside an established, absolute order of truth, separate from a world of ideas, universals, and pre-constituted elements to reveal. Indeed, only within a materialist horizon, shaped by contingency, is it possible to create, to practice *poiesis* and the ontological imagination. In a materialist universe, truth is a name and the universal is a convention, while poetry is instead a concretion, a process of construction, the conclusion of a making within the concrete, within immediacy. Thus all truth, when it becomes real, has a poetic aspect: in the sense that, extracted from the horizon of the name, confirmed in being, it happens by means of a practice and is led to a concrete determination. Nevertheless, poetry itself is emancipated from every truth, from every technique of verification, in the sense that it is immediacy. It is more than truth because it ontologically precedes truth, the density of which it immediately unveils. It anticipates truth in sensory images, not as in an aurora but in the light of high noon. The true comes after poetry and must adapt to it, since it anticipates the true. Ethical activity is situated between poetry and the true. [. . .] But ethics also comes after the truth and leads it back toward poetry [. . .]. That is the way ethics attains the status of foundational value for the metaphysics of materialism, for it accomplishes the task of mediating between the immediate and the universal, between expression and communication, in freedom, in the metaphysical void that gives sense to freedom.

Poetry moves in the void, in infinite matter, but it constructs and extracts being from nothingness. This construction of immediacy in the void, this extraction of being from nothingness, this excavation of nature with the aim of infringing upon its boundaries and restoring it to us as signification — all this is possible only within a materialist horizon from which all presuppositions, all fetishes, all foundations have been eliminated. Poetry anticipates the true because it exceeds the limits of the materiality of existence and propels the immediacy of the image forward. [. . .] The true is thereby constructed in the ethical verification. Then it returns to poetry, the ever-renewed search carried out through ethical action, until once again rupture, invention, poetic production proposes an other being. This circulation among poetry, ethical action, and truth characterises the materialist horizon, defines its harshness and hence the necessity to break it up continually, to construct signification aesthetically, to render universal [. . .] this rupture by means of ethical action, so long as the true, an other true, has not been constructed. Poetry is the moment of rupture, of liberation, that confers signification on the rest: the gentle weave, the construction of a world. [. . .]

But this terrain of life could never have been constituted if the world had not been anticipated in the poetic rupture, in the ability to affirm immediacy as the principle of weaving of every human construction. As it is given to us, the world is irrational; the historical and natural backdrop is absurd, and we are constrained to live within this irrationality. But life begins only where the full necessity of the world — of nature and history — is refused, and humankind, the subject, constructs itself otherwise. Constructing otherwise is freedom; it is the practice of ethics. [. . .] Poetry is the refusal that founds every power, every possibility of ethically enacting the world and therefore of constructing the true.

[. . .] Poetry is the immediate labour that pre-shapes every intra-mundane relation. Poetry is language, recognition of itself; it is the turn toward the enterprise of creation. Poetry is the mystery of our beginning to be. [. . .] Without the presupposition and the discovery of this poetic making, ethical action and the true would not be present in our reality. Thus poetry is radical; it founds every possible true existence on nothingness.

The great metaphysical tradition of materialism, from classical antiquity to modernity, has always offered this ontological framework to us — or rather, it has always offered it to poetry. But there is a moment when this process of materialist thought clashes with a new reality — that of the great transformation imposed by triumphant capitalism. Materialism, which has always been and still remains the schema of a dualist thought capable of highlighting dualism on the horizon of the real, must now bow to the effectiveness of the circular functioning of the human universe. Indeed, the relationship between humankind and nature, between subject and society, between production and product, between labour and the commodity has been rendered circular; and the dialectic, in its triumphal figure, seems to have substituted itself for every mechanism that ascribed agency to the subject. Poetry is dead — so declares power, speaking through Hegel. [. . .]

Indeed, the circular horizon and the dialectic want no more rupture — or rather, all the articulations of being would have to be reabsorbed, restored to the continuity without resolution of dialectical reason. Materialism becomes dialectical. But can it? There is no more need for rupture: the true has been explored to the limits of its possibilities, constructed by humankind; and now ethics can content itself with the effects of such creation — so we are told. But these effects are perverse; and wanting materialist dualism, wanting the criteria of identification of the subject and the principles of reality to resolve themselves in a dialectic is the result of mystification. Nevertheless, this mystification is real and effective. [. . .] The subsumption of all nature and every form of society within productive development is thus the given: the dialectic wants to function as the law of this radical absorption. But this subsumption, far from destroying the antagonisms, dualisms, and tensions, accentuates them. The material progression toward a complete circularity of the historical universe instead spurs the advance of chaos, global irrationality, and the lack of human signification of the real. Everything is exchangeable, but everything is thereby reduced to the neutrality of value, to equivalence, to indifference.

[. . .] Each element is indifferent and equal. Within this immense absorption of being into indifference, the capacity for ethical action to weave a web of sense and constructive intentionality between sensibility and truth seems to collapse. Ethical action is sucked into this centripetal drive, this absolutely mystifying breath of subsumed being. [. . .]

What remains of poetry in real subsumption?

The answer is found in the question. Now, only poetry is left to break out and recast the metaphysical power of ethics. Poetry is the ability to determine difference, to produce immediacy in the face of indifference and absolute mediation. The dualism of the subject is thus recreated, reconstructed, no longer on the basis of the detachment and promethean elevation of humankind, of the author, of the hero against a tragic horizon, but instead as an act of affirmation, of existence, of alternative power within the nullifying circularity of significations and their destructive indifference. [. . .] Poetry is the act of rupture. I do not define it as foundational, since poetry has none of the characteristics of foundation. It is simply rupture, rupture of indifference, allusion to an other possibility — which is neither that of the servant nor that of the slave but rather the possibility of freeing oneself. Poetry is not a foundation, for it is presupposed by a process of liberation and only in that process does the rupture become real [. . .].

To break out of the prison, to launch its own hope into the world, from an other perspective: such is the vocation of poetry. It does not resolve or close. It merely constructs a rupture, merely constructs in immediacy this path of ethics that presses toward the definition of the true. [. . .] Materialist philosophy thus makes a specific and determinate proposition for our present: in the world in which we live, poetry is an anticipation of ethics, the opening of its weave and its extension, for it is preeminently a rupture in the irrational subsumption of the world, and hence a moment of orientation, a sketch of dynamics, a gentle ontological difference.

[. . .] The old materialism stressed the time of aesthetic rupture by making it into an ethics of immediacy. The new materialism must instead expand the precipitation and violence of every rupture in a movement that is at once destructive and creative, that raises itself to the alternative: here, rupture is not merely an act of ontological opening, it is also the plenitude of an orientation, a constitutive intention, a possible communication. [. . .]

Here we must emphasise an element that further distinguishes poetic rupture in the old materialism from that in the new materialism: I am referring to the collective element, to the universality of ethical value and its function of communication. In the old materialism, the poetic rupture is individual. [. . .] In the new materialism and the social and natural situation that it registers and manifests, the moment of poetic rupture, in the density that characterises it, is invested with the highest power of universality and expressive force. [. . .] The knot that ties sensibility to imagination and poetic rupture to ethical constitution is now very tight: consequently, in reconciling the perspective of the true as well, the constitutive process manifests its communicative immediacy. The directions of communicating subjectivity converge on ontology: that is collectivity. The rupture then comprehends in itself and overthrows this density of circulation, this complexity of the horizon of exchange that the productive subsumption of the world of significations had established. [. . .] The new materialism sees the poetic rupture constitute itself in terms of community, of collective subjectivity. [. . .]

In Leopardi's experience we can confirm the passage, within the metaphysics of materialism, from the first to the second kind of situation and signification of poetry. From this viewpoint, Leopardi appears as a cultural hinge at the highest poetic level and as the theoretical anticipation of a historical passage between two different eras. It is essential to grasp in Leopardi this coincidence of a conscious poetic experience and a historical passage. Indeed, this is where the innovative and exemplary European role of his poetry lies. His is a poetry, as we have seen, that arises within materialism — sensualist materialism, worn out by too long a struggle for emancipation and yet nonetheless an instrument of revolutionary critique. It is a poetry of Enlightenment reason, in certain respects, but mitigated by a sense of the crisis of the revolution. Nevertheless, Leopardi fully experiences the myth of negative and utopian reason. For him as for Hölderlin, poetry breaks with the ideological destination of the world and thereby leaves space for ethics. [. . .] Here we come to that passage within the metaphysics of materialism that is so characteristic of Leopardi: the passage from mythology to disenchantment, from the constitution of a totalising web of poetic signification to the opposition of subjectivity and nature, second nature, true illusion. Here what stands out is the ontological preeminence of rupture, anti-dialectical affirmation in the negative purity of its expression, the negative as essence that cannot be recuperated. The poetry of modern materialism, modern poetry *tout court*, finds its birthplace here. Rimbaud and the delirium of the gods — that is what Leopardi comprehends and what his mature poetry prefigures. His mature work is in no way a poetry of serenity, of a vague modern stoicism. It is the poetry of the most profound rupture, unease, and disenchantment. But in this, precisely and only in this, it is a fundamental event, absolute modernity, avant-garde and recasting. [. . .] From the viewpoint of the history of ideas, the real passage marks not the crisis but the realisation of the Enlightenment utopia, or rather the dramatic unveiling of its dialectic. From the viewpoint of political and social history, this passage marks, in continental Europe, the victory of the revolution followed by the definitive defeat of Napoleonic imperialism, the assertion of a right adapted to a new mode of production and the revelation of that mode's terrible consequences. The new phase of struggle and development that opens up in the nineteenth century, the age of *Risorgimenti,* is also traversed by the awareness of that past and its crisis — and within the crisis by the different choices that are proposed: a reactionary choice, a reformist choice, and finally an alternative, unpolitical, and yet radically transformative choice. I cannot hide my clear preference for the alternative option: [. . .] This is a refusal of politics as abstraction and reification of the relations of power. It is a denunciation of that reality (and the economic world that corresponds to it: statistics!). Lastly, in positive terms it is the awareness that only a profound poetic rupture can open up an alternative course of ethical propositions and intentions.

[. . .] But the content of Leopardi's message is precisely not "ethics against politics." [. . .] Leopardi only extolls ethics as foundation and as alternative projection after having brought two operations to a conclusion. The first is the demystification of moral and political illusions, the discovery of nothingness as formal and actual substance of that universe, the denunciation of the mortal destiny that pervades it. The second operation is poetic: it is the complete abstraction, the radical rupture, the fundamental *epoché* that consciousness carries out with respect to this nothingness. Poetic consciousness constructs an other reality. Here there is [. . .] the opposition of an other ethics (and thus necessarily an other politics) to the nothingness of the present ethical-political universe. The political rupture thus presents itself as a profound and absolutely alternative ontological act, and it is the radicality of this rupture that best corresponds to the concreteness of the historical passage, to the wealth of its potentialities, and to the alternatives that compose it. [. . .] Here it is enough to emphasise once again that there is no possibility other than poetic denunciation in the face of the headlong transformation of utopia into despair, of hope into a prison for the mind. That is what historical reality shows, thereby signifying a tragedy of thought. It is as if there were no possibility of discriminating and rending this dialectical fabric of tragedy, no possibility of restoring to tragedy its role as foundation of the new, other than by means of a poetic act charged with the weight of the whole world. [. . .] Ethics and politics will come later; they will follow the moment of foundation. Last comes the true [. . .]. Leopardi lacks even the ambiguities that are typical of those who flirted with the dialectic — I am thinking particularly of the German materialist schools or the epigones of sensualism in France. In Leopardi the determination of this path is absolutely clear — from poetic rupture to ethics and then to a new metaphysical foundation of the true. [. . .]

We must now turn to the theme of truth. For Leopardi, the true is first of all a given, a characterisation of being that must be attained and confirmed. Thus it must be filtered through a making, an experience, in order to understand the sense of that characterisation. Here we can also grasp in Leopardi's thought an important passage between the two phases of inquiry and metaphysical conclusion. In the first phase, truth as it is given is attained and constructed as system. Yet as soon as this web of sense is comprehensively given, it is revealed as the system of indifference. [. . .] We must always keep in mind that from the materialist point of view, the discourse on truth in Leopardi always tends to be identified with the discourse on nature. The example of nature is important in that it brings to light a linear course of Leopardi's thought: the transcendence of nature is gradually destructured — the process of verification becomes increasingly rigorous, and nature ends up being considered as an immanent, abstract, reified cage that must be broken out of, whether nature or second nature. The true then constitutes an alternative to the natural true of the first epistemological approach, an alternative to the true illusion that characterises the acme of the critical experience, and lastly an alternative to the entire world — in the sense that the definition of the true corresponds to that of ontological alterity. But the definition of the true is not what permits us to attain ontological alterity; that is attained by means of the poetic rupture and its development within the web of the ethical constitution of the subject.

The true is the logic of this autonomous development, this self-valorisation. It is the result of a dialectic of ethics, thus an anti-dialectic. The true is the ultimate product of a verification that is an act of rupture of the horizon of falsity, of repetitive and sterile effectiveness, and that constructs a new reality. Leopardi's procedure gives us the sense that metaphysical time can withdraw from and oppose the time of the real, that ontology can demystify the real. [. . .] The true is constituted through an ethical process, on the basis of poetic rupture. The true is ontological alterity.

Our current experience of the world allows us to understand Leopardi's anticipation perfectly and to make it our own. How in fact does our world present itself? As a complete and self-sufficient circle of significations. Whatever the processes that gave rise to this circle may have been, it is beyond doubt that the sphere of significations includes subjects and expressions, relationships and references. Subsumption, the new determination of this signifying circle, the absolute autonomy and independence of the circuits of signification — all these phenomena that make our lives unworthy of being lived, or at very least difficult, demand a rupture, one that will draw its strength from the deep strata of ontology and open up the possibility of a recasting due to ethics. [. . .]

The mystery of this rupture is the same as that of poetry — it is poetry, the construction of new being. It is the recovery of an ontologically signifying language that is deep like the individual and collectively charged like the masses. This great game of rupture is the necessary hypothesis for an overthrow of the current inhuman conditions of the world. Then there will be a long road of ethical construction, construction on the basis of which we may even begin to think that we have made the truth. For the moment, all that remains for us to do is to start down that road with a fundamental rupture that tells us something other, that situates our humanity elsewhere. We are neither reactionaries nor progressives, neither ahead nor behind, but outside. The poetic act is revolutionary in that it constructs new collective matter.

CHAPTER 23

Massimo Recalcati (1959–)

Massimo Recalcati is a practising Italian analyst, philosopher and writer. Born in Milan on 28th November 1959, the son of flower workers, Recalcati completed his philosophical studies under the guidance of Professor Franco Fergnani, producing a theoretical thesis entitled *Desir d'être e Todestrieb. Ipotesi per un confronto tra Sartre e Freud*, in 1985. In the same year, he encountered Lacan's texts, an encounter which would irreversibly mark both his studies and his life. In 1989 he specialized in psychotherapy and defended the thesis, *Analisi terminabile ed interminabile. Note sul transfert*, with Enzo Funari. From 1988 to 2007, Recalcati carried out his analytical training between Milan and Paris with Jacques-Alain Miller.

At this time Recalcati was teaching the psychopathology of eating behaviour at the University of Pavia and psychoanalytic studies and human sciences at the University of Verona. He was also the scientific director of the School of specialization in psychotherapy IRPA – the Institute of Applied Psychoanalysis Research. In 2003, he founded *Jonas*, a non-profit-making organization, a centre devoted to the clinical psychoanalysis of new symptoms. He is a member of *Alipsi*, the Italian Association of Lacanian Psychoanalysis and *Espace Analytique*. He collaborates with several specialist Italian and international journals and the cultural section of the newspaper *La Repubblica*. His publications include *Clinica del vuoto. Anoressie, dipendenze e psicosi* (*Clinic of the Void: Anorexia, Dependencies, and Psychosis*) (2002); *Elogio dell'inconscio* (*In Praise of the Unconscious*) (2008); *Cosa resta del padre? La paternità nell'epoca ipermoderna* (*What Remains of the Father? Fatherhood in the Hypermodern Age*) (2011); *Jacques Lacan. Desiderio, godimento e soggettivazione* (*Jacques Lacan: Desire, Enjoyment, and Subjectivation*) (2012); *Il complesso di Telemaco. Il rapporto genitori e figli dopo il tramonto del padre* (2013) (English translation: *The Telemachus Complex:*

Parents and Children after the Decline of the Father, Cambridge: Polity, 2019); *Le mani della madre. Desiderio, Fantasmi ed eredità del materno* (2013) (English translation: *The Mother's Hands: Desire, Fantasy and the Inheritance of the Maternal.* Trans. Alice Kilgarriff. Cambridge: Polity, 2019); *Jacques Lacan. La clinica psicoanalitica: struttura e soggetto* (*Jacques Lacan. The Psychoanalytic Clinic: Structure and Subject*) (2016); *Il segreto del figlio. Da Edipo al figlio ritrovato* (*The Secret of the Son: From Oedipus to the New Found Son*) (2017); and *Contro il sacrificio* (*Against Sacrifice*) (2017).

Major concepts

Over the last two decades Massimo Recalcati has staked out a position that involves both an interpretation of Lacan's work and the way in which it illuminates emergent clinical problems.

His theoretical work in psychoanalysis focused initially on the psychopathology of eating disorders, thanks to which he delineated some new figures of the contemporary clinic with particular reference to pathological addiction, panic attacks, depression and un-triggered psychosis. His reflections upon these 'new symptoms' were developed in *Clinica del vuoto: anoressie, dipendenze e psicosi* (2002) and *L'uomo senza inconscio. Nuove figure della clinica psicoanalitica* (2010). Here, Recalcati explored the emergence of a new type of cultural persona: a subject disconnected from his unconscious desire, literally '*senza inconscio*', without an unconscious. In the days of Freud, the 'subject of the unconscious' was overwhelmed by desires it could hardly contain, perpetually at odds with its own place in the social order, its unconscious desire seeping out in the form of symptoms (hysteria, slips of the tongue) that served as a kind of protest against the constraints of repressive civilization.

In the late twentieth and early twenty-first centuries, this desiring subject is under threat as a result of contemporary capitalism; the subject is increasingly encouraged to escape the unconscious and to evade the dissatisfactions of desire in order to encounter enjoyment instead.

For Recalcati, the capitalist discourse promotes a subject that, bypassing castration and desire, moves directly towards enjoyment. Rather than a questioning subject, the metaphor of contemporary capitalism is an enjoying subject: a subject that does not address a question to the Other. The subject rather enacts a solution through various forms of ready-made enjoyment. The command to enjoy, to perform, however, has a detrimental effect both socially and psychically. Above all, the foreclosure of desire renders subjects unable to cope with the scale of enjoyment and produces the symptoms of the hypermodern age. Contemporary symptoms are marked by libidinal excess that discards the function of the word. They are no longer the metaphor for a repressed meaning but, bypassing the mediation of the symbol, demonstrate a somewhat mortal enjoyment, without logical reasoning in relation to the Other.

Recalcati's clinical thesis takes Lacan's work as its central point of reference. He explicates this work in two considerable volumes, *Jacques Lacan. Desiderio, godimento, soggettivazione* (2012) and *Jacques Lacan: la clinica psicoanalitica. Struttura e soggetto* (2016). In this extended work of reconstruction, he places at the heart of the matter the perpetual tension between enjoyment and desire as founding the subject of the unconscious.

From the publication of *Cosa resta del padre?* (2011) onwards, he dedicates himself to a reflection on the theme of the father's decline and absence. In *Il complesso di Telemaco* (2012), Recalcati explains his vision, stating that the contemporary scene is no longer dominated by a terrible (Oedipal) conflict between generations, nor by a (narcissistic) hedonistic and sterile self-assertion, but by a brand new need for the father, a father who is no longer the possessor of an absolute truth, but one who performs an ethical gesture. According to Recalcati (2013), in fact, 'in the case of Oedipus, the Law is an impediment to desire, and the father intervenes as if he were an adversary casually passing by; while in the case of Telemachus, the Law is that which can bring the devastating chaos of mortal pleasure back to the necessary experience of castration and desire'.

The 'Telemachus son' allows Recalcati to emphasize the theme of heritage or inheritance, not only as the conveyance of goods or genes but also as transmission in the testimony of life. Inheritance is also the key concept of another book, entitled *L'ora di lezione. Per un'erotica dell'insegnamento* (*The Time of the Lesson: Towards an Erotics of Teaching*) (2014), dedicated to the question of the transmission of knowledge in the teacher-student relationship as an essential form of legacy.

The reflection on familial relationships is completed by a consideration of the figure of the mother in *Le mani della madre* (2015) and a still deeper discussion of the process of parenting in *Il segreto del figlio* (2017).

Another of Recalcati's fields of interest is the relationship between psychoanalysis and the practice of art (cf. *Il miracolo della forma. Per un'estetica psicoanalitica*, 2007 and *Il mistero delle cose. Nove ritratti di artisti* (*The Mystery of Things: Nine Artist Portraits*), 2016). For Recalcati, psychoanalysis has to be implied *by* art and not applied *to* it. Thus he introduces an approach that should bear witness to the value of art in its radical extraneousness. Recalcati affirms that art resists interpretation and meaning, and that we should abandon the pretension exhaustively to translate a work of art into words, because art cannot be fully decoded, translated or interpreted as having one simple meaning: it is not reducible to any other discipline.

Anna Cicogna

Selected writings

Recalcati, Massimo. *L'uomo senza inconscio. Figure della nuova clinica psicoanalitica (The Man Without Unconscious: Figures of the New Psychoanalytic Clinic)*. Milan: Raffaello Cortina, 2010

Recalcati, Massimo. *Clinica del vuoto. Anoressie, dipendenze, psicosi (Clinic of the Void: Anorexia, Dependencies, and Psychosis)* [2002], 2nd edn. Franco Angeli, 2018

Recalcati, Massimo. *The Telemachus Complex: Parents and Children after the Decline of the Father* [2013], trans. Alice Kilgarriff. Cambridge: Polity Press, 2019

Recalcati, Massimo. *The Mother's Hands: Desire, Fantasy and the Inheritance of the Maternal* [2015], trans. Alice Kilgarriff. Cambridge: Polity Press, 2019

Recalcati, Massimo. *The Son's Secret: From Oedipus to the Prodigal Son* [2018], trans. Alice Kilgarriff. Cambridge: Polity, 2020

EXCERPT

Massimo   Recalcati,   *extinction   of   the   unconscious?   a   recent Anthropological Mutation*

(Massimo Recalcati, *The Man Without Unconscious: Figures of the New Psychoanalytic Clinic*. Milan: Raffaello Cortina, 2010, pp.3–14).

What type of experience is that of the subject of the unconscious? How is this experience originally articulated in the work of Freud? What kind of experience is the Freudian experience of the unconscious? It is only by trying to answer these questions that it is possible to understand which anthropological change would cause its *extinction*. Therefore, I will try to answer these questions by isolating at least three essential characteristics of the Freudian experience of the unconscious.

First characteristic: the Freudian experience of the unconscious is first of all *an experience of truth*. However, it is not an impersonal, universal, unconditional, archetypical or collective truth; the truth at stake in the analytical experience is not philosophy's transcendental truth, nor is it logic's truth without contradictions; it is not even the universal truth of religion. The truth relating to the experience of the unconscious is a truth which affects our own intimacy, our most singular being, our bizarre, weird, embarrassing, obscene and irreducible particularity. However, this truth, being forever in flight from us, never coincides with the narcissistic representation of ourselves, being always, as Lacan put it, within the subject, yet transcending the subject, it is thought to be removed from the truth because it manifests itself as an experience of decentring, of the loss of control, of the displacement of the Ego. In fact, analytical truth never assumes the ontological forms of *adaequatio intellectus et rei* because the subject can never claim to master it; it is never the subject that determines the truth, being rather, according to a key word in Lacan's teaching, 'a-subject' [*assoggettato,* subjected-*to*]. [. . .] Truth speaks only where the subject goes into eclipse, in this situation thought and being are disjoined, demonstrating that 'I' am never what I think myself to be because my being always transcends my thinking. And this is expressed in every formation of the unconscious (slip, dream, bungled actions, inadvertency, symptom): thus what I thought myself to be disintegrates when it comes face-to-face with another truth that is released in points of uncertainty and vacillation in the mastery of the ego.

Contrary to that which is established as an unquestionable certainty through the movement of the Cartesian cogito (*cogito ergo sum*), not only am I not what I think I am, but I can only approach the truth of my being through the yielding of the illusion of rational and autocratic self-control, [. . .] the truth of the Freudian unconscious speaks [. . .] where the subject does not have control of itself. In this sense, analytic truth remains absolutely eccentric to the purely theoretical dimension of the truth of the philosophical logos and to the purely formal-logical and quantitative dimension of all scientific reason.

The second characteristic of the Freudian experience of the subject of the Freudian unconscious: the experience of the unconscious is *an experience of difference*. [. . .] [I]t is the experience of the subject as difference, as absolutely singular, as non-common, incomparable and irreducible to any standard. The subject of the unconscious always emerges as *a discontinuity in the fabric constituted by universal discourse*. For this reason, the psychoanalyst accords the dignity of truth to all those expressions which are apparently the lowest and most obscene in the subject's life; the Freudian catalogue of such expressions [. . .] summarizes the experience of the unconscious as anti-universal and non-generalizable, resistant to every form of comparison, because there can be a manifestation of the unconscious – in a slip or in a dream – only when universal discourse collapses, and when the homogeneity of this discourse is destroyed by the emergence of a distinctive trait that is untameable for the 'common sense' of every already established discourse.

Third characteristic: the experience of the unconscious is an *experience of desire*: of desire, Freud specifies, as indestructible [. . .]. The movement of desire is an insistent movement of openness towards the Other. [. . .] The experience of the indestructibility of desire is an experience of openness which refutes every solipsistic rendition of the psychic apparatus. The openness of desire, its fundamental transcendence, invokes otherness as the ultimate root of the experience of the unconscious. In this sense, the encounter with the subject of the unconscious brings along with it the shattering of the moral ideal of the self-sufficiency of the Ego and all of its supposed substantial impermeability.

[. . .] This is another aspect of the indestructibility of desire: it is 'indestructible' precisely because it does not depend on the will of the Ego; the Ego neither bears it nor decides upon it; on the contrary, desire is what the will of the ego depends on, it is what bears the ego, which indeed renders it an 'a-subject' (*asujet*, in Lacan). For Freud, this places the matrix of human desire in repressed infantile experiences: elements, fragments and remnants of infancy which are never altogether extinguished; a past that never passes, a past which returns; pieces of the real that, even once they have been repressed or, if you prefer, precisely because they have been repressed, never cease returning, like anarchic spectres, on the scene of the world, claiming their ancient rights, interfering with the deceptive linear flow of our 'vulgar time'. My thesis is that a profound anthropological mutation is in progress [. . .], the experience of the subject of the unconscious as the experience of *truth*, of *difference* and of the *indestructible character of desire*, is at risk of extinction [. . .]. My thesis is that hypermodern Civilization and its prevailing symptomatic declensions (anorexia and bulimia, obesity, drug addictions, pathological dependencies, depression, panic attacks) give rise to a tendency to suppress the subject of the Freudian unconscious. In other words, my starting point consists of considering that our time [. . .] is antagonistic to the time of the subject of the unconscious. I will try to summarize the reasons for this antagonism in five points.

First point: our time is antagonistic to the experience of the subject of the Freudian unconscious because, if the experience is, as we have already seen, an experience of the incommensurable, of the absolutely singular, of desire as difference, then that which appears to dominate the big Other of the social field is instead the empire of number, of the cipher, of quantitative comparison, of scientistic quantification, of the negation of desire as that which is impossible to measure. Ours is the time of the hyper-positivist triumph of objectivity, which tends to consider the psychoanalytical unconscious as an archaic and irrational form of superstition, and surreptitiously introduces a new concept of the unconscious that is reduced to the neuronal, the cerebral, to a mere biochemical alteration of the organism, as when one wants to reduce the feeling of love to a series of fluctuations in the endorphins which mobilize in a hyperactive fashion our neuronal reactions, which are obviously destined inexorably to degrade with the passage of time.

Second point: our time is antagonistic to the experience of the Freudian unconscious because this experience demands thought and, therefore, demands the time for thinking, the readiness to lose oneself, to encounter chaos, the unforeseen, the real as impossible to think. Our time is a time insensible to the 'long' time of thought because it is the time of the rendering-maniacal of existence – of its perpetual agitation, of its intoxication through the excess of stimulation – which renders impracticable the very concept of experience, dissolving it into the compulsive tendency to 'discharge', to 'act', to the passage to the act without thought and in a way altogether de-symbolized.

[. . .] In the frantic search for new sensations and new objects of enjoyment, in the exacerbated cult of 'the new' and the continuous change of object, the hypermodern subject tries perversely to navigate his way around the rock of castration, carrying out its radical denial and looking to annul the effects of the limitation of enjoyment which symbolic castration has the beneficient power to introduce. [. . .]

Third point: our time is antagonistic to the experience of the Freudian unconscious because this experience is an experience of the indestructible character of desire in its constitutive relation with the Law. This demonstrates that without the experience of limits, of the castration of the immediacy of enjoyment, we never experience desire [. . .]. Although desire is never reducible to the Law and never fully identifies itself with it (except in the phantasmatic plan of obsessive desire which, however, is a pathology of desire), creatively to achieve desire requires the symbolic support of the Law. For this reason, Lacan has always insisted on the necessity of thinking *together*, and not in a simple and neat opposition, desire and Law, [. . .] as two sides of the same coin. For this reason, the Freudian experience of the unconscious is the experience of a hostile tension that unites and, while it unites, differentiates desire and Law. The Freudian subject is, in fact, a subject divided between the normative programme of the reality principle and the hedonistic programme of the pleasure principle. [. . .] Unlike the more recent symptomatic forms of the discontent of Civilization, these two programmes trace an unprecedented configuration of this conflict. The desire decoupled from the Law loses its propulsive force to integrate itself anonymously in a collective programme of enjoyment, disconnected from symbolic castration and deprived of satisfaction, triggered by the discourse of the capitalist. [. . .] The facilitation of access to enjoyment, the green light – deprived of the necessary passage through sublimation – granted to the discharging of drives, a sexuality operating compulsively, without veils and, therefore, without Eros, divorced from love, in short, the general effect of the desublimation of the drive induced by the new Civilization, is not at all dis-alienating and liberating, but highly repressive because it extinguishes the movement of desire, cancelling any critical dissymmetry in relation to the reality to which, instead, the subject tends to adapt itself ever more passively. The hypermodern cult of consumption [. . .] realizes a new form of human, that of the 'turbo-consumer' who freely manages their own pleasure in consuming that which most pleases their 'appetite for experiences' in moments reduced to the instantaneousness of their variegated 'desires'. [. . .] [I]t involves a collapse of desire as desire of the Other and an affirmation of a toxic enjoyment uncoupled from symbolic castration.

The unlimited freedom of consumption can thus be drastically overturned in an emotional life that renounces the encounter with the otherness of the Other and narcissistically closes around itself and the playful consumption of the futile and the random. In this sense, I affirm that our time is antagonistic to the experience of the unconscious because it tends to eliminate the critical and conflictual tension between the Law and desire in the name of a hedonism well-integrated in the system and the enthusiastic and disenchanted affirmation of *homo felix*. Our time is the time in which the Sadean imperative of unlimited enjoyment (the 'repressive desublimation' of the drive, in the language of Marcuse) has become an unheard-of social commandment, installed in the very place of the Law. Our time is a time in which everything is consumed and where everything, being consumed, is destroyed, revealing its character as thoroughly ephemeral and evanescent; and it is the closed time of the *cynicism of the monad of enjoyment.* [. . .]

Fourth point: our time is antagonistic to the experience of the unconscious because it abolishes the dimension of truth by reabsorbing it in that of biotechnological knowledge. As we have seen, the Freudian experience of the unconscious is the experience of a truth that unsettles constituted knowledge, compelling it permanently to renew itself. In Freudian theory, knowledge never exhausts being. [. . .] However, this erosion of knowledge and its certainties does not involve psychoanalysis in the rejection of knowledge. The experience of the unconscious is not the experience of a nihilistic relativism. On the contrary, the experience of analysis tries, as Lacan affirms, to reunite knowledge and truth, by affording the subject the occasion to produce a new knowledge of a truth most particular to it, a truth which touches on the intimacy of its being; it tries, in other words, to rebuild the alliance, severed by pathology, between desire and the Law.

Our time is not pressing us in this direction at all, in the direction of the rebuilding of a possible alliance between knowledge and truth; it rather seems to foster a stark distinction between them, affirming a sterile primacy of knowledge that reduces the truth of the unconscious, as Chistopher Bollas once put it, to a mere 'archaism'. The only thing that counts for our time is the power of things; knowledge as classification, anonymous cataloguing, protocol of the facts, knowledge as a manifestation of the grey and formal power of statistics. The man of the anonymous bureaucracy of hyper-specialized knowledge that adapts in a conformist way to the established order of things takes the place of the Freudian man who wants to know the mystery of the truth of his desire and who is, therefore, willing to put all of his acquired certainties at stake by challenging the established order of things.

Fifth point: the experience of the analytic cure is the experience of a transformation that takes place thanks to a *new alliance that the subject establishes with the unconscious*. Not to exorcize, negate or colonize the unconscious, but to establish a new alliance (also therapeutic) with their own unconscious. [. . .] [I]n our time, the 'psy' experience of the cure stands for an essentially disciplinary experience, as a process of orthopaedic adjustment of the subject's body or thought, as a rehabilitation of the subject to normality, to the performance principle, to the conformist assimilation of the established discourse. This is the direction in which cognitive-behavioural therapies are actually moving, therapies which are increasingly widespread and dominant on the market. We have shown how the subversive character of the experience of the unconscious is different to the Civilization of our time and how this experience is at risk of extinction and being supplanted by the scientific power of data, by the objects of enjoyment, by psycho-educative practices of a disciplinary type and by the false liberation promised by the discourse of the capitalist.

We have also stressed how this difference has generated a new psychopathology, new forms of symptom and an unheard-of psychoanalytic clinic. The foundation of this new clinic is formed by that which I have been able to define as a fundamental metamorphosis that consists in the reduction of the 'lack of being' to 'a void'. If the 'lack of being' constitutes human reality as such for Lacan and is the product of a fundamental symbolization of the void, the experience of the void is an experience of reduction, reification, ossification and substantializing of lack. In hypermodern reality, this experience appears unequivocally to impose itself upon this lack: if the human experience of the lack is the matrix of the dynamism of desire, of its function of opening towards the Other, towards symbolic exchange with the Other, then the experience of the void is an experience of annulment, nirvanization, hibernation, petrification and cancellation of desire. The lack reduced to a void would, therefore, be a *lack disconnected from desire*. This metamorphosis is effectively the sign of a sort of anthropological mutation: *the man of the clinic of the void appears as a man without unconscious.*

While the classical clinic of neurosis was centred around the fundamental conflict between the programme of desire and the programme of Civilization, the clinic of the void emphasizes the primary necessity of curbing anxiety, and hence it emphasizes *defences against anxiety more than the repression of desire*. At its core, there is no longer the programme of desire but the programme of *narcynicism* (narcissism + cynicism) of enjoyment; of the enjoyment of the One, oneyance [*uniano*] (*unien*), autistic, monadic, of enjoyment without the Other, which is opposed to symbolic exchange.

The basis of this change is social and concerns an essential modification of the commandment of the Super-Ego. [. . .] Its moral voice demanded the rejection of drives as a condition of access to Civilization; in a Hegelian fashion, the civilizing process imposed the annihilation of the animal. The hypermodern Civilization is contributing to a change of orientation in the social Super-Ego's programme: its commandment no longer speaks with the Kantian voice of the moral conscience: the hypermodern twist on the Super-Ego occurs in an unheard-of way through the promotion of enjoyment, of the 'narcynicism' of enjoyment, to a new social imperative. In other words, enjoyment is made equivalent to the Law. In this, we can discern the tendency, not simply cynical but also perverse, of the hypermodern programme of Civilization. Enjoyment assumes the form of a categorical imperative that denies castration: *You must enjoy*!

The paradigm of the clinic of the void was derived from the clinic of anorexia. It was the anorexic who taught us the heterogeneity of void and lack, but also how the enjoyment of the void can annihilate the dialectic of desire that stems from lack. We may say that the anorexic builds a wall against the wall of language. They live in mortification and appear to deprive themselves of enjoyment, just to avoid paying the price of symbolic castration; they mortify their own body, discipline it through a drastic regime of privation, but they do all of this only to escape the symbolic mortification induced by the signifier. The choice of the anorexic is, therefore, a choice antagonistic to the symbolic function of castration. In this clinical context, the experience of the void assumes a character that is particularly relevant. The subject appears to carry out a disconnection from the Other via a radical refusal that, separating itself from the Other, focuses only on the void of one's own body and on strategies aimed at its preservation. In this way, the lack of being from which desire arises becomes literally ossified in the void that the subject claims to know how to govern.

For the term '*unien*', see J. Lacan, *Television / A Challenge to the Psychoanalytic Establishment*. Trans. Denis Hollier, Rosalind Krauss, Annette Michelson, Jeffrey Mehlman & Bruce Fink. Ed. Joan Copjec. New York: Norton, 1990, p. 23. (Lacan specifies that '*unien*' is an anagram of '*ennui*', which is translated in this volume as 'annoyance'. For want of anything better, we have retained the translators' rendering, 'oneyance', which attempts the same in English, while capturing the reference to 'oneness'. The term is intended to 'designate the identification of the Other with the One'. Recalcati perhaps attempts the same in Italian by jumbling '*una*' and '*noia*' (ennui) to form '*uniano*' – Ed.)

This metamorphosis brings with it a series of implications: the narcissistic affirmation of the ideal Ego, which cuts all ties with the Other; the perverse choice of an inhuman object (the mirror image of the slim body, the void of one's own body) as a fundamental partner; practices of governing the body aimed at shielding the void; the consolidation of the idealizing identification with the image of the slim body which has a defensive aim with respect to anxiety.

The tendency to abolish the subject of the unconscious, to disconnect the subject of the unconscious, the absence of the subject of the unconscious insofar as it is the subject of desire seems consequently to condition new forms of psychopathology. In fact, the clinic of the void [. . .] is a *clinic in the absence of the unconscious*. This means that in the new psychopathology, the couple *repression-return* of the repressed, central to the clinic of neurosis, is no longer operative, but is replaced by the couple anxiety-defence.

Translated by Katherine Langley with Michael Lewis

With thanks to Lorenzo Chiesa for his advice on this translation. All responsibility for any errors and infelicities which remain lies solely with the translators.

CHAPTER 24

Emanuele Severino (1929–)

Emanuele Severino is considered by a number of prominent Italian intellectuals — such as Massimo Cacciari, Carlo Sini and Vincenzo Vitiello – to be one of the foremost contemporary philosophers.

Severino was born in Brescia in 1929. He graduated from the University of Pavia in 1950. His thesis, entitled *Heidegger e il problema della metafisica* (*Heidegger and the Problem of Metaphysics*), was supervised by Gustavo Bontadini, one of the most illustrious figures of Italian neo-scholasticism. Bontadini's philosophy will influence Severino's own intellectual development.

Severino started his academic career at the Università Cattolica del Sacro Cuore in Milan, where he lectured in philosophy from 1954 to 1969. During this period, some of his publications – notably *Ritornare a Parmenide* (*Back to Parmenides*) and *Ritornare a Parmenide. Poscritto* (*Back to Parmenides: Postscript*) – aroused a vibrant debate among Catholic intellectuals. In 1969, Severino's work was examined by a commission chaired by Cornelio Fabro, another important representative of Italian neo-scholasticism, which proclaimed the incompatibility of Severino's philosophy with the doctrine of the Catholic Church. Severino himself agreed with this verdict.

Thus, Severino had to leave the Università Cattolica del Sacro Cuore and moved to the University of Venice, where he lectured until his retirement in 2001. In this university, he was Head of the Department of Philosophy.

Severino has been teaching ontology at the University Vita-Salute San Raffaele in Milan since 2003.

Severino can be defined as an ontological thinker, insofar as his fundamental philosophical question concerns being. However, in Severino's perspective, being is every positive determination: being is the sky, the plant, the man etc. Unlike the Heideggerian discourse, Severino's philosophy does not acknowledge the difference between Being and beings.

The commencement of his entire ontology is the Aristotelian principle of non-contradiction: according to Severino, this is the firmest principle of metaphysics, as its negation is self-negation.

By acknowledging the unconditional validity of the principle of non-contradiction, Severino is led to claim that every entity is fundamentally eternal: this is the core of his philosophy and its most original thesis. Every being is eternal insofar as it cannot negate the principle of non-contradiction, which implies that being cannot be both itself and its other at once. If being cannot be its other, then it cannot become something else (non-being), but is rather bound to itself. Thus, in Severino's ontology every determined being, every single instant is inevitably eternal, as the principle of non-contradiction is the fundamental law of being.

According to Severino, this claim is not irreconcilable with the phenomenological evidence which proves that something changes. As a matter of fact, Severino contends that the transformation we experience in our own lives is the appearing and disappearing of eternal beings, which is to say that becoming does not coincide with creation or annihilation, both of which imply the identification of being with nothingness; becoming is simply the appearing or disappearing of what has never been created and will never be annihilated. This is the reason why the commission headed by Fabro proclaimed the incompatibility of Severino's philosophy with the Catholic doctrine: in this regard, the creation of the world from nonbeing is one of Christianity's principal dogmas.

Having said that, from Severino's perspective the essence of Western civilization is inevitably nihilism, as it is dominated by the conviction that being *can* become its other (nothingness). He maintains that the very essence of technology must be related to this conviction.

In 1958, Severino published his first masterpiece, entitled *La Struttura Originaria (Originary Structure)*, to which he will refer continually in his future works. Among his publications, other significant books include *Destino della necessità (The Destiny of Necessity)* (1980), *La Gloria (Glory)* (2001), *Oltrepassare (Exceeding)* (2007), *La morte e la terra (Death and the Earth)* (2011) and *Testimoniando il Destino (Witnessing Destiny)* (2019).

Andrea Soardo

Selected writings

Severino, Emanuele. *Destino delle necessità 'The Destiny of Necessity'*. Milan: Adelphi Edizioni, 1980

Severino, Emanuele. *La Gloria. Risoluzione di Destino della necessità (Glory. Resolution of 'Destiny of Necessity')*. Milan: Adelphi Edizioni, 2001

Severino, Emanuele. *Oltrepassare (Exceeding)*. Milan: Adelphi Edizioni, 2007

Severino, Emanuele. *La Terra e la Morte (Death and the Earth)*. Milan: Adelphi Edizioni, 2011

Severino, Emanuele. *La Struttura Originaria (Originary Structure)*. Brescia: La Scuola, 2014

Severino, Emanuele. *Nihilism and Destiny*, trans. Kevin William Molìn and edited by Nicoletta Cusano. Milano: Mimesis International, 2016a

Severino, Emanuele. *The Essence of Nihilism*, edited by Alessandro Carrera and Ines Testoni. London: Verso (originally 1972), 2016b

Severino, Emanuele. *Testimoniando il Destino (Witnessing Destiny)*. Milan: Adelphi Edizioni eBook, 2019

EXCERPT

Emanuele Severino, *Nihilism and Destiny*

(Emanuele Severino, *Nihilism and Destiny*. Trans. Kevin William Molìn. Ed. Nicoletta Cusano. N.p.: Mimesis, 2016, Chapter 1. 'Nihilism and Destiny', pp. 13–23.)

At the foundation of every thought and action today, there lies the persuasion that every *thing* is ephemeral, insofar as it is subject to birth and death. This persuasion, in its turn, is founded on the central trait of philosophy in our time: the thought that no 'thing' exists by necessity. We think this way, no matter how the thingness of things is understood by philosophical thought: whether the thingness is understood as reality independent of the human, or as object of experience or consciousness, or as interpretation or as language, etc.; and bearing in mind here that the word 'thing' should be understood in its broadest sense — the one in which, for instance, a 'thing' is a tree, a psychic state, a relation, a concept, a god. It is precisely in relation to this extremely wide sense of the thingness of things that already Kant, in Book II of the *Transcendental Dialectic* (Ch. III, Section IV, titled *Of the Impossibility of an Ontological Proof of the Existence of God)*, claims that 'the proposition: 'this or that thing exists' is a synthetic proposition'. This means that when we think that a thing is not in existence, 'it is not'; that is, 'it is nothing', 'in this judgement there cannot exist the least self-contradiction'. And since the existence of a thing is necessary, whenever the negation of such existence gives rise to a contradiction, no thing exists by necessity.

This Kantian thesis is perhaps the most widely shared in the philosophical thought of our time. It is essentially connected to the other Kantian thesis, that 'being is not a real predicate', about which Heidegger states it '*cannot be impugned* in its negative content' (*Basic Problems of Phenomenology)*. Just so as to give another example: Quine's critique of the distinction between analytic and synthetic propositions tends to ascribe an empirical and synthetic character even to analytic propositions. And thus, if at all possible, he reinforces the thesis that no thing exists by necessity.

Before Kant, already Hume writes at the end of *An Enquiry Concerning Human Understanding* that 'whatever is may *not be*. No negation of a fact can involve a contradiction. The nonexistence of any being, without exception, is as clear and distinct an idea as its existence'.

But that things of the world do not exist by necessity, however, is the principle lying at the core of the most ancient philosophical thought; that is, held ever since Greek philosophy conceived the infinite opposition between *being* and *nothing*. In Greek thought, entities that appear move from non-being into being, and vice versa; and this means precisely that they do not exist by necessity. The entire Western civilisation grows out of the confidence that things, *insofar as they are things*, do not exist by necessity.

For the philosophical tradition, divine things exist by necessity; but they exist by necessity not insofar as they are things, but insofar as they are divine. But then, in its deepest (and still for the most part hidden) essence, contemporary philosophy shows that divine things cannot exist (and thus, that even Kant's attempt is destined to failure, however much it tries to salvage, in the context of practical reason, those necessary and divine things which the critique of pure reason is bound to negate).

For the first time — and once and for all in the history of the West — Greek philosophy thought of the 'thing' as 'entity' or 'essent': as 'that which is'. The totality of things is the totality of entities, leaving only nothingness outside of itself. That is, leaving no entity outside of itself. It is only because Greek philosophy has thought of nothingness, in its radical meaning, that it has been able to think of the entitiness and the totality of entities. And it is only because it has thought of the entitiness and the totality of entities, that it has been able to think of nothingness as the absence of every entity and as the totality of entities. On the other hand, for Greek thought, and then for the thought of the entire West, that which is not a nothing is the entity insofar as entity. That is, it is not solely the totality of entities, but it is every entity. The 'entity' is 'that which is'; 'being' is the 'is' of that which the being of the entity. According to the West no entity, insofar as it is an entity, 'is' by necessity; and this implies the power to imagine a time in which the things that are, are not. To say 'when a certain entity is not' means to say 'when a certain entity is nothing'. To think that an entity is not, according to the West, does not entail a contradiction.

For some time, my writings have moved towards indicating another dimension to the question: pointing out, that is, that to think a time in which entities are not means to fall into the deepest, most hidden, radical and rooted contradiction, which nonetheless guides the West and already the entire Planet by now. This contradiction now implicates every aspect and instant of our existence and presents itself, in the eyes of the West and the Planet, as the supreme truth and evidence, as supremely unquestionable. Both the philosophical tradition and contemporary philosophy — and science, religion, art, in short, all forms of culture, of institutions and of the Western civilisation — are guided by the conviction that entities can be nothing and that, on the contrary, their non-being (their being the nothingness which they come from and to which they return) is unquestionably attested by the experience of becoming.

This supreme contradiction shrouds the metaphysical-religious confidence that it is out of the work of a God that something rather than nothing exists; as well as the assuredness, proper to our time, with which the world is seen as existing by chance, and the being of things as having no reason, no foundation, no explanation whatsoever. These two opposite modes of thought have the same spirit, they are shrouded by the same extreme *Folly*. This folly, however, has nothing to do with a sort of psychological or anthropological weakness that, with certain precautions, could have been avoided. What for the West is supreme evidence is supreme *Folly*. It is deeply concealed precisely because it is assumed to be the supreme evidence. As inhabitants of the West, in *ea vivimus, movemur et sumus*. This affirmation can show its own absolute necessity only within *Non-folly;* which is not the thought of one among us, nor that of a God, although it is present in the depths of each thought and, therefore, even in the thought and action that Folly consists in. Non-Folly is the authentic and radical sense of destiny. It is the sense of what — differently from every *epistéme* of the Western tradition — has always already and forever succeeded in *staying*, counter to every possible form of its negation.

Here it will be possible only to indicate, from afar, a few traits of the essential relationship between extreme Folly and Non- Folly.

Western thought finds it wholly natural to state there is the time in which entities still are not and the time by which now they are no longer; concerning itself with establishing that, when a thing is not, it is so by necessity. Already Aristotle explicitly says so, in *De interpretatione*. Still, Western thought leaves in the most profound and unexplored obscurity the meaning of the expression 'when a thing (an entity) is not" — for example, 'when this day is not' — it was still not yet and it will no longer be (or 'when man, trees, stars, the Earth, peace, war are not').

For Western thought, when this day is not and has become past, it is no longer. Insofar as it is past, this day is not. It is said that, in some way, even the past 'is' (and the same is said of the future). In such instances, we refer to the past that remains in memory and in the traces that it has left. Still — we observe — that which remains in memory and in the traces is not past: instead, it is precisely something that remains. The past, insofar as it is past, does not remain. It 'is' no longer — that is, it is non-being, nothingness.

For the Greeks and the West, nothingness, insofar as it is the absence and non-being of every entity, is not the non-being of a particular entity. Nonetheless, for this mode of thought, to state that a particular entity *is not* means to state that such particular entity is nothing. It is to state that, insofar as it is absent, it is the absence of every entity, of all that one way or another is an entity.

Apropos of non-being, without which there cannot be any becoming, Plato states in *Parmenides* (163 c–d):

When we say that something is not, we indicate the absence of being *[ousías apousía]* in that about which we say that it is not. And, by saying that something is not, we do not state that such something in a certain sense is not, and in a certain other sense it is: this saying that it is not, instead, means absolutely that what is not is not in any sense or place, and that in no sense it partakes in being. Thus it is not possible that what is not exists, nor that in any other sense that it partakes in being. But generating and perishing are nothing other than acquiring being and losing it.

It appears, from Plato's passage, that the non-being of entities is an absolute nothingness, precisely that which 'in no sense partakes in being' and 'is not in any sense or place'. For the generated entity, to acquire being is thus to come from its own having been an absolute nothingness; and to lose being is to enter into its own being an absolute nothingness. Plato and Aristotle certainly know that, within what is experienced as generating and perishing, the point of departure and arrival of becoming are not an absolute nothingness; but Plato and Aristotle state — as then the entire thought of the West will go on to state (even when it will not realise this) — that what is specifically generated and perishes, as such, comes from *its own* having been an absolute nothingness and re-entering it. 'It is, after all, the non-being that gets produced,' says Aristotle (*Metaphysics*, 1067 b 31); and thus, what perishes is that which is.

For the entirety of Western thought — and therefore also for scientific thought — becoming manifests itself as the passage of something from being into non-being. Even if the West often cannot render explicit what it thinks, the West thinks that the non-being of the entity in becoming is the absolute non-being *of such entity;* and that, however, the situation in which *a certain entity* is not — in which it is an absolute non-being — is *not* the situation in which *no entity* is. That is, it is not the situation in which *every entity* is an absolute non-being, so that in the situation in which a certain entity is not, certain other entities can be. And this is the case for Western thought, for the becoming that manifests itself in our experience. The point of departure and arrival of becoming in our experience are not, in other words, an absolute nothingness. Exactly for this reason, not only can Aristotle state that what generates itself is that which is absolutely nothing, and that what becomes absolutely nothing is that which is; but he can also state that becoming is the passage 'from something to something' — where this 'something' (point of departure and arrival of becoming) is the positive context (Aristotle calls it *substratum)* in which the entity finds itself as not being. For the West, that becoming is a passage from being into non-being (in the sense now indicated), is the originary and supreme evidence now already dominating over any other evidence — and which is experienced as evidence, even when we may not register our experiencing it in such way.

Extreme Folly is precisely this extreme plausibility that accompanies the mature form of Western ontology.

To state that, within becoming, an entity — for instance, this day — begins to be means to state that there exists a time, a time of the past, in which this day was nothing, absolutely nothing. Even when it is acknowledged that many aspects, things, and events of this day pre-exist its beginning, if it is asserted that this day begins to be, it is necessary *to negate* that *all* things, aspects and events of this day pre-exist its own beginning. If we were convinced, in fact, that *all* that which constitutes this day preexists the day's beginning, we could not state that this day begins to be. Therefore, the persuasion that this day begins to be entails by necessity the persuasion that, before this day begins to be, at least the *specific form* of this day 'is not': it does not exist, it is nothingness, absolute nothingness. This persuasion is evident, in a more or less explicit way, in all of Western thought.

The specific form of this day is the unrepeatable configuration and timbre, precisely the specific unity, which all the elements constituting it (pre-existent or not) adopt on this day. To believe that it begins to be means to believe *at the very least* that the specific form of this day was hitherto an absolute nothingness. And to believe that this day will cease to be means, at the very least, to believe that its specific form will once more become an absolute nothingness (even if many of its aspects and many things belonging to it will continue to be).

But the specific form of this day is not a nothing: it is an entity. *Therefore, to believe that this specific form has been nothing and will once more become nothing means to believe that there exists a time in which this entity, insofar as it is an entity, is nothingness. That is, it means to state that such an entity, insofar as it is an entity, is nothingness, absolutely nothingness.*

Identification of the entity with nothingness is stated in relation to all entities, which, according to the West, pass from non-being into being and vice versa. What for the West is supreme 'evidence' of this passage is, in truth, the supreme Folly whereby thought and action are guided by such thought. Folly, that is, does not appear in the eyes of the West as Folly, as identification of the entity with nothingness. Instead, it appears precisely as 'evidence', and Folly is kept outside of the consciousness that the West has of the world. Faith in the 'evidence' of becoming — that faith which is the dominant and altogether essentially hidden thought of the West — therefore necessarily entails faith in the entity, insofar as it is an entity, as being a non-entity; that is, it entails faith in the entity, insofar as it is an entity, as being nothing.

This implication subsists in spite of every attestation of fidelity that the West expresses towards the principle of non-contradiction. Because if we were to ask Western thought whether it is possible that there existed a time in which the circle had become square — and therefore a time in which the circle would be square — or whether there existed a time in which one had become, and therefore is, two, then such thought would be sufficiently prepared to answer: 'No', in no time or state of existence whatsoever is it possible that the circle would be square, or that one would be two. But this sensibility to contradiction (which characterises Western thought, even when it believes it can take distance from the principle of non-contradiction), this *horror contradictions*, disappears and is totally neutralised when it is believed, instead, that there exists a time in which this day, this non-nothing, was not, in which it was nothing; and that there will come a time in which the day will, once more, be nothing.

In the dominion of Folly, it appears that the most evident and 'natural' thing to think is that entities have been nothing and will return to nothingness. But to state that *this day is* nothing *essentially differs* from stating that *nothingness* is nothing: when one thinks that *things* become nothing and, having become nothing, *are* nothing, one is not thinking of a process in which *nothingness* becomes nothing, so that at the end of such a process nothingness would be nothing. Instead, one is thinking of a process in which, specifically, *things* have become nothing and, having become nothing, *things* are nothing. 'Life' is drama and tragedy, exactly because it is *about things* that their becoming nothing and being nothing is affirmed. *About things*: and above all about things we love and without which our lives would be unbearable. But precisely because it is *about things, and not about nothingness*, that the West thinks things come from nothing and return to it; exactly for this reason, the West is, in its essence, extreme Folly. It is the essential form of *nihilism,* that is, the persuasion that things insofar as they are things—entities insofar as they are entities — are nothing.

Non-Folly is the manifestation of the necessity that the entity is entity; the impossibility that an entity is nothing. Non-Folly is the manifestation of the impossibility that the entity insofar as it is an entity — that is, every entity — is not; it is the manifestation of the *eternity* of every entity. Eternal is every entity; therefore, above all, every state of the world, consciousness, and affectivity is eternal. Eternal is the past and the future, as is the present. The infinite entities not manifesting themselves are eternal, too.

Based on faith in the Greek sense of becoming, no immutable and eternal being, and no definitive and incontrovertible truth are possible. This is precisely what the essential thought of our time draws from that ancient faith. But Non-Folly radically questions faith in becoming: it is its most radical negation. Non-Folly is thus essentially (and eternally) *outside* the disdain, in our times, for the incontrovertibility and necessity of truth. However, it also stays outside the way in which the metaphysical-ontological tradition of the West has understood such incontrovertibility and necessity: the destiny of necessity is not the *epistéme.*

The conviction that essents come from nothingness and return to it, that is, the conviction that essents — non-nothings — are nothing, is both supreme Folly and extreme Violence. Not even the most shadowy of entities can be annihilated (or produced) by extreme Folly; but, within extreme Folly, entities are subjected to the extreme Violence that poses them as an absolutely nothing to modify the world. That is, the Violence that acts (believes itself to be acting) with the conviction that it can annihilate, produce, that which instead is impossible to annihilate, produce, or create.

Extreme Violence and Folly are the hidden root out of which the history of the West begins to grow. Based on the faith that entities oscillate between being and nothingness, entities make themselves available to forces pushing them towards nothingness and towards being: entities are seen as themselves demanding to be violated. Only if they are conceived as becoming, in the Greek sense of this word, can we think their domination, production and destruction without limit; since, in their very being dominated, their essence is not denied (the essence assigned to them by extreme Folly) but they fulfil their profoundest vocation. Nihilism is external Violence and Folly.

Non-Folly as the destiny of necessity is the negation of nihilism: negation of the authentic sense proper to nihilism, and which differs essentially from every definition of nihilism suggested by Western thought. As the negation of nihilism, Non- Folly is altogether the negation of the professed 'evidence' that the entity comes from nothingness and returns to it. Even here, we have to limit ourselves to give a summary indication.

That which is annihilated, for the West, is also something leaving the horizon of manifestation and appearance of entities. Inasmuch as it is believed that something coming from being then annihilates itself, it is necessary to believe that such something no longer appears; and, inasmuch as it is believed that something is still not yet anything, it is necessary to believe that such something does not appear yet. For the West, recollection does not manifest what has gone into nothingness, but only its image; and even foresight can only anticipate the image of what is still not yet anything. When this day will have gone into nothingness, this day — the West thinks — will not remain here before us in the flesh and bones it now manifests itself in, but only its image will be manifested in the recollection.

For the West, when something goes into nothingness, it also leaves the vault of experience, the vault of appearance. Inhabitants of the West don't say that when the sun leaves the vault of the sky, it has gone into nothingness: they don't say it, because in the morning the sun returns. But if we wanted to know from the vault of the sky what fate befalls the sun after it has set, the vault of the sky would not know how to respond; it would not be able to manifest what fate befalls that which, as the sun, has left it. In the same way, when something is thought to go into nothingness, it is impossible for one to believe that the experience, the manifestation of the entity, would show the fate befalling what, having annihilated itself, has also left the realm experience and no longer appears.

Inhabitants of the West learn that, when something goes out of their experience in certain ways — for instance, in the terrible ways of violence — the return of such a thing cannot be ascertained. It is at this point that they construct the *doctrine* that such something has become nothing. But, to be precise, the assertion of an annihilation of things is a *doctrine*: it is not the result of an experience; it is not something that appears and manifests itself. The annihilation of nothingness and the emergence from it are then opposites to an immediate or even supreme 'evidence'. Not only that, but the *doctrine* sustaining the annihilation and creation of entities is the doctrine of Folly and nihilism. It is the doctrine of the impossible, and it is impossible for the impossible to manifest itself in any experience whatsoever.

Certainly, the content of the appearance is variable; but in Non-folly the appearance of variation can neither be the appearance of the thing becoming other than itself, nor the appearance of that extreme form of becoming other which is becoming nothing (on the part of the entity) or becoming entity (on the part of nothingness). In Non-folly the appearance is not even phenomenal appearance, but it is the appearance of the entities themselves, that is, the eternals themselves. The variation that appears in Non-folly is thus the supervening of eternals in the circle of appearance, and their leaving it.

Many questions open themselves up at this point — but no longer the question asking why essents are instead of being nothing. Essents are because it would be contradictory for them not to be. Essents are because they are eternal.

But the infinite *opposition* between the essent and that which it is not, and thus between the essent and nothingness, is not an arbitrary presupposition. It is instead the destiny of every essent and every thought, because the negation of the opposition between any essent whatsoever and its other is an essent aiming to oppose itself to all that which is not, and, thus, also to nothingness. This means that negating the opposition of every essent to its other is founded upon that which it negates. That is, such negation negates itself. The opposition between every essent and its own other, and between every essent, is nothingness; it shows itself, therefore, as the necessity of the destiny of every essent and every thought.

CHAPTER 25

Davide Tarizzo (1966–)

Davide Tarizzo obtained his PhD in hermeneutic philosophy from the University of Turin in 1996, under the supervision of Gianni Vattimo and Pier Aldo Rovatti. The thesis, on philosophy and psychoanalysis, was published in 1998 with the title *Il desiderio dell'interpretazione. Lacan e la questione dell'essere (The Desire of Interpretation: Lacan and the Question of Being)*. In 1997, Tarizzo moved to Paris to further develop his research under the supervision of Jacques Derrida. In the same year, he started working for the Italian publisher Einaudi, editing and translating books by Arendt, Badiou, Cavell, Deleuze, Jankélévitch, Minkowski and Nancy. Between the late 1990s and early 2000s, Tarizzo's main focus was the question of subjectivity as viewed from the perspectives of Lacanian psychoanalysis and key thinkers in the Continental tradition. He published essays on topics such as 'L'anima in fuga. Deleuze e il piano psichico' (1996), 'L'altra verità. Heidegger e la decisione' (1998), 'La vertigine di Cartesio. Cenni sull'idiozia e la sua storia' (2000) and 'Nexus finalis. Contingenza e comicità in Kant' (2001). In 2003, he also published two monographs: *Il pensiero libero. La filosofia francese dopo lo strutturalismo (Free Thinking: French Philosophy after Structuralism)* and *Introduzione a Lacan (Introduction to Lacan)*. Shortly afterwards, in 2004, he wrote another monograph which mainly focused on Hegel's concepts of *Geist* and contingency: *Homo Insipiens. La filosofia e la sfida dell'idiozia (Homo Insipiens: Philosophy and the Provocation of Idiocy)*.

From 2002 to 2008, Tarizzo held teaching and research positions at the University of Salerno, the University of Eastern Piedmont Amedeo Avogadro and the University of Naples 'L'Orientale'. From 2005 to 2010 he was scientific secretary for the PhD in philosophy coordinated by Roberto Esposito at the Italian Institute of Human Sciences, Naples. In this period, he outlined a 'clinical approach to critical theory' thanks to which he has analysed key issues in social and political philosophy such as the question of biopolitics and that of foundations of modern democracy. These researches, still partially unpublished in English, have been presented at several Italian universities and internationally at the Cardozo School of Law, Cornell University, the University of Helsinki, the New School for Social Research, Instituto de Estudios Criticos of Mexico City, Scuola Normale Superiore of Pisa, the Slovenian Academy of Sciences and Arts and the Sorbonne, amongst others.

His research on biopolitics is most fully laid out in *Life: A Modern Invention* (2010, English translation 2017). This book marks a turning point in the field of biopolitics because it shows the fundamental importance of the theory of evolution by natural selection in the definition of what Foucault called the 'threshold of biological modernity'. Thanks to a genealogy of the modern concept of life that runs from German idealism to contemporary evolutionary biology, Tarizzo is able to trace a connection between the Kantian notion of the human will and the Darwinian concept of natural selection.

The outline of Darwin's Kantianism does not aim at saturating the entire field of contemporary evolutionary biology but, rather, at showing the teleological drift of a certain notion of biological life which Tarizzo defines as 'autonomous life'. Biological life becomes a force which expresses an absolute and pure 'will to life': as a will that wants only itself, the autonomous life wants only its own survival and reproduction. According to this view of the organic world, the evolution of life cannot be driven by the old static law of *conservation vitae*, which aims at the realization or conservation of an ultimate form of life: such a supreme given form would render the force of life incapable of establishing some other forms and would thus eliminate life's originary autonomy. The evolution of life is rather directed by a new dynamic law, the *salus vitae*, which is characterized by a struggle for the infinite enhancement of life itself. *The Biopolitical Order: Science and Society in the Age of Optimisation* (in preparation) further expands this critical inquiry, addressing the biopolitical order of contemporary societies. By focusing on concepts such as the operational definition of mental illness, the epidemiological characterization of risk and the economic approach to human behaviour, the book demonstrates how these scientific notions contribute to constituting a certain form of biopolitical power.

This research on biopolitics has gone hand in hand with the development of a 'clinical approach' to modern democracy which begins with the monograph, *Giochi di potere. Sulla paranoia politica* (2007) (*Games of Power: On Political Paranoia*) and is further developed in later contributions such as 'Quando un popolo muore' (2013), 'Populismo: sostanza o attributo?' (2015), 'Massa e popolo: Freud e Laclau' (2012) and 'What Is a Political Subject?' (2011). One of the central themes of this inquiry is the question of modern political subjects. A political subject, or a 'people', is not only the 'nation' but also the 'class' (Marxism), the 'race' (Social Darwinism), the 'civil society' (Lockean Liberalism) and so on. Shedding light on this concept means providing a definition for the two words of which it is comprised — political and subject: hence the need to outline a study at the crossroads between psychoanalysis (the 'subject') and political theory (the 'political'). *Political Grammars: The Unconscious Foundations of Modern Democracy* (2021) fills this gap by proposing a theory of modern political subjectivities. Tarizzo argues that the individual subject is a grammatical illusion because it lacks any truth-value; however, this illusion is of a particular type, necessary because, 'stronger than anything, the subject I-think-I-am imposes itself'. The *ego* is therefore a 'true fiction', and the same holds for the collective subject, the *nos*, because each person is both an individual and a collective subject. The explanation of the way in which the individual and the collective subject relate to each other not only fills a gap in current psychoanalytic theory but also serves as a basis for a 'theory of political grammars'.

Thanks to the clinical approach to political theory, Tarizzo not only inquires into the processes that allow a political subject to emerge but, in texts such as 'Ospitalità. L'esigenza dell'Europa, della filosofia, della democrazia' (2014) and 'Después del euro: soberania nacional y hospitalidad europea' (2015), he also aims at understanding the conditions necessary for the rise of new political subjects such as the European *populus*.

For many years, Tarizzo has been conducting a research project on contemporary metaphysics. In his view, contemporary metaphysics belongs mainly to physics rather than philosophy; and it is in the field of physics that the split between ontology and metaphysics emerges. The traces of such a fracture can already be detected in the works of philosophers such as Plato and Hegel in particular. The results of this work will be published in a book entitled *Metaphysics Beyond Ontology*.

Marco Piasentier

Selected writings

Tarrizzo, Davide. 'Applauso. L'impero dell'assenso' ('Applause. The Empire of Assent'), In *Forme contemporanee del totalitarismo*, edited by Massimo Recalcati, 83–105. Torino: Bollati Boringhieri (translated especially for this volume, by Katherine Langley), 2007

Tarrizzo, Davide. *Il desiderio dell'interpretazione: Lacan e la questione dell'essere (The Desire for Interpretation: Lacan and the Question of Being)* (English translation forthcoming with Bloomsbury), Reggio Calabria: La Città del Sole, 1998

Selected writings in English

Tarrizzo, Davide. *Life: A Modern Invention*, trans. Mark William Epstein. Minneapolis, MN: University of Minnesota Press, [2010] 2017

EXCERPT

Davide Tarizzo, *Applause: The Empire of Assent*
_____

(Davide Tarizzo, 'Applauso. L'impero dell'assenso'', in Massimo Recalcati (ed.), Forme contemporanee del totalitarismo. Torino, 2007. Trans. Bollati Boringhieri, pp. 83–94.

I shall skip the preliminaries so as to take my cue without delaying from an experience which has tormented me for many years now. I shall talk about this sensation of annoyance and embarrassment which grips me at the end of a lecture, a concert, a theatrical spectacle [*spettacolo*][1] or some other public event — and even, increasingly frequently, at the end of film screenings — when everybody punctually and without fail starts to applaud. Setting aside personal idiosyncrasies, so far as this is possible, I would simply like to ask myself the following questions: what sense do all of these instances of applause have and why does such punctuality make them by now both predictable and inevitable, almost as if the applause were an 'absolute'' of our everyday lives? Is it true that applause — having started out as an occasional gesture and signified appreciation of a very precisely delimited class of performances, which it was until some time ago (but how long ago, in fact?) — is becoming something new, something disoriented and disorientating, something that is truly *unheimlich* [uncanny], something that is increasingly out of place, and which is tending to assume a sense that has come to differ and is perhaps symptomatic?[2]

Let us begin with a little portable phenomenology of applause that can be divided into four points:

a)   A round of applause can be given or received, depending on whether we take the perspective of the agent or the patient, of the actor who gives a certain performance, or of a member of the audience who benefits from the performance in a more or less passive way.

b)   A round of applause is not a linguistic act, in the sense that applause does not entail the use of the spoken word (apart perhaps from shouting the word *bravo,* which is to say acclaiming someone, but in any case, this is slightly different from applause), but nevertheless, it is an act endowed, without doubt, with some linguistic or semiotic value, and it is, therefore, an act of assent [*assenso*] or approbation [*approvazione*].

c)   It is possible to participate in applause in a direct or indirect way, in the sense that if I applaud at the end of a concert, I assist with something in a personal way, whilst if I hear a round of applause on television during a chat-show or a sitcom, that is quite a different matter. Here it is possible to think that, in this case, I

am not applauding, but the matter is more complicated than it
may appear at first glance. Let's say that, after a joke made by a
television presenter, followed by applause, real or fictitious, from
the audience, similarly real or fictitious, I smile, amused. In this
case, can we really say that I am not applauding, which is to say,
that I am not demonstrating my approval [*assenso*] of that which I
see and hear, lending assistance to the 'spectacle'?

d) The final characteristic of applause: its binding force, injunctive,
imperative, which places us before a stark alternative: *in or out*
[o dentro o fuori] — either within the collectivity which applauds
[*la collettività che applaude*] or without, either within *everyone
who is applauding* [*il* tutti che applaudono] or without. An
alternative which only allows us to choose either the stupidity of
the applause or the idiocy of those who exempt themselves from
it. In fact, 'stupid', according to its Latin etymology, is someone
who is amazed or stupefied [*stupito*], delighted [by something
'stupendous']) [*ammirato*], or struck by something (from *stupeo*
are derived both *stupor* and *stupidus*), whilst 'idiotic', according
to its etymology, which is in this case Greek, is someone who
stands apart, the individual [*singolo*] that isolates itself from the
community, it is the one who, in the end, even constitutes the
figure of the inexperienced [*dell'inesperto*] or of the uncivilised
[*dello zotico*] (all of these acceptations being present in the words
idioteia, idiotes, which derive from *idios*). In light of the above,
it is not without interest that Roland Barthes remarks: 'For some
years, a unique project, apparently: to explore my own *bêtise*, or
better still: to *utter* it, to make it the object of my books. In this
way I have already uttered my *bêtise "égotiste"* and my *bêtise
amoureuse*. There remains a third kind, which I'll someday have to
get down on paper: *bêtise politique*'[3].

But, what is a round of applause? First of all, we shall try to find an answer
in the dictionary. 'Applause' is defined in the Zingarelli dictionary as a
'spontaneous and clamorous expression of both favour and approbation
[*approvazione*], expressed by clapping', from the Latin *applausus* —
made up of *ad* and *plausus* — which signifies the same thing. Therefore,
to applaud signifies simply putting your hands together in a show [*segno*]
of approbation and in a spontaneous manner. And here we straightaway
find the first discrepancy between the word and the thing that I would
like to highlight. In the age of the technical reproducibility of applause,
applause is no longer spontaneous, and is perhaps no longer even
clamorous.

As far as I know, a history of applause has not yet been written. It does
not even exist, to my knowledge, a history of the audience [*del pubblico,
dell'audience*[4]], which retraces its historical and cultural transformations,

and which reconstructs, so far as is possible, the attitudes and behaviours displayed by an audience in front of spectacular events (theatrical, musical, the circus, and so on). On the other hand, if a history of the audience were to be written one day, an important chapter should certainly be devoted to applause, namely to the various forms of approval and disapproval [*assenso e dissenso*] expressed by the audience, which always assume a historical and cultural profile.

Now, we should ask ourselves: what would we read about contemporary applause, applause as it is configured in our day, in this hypothetical universal history of the audience. We would probably read a similar observation to that of Günther Anders, thrown almost casually into the middle of some caustic observations on our current inability to take up a position when placed before an image (televisual or cinematic):

> *We are cheated of the experience and the capacity to take up a position.* Since we are not capable of taking cognisance of the vast horizon of the world that today is really 'our world' (since 'real' refers to something that we can encounter and upon which we depend) in direct sensible vision, but only through images of it, *we encounter precisely that which is more significant in the form of apparition and fantasm*, and therefore, in shrunken form, if not actually in a form altogether devoid of reality. Not as a 'world' (a world that can only be appropriated by moving around in it and experimenting) but as an *object of consumption* delivered to our homes. Those who have consumed an atomic explosion from the comfort of their own homes, in the form of an image delivered to one's home, which is to say in the guise of a mobile picture-postcard, now associate everything that one can happen to hear about any atomic situation with this domestic event of microscopic dimensions, and this entails their being cheated of the capacity to conceive of the thing itself and to take up an adequate position in relation to this thing. That which is delivered in a fluid state, which is to say, in such a way that it can immediately be absorbed, renders impossible, because superfluous, a personal experience. Actually, for the most part, the requisite position is itself kindly provided along with the image, and few things are so characteristic of broadcasting today as the free home-delivery of applause.[5]

Let us pause for a second on this particular feature of contemporary applause: most of the time, it involves indirect applause, which is neither received nor given in the first person. In other words, we assist in the applause of others, which we are called to give our assent to by way of contagion. Televised applause takes this form, yet it is still an invitation or a command — *inside or outside* [o dentro o fuori]. However, given that the only way in which to express disagreement [*dissenso*] or step outside, in a situation like this, would be to immediately turn off the television, we can conclude that for as long as the television remains switched on, we remain inside [*dentro*], we are giving our assent, we are applauding even without moving our hands. The same could be said for the laughter played in the background of jokes on a sit-com or comedy. We laugh without laughing, as long as the television is switched on, we laugh without moving our lips, and at times — indeed often, almost always, if you pay close attention — our fantasmatic laugh does not follow directly after funny jokes, but is instead urged and released by fake, televised, laughter, the task of which is to dictate the timing of the reaction and coordinate our position with respect to the programme. But if the joke is genuinely funny, why resort to such a stratagem, why intersperse witticisms with this laughter that erupts before immediately fading, in so unnatural a manner? Why force us to laugh? And why should we laugh in such a contrived manner? Why should our laughter be wrung from us by this vampiric cackle?

A few years ago, Quentin Skinner gave a memorable lecture at the Sorbonne about laughter and philosophy, reviewing some of the classic theses on the subject.[6] It is not necessary here to go into too much detail. It is enough simply to recall the importance of this theme for the philosophy, and indeed the politics, of the modern age. It is enough, for example, to remember the overt hostility of Hobbes towards an emotional reaction like laughter: 'the passion of laughter is nothing else but a sudden glory arising from sudden conception of some eminency in ourselves, by comparison with the infirmities of others, or with our own formerly'.[7] For Hobbes, laughter, in practice, is a source of disequilibrium and disorder in interpersonal relations, and it is always the expression of a suppressed hatred, of man's natural undying enmity for the other man, which undermines the established order — this is why it is a question of sterilising the disruptive force, condemning without appeal the invisible hostility of laughter. For Spinoza, the great heretic, laughter is on the contrary a benign phenomenon, a passion that should be valued, since it is the key to an increased activity of the mind and body, or of man as such — this is why it is a question of cultivating the experience and strengthening rather than diminishing its affirmative power: 'Cheerfulness [*hilaritas*] [. . .] is pleasure which, in so far as it is related to the body, consists in this, that all parts of the body are affected equally; that is [. . .], the body's power of activity is increased or assisted'.[8] Now, the historical analysis of the diverse philosophical conceptions of laughter from its origins up until today is of little importance. What is important is that laughter appears in every case to present a subversive face, the face of a man who rejoices in himself, who says 'yes' to his own mind and his own body — whether others pay the price for it (Hobbes) or whether nobody pays anything (Spinoza). This is the nomadic power of laughter, laughter's purely affirmative force, in spite of everything and everyone. The one who laughs, first of all says 'yes' to themselves. And from this point of view, the question immediately becomes political. If politics is in fact the art of inducing man to say 'yes' to an other man, *homo ridens*, the man who says 'yes' to himself, at this point creates a problem. (This explains why philosophy, and indeed politics, have in the past pursued this problem and why it is wise for philosophy and politics today to return to it).

Let us return to laughter in the third personal form of today's audience, the laugher track. This in fact provides an elegant way of escaping from our impasse. Because this laughter is not true laughter; it is applause. Those who laugh when sitting in front of a television screen do not say 'yes' to themselves, but to others, who laugh in their place. It would seem that nothing of this kind has ever truly appeared until now. The role of the chorus [coro] in ancient tragedies, which also took place between the tragic scene and the audience in the theatre, was certainly not to applaud; and during a comedy [commedia], in the past, it is plausible that one laughed differently to how one laughs today, or how one applauds today. Indeed, there was no form of laughter which anticipated our way of laughing. There was nobody who laughed in our place. Even today, given that counterfeit laughter does not belong to anybody, being disembodied and mindless, *anonymous and spectral,* there is *no one* [doing the laughing]. Therefore, responding to their bidding, we too lose body and mind. Here, our laughter becomes applause, which is to say, a modality of assent, no longer to ourselves but to others. Laughter changes its nature, and along with it, the man that laughs and says 'yes' to the *no one* who takes his place. This may appear to be an exaggeration based on a detail that is in the end marginal. However, God, as we know, hides in the details.[9] And the God in question, above all, is the last one we can still venerate, or rather applaud, even in those precious moments in which we once adored or said our prayers in rapt recollection (think, for example, of funerals). This God, our God, is the spectacle.

The spectacle laughs at itself. This is the perhaps definitive proof that we are dealing with the last God. Nietzsche had forewarned us of this: 'Gods are fond of mockery: it seems they cannot refrain from laughter even when sacraments are in progress'.[10] The God of the spectacle laughs at himself, eliminating the possibility of laughter in the first person, or rendering it ever more slight. But, where is the spectacle? There are spectacles wherever we applaud, wherever we venerate our God. This means that even the God of the spectacle, like those who preceded him, needs all of us in order to reign. Not only this, it also means that applause determines and generates the spectacle. It signifies, that is to say, that we can at this point give a formal definition of the spectacle. *A spectacle is anything that we applaud.* Not everything is a spectacle in today's world, as Guy Debord believed. If this were indeed the case, if we really lived in the realm of the 'integrated spectacle', in which one could no longer distinguish reality from the spectacle,[11] we would not be able to *see* the spectacle, we could no longer grasp its spectacular nature, and we could not give a definite and comprehensible sense to the word 'spectacle'. However, if not everything is a spectacle in today's world, this is because everything tends to be transformed into a spectacle. The index of this transformation is applause. Not only the index, but also the driver. Every time that we applaud, in the most disparate of circumstances and in situations that are increasingly unthinkable, we actually create the spectacle.

Let us try to clarify some features of today's applause.

a) *Applause creates the audience.* If we agree that in the present condition, applause generates the spectacle, or transforms ever more disparate phenomena into spectacular events, then the following is a logical consequence: applause does not just create the spectacle, but it also creates the audience, in the sense that by applauding we qualify as an audience.

b) *Applause is increasingly, invasive.* Today, the audience happens to hear and watch outbursts of applause which come from within the cinema screen, in a play of reflections between the real audience and the fictitious audience which conveys the invisible command to applaud and assent to the scene that both audiences are contemplating at that moment: the scene — for instance, a romantic kiss in the centre of a stadium, perhaps with the crowd giving a *standing ovation* [in English in the original] — becomes a surface for reflecting the real audience into the fictitious audience, or the place where the audience, oscillating at this point between reality and fiction, encounters itself.

c) *Applause is for everything and nothing* [*il contrario di tutto*]. For example, on the television, when rounds of applause occur almost continuously during a debate, expressing approval [*assenso*] first for one argument then for another, counterposed and contradictory to one another. That which remains, in the background, are not the two arguments, but applause as such, approval *qua* approval [*assenso* qua *assenso*], which makes these encounters truly 'spectacular'. Prima facie, all of this can seem trivial, and is usually explained in another way. The effects, however, seem to go far beyond the intentions of the actors and moderators of the debate. The effects, with the passing of time and the repetition of the scene, are those of an injunction [*ingiunzione*] to pure and unconditional approval [*assenso*]. It is no longer a matter of an injunction to approve [*assenso*] this or that argument, this or that joke, this or that character. With time, the injunction to approve is purified and evacuated of all content, so as to be transformed into an injunction which enjoins approval as such or the pure form of approval, the functioning of which is the only constant in this staging [*messa in scena*]: the applause of the audience in the room, which transforms the scene into a spectacle, turns each and every one of us into a member of the audience.

d) *Applause integrates, globalises or totalises that which we call the world.* Applause is an assent, it is a saying-'yes'. But, in how many languages can we say 'yes'? In response, we just need to ask ourselves: in how many languages can we applaud? In fact, applause is a universal language, it is the language which we all speak today. But who are we? There is no answer, there are no words, there is no language in which to respond to this, except the language of applause, which crosses over all national, social, cultural, ethnic and religious frontiers. In other words, the only human community which today tends to impose itself, that which we shape globally and worldwide, day in day out, swept away by an unstemmable tide, is the community of the audience [*del pubblico, dell' audience*], a community that everybody is being included in, *volens nolens*. Applause is the slender thread which holds everyone [*tutti*] together, which makes us 'all' ["*tutti*"], which makes us "us" ["*noi*"]. A slender thread but as robust as a chain. Is there any need to remember that the wall, which until a couple of years ago divided the world in two, collapsed, not through violence but beneath volleys of applause? Is there any need to remember that antennas are now spread all over the globe to capture the applause which each day echoes on a planetary scale? A famous American actor recently spoke about his journey to the Amazon, a land in which he hoped to be able to stroll in peace without being immediately surrounded by delirious fans. Vain hope, he said, amused, since even there he had quickly been identified: Aren't you the one from that ship which capsized? Applause. Installed, in the centre of this village, hidden away in a far-flung corner of the globe, a satellite dish — altar to the new God.

We could and maybe we should continue. After all, these are but fragments of an analysis of applause in its current configuration, which should be completed and perfected. Now, I should like to emphasise the idea that is behind all of this. Applause is a practice [*pratica*]; I would even say that clapping your hands is the simplest thing in the world. For this reason, one cannot think of it as a practice of power [*una pratica di potere*]. Briefly put, the idea, or my idea at any rate, is not that there are certain evil figures who covertly manipulate the society of the spectacle (the State, the multinationals, the secret [masonic] lodges and so on, as in the fantasy of some). The idea is not even that of a microphysics of practices of power (*à la* Michel Foucault) which is often short-sighted in its views when it comes to the properties and specific characteristics of the current means of communication (properties and characteristics without history, which are the random and contingent results of technological fabrication, but which turn history on its head) or the 'becoming-spectacle of the world'. The idea, to be completely frank, is that power [*potere*] is not the right concept here, that this category is no longer appropriate, at least not in the guise (or in the guises) which it has assumed until now. (To clarify this affirmation slightly, suffice it to say that in the world of unconditional assent and of the *no one*, even the category and symbolic authority of the Father tend to vanish, as Jacques Lacan noticed years ago: hence the widespread and restless interrogation of fatherhood in all of its aspects and symbolic valences, which have become a recurrent and almost obsessive theme of cinema, for adults and children). Rather, we find ourselves faced with a complex and stratified process of reorganisation of the *frames* [English in the original] within which humans experience and assert their own humanity, reconfiguring their reciprocal relationships in search of new, unpredictable balances. We are dealing with a 'systemic' process (but I am not referring to Niklas Luhmann here) in which many factors are interwoven, some old and some new: that is, background historical factors and current factors of technological renewal which are imposing relevant and sometimes dramatic modifications within human 'forms of life' ["*forme di vita*"]. From the spectacularisation of the world to the irruption of biopolitics, we are dealing with processes that are connected to technological innovation, in the face of which philosophy and politics of a traditional type appear to be ever more disorientated. (Whence the insistence on the problem of 'technology' ["*tecnica*"] on the part of some key thinkers such as Martin Heidegger, Günther Anders, Gilbert Simondon and Jacques Derrida, to name but a few). The acceleration of technological process is rendering obsolete, at least in part, the old philosophico-political categories, making it urgent and necessary to invent new ones. In fact, the agents of these processes — namely, ourselves — may be said not to be aware of them. Thus it is not that these processes are necessarily a force for evil, just as it is not the case that they are a force for good. In short, it is not a matter of expressing value judgements. If anything, it is a matter of opening our eyes to what is happening around us, of observing, describing and deciphering — employing, if it proves useful, new conceptual tools. This is the sense of the definitions that follow, which are meant to be provocative rather than exhaustive.

Thesis

Applause is today both the index of and the driver for unconditional assent [*assenso*], or assent *qua* assent.

Definitions

1) I propose to define as democratic, or participative, a political regime based on the principle of free consent [*consenso*] and legitimate dissent [*dissenso*].

2) I propose to define as a tyranny, or despotic, a political regime based on the principle of forced consent and sanctioned dissent.

3) I propose to define as totalitarian a(n) (anti-)political regime based on the principle of unconditional assent [*assenso*], which is neither a free nor a forced consent since it no longer entails an effective alternative to dissent. (It was George Orwell, who in his book *1984*, brought to light the absolute inadmissibility of dissent in a totalitarian regime, which is based quite to the contrary on the principle of unconditional assent).

3.1) Unconditional assent can refer to a precise ideological content or it can be deprived of all ideological content: in the first case, we shall speak of incomplete totalitarianism, while in the second case, we shall speak of complete totalitarianism. (These concepts are coextensive with those of 'concentrated spectacle' and 'diffuse spectacle', proposed in their day by Debord, though they are not synonyms of the latter).

3.1.1) Unconditional assent [*assenso*], from which it is impossible to dissent in any respect, may be opposed only by dissidence: a totalitarian regime is a political regime which fights against dissidence.

3.1.2) To unconditional assent, which can assume the guise of ideological assent or pure assent, corresponds two forms of dissidence: ideological dissidence and pure dissidence.

3.2) Dissidence is not a refutation or negation of assent but rather the suspension of assent: in a totalitarian regime, every refutation or negation of assent is nullified by the game of unconditional assent. (Ludwig von Mises was the first to bring this game of unconditional assent to light, alluding precisely to this when he spoke of the 'polylogism' of totalitarian regimes).

3.2.1) Dissidence is not dissent: an incomplete totalitarian regime rules out the very possibility of dissent on the basis of Ideology; a complete totalitarian regime does the same thing through the Spectacle.

3.2.2) Dissidence is questioning: in the case of a totalitarian regime of Ideology, we shall speak of partisan dissidence; in the case of the totalitarian regime of the Spectacle, of nomadic dissidence.

I propose to call philosophy every discourse that revokes the unconditional by means of questioning: philosophy is pure dissidence.

Translated by Katherine Langley with Michael Lewis

Notes

1   A crucial – technical – word in the present text, which is why we take the liberty of translating it literally as 'spectacle' throughout, even if something less impressive might sometimes be apt.

2 The following reflections are strictly related to Tarizzo, *Homo insipiens. La filosofia e la sfida dell'idiozia (Homo Insipiens: Philosophy and the Challenge of Idiocy)*. Milan: Franco Angeli, 2004.

3 Roland Barthes, *The Rustle of Language*. Trans. Richard Howard. Berkeley & Los Angeles: University of California Press, 1989 [1984], p. 366 ('Deliberation', Journal entry of 22 July 1977). Translation slightly modified.

4 'Audience' in Italian is an Anglicism which we have elided here and on another later occasion, which we have nevertheless marked. Throughout, we have translated '*pubblico*' as 'audience' in occasional adjectival forms.

5 G. Anders, *L'uomo è antiquato II. Sulla distruzione della vita nell'epoca della terza rivoluzione industrial [The Obsolescence of the Human. On the Destruction of Life in the Age of the Third Industrial Revolution]*. Turin: Bollati Boringhieri, 1992, pp. 232–3. Original: *Die Antiquiertheit des Menschen, Band II: Über die Zerstörung des Lebens im Zeitalter der dritten industriellen Revolution*. Munich: Beck, 1988 [1980].

6 Of the many other reviews in existence, one could cite as an example – to mention but one – the entry on *Humour and Wit* written by Arthur Koestler for the *Encyclopaedia Britannica*.

7 Thomas Hobbes, *The Elements of Law, Natural And Politic: Part I, Human Nature, Part II, De Corpore Politico*, with *Three Lives*. Ed. J. C. A. Gaskin. Oxford: Oxford University Press, 1999, pp. 54–5 (Ch. IX, 13).

8 Baruch Spinoza, *Ethics; Treatise on the Emendation of the Intellect; and Selected Letters*. Trans. Samuel Shirley. Ed. Seymour Feldman. Indianapolis: Hackett, 1992, Part IV, Prop. 42.

9 See also the comments on '[a] meticulous observation of detail, and at the same time a political awareness of these small things, for the control and use of men', in M. Foucault, *Discipline and Punish: The Birth of the Prison*. Trans. Alan Sheridan. London: Penguin, 1991, p. 141.

10 F. Nietzsche, *Beyond Good and Evil*. Trans. R. J. Hollingdale. London: Penguin, 1990, §294.

11 G. Debord, *Society of the Spectacle*, Trans. Donald Nicholson-Smith. New York: Zone, 1994, pp. 8, 13–14

CHAPTER 26

Mario Tronti (1931–)

Mario Tronti's intellectual and political trajectory spans some sixty years, but it is for his leading role in Italian *Operaismo* (Workerism) that he is best known. This heretical 1960s Marxist current sought to theorize and intervene in the new wave of factory-based militancy that was turning against the traditional workers' movement and the discipline and subjectivity of work. As Tronti later reflected, *Operaismo* championed a working-class politics 'capable of contesting and putting into crisis the mechanism of capitalist production' (2010, 186). This bold assertion of the antagonistic form and standpoint of the working class is typical of *Operaismo*, which was a fierce opponent of neo-Gramscian ideas of the 'national-popular', the 'organic intellectual', cross-class alliances and socio-economic planning, ideas which had dominated the culture and institutions of post-war Italian socialism and the Italian Communist Party.

Tronti's writings of this period are collected in his 1966 book *Operai e capitale* (*Workers and Capital*) (Tronti 2019), although they first appeared as essays in the journal *Quaderni rossi* (Red Notebooks) and the newspaper *Classe operaia* (Working Class), collective publishing projects that served as the crucible for *Operaismo*. Among Tronti's achievements are two of the three most significant conceptual and methodological innovations of *Operaismo* – the *primacy of workers' struggles* and the *social factory*, which I shall sketch out in a moment. The third, *class composition*, was the cornerstone of *Quaderni rossi* (1961–6), a concept and methodology that sought to understand the dynamic nature of the industrial working class through research on factory conditions and workers' struggles, combining sociological methods and 'co-research' with workers themselves (Wright 2017). Focusing on the vast automotive and petrochemical factories in the industrial north, *Quaderni rossi* became increasingly divided into two factions: a 'sociological' faction, led by the journal's founder, Raniero Panzieri, was reluctant to make the leap into the direct political intervention that would soon characterize *Operaismo*'s mode of research, causing the more 'interventionist' faction, led by Tronti and including Antonio Negri, Alberto Asor Rosa and Romano Alquati, to split with *Quaderni rossi* and found *Classe operaia* (1964–7).

Of all *Operaismo*'s theoretical innovations, it is best known through Tronti's assertion that *workers' struggles determine the course of capitalist development*. Reversing the received wisdom that *capital* was the active party in the capital-labour relation, this 'Copernican revolution' was set out most decisively in Tronti's essay, 'Lenin in England', which was published as the editorial to the first issue of *Classe operaia*. Here Tronti argued:

> We too have worked with a concept that puts capitalist development first, and workers second. This is a mistake. And now we have to turn the problem on its head, reverse the polarity, and start again from the beginning: and the beginning is the class struggle of the working class. At the level of socially developed capital, capitalist development becomes subordinated to working class struggles; it follows behind them, and they set the pace to which the political mechanisms of capital's own reproduction must be tuned. (Tronti 1979, 1)

There are two main thrusts to Tronti's thesis here. First, it places workers' struggles against capitalist domination in work at the centre of political praxis, where workers are neither passive recipients of capitalist control nor marginal to the manoeuvring of political parties but leading agents of social change. It compels at once an affirmation of workers' struggles and close attention to their changing forms and effects, as capitalism reconfigures its technological and social forms under pressure to contain workers' disruption.

However, this is not a timeless battle between oppressor and oppressed vying to gain the upper hand, because Tronti understood workers' struggles to have become the *internal motor of capitalist development*. This is the second thrust of his argument. Capitalist society, initially unable to manage its interests as a whole, interests which frequently conflict with those of individual capitalists, comes to develop its collective interest through its response to the collective pressure from workers' struggles, struggles that in the course of the twentieth century become progressively more integrated into capitalist planning. This is the role of the classical workers' movement, which in exchange for gains in wages, conditions and democratic representation, becomes the main driver of capitalist modernization (until the early 1970s, when this arrangement breaks down and capitalism restructures itself around global supply chains, financialization and precarity). As Tronti put it, 'the objective needs of capitalist production are presented in the end in the form of workers' subjective demands; the union proposes a platform of demands, and that platform is nothing other than the reflection of the objective needs of capitalist production' (cited in Filippini and Macchia 2012, 26).

As a consequence, workers' struggles had to break out of this internal mechanism of capitalist modernization. And this is what *Operaismo* observed in the 1960s, as it articulated in theory those workplace struggles that were simultaneously struggles *against the institutions of the workers' movement*, struggles whose features included organized passivity, disaffection with work, sabotage on the assembly line, insubordination, non-collaboration with the unions. This was known in *Operaismo*, and in the subsequent social and intellectual movement of *Autonomia* (Autonomy), as the 'refusal of work'.

Politics was not to be a question of the better *management* of work and a more *equitable distribution* of its product – as it was for the historical workers' movement and the traditional Marxism of Lenin, Trotsky and Mao. Instead, communist practice was located *within the sphere of production* itself and in the reproduction of social relations necessary for the perpetuation of that production. Put otherwise, this was a politics *within and against the structure of work and the subjectivity of the worker*. Retrieving a formulation that was first mooted by Marx and Engels (1975, 36), for whom the proletariat was the class of *self-abolition*, 'dissolved and self-dissolving private property', Tronti wrote that the working class 'need only *combat itself* in order to destroy capital. It has to recognise itself as a political power and negate itself as a productive force' (Tronti 2019, 274, my emphasis). In this formulation, there is no positivity to be retrieved in work and the class condition. As Tronti argues in the text from *Operai e capital* included in this volume, 'the worker *creates* capital, not only insofar as she sells labour power, but also insofar as she *bears* the class relation', that is, bears the relations of capital in the very condition of being working class. As such, the working class as a political force can exist *only* as antagonism and negation: 'The working class cannot constitute itself as a party within capitalist society without preventing capitalist society from functioning. As long as capitalist society does continue to function, the working-class party *cannot* be said to exist.'

The thesis of the *social factory*, the second of Tronti's most significant contributions to *Operaismo*, was developed a little earlier, in his essays 'La fabbrica e la società' (Factory and Society) and 'Il piano del capitale' (The Plan of Capital), published in the second and third issues of *Quaderni rossi* in 1962 and 1963. Here Tronti advanced the thesis that as capitalist production, distribution and exchange supplants all pre-capitalist formations, capitalism develops a specifically capitalist form of *society*, where all social structures and domains become increasingly subordinated to capitalist imperatives. As he writes, 'At the highest level of capitalist development, this social relation becomes a *moment* of the relation of production, the whole of society becomes an *articulation* of production, the whole society lives in function of the factory and the factory extends its exclusive domination over the whole society' (Tronti 2019, 26).

Tronti's social factory thesis drew attention not only to the capitalist structure of the state and social democracy, as was a significant critical stream in *Operaismo* and *Autonomia*, but also to the way in which domains and forms outside of the wage-relation became integrated in the reproduction of capitalism. Here was a compelling analytic figure that could aid in grasping emerging sites of class composition outside the direct sphere of the workplace – the home, the school and university, housing, the city, the circulation of goods and people.

However, as Steve Wright notes, Tronti and *Operaismo* did not take this path themselves, staying firmly rooted on the factory shop floor (2017, 37). It illustrates one of the impasses of *Operaismo*, in that the privileging of value-producing activity and the sphere of production – for all that foregrounding the 'refusal of work' was a crucial development – tended to reproduce a hierarchy between workplace and non-workplace struggles. Hence it carried, without sufficient critique, the concomitant hierarchies of gender and racialization, hierarchies that are integral to the reproduction of capitalism.

In grappling with this impasse, the social factory thesis was developed by feminist struggles within and against *Autonomia*, notably *Lotta Femminista* and the demand for 'wages for housework'. Instead of challenging *Operaismo*'s focus on value-producing activity, they *expanded it* to cover also the sphere of *reproduction* – namely, the role of unpaid gendered work in the home, work that is necessary for the reproduction of labour-power and yet is naturalized by discourses of family, gender and love as a domain outside of capitalist structures (Dalla Costa and James 1972; Fortunati 1995).

If stretching Marx's category of productive labour in this way could so effectively challenge the role of capitalist accumulation and the workers' movement in the oppression of women, it was of course a useful heresy. However, in the development of the social factory thesis in more recent post-*Operaismo* work, notably in Hardt and Negri, stretching the category of value-producing activity has been less effective, as the analysis of the complex differentiation, functionality and tension of different domains of capitalist accumulation is replaced with an amorphous productivity of all and any social activity. As Hardt and Negri lose analytic precision here, they also drop Tronti's insistence that the form of labour is immanently conditioned by capital, favouring instead more traditional Marxist ideas of the self-management of labour, and not its negation (Thoburn 2001).

The impasse that concerned Tronti himself was the role and function of the Marxist 'small group', which during the course of *Classe operaia* he came to see as not only ineffectual but a block to revolutionary renovation of the established workers' movement. Breaking with Negri and others who went on to become protagonists of the organization Potere Operaio (Workers' Power) and, later, *Autonomia*, Tronti precipitated the demise of *Classe operaia* in 1967 and returned to the fold of the Communist Party, seeking in vain to contribute to its radicalization. Ironically, classical *Operaismo* came to an end, then, just as ten years of struggles against work and the social factory were about to kick off with the 1969 'Hot Autumn'.

Nicholas Thoburn

Cited texts and selected writings

Dalla Costa, Mariarosa. and Selma James. *The Power of Women and the Subversion of the Community*. London: Falling Wall Press, 1972

Filippina, Michele. and Emilio Macchia. *Leaping Forward: Mario Tronti and the History of Political Workerism*. Maastricht: Jan van Eyck Academie, 2012

Fortunati, Leopoldina. *The Arcane of Reproduction: Housework, Prostitution, Labor and Capital*, trans Hilary Creek. New York: Autonomedia, 1995

Marx, Karl. and Frederick Engels. *The Holy Family; or Critique Of Critical Criticism*. In *Collected Works*, Volume 4. London: Lawrence and Wishart, 1975

Thoburn, Nicholas. 'Autonomous Production? On Negri's "New Synthesis"'. *Theory, Culture and Society* 18, no. 5 (2001): 75–96.

Tronti, Mario. 'Lenin in England'. In *Working Class Autonomy and the Crisis: Italian Marxist Texts of the Theory and Practice of a Class Movement: 1964–79*, edited by Red Notes. London: Red Notes and CSE Books, 1979

Tronti, Mario. 'Workerism and Politics'. *Historical Materialism* 18 (2010): 186–189.

Tronti, Mario. 'Our Operaismo', trans. Eleanor Chiari, *New Left Review* 73 (2012): 118–39.

Tronti, Mario. *Workers and Capital*, trans. David Broder. London: Verso, 2019

Wright, Steve. *Storming Heaven: Class Composition and Struggle in Italian Autonomist Marxism*, 2nd edn. London: Pluto Books, 2017

EXCERPT

Mario Tronti, *The strategy of refusal*

(Mario Tronti, 'Strategy of Refusal'.)

Adam Smith says — and Marx notes the accuracy of his observation — that the effective great development of labour's productive power begins when labour is transformed into wage-labour; that is, when the conditions of labour confront it in the form of capital. One could go further and say that the effective development of labour's political power really begins from the moment that labourers are transformed into workers; that is, when the whole of the conditions of society confront them as capital. We can see, then, that working-class political power is intimately connected to the productive power of wage-labour. The power of capital, conversely, is primarily a social power. Working-class power is a potential power over production — that is, over a particular aspect of society. Capitalist power is a real dominion over society in general. But such is the nature of capital that it requires a *society centred on production*. Production, a particular aspect of society, thus becomes the aim of society in general. Whoever controls and dominates it controls and dominates everything. Even if factory and society were to become perfectly integrated at the economic level, at a political level they would, nonetheless, forever continue to be in contradiction. One of the highest and most mature points of the class struggle will be precisely the frontal clash between the *factory as working class* and society *as capital*. To deny capital's interests a way forward in the factory is to block the functioning of society itself — and the way is then open to overthrow and destroy the power of capital. To instead seek to take over the running of the 'general interests of society' would, however, mean simplistically reducing the factory itself to capital, indeed by reducing the working class — a part of society — to society as a whole. But, if the productive power of labour makes a leap forward when it is put to use by the individual capitalist, it is also true that it makes a political leap forward when it is organised by social capital. This political leap forward may not express itself in organisational terms, and hence, from the outside, one might conclude that it has not happened at all. Yet it still exists as a material reality, and the fact of its spontaneous existence is sufficient for the workers to refuse to fight for old ideals — though it may not yet be sufficient for the working class to take on the initiative in elaborating a new plan of struggle, based on new objectives. So, are we still living through the long historical period in which Marx saw the workers as a 'class against capital', but not yet as a 'class for itself'? Or should we not perhaps say the opposite, even if it means muddying the waters of Hegel's triad a little? That is, that initially, faced with the direct boss, the workers *immediately* become 'a class for itself' and indeed are recognised as such by the first capitalists. And only afterwards, through a historical travail which is perhaps not yet over, passing through terrible practical experiences which are still ongoing, do the workers arrive at the point of being actively, subjectively, 'a class against capital'. For this transition to take place there needs to be political organisation, the party, which demands all power. In the period in between there is the workers' collective, mass refusal, expressed in passive forms — to reveal themselves as a 'class against capital' before they have this organisation of their own, before they have this total demand for power. The working class *makes* its own existence. But it is, at the same time, an *articulation* and *dissolution* of capital. Capitalist power seeks to use the workers' antagonistic will-to-struggle as a motor for its own development. The working-class party must take this real working-class mediation of capital's interests and organise it in an antagonistic form, as the tactical terrain of struggle and as a strategic destructive potential. Here, there is only one point of reference, only one set of bearings, for the opposed viewpoints of the two classes — and it is the class of workers. Whether one's aim is to stabilise the development of the system or to destroy it forever, it is the working class that decides. The society *of capital* and the *working-class party* find themselves to be two opposite forms with one and the same content. And in the struggle over that same content, the one form excludes the other. They can only both coexist during the brief period of the revolutionary crisis. The working class cannot constitute itself as a *party* within capitalist society without preventing this society from continuing to function. As long as it continues to function, this party is *not* the working-class party.

Remember: 'the existence of a class of capitalists is based on the productive power of labour'. Productive labour, then, stands in relation not only to capital, but also to the capitalists as a class; in this latter relationship, it exists as the working class. This is probably a historical transition: it is productive labour which produces capital; it is capitalist production that 'organises' the working class, through industry; it is the organisation of industrial workers into a class that prompts the capitalists in general to constitute themselves as a class. At an average level of development, workers thus already present themselves as a social class of *producers:* industrial producers of capital. At this same level of development, the capitalists present themselves as a social class not so much of *entrepreneurs* as of *organisers:* that is, the organisers of workers by means of industry. A history of industry cannot be conceived other than as a history of the capitalist organisation of productive labour, and thus as a working-class history of capital. There is no forgetting the 'industrial revolution' here. Our research must start out from this point, if it is ever to get to grips with the contemporary forms of capital's dominion over workers — which is, indeed, increasingly exercised through the objective mechanisms of industry — and then investigate the possible working-class uses of them. This is the point at which the development of the relationship between living labour and the constant part of capital is violently subordinated to the emergence of the class relationship between the collective worker and the whole of capital, as social conditions of production. Every technological change in the mechanisms of industry thus turns out to be determined by the specific moments of the class struggle. Proceeding along this path would achieve two things: first, we would escape the trap of the apparent neutrality of the relationship between humanity and machinery; and, second, we would locate this same relationship in the combined history of working-class struggles and capitalist initiative. It is wrong to define modern society as 'industrial civilisation'. The 'industry' mentioned therein is just a means to be used. In truth, modern society is the civilisation of labour. And a capitalist society can never be anything but this. Precisely for this reason, in the course of its historical development, it can even take on the *form* of 'socialism'. So, we have not an industrial society — the society of capital — but the society of industrial labour, and thus the society of working-class labour. We must find the courage to fight capitalist society on these terms. Are the workers doing anything else when they struggle against the boss? Are they not above all fighting against labour? Are they not first and foremost saying 'no' to the transformation of labour-power into labour? Are they not, more than anything, refusing to *receive* work from the capitalist? Stopping work does not in fact mark a refusal to *give* capital the use of one's labour-power, since it has already been given to capital through the legal contract stipulating the sale and purchase of this particular commodity. Nor is it a refusal to hand capital the products of labour, since this is legally already capital's property, and the worker does not in any case know what to do with this property. Rather, stopping work — the strike, as the classic form of working-class struggle — is a refusal of capital's command, its role as organiser of production. It is a way of saying 'no' to the offer of concrete labour at a particular point in the process, a *momentary* blockage of the labour process as a recurrent threat which cuts into the process of value creation. The anarchosyndicalist 'general strike', which was meant to provoke the collapse of capitalist society, is doubtless a romantic naivety owing to a primitive phase. It in fact already implies a demand, which it appears to oppose — that is, the Lassallean demand for a 'fair share of the fruits of one's labour' — in other words, a fairer 'stake' in capital's profits. In fact, these two perspectives converge in that incorrect correction which was imposed on Marx, and which has subsequently enjoyed such success within the practice of the official workers' movement — namely, the idea that those who really 'create work' are 'working people' and that it is their concern to defend the dignity of this thing which they provide, against all those who would seek to debase it. No, the commonplace terminology is correct, and it really is the capitalist who creates work. The worker is the *creator of capital*. She in fact possesses a unique, particular commodity that is the condition of all the other conditions of production. For, as we have seen, at first all these other conditions of production are but capital in itself — a dead capital which, in order to come to life and develop into a social relation of production, needs to subsume labour-power as an activity under itself, as a subject of capital. But as we have also seen, it cannot become a social relation of production unless the class relation is introduced into it, as its content. And the class relation is imposed from the proletariat's very *first* self-constitution as a class confronting the capitalist. Thus, the worker *creates* capital, not only insofar as she sells labour-power, but also insofar as she *bears* the class relation. Just like the sociality implicit within labour-power, this is another thing the capitalist does not pay for, or rather pays the cost (never subject to contract) of the working-class struggles which periodically shake the production process. Not by chance, the workers choose this as the terrain on which to attack the employers, out of their own tactical interest, and this is thus the terrain on which the employer is forced to respond with continual and disruptive technical developments in the organisation of work. In this whole process, the only thing that does not come from the worker's side is, precisely, work. From the outset, the *conditions of labour* are in the hands of the capitalist. And the only things in the worker's hands from the outset are the *conditions of capital*.

This is the historical paradox which marks the birth of capitalist society, and, indeed, an 'eternal rebirth' that will continue throughout its development. The worker cannot be *labour* other than in relation to the capitalist that stands against her. The capitalist cannot be *capital* other than in relation to the worker that stands against him. It is often asked what a social class really is. The answer is: these *two* classes. The fact that one is dominant does not imply that the other becomes subaltern. Rather, it implies a struggle, on equal terms, to break that domination and to reverse it into new forms, into a domination over those who have thus far dominated. We urgently need to resume circulating an image of the working-class proletariat that represents it as it really is — 'proud and menacing'. It is high time for a fresh comparison, in a new historical experience that directly sets the working class against capital [. . .].

If all of this is the case, then we can conclude that the capitalist class, from its birth, is in fact subordinate to the working class. Hence the need for exploitation. Working-class struggles against the iron laws of capitalist exploitation cannot be reduced to the eternal revolt of the oppressed against their oppressors. For the very same reason, the concept of exploitation cannot be reduced to the individual employer's desire to enrich himself by extracting the maximum possible amount of surplus-labour from the bodies of his workers. [. . .] Exploitation is born, historically, from capital's need to escape from its de facto subordination to the class of worker-producers. It is in this very specific sense that capitalist exploitation in turn provokes working-class insubordination. [. . .] Now it is the working class's directly political thrust that imposes economic development on capital — a development which, starting from the site of production, extends to the general social relation. But this political vitality on the part of its antagonist — which it can also not do without — is, at the same time, the most fearsome threat to capital's power. We have already envisaged the political history of capital as a succession of attempts by capital to free itself from the class relation as a normal moment of 'separation'. Now we can envisage it at a higher level as the *history of the capitalist class's successive attempts to emancipate itself from the working class,* through the medium of the various forms of capital's political domination over the working class. This is the reason capitalist exploitation, a permanent form of the extraction of surplus-value within the production process, has throughout the history of capital been accompanied by the development of ever more *organic* forms of political dictatorship at the level of the state. In the society of capital, there is a truly economic need for political power: namely, the need forcibly to make the working class renounce its own social role as the dominant class. From this point of view, the present forms of economic planning are nothing more than an attempt to impose this *organic* form of dictatorship within democracy as the modern political form of a class dictatorship. [. . .].

When does the political state start to direct at least part of the economic mechanism? When this economic mechanism can begin to use the political state itself as an *instrument of production;* in other words, in the sense that we have used it thus far, as a moment of the *political reproduction* of the working class. The 'end of laissez-faire' means, in substance, that working-class articulation of capitalist development can no longer function on the basis of spontaneous objective mechanisms; rather, it must be subjectively imposed by way of the political initiative of the capitalists themselves, as a class. [. . .] The capitalists have still not invented — and in fact, will obviously never be able to invent — a non-institutionalised political power. That type of political power is specific to the working class. The difference between the two classes at the level of political power is precisely this: the class of capitalists does not exist independently of the formal political institutions through which, in different but permanent ways, it exercises its domination. For this very reason, the smashing of the bourgeois state marks the true destruction of the capitalists' power, and, indeed, it is only possible to destroy that power by smashing the state machine. [. . .] By its very nature, capital is immediately and only an *economic* interest, and, at the beginning of its history, it was nothing more than the egotistical point of view of the individual capitalist. But, faced with the threat posed by the working class, it is forced to organise itself into a *political force* and to subsume under itself the whole of society in its own self-defence. It becomes the class of capitalists or, equivalently, it organises itself into a repressive state apparatus. If it is true that the concept of class is a political reality, then no capitalist class exists without the state of capital. And the so-called bourgeois 'revolution' — the conquest of political power by the 'bourgeoisie' — amounts to nothing more than the long historical transition through which capital constitutes itself as a class of capitalists in antagonistic relation to the workers. [. . .] [T]he development of the working class is totally the opposite: [. . .] At the outset, the proletariat is nothing more than an immediate *political interest* in the destruction of all that exists. In its internal development, it has no need for 'institutions' to bring its essence to life, since this essence is nothing other than the *living force* of that immediate destruction. Yet the proletariat does need *organisation* in order to objectify the political power of its antagonism against capital; in order to articulate this power within the material reality of the class relationship in any given moment [. . .]. Marx discovered the existence of the working class long before any forms existed to express it politically: thus, for Marx, there is *a class even in the absence of the party.* On the other hand, the very existence of the Leninist party created the real illusion that a specific process of working-class revolution was already underway; for Lenin, in fact, *when the class organises itself into a party, it becomes revolution in action.* Here are two mutually complementary theses, just as the figures of Marx and Lenin are complementary. What do these two figures fundamentally represent for us today if not admirable anticipations of the class's future?

If the class is not identical to the party and yet we can speak of class only at a political level; if there is class struggle in the absence of the party, and yet every class struggle is nonetheless a political struggle; if the class makes the revolution through the party — or, in other words, puts into action what it is — by dissolving *in practice* everything that it must dissolve in theory, *taking the leap* from strategy to tactics, and only by these means *seizes* power from those in whose hands it previously lay, before organising that power in its own hands, in new forms. . . if all of this is true, then we must draw the conclusion that the class-party-revolution relationship is far tighter, more determinate and much more historically specific than is currently presented, even by Marxists. We cannot split the concept of revolution from the class relation. But a class relation is posed for the first time by the working class. *The concept of revolution and the reality of the working class thus become the same thing.* [. . .]. Nothing is more alien to the working-class point of view than the opportunistic cult of historical continuity, and nothing more repugnant to it than the concept of 'tradition'. Workers recognise only one continuity — that of their own, direct political experiences; and only one tradition — that of their struggles. [. . .] We [. . .] think that the time has come to begin the work of reconstructing the facts, the moments, the transitions, which the inner reality of capitalism reveals — and can only reveal — precisely to the working-class viewpoint. It is now time to start building that *working-class history of capitalist society,* which alone can provide rich, fearsome, decisive weapons of theory to this moment of practical overthrow. Theoretical reconstruction and practical destruction can henceforth run only together, as the two legs of that single body which is the working class. [. . .] Because the working class is what it is, because of the point where it acts, because of the mode in which it is forced to fight — only the working class can be a *revolutionary process.* [. . .] When it was attempted to apply the model of the bourgeois revolution to the course of working-class revolution, this led to the strategic collapse of the movement. And we must always bear this in mind. Copying this model, the workers would supposedly demonstrate in practice their ability to manage society economically — naturally having far more ability than the capitalists, in this regard — and on this basis lay claim to direct the state. This was to see the working-class management of capital as the highest, most 'classic' road to socialism. From the viewpoint of historical materialism, social democracy is theoretically the most orthodox workers' movement. The communist movement has fundamentally done nothing other to break and overturn in certain aspects of its practice, as necessity demanded, the logic of this essentially social-democratic theory.

And yet, at the beginning the dividing line between social democracy and the communist movement was clearly established. And if an internal history of the working class is to be reconstructed — alongside the history of capital — it will certainly include both of these organisational experiences, although they cannot be conceived at the same level or attributed the same significance. [. . .] The problem is the price we might pay at the level of theory if we adopt the communist movement's tradition of struggles as our own, and any answer to this problem is circumscribed by the question of what immediate practical results are to be achieved by taking this path. At this point, we must guard against the subjective illusion that conceives the strategic overthrow here proposed as the birth *first* of working-class science and *subsequently* as the first real possible organisation of the class movement. Instead, we must set our minds on a specific type of internal development of the working class, a political growth of its struggles, and use this as a lever for a further *leap forward*. [. . .] Man, Reason, History ... these monstrous divinities must be fought and destroyed just like the boss's own power. It is not true that capital has abandoned these ancient gods. It has simply turned them into the religion of the official workers' movement: that is how they actively continue to govern the world. Meanwhile, the negation of these gods, which, in itself, presents a mortal danger for capital, is in fact managed directly by capital. Thus, antihumanism, irrationalism, antihistoricism become not practical weapons in the hands of the working-class struggle but cultural products in capitalist ideologies. In this way, culture — not because of the particular guise that it momentarily assumes in the contemporary period, but precisely through its ongoing form, *qua* culture — becomes a mediation of the social relation of capitalism, a function of its continued conservation. 'Oppositional' culture does not escape this fate, either; it merely presents the body of the workers' movement ideologies in the common clothing of bourgeois culture. Here, we are not interested in whether or not the historical figure of the intellectual-on-the-side-of-the-working-class could have existed at some point. Because what is decidedly impossible is for such a political figure to exist *today*. The organic intellectuals of the working class have, in reality, become the only thing that they could be: organic intellectuals of the workers' movement. The old party, the old form of organisation outside of the class, needs them. For decades, they have assured the relationship between the party and society without passing through the medium of the factory. And now that the factory is imposing itself, now that capital itself is calling them back into production, they become the objective mediators between science and industry. Such is the new form that is being assumed by the traditional relationship between intellectuals and the party. [. . .] There is no culture, no intellectuals, apart from those who serve capital. This is the counterpart of our solution to the other problem: there can be no working-class reenactment of the bourgeois revolution, no retracing of its path by the working class. For there is no revolution, ever, outside of the working class, outside of what the class is, and thus outside of what the class is forced to do. A critique of culture means a *refusal to become intellectuals*. A theory of revolution means the direct practice of class struggle. This is the same relation as the one between working-class science and the critique of ideology. And between these two things is the moment of subversive praxis. We said earlier that the working-class point of view cannot be separated from capitalist society. We should add: it cannot be separated from the practical necessities of the class struggle within capitalist society.

What, then, are these necessities? And, most importantly, is a *new strategy* needed? [. . .] A new form of antagonism must take to the level of working-class science, bending this science toward new ends and then transcending it in the wholly political act of practice. The form of this struggle is the refusal, the organisation of the working class 'No': the refusal to collaborate actively in capitalist development, the refusal to put forward a positive programme of demands. We can identify the germ of these forms of struggle and organisation right from the very start of the working-class history of capital, right from the time that the first proletarians were constituted as a class. But the full development, the real significance of these forms, comes much later, and they still exist as a strategy for the future. Their possibilities of material functioning increase as the working class grows quantitatively, as it becomes more concentrated and unified, as it gradually develops in quality and becomes internally homogeneous, and as it increasingly succeeds in organising itself around the movements of its own total power. These forms thus presuppose a process of accumulation of labour-power, which — unlike the accumulation of capital — has a directly political meaning. It implies the concentration and growth not of an economic category, but of the class relation which underlies it; an accumulation, therefore, of a political power which is immediately alternative, even before it comes to be organised through its own particular 'great collective means'. The refusal is thus a form of struggle which grows simultaneously with the working class. And the working class is, at the same time, both a political refusal of capital and the production of capital as an economic power. This explains why the working class's political struggle and the terrain of capitalist production always form a single whole. Insofar as they could not be absorbed by the capitalist, the very first proletarian demands objectively functioned as forms of refusal which put the system in jeopardy. Whenever the workers' positive demands go beyond the capitalist-granted margins, they repeat this function — the objective, *negative* function of a pure and simple political blockage in the mechanism of economic laws. Every conjunctural transition, every structural advance in the economic mechanism, must therefore be studied in terms of its specific moments — but only so as to ask from the working-class point of view what capital cannot now give. In such circumstances, the *demand-as-refusal* sets off a chain of crises in capitalist production, each of which demands the tactical ability to drive forward the level of working-class organisation.

[. . .] In the beginning, the content of the class struggle had two faces — that of the working class and that of the capitalists — which were not yet separated by any radical division. The struggle for the limiting of the working day is instructive in this respect. Moreover, the platforms of demands which workers have for decades presented to the capitalists have had — and could only have had — one result: the improvement of exploitation. Better living conditions for the workers were inseparable from a greater economic development of capitalism. [. . .]

The masses of working-class demands thus become ever more simple and united. There must come a point where all of them will disappear, except one — the demand for power, all power, to the workers. This demand is the highest form of refusal. It already presupposes a de facto inversion of the relation of domination between the two classes. In other words, it presupposes that henceforth it will be the capitalist class that makes demands, issues positive requests and presents its bill of rights — in the name, naturally, of the general interests of society. And it will be the workers who are rejecting what is asked of them. There must also be a point, here, where all the requests and demands will come explicitly from the capitalists and only the 'no' will be openly working class. These are not stories from some far-off future — the tendency is already under way and we must grasp it as it emerges in order to be able to control it.

[. . .] The platform of demands that the trade union puts forward is reviewed and checked by the very people on whom it is supposed to be imposed — the same bosses who are supposed to take it or leave it. Through the trade-union struggle, working-class demands can do nothing more than reflect capital's own needs. And yet capital cannot pose this necessity directly, all by itself — not even if it wanted to, not even when it reaches its highest point of class consciousness. Rather, at this point, it acquires precisely the opposite consciousness: it *must* find ways to have its own needs put forward by its enemies, it *must* articulate its own movement via the organised movements of the workers. We might ask: what happens when the form of working-class organisation takes on a wholly alternative content? When it refuses to function as an articulation of capitalist society?

When it refuses to *shoulder* capital's needs through meeting working-class demands? The answer is that, at that moment and starting from that moment, the system's whole development mechanism is blocked. This is the new concept of the *crisis of capitalism* that we must start to circulate: there will no longer be an economic crisis, a catastrophic collapse, a *Zusammenbruch,* however momentary, that is owed to the impossibility of the system's continued functioning. Rather, it will become a political crisis imposed by the subjective movements of the organised workers, through a chain of critical conjunctures provoked by the working-class strategy of refusing to resolve the contradictions of capitalism and by the tactic of organisation within the structures of capitalist production, but outside of and free from its political initiative. Of course, it remains necessary to block the economic mechanism and, at the decisive moment, to incapacitate it. [. . .] Obviously, non-collaboration must be one of our starting points, and mass passivity at the level of production is the material fact from which we must begin. But at a certain point, all this must be reversed into its opposite. When it comes to the point of saying 'no', the refusal must also become political, and therefore active, subjective and organised. It must once again become an antagonism — this time, at a higher level. It is impossible to think of initiating a revolutionary process without this. This is not a matter of instilling in the mass of workers the consciousness that they must fight against capital and for something that will transcend it in a new dimension of human society. What is generally known as 'class consciousness' is, for us, nothing other than the moment of organisation, the function of the party, the problem of tactics — the channels which must carry the strategic plan through to a point of practical breakthrough. And at the level of pure strategy, there is no doubt that this point is provided by the very advanced moment in which this hypothesis of struggle becomes a reality: the working-class refusal to present demands to capital, the total rejection of the whole trade-union terrain, the refusal to limit the class relation within a formal, legal, contractual form.

CHAPTER 27

Gianni Vattimo (1936–)

Gianni Vattimo first achieved worldwide renown as part of the original tripartite theoretical appropriation of postmodernism by philosophy, through his own *The Transparent Society* (1989; 1992), alongside Lyotard's *The Postmodern Condition* (1979) and Jameson's *Postmodernism: The Cultural Logic of Late Capitalism* (1984; 1991). Vattimo's own particular role in that trio was to see postmodernity not as a loss, or chaos, but as an epoch of affirmative nihilism, to be celebrated since it renders actual liberating, hermeneutical ethics. Born in Turin and spending most of his academic life there under his mentor, Luigi Pareyson, Vattimo did spend two formative years with Gadamer in Heidelberg, resulting in the Italian translation of *Truth and Method*.

Vattimo's philosophical position is an oscillation between Heidegger's conservatism and Nietzsche's nihilism. He stresses again and again the need to avoid the caricatural reading of Nietzsche as a strong nihilist. It is not the case that the death of God leads to the Dostoievski moment or the destructive chaos of the unconstrained existentialist subject. The consequence of nihilism as a way of life is the view that there is a connection between knowledge and domination both inside and outside of the subject. Positive or weak nihilism is the re-evaluation of values in terms not of some metaphysical reality but of the purpose which they serve. This discovery does not lead to an unhealthy strong nihilism, nor is it an emancipation via the de-masking or demystification of power-knowledge constructs (ideologies). Rather, Vattimo proposes that we cast a 'friendlier' eye on the discursive procedures and symbolic forms of one's world or form of life – accepting them as one possible experience of being.

The subject of 'weak thought' (*il pensiero debole*) is aware of the conditions of understanding as perspectives and as such liberates itself from the power of absolute claims (a dreamer knowing that they are dreaming). Vattimo offers a serious consideration of the Marxist-Nietzschean insight that the belief that conditions of understanding are absolutely true is a myth propagated in the interests of the one served by such conditions. One's conditions of understanding the world are not true absolutely but originate from one's historical and geographical situation. Vattimo's pluralism is a form of perspectivism: perspectives are necessary to form judgements, but they are metaphysically groundless and contingent (if one ignores the history of Being here), and the subject is free to move from one perspective to the next. A society which affirms nihilism makes such perspectivism possible and weakens the hold of absolutist metaphysics.

The defining tenet of metaphysical absolutism is that there is but one reality and one language to describe it. Vattimo's mistrust of metaphysics is Heideggerian in nature: truth is not fixed in the way that the philosophical tradition believes, but rather Being gives itself historically. One can describe a perspective upon Being but not capture it in its totality. However, metaphysics and its world view (the technological–scientific world of Western capitalism) privilege one perspective over all others, avowing it to be the whole truth. It is in this way that science can claim to be truer than the moral and human sciences, even though their respective truth values are in a certain sense incommensurable. They are different perspectives upon, sometimes but rarely, the same object.

The Heideggerian critique holds that metaphysics is a form of violence against thought: it illegitimately restricts thinking. One must think in a certain way, one must see a certain perspective as absolute or else one is silenced as irrational. Yet, every description is made possible only through an ungrounded appropriation of conditions for the possibility of experience. As such, any description implicitly contains these conditions not only as the possibility for experience but also as the limit or horizon of experience. And the choice of an origin or of axiomatic presuppositions that determine truth is a case of might rather than right – an expression of one group's dominance over others.

And so, a society which affirms nihilism is one characterized by Heidegger's end of metaphysics. As such, the subject – truly to know itself – has to interrogate and interpret rather than merely process the world. Instead of rationally interrogating the world, one must interrogate the world hermeneutically. The conditions through which the subject understands reality are hidden from it; be they in its unconscious or the structures of meaning it uses to express its understanding. Only through the act of expressing *its* world can it disclose those categories which shape its perception of the world. Understanding is a fundamental way in which the subject relates itself to the world: the conditions which make experience possible are cultural givens which are revealed through the subject's interpretation of the representation of the world. The categories and concepts through which understanding ourselves, others and our situation is possible are inherited through our community, tradition or language – which is to say, our historical and geographical location into which we were 'accidentally thrown'.

Vattimo's weak or enfeebled thought depends upon the distinction between the strong nihilism outlined earlier and a weak nihilism: the capacity to negate what is absolute, yet simultaneously recognize a new, 'weaker' truth in the structures of meaning and orders of values found in the world, for without the concepts and categories of a tradition, the subject would not perceive the world at all. Such interpretation, coupled with the linguistic representation of truths, can lead to the realization of that which is true in an important sense, and that which is contingent or purely symbolic: unjustified or inappropriate perspectives restrict and corrupt one's experience in the interests of an outmoded institutional or economic power. The subject–object relation is one such perspective and only a conditional possibility of knowledge if the subject is ethically impartial and epistemologically objective, but, in postmodern thought, it is no longer a question of what is said but always of who is speaking; every pretence at impartiality or objectivity is the hidden and perhaps unconscious expression of a group or individual world view which is but one truth among many. Postmodern society manifests this weakening of truth in the theoretical demystification of demystification (the world was disenchanted by scientific rationalism, but this rationalism is itself justified by progress which is the corrupted Judeo-Christian myth of salvation); and the sociological rise of mass media which plays a determinant role in complexifying visions of the world and interpretations of human experience.

For Vattimo, however, since pluralism is not an empirical condition but a transcendental condition of knowledge, tolerance is an *a priori* normative requirement for free and sincere thinking. One finds at the heart of Vattimo's endeavour a coincidence between the aspirations of modernity (the refusal of blind obedience to authority) and liberalism (the values of liberty, equality, respect and tolerance). The values of liberalism resist the reduction of dialogue and discourse to the level of might is right where the preferences of those who are more powerful or violent prevail. Vattimo proposes an ethics of interpretation to avoid violence. The first characteristic of this ethics of interpretation is in the recognition and negation of the contextual, embedded nature of the self. This is the recognition that those motivations and values which impinge upon the agent's practical reason in a concrete situation must be put in question in order to ensure both their validity and their relevance to the matter in hand. The step back is the disentanglement of the moral self from the particular self, achieved in liberalism by the divorce of the universal from the contingent. However, Vattimo rejects the idea that such a step back leads to some prior or privileged epistemic or moral position. Ethical norms may not be prescribed from nowhere or from the perspective of the void. The subject of liberalism is unencumbered and hence rationality is replaced by the affirmation of mere preferences or partial interests. The stepping back cannot be a denial of finitude. In other words, the situation of the speaker – the voice and its tradition – is equivalent to comprehensive values: it is impossible to negate these values and still make substantial political or ethical commitments. So, liberty and respect, among others, must be both formal and substantive: formal in order to allow free and open dialogue to be possible; substantive otherwise in cases of conflict between political values and comprehensive ones; there is no reason for the former to carry greater weight. Therefore, a universal requirement of a doctrine, if it is to be considered a partner in consensus, is *respect*. The grounding norm is one of autonomy: treat others with respect.

Weak thought is a form of positive nihilism: one realizes that one's values and beliefs are grounded in an interpretation of reality, but an interpretation is not mere fiction or inconsequential, but it is one truth among many. When the dichotomy of truth and fiction is deconstructed, one is left with neither truth nor fiction, and the raising up of the epistemic status of political values together with the levelling down of the epistemic status of comprehensive values leads to a coincidence in their weight. Vattimo speaks explicitly of a responsible interpretation of one's own moral fabric with all its inherent values, and the recognition that such values derive from a world view and not from incontrovertible, absolute truth. The values which are to be preferred are those which – although derived from a particular tradition – are judged by the criteria of tolerance (the reduction of violence) and consensus (the recognition that agreement is not grounded in the legitimacy of one comprehensive doctrine in relation to others, but in the recognition of the finitude of one's own position and the other's).

The subject is an historical product immediately motivated by the comprehensive values of its tradition, which are true if they cohere with the standard of rationality characterizing that tradition. Yet, the hermeneutic subject is more: reason is no longer adherence to the principles which originate from a world view, but the rationality of an open dialogue between versions or aspects of the truth in order to garner agreement and reduce violence. On the one hand, one is committed to consistency; on the other, one is committed to consensus. For this hermeneutical truth, the embedded subject must also be committed to a certain precondition that makes free and transparent dialogue possible in order to rule out the violence of metaphysics. The conditions that a doctrine must meet in order to enter into dialogue are that it sincerely expresses the criteria of respect and tolerance and that it be aimed at consensus.

So, it seems that Vattimo is claiming that respect, tolerance, liberty and equality are normative commitments for the subject who inhabits the contemporary fabric of nihilistic society. The normative commitments of an ethics of interpretation coincide with the values of political liberalism and, moreover, explain why the political is privileged over and above the comprehensive, since it supplies a rational basis – acceptable to all – for intercultural dialogue. These values are ethical and necessary in order to produce a subject who can offer a responsible interpretation. Such a subject is not a knowing subject who seeks to affirm the correspondence of an object with its conditions for being experienced. The hermeneutic subject is ethical because the norms which oblige him or her should guarantee the absence of violence: one must be able to step back, that is, not be coerced or irrevocably bound to one's tradition (liberty), one must recognize the finitude of one's position and that of others (tolerance) and one must recognize the right of all individuals to their own responsibly articulated and interpreted tradition (equality and respect).

Postmodernity, in some sense, can be understood as the end of history and the fulfilment of the Enlightenment. It seems that Vattimo is committed to the autonomy of the subject and its liberation, even if such a liberation is no longer transparently easy – a matter of the imposition of universal reason. The postmodern condition is, peculiarly and surprisingly, a commitment to the universality not of individual reason but of social dialogue. The overriding norm is liberation from idols, from superstition, that is, not simply false beliefs but specifically those false beliefs used for political and ethical manipulation. The reflective and secular nature of our society is universally desirable. The privilege of liberal values does not lie in moral realism but in a commitment to one substantial good: freedom – the political freedom to make one's own choice. There is no one truth or way of life which is intrinsically universally better than all others. Oddly, this commits one to a form of life which allows all interests to be expressed and considered with respect. That is, a liberal form of life.

David Rose

Selected writings

Vattimo, Gianni. *The End of Modernity: Nihilism and Hermeneutics in Postmodern Culture*, trans. J. R. Snyder. Baltimore: John Hopkins University Press, 1988a.

Vattimo, Gianni., 'Metaphysics, Violence, Secularisation'. In *Recoding Metaphysics: The New Italian Philosophy*, trans. B. Spackman and edited by G. Borradori, 45–61. Evanston: Northwestern University Press, 1988b.

Vattimo, Gianni. 'Toward an Ontology of Decline Recoding Metaphysics.' In *Recoding Metaphysics: The New Italian Philosophy*, trans. B. Spackman and edited by G. Borradori, 62–73. Evanston: Northwestern University Press, 1988c.

Vattimo, Gianni. *The Transparent Society*, trans. D. Webb. Cambridge: Polity Press, 1992.

Vattimo, Gianni. *The Adventure of Difference: Philosophy after Nietzsche and Heidegger*, trans. C. P. Blamires and T. Harrison. Cambridge: Polity Press, 1993.

Vattimo, Gianni. *Beyond Interpretation: The Meaning of Hermeneutics for Philosophy*, trans. D. Webb. Cambridge: Polity Press, 1997.

Vattimo, Gianni. With J. Derrida. *Religion*. Stanford: Stanford University Press, 1998.

Vattimo, Gianni. *Belief*, trans. L. D'Isanto and D. Webb. Cambridge: Polity Press, 1999.

Vattimo, Gianni. *Nietzsche: An Introduction*, trans. N. Martin. Stanford: Stanford University Press, 2002.

Vattimo, Gianni. *After Christianity*, trans. L. D'Isanto. New York: Columbia University Press, 2002.

Vattimo, Gianni. *Nihilism and Emancipation: Ethics, Politics, and Law*. Foreword by Richard Rorty, edited by Santiago Zabala and trans. William McCuaig. New York: Columbia University Press, 2004.

Vattimo, Gianni. With R. Rorty. *The Future of Religion*, edited by Santiago Zabala. New York: Columbia University Press, 2005.

Vattimo, Gianni. *Dialogue with Nietzsche*, trans. William McCuaig. New York: Columbia University Press, 2006.

Vattimo, Gianni. With John D. Caputo. *After the Death of God*, edited by Jeffrey W. Robbins. New York: Columbia University Press, 2007.

Vattimo, Gianni. With Piergiorgio Paterlini. *Not Being God: A Collaborative Autobiography*, trans. William McCuaig. New York: Columbia University Press, 2009.

Vattimo, Gianni. With René Girard. *Christianity, Truth and Weakening Faith: A Dialogue*, edited by Pierpaolo Antonello. New York: Columbia University Press, 2010a.

Vattimo, Gianni. *The Responsibility of the Philosopher*, edited by Franca D'Agostini and trans. William McCuaig. New York: Columbia University Press, 2010b.

Vattimo, Gianni. *A Farewell to Truth*, trans. William McCuaig, with a foreword by Robert T. Valgenti. New York: Columbia University Press, 2011a.

Vattimo, Gianni. With Santiago Zabala. *Hermeneutic Communism: From Heidegger to Marx*. New York and Chichester: Columbia University Press, 2011b.

EXCERPT

Gianni Vattimo, *Ethics of communication or ethics of interpretation?*

(Gianni Vattimo, *The Transparent Society*. Trans. David Webb. Cambridge: Polity Press, 1992, pp. 105–19.)

The reasons one might have for saying that hermeneutics is distinctly inclined towards ethics seem at the same time to stand in the way of such an inclination being fully expressed. [. . .] [I]t may be that the increasingly central position of hermeneutics in the present philosophical scene depends precisely on its orientation towards ethics and the way it affirms ethics as a positive element in the critique of traditional metaphysics and of the scientism that is its most recent configuration. [. . .] Indeed, the horizon within which [Hans-Georg Gadamer's] *Truth and Method* proclaimed the significance of truth in those fields of experience which are irreducible to the positive sciences, and which even 'include' these very sciences as a moment or part of themselves, was precisely that of sociality thought as 'reason in act', as *logos*, given primarily in the natural language of a determinate historical community. The horizon is that of ethics, qua *ethos*, custom, the shared culture of an epoch and a society, and that which ultimately 'belies' scientism and its purported reduction of truth to single statements experimentally confirmed via the methodology of mathematical and natural science. [. . .]

As the philosophically richest and most consistent expression and interpretation of the anti-scientific fever, hermeneutics is constituted from the very beginning as a philosophy led by an inclination for ethics [. . .] The ethics that hermeneutics makes possible seems to be primarily an ethics of goods, to use Schleiermacher's expression, more than an ethics of imperatives. Or better still, if there is an ethics delineated in hermeneutics, it is one in which, taking interpretation as an act of translation [. . .], the various *logoi* — discourses of specialised languages, but also spheres of interest, regions of 'autonomous' rationality — are to be referred back to the *logos*-common consciousness, to the cradling substratum of values shared by a living historical community and expressed in its language. [. . .] To be sure, according to this view, ethics seems to be static (or simply reactionary, and at least traditionalist), and this impression is reinforced the more one forgets — as Gadamer does *not* — that the bounds of the *logos*, of the common language-consciousness within which we are thrown and to which we must appeal in 'rationalising' our choices, cannot be rigidly defined. Indeed, and this is simply another aspect of hermeneutics as *koine*, it seems that reason can be recognised as the *logos*-common consciousness only today, when natural languages, and the historical communities that speak them and that are spoken by them, are beginning to lose all stable boundaries and fixed identities. Accordingly, we must recognise that if Gadamer [. . .] understands the Socratic 'leap into the *logoi*' as the transition to the *logos*-common consciousness from specialist languages and particular spheres of interest (which become ethically reprehensible when they prevail in isolation), he can do so only insofar as the horizon of reference, the *logos* understood as reason in act in language, increasingly becomes only a limited idea, the regulative ideal of a community that is always in the course of making itself and which can never be identified with a factual historical society, whose established values would have to be accepted as canonical.

The conservative and reactionary appearance of the ethics inspired by hermeneutics thereby reveals itself to be, in fact, merely an appearance. Yet, and for these very same reasons, the transition to the *logos*-common consciousness, as a normative moral ideal, seems to be reduced to too little. To the precise extent that it is not thought of as an inherited body of values defined once and for all, this *logos* is ultimately identified with the pure and simple demand for universalisation that philosophy raises formally, but to whose contents, meanings and actual criteria for choice it seems unwilling to commit itself. On the face of it, this amounts to a recognition that the values on the basis of which a preference is sometimes declared in social dialogue for one choice over another are radically historical. This is clearly right. But in considering itself a kind of meta-theory or meta-ethics, this philosophy represents itself to itself as non-historical, illusorily placed in an external viewpoint (a 'view from nowhere', as the title of a recent work by Thomas Nagel has it). Such a viewpoint does not exist, at least not if the hypothesis of a radical historicality characterising the *logos* and the values by which it is constituted holds true.

What I propose to call an ethics of communication, in contrast to an ethics of interpretation, falls entirely within such a perspective still dominated by a transcendental-metaphysical prejudice whose view of historicality is by no means radical enough, at least from the point of view of hermeneutics, In spite of the undeniable differences, brought out in discussions and polemics, separating hermeneutics in its canonical Gadamerian form from the ethics of communication of writers such as Apel and Habermas, these positions are not really so far apart. To be precise, Apel and Habermas make explicit a transcendental attitude that Gadamer rejects, but which nonetheless remains as an almost unavoidable risk for his philosophy, at least insofar as he seems to refuse a radical recognition of the historicality of hermeneutics itself. In other words, the ethics inspired by hermeneutics, at least in its Gadamerian formulation, is faced by only two paths. It either ossifies, and determines the physiognomy of the *logos* unambiguously as the ensemble of values shared by an actual historical community [. . .], in which case it inevitably becomes a conservative ethic, taking accepted values and the existing order as its criteria; or else, as tends to happen on the whole, it recognises the *logos*-language in actual conditions as a limit-idea, and ultimately presents itself as a pure demand for universalisation via communication, not unlike that which is heard, in the light of an explicit return to Kant, in Apel and Habermas.

[. . .] [F]rom the point of view of hermeneutics, these positions propose, at least implicitly, the restoration of metaphysics. This is not solely, or not so much, because the subject whose transparency is to be promoted (against the opacity of an existence conditioned by the division of labour, neuroses, various forms of institutional violence, etc.) is modelled on the subject of metaphysics and modern scientism, whose ultimate form is that of full self-consciousness. Above all, it is because the normative ideal of unrestricted communication displays its categorical character in its recognition of an essential structure, holding for every historical experience, but itself withdrawn from becoming. Despite not insignificant differences in their views, Apel and Habermas agree in recognising that experience is made possible, in the final analysis, by the a priori of unrestricted communication or communicative action. As the condition for the possibility of experience, it is also, immediately and according to the classical overturning of being (permanent, structural) into value, the norm for action. [. . .] The 'intersubjective' essence of the I, then, does not bind the I to concrete historical conditions, but is affirmed only as a function of the specific normativity of the 'collective' as the site of communication-universalisation. [. . .] [T]his confirms, if there were any need (and Habermas certainly does not deny it), the profound link between the ethics of communication and modern metaphysics, oriented towards the full explication of the subject. This explication never ceases to be couched in Cartesian terms as self-transparency, even when associated with the idea of community. Indeed, the latter is (even as the myth of the organic community) the self-transparency of the subject translated onto the social plane.

Habermas believes that by affirming the intersubjective constitution of the I he is doing justice to the finitude of the subject and breaking with idealism, understood primarily as creeping solipsism [. . .]. In reality, however, his principal concern is to reflect the finitude of the subject which results from its having become an object of positive knowledge. The finitude that Habermas guarantees the subject is therefore only that which belongs to objects of science,[3] and not that of historical existence. [. . .] By contrast, hermeneutics 'deposes' the idealist subject, but not in order to lay it open to investigation by the positive sciences. For Habermas, the fact that the I is 'ascribed' to its relations with others means that it is finite insofar as it can thereby become the object of the human sciences. For hermeneutics, that the I is ascribed to intersubjective constitution (or, with Heidegger, 'thrown' into a world) means that nothing that concerns it can be the object of structural description, but may be given only as destiny. To be sure, the human sciences may form a part of this destiny as well, but in this case they are presented in a very different light. [. . .] If one wishes to execute the turn modernity demands of thought, one must renounce the metaphysical ideal of knowledge as the description of objectively given structures. Habermas's intersubjective I is wholly the I of modern metaphysics-science. It is the object of the human sciences and the equally ahistorical subject of the laboratory.

These ahistorical traits are such that the ethics of communication cannot be considered a fitting outcome for the moral inclination of hermeneutics.

In fact, the latter has sought, for ethical reasons, to affirm historicality as *belonging*: the experience of truth does not occur in the reflection of an object by a subject committed to self-transparency, but rather as the articulation — or interpretation — of a tradition (a language, a culture), to which existence belongs, and which it reformulates in new messages sent to other interlocutors. Ethical life and historicality coincide here. Hermeneutics can live up to its ethical inclination in an appropriate fashion only by remaining faithful to the instance of historicality. But how? Principally, by thinking of itself not as an ultimately metaphysical descriptive theory of the hermeneutic constitution of existence, but rather as an event of destiny. Hermeneutics must recognise itself as the thought belonging to the epoch of the end of metaphysics, and nothing more. Hermeneutics is not the adequate description of the human condition, which is finally making headway only at a certain point in history, thanks to a particular thinker or a series of fortuitous circumstances. It is the philosophical thought of secularised Europe. The fact that its source lies in the world of the Protestant Reformation, the religious wars, the classicist dream of a recovery of the tradition of literature and art of antiquity, is far more important for hermeneutics than is generally recognised. [. . .] If it theorises that the experience of truth is belonging and not reflection, it must also say to which epoch, world or provenance it itself as theory belongs.

It cannot lie back, believing itself to have finally presented an adequate description of existence, of its interpretative constitution. Within these bounds, hermeneutics would appear as a hopelessly banal metaphysical theory, even as the most banal and futile. In fact, it says that there is no such thing as truth as a stable structure of being reflected in propositions, only many horizons and the many different cultural horizons within which experiences of truth occur, as internal articulations or interpretations. Even if we go further still, singling out the regulative ideal of promoting dialogue between different horizons and cultural universes, we do not get far; *what* will hermeneutics have to say once dialogue has been established?

If, however, the 'trivial' and weak hermeneutic thesis recognises itself as *belonging*, instead of disguising itself as a metaphysical description, then it will see itself as a destiny (a provenance) and will become capable of choice, that is, of morality. Hermeneutics will recognise its destiny, if it understands the *nihilistic* character of its constitution. Even for hermeneutics itself as theory, truth does not consist in reflecting a given fact, but in responding to a destiny. This destiny is that of the epoch of the end of metaphysics, in which, as Heidegger says, the first lightning flash of the event of being lights up inasmuch as in this moment man and being lose the characteristics ascribed to them by metaphysics (which is the thought of presence, of objectivity, of the will to power). Hermeneutics [. . .] cannot but legitimate itself as corresponding to a destiny that we call modernity; it certainly cannot see itself as an adequate description of some kind of structure of existence. In simple terms, one can say that if there is any reason for listening to the discourse of hermeneutics, it can only lie in the fact that hermeneutics is presented as belonging to the age in which we live, as its theory, and so only in a certain sense 'adequate'. It is in the world of public opinion, of the mass media, of Weberian 'polytheism', of the technical and potentially total organisation of existence, that a theory of truth not as correspondence but as interpretation may be found. [. . .] From a rigorously Heideggerian standpoint, hence one that is radically faithful to the historicality at the origin of hermeneutics, the latter cannot seriously take itself to be an alternative to modernity, since this would require that it legitimate itself as founded on some *evidence* that modernity had neglected or forgotten. Instead, it must present itself as the thought of the epoch of the end of metaphysics, that is, as the thought of modernity and its consummation, and nothing more. Now Heidegger teaches us that modernity is accomplished as nihilism, *Ge-stell*, the world of technological and scientific rationalisation, the world of the conflict between the *Weltbilder* [world pictures]. [. . .] In what sense, though, can it be said more specifically that hermeneutics, as that thought which places itself outside metaphysics, is made possible by modernity itself as universal technological domination and the accomplishment of nihilism? In the first place, such a thesis seems to conflict with explicit remarks made by Heidegger, who only rarely [. . .] allows a glimpse of the possibility that the nihilistic traits of modernity itself may herald a new thought that is no longer metaphysical. This possibility, only glimpsed by Heidegger, might become explicit and recognisable only with the profound modification undergone by *Ge-stell*, the world of the technical, with the transition from mechanical technology to information technology. It is well known that today the distinction between developed and undeveloped countries is no longer made in terms of the possession of mechanical technology capable of bending, concentrating and overcoming the forces of nature, of shifting, dismantling and rebuilding. It is no longer a question of engines, but of computers and the networks connecting them which make it possible to control the more 'primitive' machines, that is, the mechanical ones. It is not in the world of machines and engines that humanity and being can shed the mantles of subject and object, but in the world of generalised communication. Here the entity dissolves in the images distributed by the information media, in the abstraction of scientific objects (whose correspondence with real 'things' open to experience can no longer be seen) or technical products (that do not even make contact with the real world via their use value, since the demands they satisfy are increasingly artificial). Whereas the subject, on its part, is less and less a centre of self-consciousness and decision-making, reduced as it is to being the author of statistically predicted choices, playing a multiplicity of social roles that are irreducible to a unity. In the *Ge-stell* of information, the world of images of the world, the true world, as Nietzsche said, becomes a fable; or, to use the Heideggerian term, *Sage*. Hermeneutics is the philosophy of this world in which being is given in the form of weakening or dissolution. The thesis 'there are no facts, only interpretations' has a reductive sense, of the loss of reality, which is essential to hermeneutics.

On the ethical plane, the effect of all this is to replace an ethics of communication with an ethics of interpretation. [. . .] [I]n the classical Heideggerian definition interpretation means the 'articulation of what is understood', the unfolding of a knowledge in which existence is always already thrown, according to its destining: primarily, then, to look for the guiding criteria of choice in the provenance and not in a structure of existence, not even the hermeneutic structure. Hermeneutics, as an awareness that truth is not reflection but belonging, is not born out of the correction of an error, or the rectification of a perspective. It arises from modernity as the epoch of metaphysics and of its accomplishment in the nihilism of the *Ge-stell*. Recognising its own nihilistic destiny, hermeneutics paves the way for an ethics founded on an ontology of reduction and dilution — or, if one prefers, of dissolution. [. . .]

Accepting its own nihilistic destiny, and inspired by an ontology of reduction — which carries to its natural conclusion the Heideggerian idea of being that can never be given as full presence, but only as trace and memory (and which thus cannot provide a foundation, authority, sovereignty) — hermeneutics eludes a further risk that does not seem entirely ruled out by the ethics of communication. The latter can in fact try to avoid the accusation of still being a transcendental metaphysics (which posits as a normative foundation of morality the *fact* that experience is made possible by the a priori of unlimited communication) by stressing the pure formality of its conception; it excludes all metaphysical rigidity to the extent that it conceives morality to be negotiation, persuasion by way of rational argumentation, not limited by any necessary metaphysical structure. In this respect, the ethics of communication presents itself as a rigorously egalitarian ethics. But at the same time, it shows itself unable to exclude the possibility that the egalitarianism and the negotiation come to be understood in the sense of a pure escalation of social conflict. Why, in the end, if there are no metaphysical principles, should we prefer rational argumentation to physical confrontation? [. . .] Habermas would respond that the method of rational argument is the most favourable to life and its development (nonetheless it is always a hypothetical imperative: if we want to live . . .). Alternatively, he would reply, shifting ground slightly, by theorising that man is 'by nature' an intersubjective and communicative I [. . .]. However paradoxical it may seem, there is in the ethics of communication no sufficient 'foundation' for morality. Again paradoxically, it is the ethics of interpretation that furnishes morality with the more substantial rationale — though not, to be sure, with a foundation. To the extent that hermeneutics recognises itself as provenance and destiny, as the thought of the final epoch of metaphysics and thus of nihilism, it can find in 'negativity', in dissolution as the 'destiny of Being', given not as presence of the *arche* but only as provenance, the orienting principle that enables it to realise its own original inclination for ethics whilst neither restoring metaphysics nor surrendering to the futility of a relativistic philosophy of culture.

CHAPTER 28

Paolo Virno (1952–)

Like a number of contemporary Italian philosophers, Virno takes as seriously as may be imagined Aristotle's definition of the human being as the animal possessed of language. Everything there is to say about man's contemporary political situation and the manner in which this political situation might be transformed is contained within language and our relation to it.

What singles out Virno's approach is perhaps the *biological* and *anthropological* character of his interpretation of language. He interprets the latter as a natural faculty which belongs to what he is quite content to call 'human nature'. He moves beyond such thinkers as Noam Chomsky who will have trodden this path before him by transforming their conception of a 'faculty' into a 'power' with the help of the philosophical category of 'potentiality' (*dynamis*).

Such a transformation is necessary if one is to understand either our position with respect to contemporary capitalism or the way out of it. It is tempting to read Virno's entire philosophy and anthropology as a retrospective construction built exclusively on the basis of the contemporary moment and its politico-economic character: this character Virno describes as 'biolinguistic', and the system in which labour and production take place as 'biolinguistic capitalism'. In other words, the contemporary labour market values not any particular skill or ability but the very ability to learn *new* abilities: in other words, 'flexibility' or 'plasticity' – and in Virno's terms, sheer 'potential'. The most valuable commodity which labourers can now possess is potentiality itself. Labour power is itself to be understood as potential. And in particular, given the *communicative* nature of most labour in developed Western countries, in the period Virno often describes as 'post-Fordist' (although in his very most recent work he expresses certain reservations as to the aptness of this term), which is to say, after the moment of standardized, rationalized, factory labour has declined or been exported to territories less particular about employment practices and human rights, this potential will be above all *linguistic*. Language as a biological or vital faculty: hence 'biolinguistic capitalism'.

This allows us to understand Virno's conception of history: it is one in which the most elementary facets of human nature are manifested within a particular epoch in a certain way: either, as in traditional societies, in the state of exception (or emergency) and hence rarely, or today, in what Agamben – and Virno implicitly – will describe as a 'permanent' state of exception, in everyday life and work. Such is perhaps the ultimate cause of the collective anxiety which dogs the precarious labourers of our age. Investigating history understood as the manifestation of human nature – the appearance of the transcendental conditions *for* appearance – is the task of the discipline which Virno calls 'naturalist historiography'.

What is curious about Virno's conception of the transcendental is that it is something wholly material, entirely 'empirical': the physical properties of the human being's physiognomy that allow it simply to speak. Indeed, Virno, for all his extremely subtle attempts to deconstruct the transcendental-empirical divide, describes his work as an 'empiricism to the nth power'.

While resisting the idea, which he finds in such politically disparate figures as Carl Schmitt and Noam Chomsky, of deriving a politics directly from a theory of human nature, he nevertheless considers politics to be absolutely inseparable from anthropology for the reason that our historical moment involves an all-out exploitation of man's biological nature. Any worthwhile attempt at a revolutionary politics will involve rethinking the linguistic potential of man in a way that Chomsky failed to do. For Chomsky, language was ultimately, even unwittingly, conceived as private and individual and its quasi-transcendental form was secretly modelled upon an actual determinate historical language (in terms of grammar). Virno insists that we conceive it as public, transindividual and properly potential, in the sense – freed from the model of actuality – that Heidegger, Deleuze and Agamben will have attempted to bestow upon it.

This is related to the manner in which Virno exceeds Schmitt's construal of the relation between anthropology and politics, for which an anthropology of evil and danger (man as a wolf to man) will necessitate a strong state, even an authoritarian one, while an anthropology of goodness and meekness is employed by an anarchistic tendency which calls for the abolition of the state and the elimination of the *archē* of a single sovereign. Virno wishes chiasmically to reverse this set of alignments and to argue for an anthropology of evil while nevertheless advocating the abolition of the state and its capitalistic mode of production. This anthropology he understands less in terms of man's natural individual competitiveness and violence – although such aggression does exist – and more in terms of the danger that threatens the human being from the *outside* due to its initial unpreparedness for life which has in the twentieth century taken the name of neoteny. This leads to a permanent lack of adaptation with respect to its environment in the sense that its unspecialized instincts and non-automatic, non-biunivocal perceptual and motor responses lay it infinitely open to an overwhelming flood of data stemming from its 'world'. Virno derives this anthropology largely from the work of Arnold Gehlen, in particular, but also with reference to Helmuth Plessner, Louis Bolk, Adolf Portmann and, most recently, Stephen Jay Gould, while acknowledging that its roots extend much further back, to J. G. Herder at least.

He considers this anthropological-political gesture to involve a transformation of what he calls, following Hobbes and Spinoza, the *People* into the *Multitude*. The People he considers to be a collectivity fused together to form a unity by means of a single transcendent instance which might be described as the sovereign, while a Multitude would be a collectivity unified without recourse to such sovereignty and without a state. Virno considers this unification to take place precisely by means of the public, transindividual, potential character of *language*.

Thus, to achieve this revolutionary transformation, anarchistically perhaps, and to shift the *polis* away from the sovereign state and its biolinguistic capitalism, it is the philosopher-linguist-anthropologist's task to rethink the nature of language, and thus the nature of man as a 'linguistic animal'. In this way, the philosopher will perhaps discover a new sense to Aristotle's other definition of man, as the 'political animal', which places it in an intimate relation with the first. This extremely novel and yet remarkably traditional intertwining of anthropology, philosophy and linguistics, together with the politics one may derive from the conjunction of all three, defines Virno's work.

Michael Lewis and Zoe Waters

Selected writings

Virno, Paulo. 'Dreamers of a Successful Life', trans. Jared Becker, 'On Armed Struggle', trans. Robert Zweig. In *Autonomia: Post-Political Politics*, edited by Sylvère Lotringer and Christian Marazzi. Los Angeles, CA: Semiotext(e), 2007 [1980].

Virno, Paulo. *Convention & Materialism: Uniqueness without Aura*, trans. L. Chiesa. Cambridge, MA: MIT Press, 2021. *Convenzione e materialismo: L'unicità senza aura* Rome: DeriveApprodi 1986. Revised and corrected edition, 2011.

Virno, Paulo. *The Idea of World: Public Intellect and Use of Life*. trans. L. Chiesa. Cambridge, MA: MIT Press, 2022. *Mondanità. L'idea di 'mondo' tra esperienza sensibile e sfera pubblica* Rome: Manifestolibri, 1994. Expanded edition, entitled, *L'idea di mondo. Intelletto pubblico e uso della vita,* incorporating the essay, 'The Use of Life' (Macerata: Quodlibet, 2015).

Virno, Paulo. *Parole con parole. Poteri e limiti del linguaggio*. Rome: Donzelli, 1995.

Virno, Paulo. 'The Ambivalence of Disenchantment', 'Virtuosity and Revolution: the Political Theory of Exodus' (extracted from *Mondanità*, 1994), and (with Lucio Castellano et al.) 'Do You Remember Revolution?' in *Radical Thought in Italy: A Potential Politics*, edited by Paolo Virno and Michael Hardt. Minneapolis, MN: University of Minnesota Press, 1996.

Virno, Paulo. *Déjà Vu and the End of History*, trans. David Broder. London: Verso, [1999] 2015. *Il ricordo del presente: Saggio sul tempo storico.* Turin: Boringhieri, 1999.

Virno, Paulo. *A Grammar of the Multitude: For an Analysis of Contemporary Forms of Life*, trans. Isabella Bertoletti, James Cascaito, and Andrea Casson. Los Angeles, CA: Semiotext(e), 2004. Grammatica della moltitudine. *Per una analisi delle forme di vita contemporanea.* Rome: DeriveApprodi, 2002/2014.

Virno, Paulo. *Motto di spirito e azione innovativa. Per una logica del cambiamento.* Turin: Boringhieri, 2005. (Translated as part of Virno 2008, infra.)

Virno, Paulo. *Multitude: Between Innovation and Negation*, trans. Isabella Bertoletti, James Cascaito, and Andrea Casson. Los Angeles, CA: Semiotext(e), 2008. (Partial Translation of Virno 2010, *E Così Via, All'Infinito: Logica e Antropologia* and full translation of *Motto di spirito e azione innovativa*, with a new Appendix not included in either).

Virno, Paulo. *When the Word Becomes Flesh: Language and Human Nature*, trans. Giuseppina Mecchia. South Pasadena, CA: Semiotext(e), 2015. *Quando il verbo si fa carne. Linguaggio e natura umana.* Turin: Boringhieri, 2003.

Virno, Paulo. 'Post-Fordist Semblance' trans. Max Henninger, *SubStance 112* 36, no. 1 (2007): 42–46.

Virno, Paulo. 'Natural-Historical Diagrams: The "New Global" Movement and the Biological Invariant'. In *The Italian Difference: Between Nihilism and Biopolitics*, edited by Lorenzo Chiesa & Alberto Toscano. Melbourne: re.press, 2009.

Virno, Paulo. *E così via, all'infinito: Logica e antropologia [And So On, Ad Infinitum: Logic and Anthropology].* Turin: Boringhieri, 2010. (Partially translated in Virno 2011, infra, and Virno 2008).

Virno, Paulo. 'The Anthropological Meaning of Infinite Regression', trans. Lorenzo Chiesa in *Angelaki* 16, no. 3 (September 2011): 63–76. (Partial Translation of Virno 2010.

Virno, Paulo. *An Essay on Negation: For a Linguistic Anthropology*, trans. Lorenzo Chiesa. London; Calcutta: Seagull, 2018. *Saggio sulla negazione: Per una antropologia linguistica.* Turin: Boringhieri, 2013.

EXCERPT

Paolo Virno
—————

(Paolo Virno, 'Natural-Historical Diagrams: The "New Global" Movement and the Biological Invariant' in Lorenzo Chiesa and Alberto Toscano (eds.), *The Italian Difference: Between Nihilism and Biopolitics*. Melbourne: re.press, 2009, pp. 131–47.)

1. Always already just now

The content of the global movement which ever since the Seattle revolt has occupied (and redefined) the public sphere is nothing less than human nature. The latter constitutes both the arena of struggle and its stake. The arena of struggle: the movement is rooted in the epoch in which the capitalist organization of work takes on as its raw material the differential traits of the species (verbal thought, the transindividual character of the mind, neoteny, the lack of specialized instincts, etc.). That is, it is rooted in the epoch in which human praxis is applied in the most direct and systematic way to the ensemble of requirements that make praxis human. The stake: those who struggle against the mantraps placed on the paths of migrants or against copyright on scientific research raise the question of the different socio-political expression that could be given, here and now, to certain biological prerogatives of *Homo sapiens*.

We are therefore dealing with a historically determinate subversive movement, which has emerged in quite peculiar, or rather unrepeatable, circumstances, but which is intimately concerned with that which has remained unaltered from the Cro-Magnons onwards. Its distinguishing trait is the extremely tight entanglement between 'always already' (human nature) and 'just now' (the bio-linguistic capitalism which has followed Fordism and Taylorism). This entanglement cannot fail to fuel some Rousseauian conceptual muddles: the temptation to deduce a socio-political ideal from the biological constitution of the human animal seems irrepressible, as does the idea of a naturalist corrective to the distortions produced by an irascible history. Think of the political Chomsky, for whom the crucial point is to constantly reaffirm some innate capabilities of our species (for example, the 'creativity of language'), against the claims, unjust because *unnatural,* of this or that system of power. To my mind, there is both truth and falsehood in the 'Chomskyianism' that pervades the common sense of the movement. Truth: it is absolutely realistic to hold that the biological invariant has today become a fulcrum of social conflicts, in other words that immutable metahistory surges up at the centre of the most up-to-date labour and communicative processes. Falsehood: the biological invariant becomes the raw material of social praxis only because the capitalist relation of production mobilizes to its advantage, in a historically unprecedented way, the species-specific prerogatives of *Homo sapiens*. The undeniable preeminence of the meta-historical plane entirely depends on a contingent state of affairs.

To clarify the link between global movement and human nature it is necessary to tackle, be it tangentially, some tricky problems. First (§2), an apodictic thesis: how and why is human nature, far from being only the condition of possibility of historical praxis, also at times its manifest content and operational field. Second (§3), a synoptic definition, itself also apodictic, of those phylogenetic constants which are simultaneously the condition of possibility and the manifest content of historical praxis. On the basis of these premises, the real discussion begins. It consists (§§4-5) in confronting the rather different ways in which the background, that is human nature, comes to the foreground, in the guise of an empirical phenomenon, in traditional societies and in contemporary capitalism. This crucial difference helps us to better understand the specific weight which the political action of the global movement carries, or could carry (§6).

2. Maps of human nature

The decisive question is broadly the following: can human beings *experience* human nature? Note that experiencing something, for instance an object or an event, does not at all mean representing it with some degree of scientific precision. Rather, it means perceiving it in its phenomenal manifestness, being emotionally involved, reacting to it with praxis and discourse. If that is so, our case immediately confronts us with a difficulty: the expression 'human nature' effectively denotes the ensemble of innate dispositions that guarantee the very possibility of perceiving phenomena, to be emotionally involved, to act and discourse. Accordingly, the decisive question takes on a paradoxical air: is it possible to experience, in the full sense of the term, that which constitutes the presupposition of experience in general?

The answer depends on the way in which we conceive of eternity in time. Make no mistake: by 'eternal' I simply mean that which displays a high degree of invariance, not being subject to social and cultural transformations. In this mild acceptation, 'eternal', for instance, can be said of the language faculty. There are basically two ways, opposed to one another, of conceiving the eternal in time. The first, which I reject, can be loosely defined as 'transcendental'. Its point of honour lies in arguing that the invariant presuppositions of human nature, on which really experienced facts and states of affairs depend, never present themselves in turn as facts or states of affairs. The presuppositions remain confined in their recondite 'pre-'. That which grounds or permits all appearances does not itself appear. This approach rules out that human beings may experience human nature. The second way of considering the eternal in time can be defined, once again loosely, as 'natural-historical'. It consists in demonstrating that the conditions of possibility of human praxis possess a peculiar empirical counterpart. In other words, there are contingent phenomena which reproduce point-by-point the inner structure of the transcendental presupposition. Besides being their foundation, the 'eternal' exposes itself, as such, in such and such a given socio-political state of affairs. Not only does it *give* rise to the most varied events, but it also *takes* place in the flow of time, taking on an evental physiognomy. In other words, there are historical facts which show in filigree the conditions that make history itself possible. This second approach, which I share, implies that human beings can experience human nature.

I call *natural-historical diagrams* the socio-political states of affairs which display, in changing and rival forms, some salient features of anthropogenesis. The diagram is a sign that imitates the object to which it refers, meticulously reproducing its structure and the relation between its parts. Think of a map, a mathematical equation, a graph. However, the contingent historical fact, which offers the abridged image of a biological condition, is not a necessary condition of the latter, since its roots lie instead in a particular social and cultural conjuncture. The diagram faithfully reproduces the object that it stands for but, unlike an index, it is *not* caused by it. A geographical map is something other than the knock on the door which attests to the presence of a visitor.

Recall the question we formulated above: is it possible to experience, in the full sense of the term, that which constitutes the presupposition of experience in general? I can now reply: yes, if and when there are adequate phenomenal diagrams of this presupposition; yes, if and when a historical event offers the map or the equation of certain fundamental meta-historical constants. The diagrams of human nature institute an endless circularity between the transcendental and the empirical, the condition and the conditioned, the background and the foreground. To get an approximate idea of the diagram, consider this observation by Peirce on self-reflexive diagrams (I thank Tommaso Russo for having brought it to my attention): 'On a map of an island laid down upon the soil of that island there must, under all ordinary circumstances, be some position, some point, marked or not, that represents *qua* place on the map the very same point *qua* place on the island'. The map is the diagram of a territory, part of which is constituted by the diagram of that territory, part of which. . . to infinity. The same happens, in effect, when you formulate a mental image of your own mind; accordingly, the image of the mind includes an image of the mind that includes an image . . . to infinity. Unlike the map discussed by Peirce, the diagrams of human nature are not scientific constructions or conventional signs; they are concrete phenomena, socio-political states of affairs, historical events. What's more, the paradoxical oscillation implied by these diagrams is not spatial but temporal. That is, it consists in the infinite circularity between 'just now' and 'always already' (experienced facts and conditions of possibility of experience); not in the circularity between part and whole, as in the case examined by Peirce.

Natural history, in the particular sense I am giving to it here, meticulously collects the multiple socio-political *diagrams* of the biological invariant. Accordingly, it concerns itself with all the circumstances, rather different over the course of time, in which *anthropos,* working and speaking, retraces the salient stages of anthropogenesis. Natural history inventories the ways in which human beings *experience* human nature. Having the latter as its content, the global movement should be considered as an episode of natural history. It can rightfully be compared to the map of an island which is laid down on a precise point on the island itself.

3. The potential animal

Our theme is and remains the existence of natural-historical facts that have the value of diagrams (graphs, maps, etc.) of human nature. However, in order to discuss these diagrams with greater precision, it is necessary to establish some aspect of the object that they designate. What are we speaking about when we speak of species-specific prerogatives, of phylogenetic metahistory, of biological invariant? The following annotations are merely offered by way of orientation: nothing more than a road sign. Whoever doesn't share them, or thinks they fall short, can replace or complement them at will. The crucial point, I repeat, is not an exhaustive definition of that which in *Homo sapiens* remains unaltered from the Cro-Magnons onwards, but the ways in which the mutable course of history sometimes thematises the 'eternal', even exhibiting it in concrete states of affairs.

The biological invariant that characterises the existence of the human animal can be referred back to the philosophical concept of *dynamis*, power. From a temporal angle, power means *not-now,* untimeliness, a deficit of presence. And we should add that if there were no experience of the not-now, it would also be impossible to speak of a 'temporal angle'; it is precisely *dynamis* which, by dissolving the 'eternal present' of God and the nonhuman animal, gives rise to historical time. The potentiality of *Homo sapiens:* (a) is attested by the language faculty; (b) is inseparable from instinctual non-specialization; (c) originates in neoteny; (d) implies the absence of a univocal environment.

The language faculty is something other than the ensemble of historically determinate languages. It consists in a body's inborn capacity to emit articulate sounds, that is in the ensemble of biological and physiological requirements which make it possible to produce a statement. It is mistaken to treat the indeterminate power-to-speak as a proto-language spoken by the entire species (something like a universal Sanskrit). The faculty is a generic disposition, exempt from grammatical schemas, irreducible to a more or less extended congeries of possible statements. Language faculty means language *in potentia* or the power of language. And power is something non-actual and still undefined. Only the living being which is born aphasic has the language faculty. Or better: only the living being which lacks a repertoire of signals biunivocally correlated to the various configurations — harmful or beneficial — of the surrounding environment.

The language faculty confirms the instinctual poverty of the human animal, its incomplete character, the constant disorientation that sets it apart. Many philosophers argue that the language faculty is a highly specialized instinct. But they go on to add that it is a specialization for polyvalence and generalization, or even — which amounts to the same — an instinct to adopt behaviours that have not been preset. Now, to argue that the linguistic animal is supremely able in. . . doing without any particular ability is really to participate in the international festival of the sophism. Of course, the language faculty is an innate biological endowment. But not everything that is innate has the prerogatives of a univocal and detailed instinct. Despite being congenital, the capacity to speak is only *dynamis*, power. And power properly speaking, that is as distinguished from a well-defined catalogue of hypothetical performances, coincides with a state of indeterminacy and uncertainty. The animal that has language is a potential animal. But a potential animal is a *non-specialized* animal.

The phylogenetic basis of non-specialisation is *neoteny*, that is the 'retention of formerly juvenile characteristics produced by retardation of somatic development'. The generic and incomplete character of the human animal, the indecision that befalls it, in other words the *dynamis* which is consubstantial with it, are rooted in some of its organic and anatomical primitivisms, or, if you prefer, in its congenital incompleteness. *Homo sapiens* has 'a constitutively premature birth', and precisely because of this it remains an 'indefinite animal'. Neoteny explains the instability of our species, as well as the related need for uninterrupted learning. A chronic infancy is matched by a chronic non-adaptation, to be mitigated in each case by social and cultural devices.

Biologically rooted in neoteny, the potentiality of the human animal has its objective correlate in the lack of a circumscribed and well-ordered environment in which to insert oneself with innate expertise once and for all. If an environment [*ambiente*] is the 'ensemble of conditions [. . .] which make it possible for a certain organism to survive thanks to its particular organization', it goes without saying that a non-specialized organism is also an *out-of-place* [*disambientato*] organism. In such an organism perceptions are not harmoniously converted into univocal behaviours, but give rise to an overabundance of undifferentiated stimuli, which are not designed for a precise operational purpose. Lacking access to an ecological niche that would prolong its body like a prosthesis, the human animal exists in a state of insecurity even where there is no trace of specific dangers. We can certainly second the following assertion by Chomsky: 'the way we grow does not reflect properties of the physical environment but rather our essential nature'. Provided we add, however, that 'our essential nature' is characterized in the first place by the absence of a determinate environment, and therefore by an enduring disorientation.

We said that the primary task of natural history consists in collecting the social and political events in which the human animal is put into direct relation with metahistory, that is with the unmodifiable constitution of its species. We call natural-historical those maximally contingent phenomena which offer plausible *diagrams* of an invariant human nature. The terse definitions we proposed above allow us to specify the overall argument. The questions that natural history must face up to are accordingly the following: In what socio-political situations does the non-biological specialization of *Homo sapiens* come to the fore? When and how does the generic language faculty, as distinct from historical languages, take on a leading role within a particular mode of production? What are the *diagrams* of neoteny? Which are the maps or graphs that will adequately portray the absence of a univocal environment?

The answer to these questions will shed light on an essential difference between traditional societies and contemporary capitalism. In other words, it will shed light on the unprecedented features of the historical situation in which the global movement of Genoa and Seattle finds itself operating.

4. Cultural apocalypses

In traditional societies, including to some extent in classic industrial society, the potentiality (non-specialization, neoteny, etc.) of the human animal takes on the typical visibility of an empirical state of affairs only in an emergency situation, that is in the midst of a *crisis*. In ordinary circumstances, the species-specific biological background is instead concealed, or even contradicted, by the organization of work and solid communicative habits. What predominates thus is a robust discontinuity, or rather an antinomy, between 'nature' and 'culture'. Anyone who would object that this discontinuity is merely a mediocre cultural invention, to be chalked up to the bilious anthropocentrism of spiritualist philosophers, would be making his own life too easy, neglecting what is by far the most interesting task: to individuate the *biological* reasons for the enduring bifurcation between biology and society. A programme to naturalize mind and language that would forsake a *naturalist* explanation of the divergence between 'culture' and 'nature', preferring to reduce the whole affair to a. . . clash of ideas, would be shamelessly incoherent.

Let's stick with well-known, even stereotypical formulations. We call potential the corporeal organism which, lacking its own environment, must wrestle with a vital context that is always partially undetermined, that is with a *world* in which a stream of perceptual stimuli is difficult to translate into an effective operational code. The world is not a particularly vast and varied environment, nor is it the class of all possible environments: rather, there is a world *only* where an environment is wanting. Social and political praxis provisionally compensates for this lack, building *pseudo-environments* within which omnilateral and indiscriminate stimuli are selected in view of advantageous actions. This praxis is thus opposed to its invariant and meta-historical invariant. Or rather, it attests to it to the very extent that it tries to rectify it. If we wanted to turn once again to a concept drawn from Charles S. Peirce's semiotics, we could say that culture is a 'Sign by Contrast' of a species-specific instinctual deficit: a sign, that is, which denotes an object only by virtue of a polemical reaction to the object's qualities. Exposure to the world appears, above all and for the most part, as a necessary immunization from the world, that is as the assumption of repetitive and predictable behaviours. Non-specialization finds expression as a meticulous division of labour, as the hypertrophy of permanent roles and unilateral duties. Neoteny manifests itself as the ethico-political defence of neotenic indecision. As a device which is itself biological (that is, functional to the preservation of the species), culture aims at stabilizing the 'indefinite animal', to blunt or veil its disorientation [*disambientamento*], to reduce the *dynamis* that characterizes it to a circumscribed set of possible actions. Human *nature* is such as to often involve a contrast between its expressions and its premises.

On this background, which we've evoked with all the brevity of a musical refrain, there stands out a crucial point, which is instead redolent with nuances and subtleties. We've already alluded to it: in traditional societies, the biological invariant (language as distinct from languages, raw potentiality, non-specialization, neoteny, etc.) acquires a marked historical visibility when, and only when, a certain pseudo-environmental setup is subjected to violent transformative traction. This is the reason why natural history, if it is referred to traditional societies, coincides for the most part with the *story of a state of exception*. It scrupulously describes the situation in which a form of life loses any obviousness, becoming brittle and problematic. In other words, the situation in which cultural defences misfire and one is forced to return for a moment to the 'primal scene' of the anthropogenetic process. It is in such conjunctures, and only in such conjunctures, that it is possible to garner vivid *diagrams* of human nature.

The collapse of a form of life, with the ensuing irruption of metahistory into the sphere of historical facts, is what Ernesto de Martino, one of the few original philosophers in twentieth-century Italy, called a 'cultural apocalypse'. With this term he designated the historically determinate occasion (economic disruption, sudden technological innovation, etc.) in which the very difference between language faculty and languages, inarticulate potentiality and well-structured grammars, world and environment, becomes visible to the naked eye, and is dramatically thematized. Among the multiple symptoms which for De Martino presage an 'apocalypse', there is one which possesses strategic importance. The undoing of a cultural constellation triggers, among other things, 'a semantic excess which is not reducible to determinate signifieds'. We witness a progressive indetermination of speech: in other words, it becomes difficult to 'bend the signifier as possibility towards the signified as reality'; untied from univocal referents, discourse takes on an 'obscure allusiveness', abiding within the chaotic domain of the power-to-say (a power-to-say that goes beyond any spoken word). Now, this 'semantic excess not reducible to determinate signifieds' is entirely equivalent to the language *faculty*. In the apocalyptic crisis of a form of life, the biologically innate faculty fully exhibits the gap which forever separates it from any given language. The primacy attained by an undulating power-to-say is matched by the abnormal fluidity of states of affairs and the growing uncertainty of behaviours. As De Martino writes: 'things refuse to remain within their domestic boundaries, shedding their quotidian operability, seemingly stripped of any memory of possible behaviours'. No longer selectively filtered by a complex of cultural habits, the world shows itself to be an amorphous and enigmatic context. The conflagration of the ethico-social order thus reveals two correlated aspects of invariant 'human nature': a language faculty distinct from languages and a world opposed to any (pseudo-)environment whatsoever.

This twofold revelation is nevertheless transitory and parenthetical. The ultimate outcome of the apocalypse or state of exception is the institution of new cultural niches, capable of concealing and blunting once again the biological 'always already', that is the inarticulate and chaotic *dynamis*. Rare and fleeting are the apocalyptic diagrams of human nature.

5. Metahistory and social praxis

What was said in the preceding section only counts for traditional societies. Contemporary capitalism has radically modified the relation between unalterable phylogenetic prerogatives and historical praxis. Today, the prevailing forms of life do not veil but rather flaunt without any hesitation the differential traits of our species. In other words: the prevailing forms of life are a veritable inventory of *natural-historical diagrams*. The current organization of work does not allay the disorientation and instability of the human animal, but on the contrary takes them to their extreme and systematically valorizes them. Amorphous potentiality, that is the chronic persistence of infantile characteristics, does not menacingly flare up in the midst of a crisis. Rather it permeates every aspect of the tritest routine. Far from dreading it, the society of generalized communication tries to profit from the 'semantic excess not reducible to determinate signifieds', thereby conferring the greatest relevance upon the indeterminate language faculty. According to Hegel, philosophy's first task is to grasp its time with thought. This proverbial precept, akin to the chalk that grates against the blackboard for those who delight in studying the ahistorical mind of the isolated individual, needs to be updated in the following way: the paramount task of philosophy is to come to grips with the unprecedented superimposition of the eternal and the contingent, the biologically invariant and the socio-politically variable, which exclusively connotes the current epoch.

Let it be noted in passing that this superimposition accounts for the renewed prestige which for some decades now has been accorded to the notion of 'human nature'. It does not depend on the impressive tectonic shifts within the scientific community (Chomsky's pitiless critique against Skinner's *Verbal Behavior* or suchlike) but on an ensemble of social, economic and political conditions. To believe the opposite is yet another demonstration of culturalist idealism (of a very academic sort, to boot) on the part of those who nonetheless never fail to toot the horn of the programme to naturalize mind and language. Human nature returns to the centre of attention not because we are finally dealing with biology rather than history, but because the biological prerogatives of the human animal have acquired undeniable historical relevance in the current productive process. That is, because we are confronted with a peculiar empirical manifestation of certain phylogenetic, which is to say metahistorical, constants that mark out the existence of *Homo sapiens*. If a *naturalist* explanation of the autonomy enjoyed by 'culture' in traditional societies is certainly welcome, so is a *historical* explanation of the centrality attained by (human) 'nature' in the midst of post-Fordist capitalism.

In our epoch, the object of natural history is not a state of emergency, but everyday administration. Instead of dwelling on the erosion of a cultural constellation, we now need to concern ourselves with the way it is fully in force. Natural history does not limit itself to scavenging through 'cultural apocalypses'. Instead it tightens its grip on the totality of contemporary events. Because biological metahistory no longer surges up at the edges of forms of life, where they get stuck and idle, but installs itself durably at their geometric centre, testifying to their regular functioning, all social phenomena can be rightfully considered as *natural-historical phenomena*.

The dearth of specialized instincts and the lack of a definite environment, which have been the same from the Cro-Magnons onwards, today appear as noteworthy economic resources. It is not difficult to register the patent correspondence between certain salient features of 'human nature' and the sociological categories which are best suited to the current situation. The biological non-specialization of *Homo sapiens* does not remain in the background, but gains maximal historical visibility as the universal *flexibility* of labour services. The only professional talent that really counts in post-Fordist production is the habit not to acquire lasting habits, that is the capacity to react promptly to the unusual. A univocal competence, modulated in its last detail, now constitutes an authentic handicap for those obliged to sell their labour-power. Again, neoteny, that is chronic infancy and the related need for continual training, translates, without any mediation, into the social rule of *permanent formation*. The shortcomings of the 'constitutively premature birth' are converted into productive virtues.

What matters is not what is progressively learned (roles, techniques, etc.) but the display of the pure power to learn, which always exceeds its particular enactments. What's more, it is entirely evident that the *permanent precarity* of jobs, and even more the instability experienced by contemporary migrants, mirror in historically determinate ways the congenital lack of a uniform and predictable habitat. Precarity and nomadism lay bare at the social level the ceaseless and omnilateral pressure of a *world* that is never an environment. They induce a paradoxical familiarity with the stream of perceptual stimuli that do not allow themselves to be translated into univocal actions. This overabundance of undifferentiated solicitations is no longer true only in the final analysis, but it is true in the first analysis. It is not a disturbance to be dispelled, but the positive soil on which the current labour-process develops. Lastly, what is perhaps the most relevant and comprehensive point: inarticulate power, which is not reducible to a series of preset potential acts, acquires an extrinsic, or better pragmatic aspect in the commodity *labour-power*. This term effectively designates the ensemble of generically human psycho-physical faculties, which are precisely considered as mere *dynameis* that have yet to be applied. Today labour-power largely coincides with the language faculty. And the language faculty, qua labour-power, unmistakably shows its difference with regard to grammatically structured languages. Language faculty and labour-power lie on the border between biology and history—with the added proviso that in our epoch this very border has taken on precise historical lineaments.

To affirm that contemporary forms of life have as their emblem the language faculty, non-specialization, neoteny, loss of environment, does not at all entail arguing that they are unruly. Far from it. Being conversant with omnilateral potentiality demands, as its inevitable counterpoint, the existence of far more detailed norms than the ones which are in force in a cultural pseudo-environment. Norms so detailed that they tend to hold for a single case, for a contingent and non-reproducible occasion. The flexibility of labour services implies the unlimited variability of rules, but also, for the brief period in which they remain in force, their tremendous rigidity. These are ad hoc rules, of the kind that prescribe in minute detail the way of carrying out a certain action and only that action. Precisely where it attains the greatest socio-political relevance, the innate language *faculty* mockingly manifests itself as a collection of elementary *signals,* suited to tackling a particular eventuality. The 'semantic excess which is not reducible to determinate signifieds' often flips over into a compulsive reliance on stereotyped formulae. In other words, it takes on the seemingly paradoxical guise of a semantic *deficit*. In both of its polarities, this oscillation depends on the sudden absence of stable and well-articulated *pseudo-environments*. No longer screened by a protective cultural niche, the world is experienced in all its indeterminacy and potentiality (semantic excess); but this patent indeterminacy, which each time is to be contained and diluted in different ways, provokes by way of reaction halting behaviours, obsessive tics, the drastic impoverishment of the *ars combinatoria,* the inflation in transient but harsh norms (semantic defect). Though on the one hand permanent formation and the precarity of employments guarantee the full exposure to the world, on the other they instigate the latter's recurrent reduction to a spectral or mawkish doll's house. This accounts for the surprising marriage between generic language faculty and monotonous signals.

6. The demand for the good life

Let's sum up. In traditional societies, the biological invariant was thrust to the fore when a form of life imploded and came undone; in contemporary capitalism, when everything functions regularly. Natural history, usually busy registering with seismographic precision crises and states of exception, is instead concerned today with the ordinary administration of the productive process. In our epoch, the biological requirements of *Homo sapiens* (language faculty, non-specialization, neoteny, etc.) match up point-by-point with the most significant sociological categories (labour-power, flexibility, permanent formation, etc.).

Two phrases by Marx, taken from the *Economic and Philosophical Manuscripts of 1844,* are perfectly suited to the current situation. The first says: 'It can be seen how the history of *industry* and the *objective* existence of industry as it has developed is the *open* book of the essential powers of man, man's psychology present in tangible form. [. . .] A *psychology* for which this book [. . .] is closed can never become a *real* science'. To paraphrase: today's industry—based on neoteny, the language faculty, potentiality—is the externalized, empirical, pragmatic image of the human psyche, of its invariant and metahistorical characteristics. Today's industry therefore constitutes the only dependable textbook for the philosophy of mind. Here is Marx's second phrase: 'The whole of history is a preparation, a development, for *"man"* to become the object of *sensuous* consciousness'. Once we expunge the eschatological emphasis (history doesn't prepare anything, let it be clear) we can paraphrase as follows: in the epoch of flexibility and permanent formation, human nature now constitutes an almost perceptual evidence, as well as the immediate content of social praxis. In other words: every step they take, human beings directly experience that which constitutes the presupposition of experience in general.

The raw material of contemporary politics is to be found in natural-historical phenomena, that is in the contingent events in which the distinctive traits of our species come to light. I say *raw material*, not a canon or a guiding principle. All political orientations are effectively faced with a situation in which human praxis is systematically applied to the ensemble of the requirements that make praxis human. But they do so in the name of contrasting interests. The shared attention to the differential traits of the species gives rise to diametrically opposed aims, whose realization depends on the balance of forces they enjoy, not on their greater or lesser conformity to 'human nature'. It is in vain that Chomsky appeals to the unalterable biological endowment of *Homo sapiens* to rectify the inherent injustice of contemporary capitalism. Rather than constituting the platform and parameter for a possible emancipation, the congenital 'creativity of language' appears today as an ingredient in the despotic organization of work; or better, it appears as a profitable economic resource. To the extent that it attains an immediate empirical consistency, the biological invariant is part of the problem, and certainly not the solution.

The global movement is inscribed in this context. Not unlike its enemies, that is not unlike the politics that prolongs oppression, it too has considerable familiarity with the metahistory that incarnates itself in contingent states of affairs. But it strives to discern the various forms that could take on the manifestation of the 'always already' in the 'just now'. That the congenital *potentiality* of the human animal fully manifests itself at the socio-economic level is an irreversible matter of fact; but that in manifesting itself, this potentiality is obliged to take on the features of the commodity *labour-power* is by no means an inescapable fate. On the contrary, it is a momentary outcome, which one should intransigently struggle against. Likewise, it is not set in stone anywhere that the phenomenological correlate of the biological *non-specialization* of our species will continue to be, always and regardless, the servile *flexibility* flaunted by the contemporary labour-process. The socio-historical prominence of human nature does not attenuate but rather immeasurably enhances the specific impact (and the irreparable contingency) of political action.

The global movement is the conflictual interface of biolinguistic capitalism. It is precisely because (and not in spite) of this that it presents itself on the public stage as an *ethical* movement. The reason for this is easy to intuit. We have said that contemporary production implicates all the attitudes that distinguish our species: language, reflexivity, instinctual deficiency, etc. With a simplifying but not empty formula, we could even say that post-Fordism puts to work *life* as such. Now, if it is true that biolinguistic capitalism appropriates 'life', that is the set of specifically human faculties, it is pretty obvious that insubordination against it must focus on this same fact. The life that is included in flexible production is countered by the demand (which is pertinent because it is itself 'non-specialized') of a *good life*. And the search for the *good life* is the only concrete theme of the 'science of mores'. As numerous as its misfortunes may be, it is beyond doubt that the global movement has indicated the point of intersection between natural history and ethics.

Translated by Alberto Toscano

CHAPTER 29

Timeline

Zoe Waters (with Michael Lewis and David Rose)

The thinkers comprised in this book have been selected in large measure according to the principles set out in the Introduction. In other words, the limits of 'Italian philosophy' were drawn, temporarily and strategically, to accord for the most part with a definition of Italian philosophy borrowed from Roberto Esposito. To encompass some of those philosophers whom this account – or at least our rendering of it – misses out, we include here a timeline that very briefly outlines the work of a number of other Italian thinkers and writers.

The terrain is quite immense (Eugenio Garin's *History of Italian Philosophy* should be consulted as a first resort to get some sense of just *how* vast), and we have still no doubt elided many important figures. We invite readers to suggest significant omissions, care of the publishers. (See the Introduction and Excerpts, *supra* for all entries here left blank.)

* * *

Dante Alighieri (1265–1321)

Francesco Petrarca (Petrarch) (1304–74)

Better known today as a poet and a writer rather than an original systematic philosopher, and perhaps best known in English-speaking countries for his poems, the *Canzoniere*. He was considered one of the finest moral philosophers and scholars of his age, a humanist who profoundly influenced the formation of the Modern mindset (from the very notion of landscape, the invention of which is often attributed to his *Ascent of Mount Ventoux*, to the interpretation and treatment of historical sources (cf. Cassirer et al., 1948, 25)). Averse to scholasticism and in particular to the naturalism, rationalism and scientific interests of the Averroists (see Pomponazzi, *infra*), and even somewhat deaf to the works of Plato and Aristotle (he lacked a serious command of Greek), he was content to abide by the authority of the Church in the manner of St. Augustine, from whose Christianized neo-Platonism he nevertheless learnt a good deal of the fundamental attitude of the Greek philosopher. He venerated Cicero and the eloquence of his Latin, bringing certain of his works back into circulation and assisting thereby in the fourteenth-century renaissance of classical humanism. Among the ancient Romans and Hellenistic philosophers, he also revered the Stoics, as was common among Renaissance humanists, with an especial fondness for Seneca (cf. Cassirer et al., 1948, 23ff).

Catherine of Siena (1347–80)

Scholastic philosopher and theologian, celebrated as a feminist, mystic and activist, later declared a saint. Best known for *The Dialogue of Divine Providence* (1378) concerning the relation between love and truth, virtues and defects, desire, guilt and punishment. Aside from this treatise, Catherine dictated (and wrote from 1377 onwards) 26 prayers and at least 300 letters, including several to the Pope.

Christine de Pizan (1364–1430)

Italian born, Christine de Pizan achieved renown as a moralist and political writer in mediaeval France. She advanced a surprisingly modern notion of gender equality in works that are among the first instances of feminist literature known to us, and she is credited with being Europe's first professional woman of letters (Schaus, 2006, 133).

Pizan is known for her critiques of misogyny in popular novels, but her most famous works are *The Book of the City of Ladies* (1405) and *Treasure of the City of Ladies* (1405) in which she depicts a symbolic community of women and sets up a dialogue between three allegorical 'daughters of God' (cf. Campbell, 2003, 6). Pizan instructs women on the qualities to be cultivated if one is to ensure sexual equality, an equality of capacity guaranteed by the fact that both sexes are created in God's image. The figure of Lady Reason invoked by Pizan seeks to refute the traditional stereotype of women as irrational, and she pursues the idea that women's success depends upon their ability to speak and write (Redfern, 1995, 74).

Lorenzo Valla (1405–1457)

Perhaps the most philosophical and original of the later Italian Humanists. He shares the general Humanist antipathy towards Aristotle, dialectic and scholastic thought, and even, more unusually, resisted Stoicism and the neo-Platonism that Ficino would embrace. He breaks with the attempts made by both scholasticism and other Humanists to reconcile pagan Greek antiquity with Christianity, vigorously asserting the distinction between reason and faith, philosophy and theology, which also implies paganism and Christianity. Valla set himself to prove that human freedom was not incompatible with Divine prescience (Cassirer et al., 1948, 149f).

Marsilio Ficino (1433–99)

The great Florentine Renaissance humanist and Platonist, he translated the majority of Plato's dialogues and many later Platonistic writings from Greek into Latin, deploying Platonism in order to rearticulate the theses of humanism and to resolve certain of the problems which had arisen within its doctrines. Ficino attempted a comprehensive synthesis of Platonism as a whole – a synoptic view made possible only recently by the rediscovery of the whole Platonic corpus – with Christianity, following Augustine and others and yet going further than any of them so as to render Christian doctrine sufficiently rational that a sceptical and atheistic mindset might find it palatable (cf. Cassirer et al. 1948, 186–7). Ficino endorses the tenet of Humanism according to which human beings were universally able to aim at the highest good, Plato's *'idea tou agathou'* or 'idea of the Good', the *summum bonum*, which Christianity interpreted as God, a god which Ficino in turn understood as the object of desire on the part of all those parts of creation which stood below God in the cosmic hierarchy, with man himself at its summit.

Pietro Pomponazzi (1462–1525)

Towards the end of the fifteenth century, Averroism reigned supreme in Italian universities. Averroes, the Arabic commentator of Aristotle, had promoted an impersonal and collective vision of the soul. This involved a particular interpretation of Aristotle's notion of the passive or potential intellect: immortal, unitary and participated in (to a limited extent) by each finite *individual* intellect, the individual's vision of truth being distorted by the possession of a sensuous body, which individuated it.

In opposition to this, a revolutionary within the tradition of Italian Aristotelian philosophers, less willing than the others to identify Aristotle with Averroes's interpretation of him, Pomponazzi – 'the last Scholastic and the first man of the Enlightenment' (Cassirer et al. 1948, 267–8) – promoted in its stead a humanistic notion of the individual, personal soul, which had its own intrinsic value and dignity. He took the question of the unity of human nature, the connection between the immortal soul and the mortal body, as his problem, to be solved in the remarkably prescient form of a theory which demonstrated the way in which the finite natural body can provide a site for the infinite truths of reason, the soul being both inseparable from the body and yet capable of insight into the universal and immaterial realm of truth.

Contrary to the Platonists, such as his rival, Ficino, who attributed dignity to the individual soul by assigning it a desire which extended *beyond* nature, towards God or the Good, Pomponazzi attempted to situate the individual soul firmly *within* nature, following a certain impulse towards naturalism and the sciences derived from Aristotle himself. The soul is – at least according to human reason if not faith – mortal, the intellect extended and divisible. The happiness of human existence is not to be found simply in contemplation but also in the practical life of virtuous behaviour, which all human beings were capable of participating in (Cassirer et al. 1948, 257, 271–3, 15–16).

Giovanni Pico della Mirandola (1463–94)

Laura Cereta (1469–99)

Fifteenth-century humanist and feminist, by the end of her life she was a well-known scholar in Italy. Her letters deal with characteristically humanist themes including marriage, war, the death of loved ones and the instability of fortune. Her writings on women's education reflect the works of Christine de Pizan and argue that women ought not to waste their time on inconsequential and trivial activity. Cereta was also interested in moral philosophy, particularly Epicurus and his notion of virtue.

Niccolò Machiavelli (1469–1527)

Tullia d'Aragona (1510–56)

One of the most accomplished female intellectuals of the Renaissance, her poems, letters and philosophical works concern the concepts of love and sexuality. D'Aragona is best known for her *Dialogue on the Infinity of Love* (1547) which uncovers the misogyny of the prevailing religious dogma and declares the female sex-drive to be as fundamental as the male's so as to condemn the repression of female sexual experience. She also insists that female rationality should not be belittled. D'Aragona ponders the possibility of an ethics of love that would restore the female subject to intellectual and sexual parity with men. Every human is both soul and body, possessed of both intellect and sensibility, loving and sexual, and therefore, for d'Aragona, the only moral form of love is one that recognizes the needs of both parts.

Giordano Bruno (1548–1600)

Moderata Fonte (1555–92)

The pseudonym of Modesta di Pozzo di Forzi, a Venetian poet and feminist who wrote religious and romantic poetry, along with dramatic dialogues, but who remains best known for the posthumously published, *The Worth of Women* (1600). In this text, she considers the role of female figures in biblical narratives with the intention of disclosing the repression of women.

She imagines, following the example of Christine de Pizan, a 'city of women', where women will be safe and flourish in the total absence of men.

Galileo; or Galileo Galilei (1564–1642)

Physicist and astronomer whose most enduring contributions as far as later philosophy is concerned were his proposals that nature should be understood mathematically, and that, thanks to discoveries made with the use of the newly developed telescope, Copernican heliocentrism could no longer be denied: the Aristotelian–Ptolemaic cosmology was refuted. Also of great significance to philosophy was his work on motion, which displaced Aristotelian physics once and for all, not least by denying a connection between the weight of a body and the rate at which it falls and asserting the parabolic character of projectile motion.

Tommaso Campanella; born Giovanni Domenico Campanella (1568–1639)

Natural philosopher and poet, he advocated a philosophy of nature that opposed prevailing interpretations of Aristotelianism which attended slavishly to the words of the Stagirite rather than whatever could be discerned in the book of nature by the bodily senses. For Campanella, our knowledge must be derived solely from the things themselves, natural entities in which the activity of God may always be read.

Also interested in magic and prophecy, he perceived the natural world as a living organism, whose parts lived and sensed. His best-known work is *The City of the Sun*, which describes the ideal city as being designed in harmony with a nature that manifests God's benevolence and wisdom, a body politic modelled upon the living organism, which above all things evinced God's benign creative intention. Thus the solar city – its walls painted with beautiful and instructive images – would avoid the injustice and unhappiness into which real earthly cities had fallen precisely by deviating from the natural order. Such a society would be one in which private property may barely be said to exist, with all things held in common among its citizens, and labour would be limited to only a few hours each day.

Lucrezia Marinella (1571–1653)

Lucrezia Marinella wrote prose, verse and philosophical polemics, including one of the first polemical treatises concerned with the worth of women, entitled *The Nobility and Excellence of Women and the Defects and Vices of Men* (1600).

Giambattista Vico (1668–1744)

Giuseppa Eleonora Barbapiccola (1702–40)

Credited with introducing Cartesian thought into Italy through her translations, the interweaving of Descartes' theoretical notions with the theme of the education of women comprises Barbapiccola's project. She argues that women are not naturally intellectually inferior to men but appear so only as a result of a lack of education. Women should be granted access to the reason that Descartes demonstrates, rather than being constrained to menial private activities in the home (Accademia de' Ricovrati 2007). In later life, Barbapiccola became closely associated with Vico's intellectual circle.

Pasquale Galluppi (1770–1846)

Epistemologist and moral philosopher who taught at the University of Naples, he was strongly influenced by Christian Wolff, René Descartes and John Locke and engaged with problems of logic, metaphysics and mathematics. He began a study of Kant but soon discarded the Kantian philosophy.

Antonio Rosmini (1797–1855)

Attempted to adjust the balance between reason and faith that, for him, had tipped too far in favour of the former in the Age of Enlightenment: philosophy was to serve theological ends. Affirmed the transcendent dignity of the human person at least partly on the grounds of our innate insight into Being. Founded the religious order known as the Rosminians in 1828. Rosmini wrote a number of significant and widely read essays on Kant's philosophy.

Ottavio Colecchi (1773–1848)

Ottavio Colecchi subscribed to the philosophy of Kant, teaching and promoting his work in the private school of philosophy that he founded. He taught the likes of Francesco De Sanctis and the brothers Bertrando and Silvio Spaventa. Alongside his work on Kant, he specialized in German Idealist philosophy.

Giacomo Leopardi (1798–1837)

Much admired and prodigious linguist, philologist, poet – perhaps the greatest of the modern age in Italy – and philosopher, although still little known in the English-speaking world. Of extraordinary erudition, acquired at an exceptionally young age, he was known first for his extraordinary philological work and only later for his poetry and philosophy.

His major works of philosophical interest include the *Operette morali* and the *Pensieri* (*Thoughts*), along with his magnum opus, very recently translated in its entirety into English, the *Zibaldone*. His extensive correspondence also offers a great many insights into his philosophical project.

Important to Schopenhauer and Nietzsche, and the subject of an enormous volume by Antonio Negri, the second book he composed while in prison, which sought to restore Leopardi to his rightful place in the history of European philosophy. Negri identifies Leopardi as precisely one of Nietzsche's precursors – an ontologist, a materialist, working out, as Negri himself was at many points in his career, how to respond to defeat without despair, attacking Hegelian dialectics and positivism equally, replacing them with a materialism that focuses on the body, affects and the imagination, in their creative capacities.

Francesco De Sanctis (1817–83)

Predominantly a literary critic and historian of Italian literature who, however, made a significant contribution to aesthetics, he affirmed the autonomy of art from other disciplines, discourses and requirements, a thesis which had a great impact on his most famous disciple, Benedetto Croce.

Bertrando Spaventa (1817–83)

Along with his brother, Silvio, trained in a small liberal circle alongside Ottavio Colecchi, he began his career teaching the latter's Kantian and socialist philosophy. Spaventa also studied Rosmini's work on Kant but argued that the true significance of Kant's work was only to be uncovered by German idealism, and Hegel in particular. Spaventa's account of Hegel was original in its day and stressed above all the importance of the *Phenomenology* and the disregarding of religious interpretations.

Anna Kuliscioff (1857–1925)

Woman's activist and political revolutionary who, after being expelled from her homeland in Russia, became well established in Italy as a leader of the Italian Socialist Party (PSI). Initially, Kuliscioff was tempted by anarchism before shifting towards Marxist socialism. Her Marxist views influenced the Italian sociologist Filippo Turati, her partner, alongside whom she led the PSI. Kuliscioff ended up something of a reformist and came to believe that socialism could be actualized through education, trade unions and parliamentary action.

Benedetto Croce (1866–1952)

Giovanni Gentile (1875–1944)

Antonio Banfi (1886–1957)

Originally influenced by German Neo-Kantianism and Husserlian phenomenology – which he imparted to Enzo Paci who was responsible for its wider dissemination in Italy – he later turned away from its perceived idealism and embraced a rather orthodox form of Marxist historical materialism and joined the Italian Communist Party in 1947.

Carlo Michelstaedter (1887–1910)

Known for his existential, idealistic and nihilist philosophy. His sole work was his doctoral thesis *Persuasion and Rhetoric* (1910). He committed suicide shortly after its competition, at the age of just twenty-three. Interwoven with this philosophical treatise are accounts of personal matters, with Michelstaedter attempting to develop a conception of contemporary existence.

Antonio Gramsci (1891–1937)

Palmiro Togliatti (1893–1964)

More a political activist than a thinker, Togliatti was a founding member and leader of the Communist Party of Italy from 1927 until his death and has the dubious honour of having a Russian city named after him. He was part of the Gramscian group, *L'Ordine Nuovo*, formed after the First World War, and moved to the Soviet Union to avoid persecution.

Galvano Della Volpe (1895–1968)

Volpe was a Marxist philosopher, from the historicist tradition of Gentile and Croce, and proposed a scientific alternative to Gramscian Marxism. Alongside political philosophy, he also wrote on aesthetics and film.

Aldo Capitini (1899–1968)

Political activist, anti-Fascist and founder of the non-violence movement in Italy, he is recognized as one of the first Italians to disseminate and develop Mahatma Gandhi's philosophy of non-violence.

Nicola Abbagnano (1901–90)

Italian existentialist who sought to avoid what he perceived as the negative aspects of Heidegger in the pragmatism of Dewey. He was also interested in the history of philosophy in an Italian context and edited one of the main encyclopaedias used in teaching the subject.

Norberto Bobbio (1909–2004)

Hugely influential legal and political philosopher and one of the founders of the Italian Analytic School of philosophy and law, Bobbio's philosophical studies are far-reaching, spanning the political sciences, existentialism, jurisprudence, legal positivism, Locke, Kant, Popper and the Marxist Galvano Della Volpe.

Enzo Paci (1911–76)

Luigi Pareyson (1918–91)

Pier Paolo Pasolini (1922–75)

Best known outside of Italy as a filmmaker, Pasolini was nevertheless a poet, novelist and an important writer on social, cultural and philosophical issues. A lifelong catholic (though critical of the institution of the Church), he proposed the sacredness of life as a means by which to resist consumer capitalism. This sacred life was a life shared in common among all humanity and thus formed the basis of a resistance to capitalism – for which nothing is sacred – and the ground of a certain communism. Thus Pasolini foreshadows certain debates which would later be resumed under the heading of 'biopolitics' and 'bioethics'. He was also concerned with the possibilities and limits of transgressive action and with the problem of emancipation. He was concerned that freedom, in the 1960s in particular, was understood all too exclusively in terms of sexual freedom (the tolerance of which Pasolini would come to understand as, in the end, a false or 'repressive' tolerance that only served to reinforce the *status quo*), and more generally in the form of the (purely) individual liberty claimed by the progressive, liberal bourgeoisie whose response to post-war consumer capitalism erupted in the student revolts of the 1960s, of which Pasolini was – unusually for a Leftist – a critic.

Lucio Colletti (1924–2001)

Western Marxist and critic of Hegel, inspired by Galvano Della Volpe, who later repudiated Marxism. Such a move was typical of his flexibility towards doctrine, and he finally ended up as a member of Berlusconi's *Forza Italia*.

Uberto Scarpelli (1924–93)

Co-founded the Italian Analytic School with Norberto Bobbio. Like his colleague, he was interested in the philosophy of law.

Nicola Badaloni (1924–2005)

Politician and historian of Italian philosophy. A Marxist, he made extensive studies of Vico, Campanella, Bruno and Gramsci.

Elvio Fachinelli (1928–89)

A psychoanalyst, writing some near-popular works on Freud and the relation between psychoanalysis and philosophy, partly responsible for the dissemination of Freudian thought in Italy; in hindsight, his work might be said to form a missing link between the Freudo-Marxists and Žižek, whose work his own at times resembles and yet predates.

Gennaro Sasso (1928–)

Historian of philosophy, with interests in the relation between politics and ethics. Author of a number of works on Italian philosophy and culture but studied Machiavelli and Benedetto Croce most extensively.

Tullio Gregory (1929–2019)

Historian of mediaeval philosophy and early modern philosophy, known for his attempt to synthesize the two.

Emanuele Severino (1929–)

Giuseppe Riconda (1931–)

Concerned with the problem of evil in modernity, philosophical historiography and personalism (Riconda in Benso 2017, p. 274). Best known for his work *Tradizione e avventura* (2001), where he formulates a notion of truth and tradition inspired by Revelation.

Virgilio Melchiorre (1931–)

Attempts to synthesize transcendental phenomenology – particularly fundamental ontology and existential thought – with themes from classical metaphysics (Melchiorre in Benso 2017, p. 220).

> The encounter with personalism and existentialism has led me to reflect on the combinability of the high points of metaphysics with the existential possibilities of being human. With respect to this, my research has developed within the lines of the relation between the fundamental themes of metaphysics and anthropology and the theme of language. (ibid., p. 219)

Melchiorre argues that the notion of analogy 'constitutes the essential condition for a metaphysically concrete understanding of and within what exists' (ibid.).

Carla Lonzi (1931–82)

An art critic turned feminist activist who helped create the Italian feminist collective *Rivolta Femminile* (*Feminine Rebellion*) in 1970. A founder of the movement that came to be known as the 'feminism of difference' inspired by Luce Irigaray, which stresses female sexual *difference* as opposed to *equality*, an escape from the very terms of the debate set by the symbolic order of rationality and language that was ultimately a tool of masculine domination ('phallo-logo-centrism'). Among the most significant figures to be opposed in this regard is Hegel, whom Lonzi critiques in her work from 1970, 'Let's Spit on Hegel'. In *The Clitoridian Woman and the Vaginal Woman* (1971), she critiques Freud and Wilhelm Reich's psychoanalytic theory for its patriarchal understanding of female sexuality and its advocacy of the idea of the largely 'mythical' vaginal orgasm.

Mario Tronti (1931–)

Umberto Eco (1932–2016)

Professor of semiotics, inspired by C. S. Peirce, he presented his work in both academic form and the guise of novels which enjoyed enormous popularity. These latter works were intended to dramatize and enact his philosophical ideas – narration, along with fiction and its truth, being key concerns. *The Name of the Rose*, which relates the pursuit of a lost book that kills (Aristotle's volume on comedy), is among the most famous. Eco's ideas revolve around the interpretation of signs, into which their reader must enter. As to the purely theoretical work, his first major text, *The Open Work* (1962), remains foundational.

Gabriele Giannantoni (1932–98)

Historian and philologist, with interests in Aristotelian logic and the philosophy of language, as well as the philosophy of state education.

Carlo Sini (1933–)

Antonio Negri (1933–)

Alberto Asor Rosa (1933–)

Italian Marxist, a former deputy of the Italian Communist Party and director of the journal *Contropiano*, disseminating Marxist ideas close to Mario Tronti's workerism. A literary critic and professor of literature, he became a fiction writer following his retirement. Of particular concern to him is the relation between literature and ideology.

Giovanni Ferretti (1933–)

Attempts to rekindle the dialogue between philosophy and theology in a context of secularization. Ferretti is mostly interested in twentieth-century Christian theology and is influenced by Ernst Bloch whose 'utopian-humanistic key' and work on messianic eschatology in the context of existential human experience he admires (Ferretti in Benso, 2017, p. 263). He employs the phenomenological method in order to discern the distinct forms of intentionality specific to religious experience.

Evandro Agazzi (1934–)

A philosopher of science known for his theory of scientific objectivity named 'Objectualism'. Agazzi makes the distinction between common 'things' and scientific 'objects', defining the latter by a set of 'attributes' which comprise what science would consider to be 'real'. He embraces the 'analytic' tag but argues that hermeneutic and historicist approaches are equally important (Agazzi in Benso, 2017, p.159). In his recent work, he deploys phenomenological notions such as intentionality and applies them to AI, arguing that intentionality is the only distinguishing factor of human operations as distinct from machines.

Enrico Berti (1935–)

A renowned scholar of Aristotle, he, like many Italian thinkers, saw philosophy as exceptional because of its dialectical structure and sought to reinvigorate metaphysics, albeit in a weak form (Berti in Benso, 2017)

Vincenzo Vitiello (1935–)

Influenced by the German idealists and Heidegger, Vitiello's most significant contribution to philosophy is his formulation of topology which he develops in *Topologia del moderno* (*Topology of the Modern*), arguing that time and space are in some sense the same and constitute a permanent horizon within which all events flow.

Gianni Vattimo (1936–)

Mario Costa (1936–)

Develops Walter Benjamin's idea of reproducibility in light of the impact of contemporary digital and electronic technologies. In his text, *Il sublime tecnologico* (1990), Costa argues that these media offer the possibility for the self-manifestation of the sublime, which overcomes the modern subject in favour of a hyper-subject of the internet.

Fulvio Tessitore (1937–)

Fulvio Tessitore promotes an ethics based on individual responsibility, springing from a sense of solidarity grounded in history. He develops an anti-metaphysical, relational pluralism which stresses the centrality of the historical existence of the individual.

Mario Vegetti (1937–2018)

A historian of Ancient Philosophy, with interests in a broad range of subjects from medicine, historiography and subjectivity, to anthropology.

Remo Bodei (1938–)

Bodei is a scholar of Marxist utopianism who, influenced by Freud, seeks to delineate the dialectical conflict of reason and passion in history. In *Geometria della passioni* (1991), Bodei considers the potential conflict and compatibility of reason and passion in both the individual and the community, together with the role played by delusion as a challenge to the metaphysical categories of truth, reason and reality.

Teresa de Lauretis (1938–)

Versed in semiotics, poststructuralism, psychoanalysis, feminism, queer studies and film theory, de Lauretis seeks to redress theoretical discourse's failure to include the female subject and body. Abiding by Pier Paolo Pasolini's words according to which we are at once actors and spectators, she understands gender as a construction and performance.

Angela Ales Bello (1939–)

Ales Bello has written extensively on Husserl and his student Edith Stein. She is best known for *The Divine in Husserl and Other Explorations* (2008), which aims to reveal the religious concerns underlying Husserl's phenomenological method and to supplement Husserl's philosophy with Edith Stein's anthropology, thus initiating a phenomenologically grounded investigation into religious experience.

Mario Ruggenini (1940–)

Ruggenini posits radical hermeneutics as the tool to overcome the nihilism characteristic of modern Western culture and argues that truth is exposed in conversation with the 'Other'. Truth is that which opens human existence to the sacred, and God is the principle that calls humans into conversation. Ruggenini's interest in language extends to mass communication in the modern age of the techno-sciences and globalization, along with the ethical and political conflicts that arise in this era.

Luisa Muraro (1940–)

Eugenio Lecaldano (1940–)

An analytic moral philosopher, influenced by Hume, and concerned with the origin of ethical judgements and their justification, leaning towards naturalistic solutions grounded in attitudes of pride and self-esteem.

Carmelo Vigna (1940–)

Vigna seeks to reconcile ontology and ethics through transcendental anthropology and a study of the dynamics of intersubjective relations (Vigna in Benso 2017, p.67). At the most basic level of intersubjectivity, the human exists both in a relationship with itself and within a horizon of relations to the Other.

Salvatore Natoli (1941–)

Salvatore Natoli carries out an ethical, hermeneutic investigation into the problematic of maintaining happiness in light of the agent's necessarily finite existence, deriving individual responsibility from guilt and its relation to both the objectivity of damage and the subjectivity of pain. His interest in diverse religious experiences of pain also leads to speculation as to how time and finitude might be experienced differently by people from different religious backgrounds.

Mario Perniola (1941–2018)

A well-known aesthetician and political thinker, influenced by Marx and Guy Debord whom founded the movement known as Situationism. Perniola focused on the novel, mass communication and eroticism, themes bound together by the notions of shadow, artificiality and simulation.

Pier Aldo Rovatti (1942–)

Pier Aldo Rovatti studied phenomenology under Enzo Paci, and his extensive work encompasses much of the panorama of continental thought from phenomenology to Lacanian psychoanalysis. Rovatti remains best known for his work with Vattimo on the notion of 'weak thought' (*pensiero debole*).

Giorgio Agamben (1942–)

Silvia Federici (1942–)

Marco Maria Olivetti (1943–2006)

Concerned with the relationship between faith and reason, Olivetti's work may be situated in the lineage of Emmanuel Levinas and Jean-Luc Marion. He adopts a Marxist, historicist and post-idealist approach to human subjectivity and develops an 'irreal' account grounded in ethics understood as first philosophy.

Salvatore Veca (1943–)

A social and political theorist, Veca formulates an idea of a reasonable society heavily influenced by Kantian and Rawlsian theories of justice, which validates the reasonableness of its maxims through a regulative ideal of utopia.

Paolo Parrini (1943–)

An analytic thinker who has developed a new interpretation of logical positivism and is mainly concerned with issues of realism and epistemological warrant.

Sergio Givone (1944–)

An aesthetician interested in the possible transcendence of thought through experiences such as dreams, fables and poetry – experiences normally excluded from philosophical thinking.

Massimo Cacciari (1944–)

Giulio Giorello (1945–)

With a broad range of interests in the philosophies of science, mathematics and ethics, Giorello has written on human passions, virtues and sins. In his best-known work, *Di nessuna chiesa* (*Of No Church*) (2005), Giorello proposes atheism as a practical philosophy which grounds the liberal rights of the individual in a resistance to religious authority.

Giacomo Marramao (1946–)

Deploying Karl Löwith's historical–philosophical and political–theological approach to 'Christian' secularization, Marramao interprets the crisis of the modern state by performing a genealogy of the presuppositions of Western rationalism.

Adriana Cavarero (1947–)

Marco Vannini (1948–)

One of the major interpreters of Christian mysticism, especially Meister Eckhart, Vannini sees the mystical experience as a dialectical journey towards grace. Most significantly, he argues that all religious language and production must be understood within the context of the original, direct experience of the mystic.

Sebastiano Maffettone (1948–)

Political philosopher, applied ethicist and bioethicist who translated Rawls's *A Theory of Justice* into Italian. His liberalism has led him to offer an alternative to cosmopolitanism in International Relations theory, understood as pluralistic integration.

Franco 'Bifo' Berardi (1949–)

Examines media and information technology in post-industrial capitalism from an autonomist Marxist perspective that draws on psychoanalysis and communication theory.

Roberto Esposito (1950–)

Paola Ricci Sindoni (1950–)

A scholar of twentieth-century German philosophy (particularly phenomenology), feminist thought, philosophy of religion (specifically mysticism and Judaism), moral philosophy and bioethics. She has written extensively on figures that include Edith Stein, Hannah Arendt and Karl Jaspers.

Christian Marazzi (1951–)

Paolo Virno (1952–)

Franco Volpi (1952–2009)

Historian of philosophy who wrote extensively on Heidegger, Aristotle, Schmitt, Jünger and Schopenhauer, and who was developing an original philosophical approach at the time of his premature death.

Alessandro Ferrara (1953–)

Ferrara uses a reconstructed version of Kant's reflective judgement to formulate an alternative to both proceduralist and neo-transcendental approaches to legitimation in political philosophy. His strategy is to show how normativity can transcend context and locality if value judgements are derived from authenticity and exemplarity.

Maurizio Lazzarato (1955–)

Donatella Di Cesare (1956–)

Di Cesare writes on Jewish philosophy and the dehumanization that takes place in events such as the Holocaust and relates these to globalization issues such as citizenship and exile. She was Hans-Georg Gadamer's last student and vice-president of the Martin Heidegger Society until 2015 when she resigned in response to the publication of his *Black Notebooks*. Di Cesare has since criticized Heidegger extensively, claiming a form of metaphysical anti-Semitism to lie at the root of his philosophy.

Maurizio Ferraris (1956–)

Simona Forti (1958–)

Andrea Fumagalli (1959–)

A left-wing economist inspired by workerism (the attempt to bypass the traditional organs of working class power such as the labour party and the trade unions in order to engage directly with workers on the factory floor), who identifies the nature of contemporary capitalism as 'cognitive bio-capitalism' (exploiting knowledge, language and communication understood as invariant biological traits of the human being). Cognitive bio-capitalism constitutes the final (or at least the most recent) link in a chain that extends from the Post-Fordist period of the 1970s up until the 1990s, the 'cognitive capitalism' that characterized the last decade of the twentieth century, and the 'bio-capitalism' and 'bio-economy' which followed it (in which capitalism seeks to invest the natural living faculties of human beings, their very life and even their 'bare life'). Cognitive bio-capitalism encompasses the two paradigms which most immediately precede it. The commons of life and knowledge (the general intellect) are privatized, owned and so subjected to both power and the ability to extract profit.

Massimo Recalcati (1959–)

Francesca Alesse (1960–)

Historian of philosophy, specializing in Ancient Greek thought and the origin and development of prescriptive and regulative norms in Hellenistic ethics.

Davide Tarizzo (1966–)

Elettra Stimilli (1966–)

Biopolitical thinker inspired by Weber and Foucault to rethink the theological heritage of our concepts of economy and politics, with specific attention to the problem of debt and its origins; close to, if not a part of, the tradition of Agamben and Esposito which advocates a certain form of political theology.

Works cited and further reading

Accademia de' Ricovrati, M. Agnesi, D. Faini and A. Savini de' Rossi. "Giuseppa Eleonora Barbapiccola." *The Contest for Knowledge: Debates over Women's Learning in Eighteenth-Century Italy*, edited by and trans. Rebecca Messbarger and Paula Findlen. Chicago, IL: University of Chicago Press, 2007, 37–66.

Agazzi, Evandro. 'Mathematics, Sciences, Objectivity and System Theory — Evandro Agazzi'. In *Viva Voce: Conversations with Italian Philosophers*, edited by Silvia Benso, 159–74. Albany, NY: SUNY Press, 2017

Agnesi, M., D. Faini, A. Rossi and A. Ricovrati. "Giuseppa Eleonora Barbapiccola." *The Contest for Knowledge: Debates over Women's Learning in Eighteenth-Century Italy*. Chicago, IL: University of Chicago Press, 2007, 37–66.

Ales Bello, Angela. *The Divine in Husserl and Other Explorations*, trans. Antonio Calcagno. Dordrecht: Springer, 2009

Benso, Silvia. and Brian Schroeder. 'Italian Philosophy between 1980–1995'. In *After Poststructuralism: Transitions and Transformations*, edited by Rosi Braidotti, 83–110. London and New York: Routledge, 2014.

Benso, ed., *Viva Voce: Conversations with Italian Philosophers*. Albany, NY: SUNY Press, 2017

Benso, Silvia. and Brian Schroeder, eds, *Contemporary Italian Philosophy: Crossing the Borders of Ethics, Politics, and Religion*. Albany, NY: SUNY Press, 2007

Berti, Enrico. 'Metaphysics, Experience, and Transcendence — Enrico Berti'. In *Viva Voce: Conversations with Italian Philosophers*, edited by Silvia Benso, 203–14. Albany, NY: SUNY Press, 2017

Bodei, Remo. 'Logic of Delusion, Passions and Time: A Conversation with Remo Bodei'. In *Viva Voce: Conversations with Italian Philosophers*, edited by Silvia Benso, 17–26. Albany, NY: SUNY Press, 2017

Campbell, Karlyn K. *Three Tall Women: Radical Challenges to Criticism, Pedagogy, and Theory*. Boston: Pearson, 2003

Cassirer, Ernst, Paul Oskar Kristeller, and John Herman Randall., eds, *The Renaissance Philosophy of Man*. Chicago: University of Chicago Press, 1948

Chiesa, Lorenzo. and Alberto Toscano, eds, *The Italian Difference: Between Nihilism and Biopolitics*. Melbourne: re.press, 2009

Chiesa, Lorenzo., ed., '*Italian Thought Today*. Angelaki 16, no. 3 (September 2011)

Costa, Mario. 'Technology, Communication, and Aesthetics of the Sublime — A Conversation with Mario Costa'. In *Viva Voce: Conversations with Italian Philosophers*, edited by Silvia Benso, 125–36. Albany, NY: SUNY Press, 2017

D'Aragona, Tullia. *Dialogue on the Infinity of Love*, trans. and edited by Rinaldina Russell and Bruce Merry. Chicago: University of Chicago Press, 1997

De Lauretis, Teresa. *Alice Doesn't: Feminism, Semiotics, Cinema*. Bloomington: Indiana University Press, 1984

De Lauretis, Teresa. *Technologies of Gender: Essays on Theory, Film and Fiction*. Bloomington: Indiana University Press, 1987

De Lauretis, Teresa. *The Practice of Love: Lesbian Sexuality and Perverse Desire*. Bloomington: Indiana University Press, 1994

Fonte, Moderata. *The Worth of Women: Wherein is Clearly Revealed Their Nobility and Their Superiority to Men*, trans. Virginia Cox. Chicago: University of Chicago Press, 1997

Fumagalli, Andrea. 'Twenty Theses on Contemporary Capitalism (Cognitive Biocapitalism)' trans. Sabrina Ovan. *Angelaki* 16, no. 3 (September 2011): 7–17.

Garin, Eugenio. *History of Italian Philosophy*, Vol 1, trans. and edited by Giorgio Pinton. Amsterdam, New York: Rodopi, 2008

Giorello, Giulio. 'Mathematics, Freedom, and Conflictual Democracy — Giulio Giorello'. In *Viva Voce: Conversations with Italian Philosophers*, edited by Silvia Benso, 175–84. Albany, NY: SUNY Press, 2017.

Givone, Sergio. 'Philosophy, Poetry and Dreaming'. In *Contemporary Italian Philosophy: Crossing the Borders of Ethics, Politics, and Religion*, edited by Silvia Benso and Brian Schroeder, 33–46. Albany, NY: SUNY Press, 2007

Givone, Sergio. 'Some Reflections on Narrative Thought'. *Iris* 3, no. 6 (2011): 75–88.

Givone, Sergio. 'Freedom, Guilt, Nihilism and Tragic Thought, A Conversation with Sergio Givone'. In *Viva Voce: Conversations with Italian Philosophers*, edited by Silvia Benso, 137–46. Albany, NY: SUNY Press, 2017

Green, Karen and Constant Mews. *Virtue Ethics for Women 1250–1500*. 1st ed. New York: Springer Verlag, 2011

Lecaldano, Eugenio. 'Ethics, Bioethics, and Ethical Sentimentalism — A Conversation with Eugenio Lecaldano'. In *Viva Voce: Conversations with Italian Philosophers*, edited by Silvia Benso, 27–36. Albany, NY: SUNY Press, 2017

Malpezzi Price, Paolo. 'Lucrezia Marinella'. In *Italian Women Writers: A Bio-Biographical Sourcebook*, edited by Rinaldina Russell, 234–42. Westport, CT: Greenwood, 1994a

Malpezzi Price, Paolo. 'Modereta Fonte'. In *Italian Women Writers: A Bio-Biographical Sourcebook*, edited by Rinaldina Russell, 128–37. Westport, CT: Greenwood, 1994b

Marramao, Giacomo. 'Ontology of Contingency, Power and Historical Space-Time — A Conversation with Giacomo Marramao'. In *Viva Voce: Conversations with Italian Philosophers*, edited by Silvia Benso, 81–92. Albany, NY: SUNY Press, 2017

Masson, Georgina. 'Tullia d'Aragona, Intellectual Courtesan'. In *Courtesans of the Italian Renaissance*, edited by G. Masson, 88–131. London: Secker and Warburg, 1975

Melchiorre, Virgilio. 'The Absolute, Finite Beings, and Symbolic Language — Virgilio Melchiorre'. In *Viva Voce: Conversations with Italian Philosophers*, edited by Silvia Benso, 215–22. Albany, NY: SUNY Press, 2017

Natoli, Salvatore. 'Life, Suffering, Happiness, and Virtue — A Conversation with Salvatore Natoli'. In *Viva Voce: Conversations with Italian Philosophers*, edited by Silvia Benso, 37–50. Albany, NY: SUNY Press, 2017

Olivetti, Marco Maria. 'Transcendental without Illusion: Or, The Absence of the Third Person'. In *Contemporary Italian Philosophy: Crossing the Borders of Ethics, Politics, and Religion*, edited by Benso Silvia and Brian Schroeder, 149–60. Albany, NY: SUNY Press, 2007

Parrini, Paolo. 'Science, Knowledge, Rationality and Empirical Realism — Paolo Parrini'. In *Viva Voce: Conversations with Italian Philosophers*, edited by Silvia Benso, 185–202. Albany, NY: SUNY Press, 2017

Perniola, Mario. 'Imagination, Rituality, and Transit – A Conversation with Mario Perniola'. In *Viva Voce: Conversations with Italian Philosophers*, edited by Silvia Benso, 147–58. Albany, NY: SUNY Press, 2017

Rabil, Albert, Jr, 'Laura Cereta'. In *Italian Women Writers: A Bio-Biographical Sourcebook*, edited by Rinaldina Russell, 67–75. Westport: Greenwood, 1994

Redfern, Jenny. 'Christine de Pisan and The Treasure of the City of Ladies: A Medieval Rhetorician and Her Rhetoric'. In *Reclaiming Rhetorica: Women and in the Rhetorical Tradition*, edited by Andrea A. Lunsford. Pittsburgh: University of Pittsburgh Press, 1995

Romani, Roberto. *Sensibilities of the Risorgimento: Reason and Passions in Political Thought*. Leiden: Koninklijke Brill, 2018

Rovatti, Pier Aldo. 'Praise of Modesty'. In *Contemporary Italian Philosophy: Crossing the Borders of Ethics, Politics, and Religion*, edited by Benso Silvia and Brian Schroeder, 173–92. Albany, NY: SUNY Press, 2007

Ruggenini, Mario. 'The Truth and Existence of the Sacred (*ethos anthropoi daimon*)'. In *Contemporary Italian Philosophy: Crossing the Borders of Ethics, Politics, and Religion*, edited by Benso Silvia and Brian Schroeder, 127–48. Albany, NY: SUNY Press, 2007

Russell, Rinaldina. 'Tullia d'Aragona'. In *Italian Women Writers: A Bio-Biographical Sourcebook*, edited by R. Russell, 26–34. Westport: Greenwood, 1994

Schaus, Margaret C. *Women and Gender in Medieval Europe: An Encyclopedia*. New York: Routledge, 2006

Sini, Carlo. 'Truth, Figures of Truth, and Practices of Life — A Conversation with Carlo Sini'. In *Viva Voce: Conversations with Italian Philosophers*, edited by Silvia Benso, 51–62. Albany, NY: SUNY Press, 2017

St. Catherine of Siena, *The Dialogue of St. Catherine of Siena*, trans. Algar Thorold. NC: TAN Books, 2010

Tessitore, Fulvio. 'Philosophy of Right, Historiography and Individuality — A Conversation with Fulvio Tessitore'. In *Viva Voce: Conversations with Italian Philosophers*, edited by Silvia Benso, 93–106. Albany, NY: SUNY Press, 2017

Vattimo, Gianni. 'Interpretation, History, and Politics — A Conversation with Gianni Vattimo'. In *Viva Voce: Conversations with Italian Philosophers*, edited by Silvia Benso, 107–12. Albany, NY: SUNY Press, 2017

Veca, Salvatore. 'Two Concepts of Utopia and the Idea of Global Justice'. In *It's 'Contemporary Italian Philosophy Crossing the Borders of Ethics, Politics, and Religion*, edited by Silvia Benso, 245–58. Albany, NY: SUNY Press, 2007

Veca, Salvatore. 'Global Justice, Democracy, Uncertainty and Incompleteness — A Conversation with Salvatore Veca'. In *Viva Voce: Conversations with Italian Philosophers*, edited by Silvia Benso, 113–24. Albany, NY: SUNY Press, 2017

Vigna, Carmelo. 'Metaphysics, Ethics, and Applied Ethics — A Conversation with Carmelo Vigna'. In *Viva Voce: Conversations with Italian Philosophers*, edited by Silvia Benso, 63–72. Albany, NY: SUNY Press, 2017

Vitellio, Vincenzo. 'Topology, Nothingness, and the Possible God'. In *Contemporary Italian Philosophy Crossing the Borders of Ethics, Politics, and Religion*, edited by Silvia Benso, 243–254. Albany, NY: SUNY Press, 2017

INDEX

9 781350 112834